CHILD'S TICKET
MACKSVILLE TO SYDNEY
Via STRATHFIELD
First Class
CHILD'S TICKET
MINTO TO CAMPBELLTOWN
SECOND CLASS
№ 5521
BROOKLYN — PATONGA
D. Govt. Trans., N.S.W. & Syd. Har. Ferries Pty. Ltd.
FERRY and BUS
Available between Quay and Balmoral Beach or Clifton Gardens via Taronga Park Wharf.
Not transferable. Must be shown when passing through barrier at Cir.Qy. Available only on trip for which coupon is detached.
15c-1/6
GOLD COAST MOTORAIL EXPRESS
Your Breakfast Sitting Commences at
7.10 A.M.
Please present this card to the Stewardess in the Dining Car.
Passengers are requested to attend at the time shown as another sitting, for which this ticket is not available, commences 35 minutes later.
MELBOURNE & METRO. TRAMWAYS BOARD
CITY PLUS ONE SECTION
CONCESSION CARD $1·00
Valid for 5 journeys of 2 sections commencing or finishing within the area bounded by Flinders, Spencer, Victoria and Spring Streets.
This card must be tendered to the Conductor who will punch it in the next available space and issue a Concession Check Ticket.
Both must be shown on demand or another fare paid.
PASSENGER TICKET
NAME OF PASSENGER
PORT
FLIGHT
SEAT
N.S.W. OMNIBUS PROP. ASS.
Ticket entitles passenger to travel into section indicated by punch. Must be shown on demand or another fare paid.
27c
41203
ANSETT PIONEER
Australia's National Coachline
Boarding Check
Please present on departure
Check-in time
COACH TICKET
Department of Railways, N.S.W.
RESERVED SEAT
CHATSWOOD
The holder is entitled to a seat on the Train from On the date shown hereon
Seat No. Car No.
CONDONG ROAD
MURWILLUMBAH
THIS TICKET IS ISSUED SUBJECT TO CONDITIONS ON BACK HEREOF
AS № 10889

SOUTH GRAFTON
PLATFORM TICKET
ONLY
This Ticket is not transferable, and is available to attend one train only on date of issue, and must be handed to the Collector at Barrier. Holder of this ticket is prohibited from occupying a seat on train.
28 AUG 71
31842
Department of Railways, N.S.W.
RESERVED SEAT
SOUTH GRAFTON
14634
Country Time-Tables
Victorian Railways
NOVEMBER 1954
PRICE 1/-
6d. B
NCQ
24531
6d. B
45007
3d. B
WBD
72231
B
WBE
45736
B
LQ
56714
STATE ELECTRICITY COMMISSION OF VICTORIA
PROVINCIAL TRAMWAYS
NOT TRANSFERABLE
THIS CHECK MUST BE SHOWN ON DEMAND OR ANOTHER FARE PAID
13c
ISSUED SUBJECT TO THE BY-LAWS
A 029796
Sandringham
TO
MELBOURNE
SINGLE
49668
N.S.W. GOVERNMENT TRAMWAYS
1st SECTION.
Not Transferable. Available on trip of issue only. Must be shown on demand, or another fare paid.
PLEASE DESTROY ON ALIGHTING.
3d. A
27927
1st AND 3rd Sections
PLEASE DESTROY ON ALIGHTING.
6d. B
86385

TRANSPORT

Dr Robert Lee is Associate Professor at the University of Western Sydney where he has taught history since 1979. He has published many books on transport, especially trains, including *The Railways of Victoria 1854–2004*, which was shortlisted for the NSW Premier's History Award in 2007; and *Colonial Engineer: John Whitton (1819–1898) and the Building of Australia's Railways.*

Sydney First Fleet class ferry *Friendship*, named after a vessel in the First Fleet which arrived at this spot in January 1788, heads out from Circular Quay past P&O's cruise liner *Pacific Jewel* in March 2010. (Jason Antony)

ROBERT LEE

TRANSPORT

AN AUSTRALIAN HISTORY

UNSW PRESS

A UNSW Press book

Published by
University of New South Wales Press Ltd
University of New South Wales
Sydney NSW 2052
AUSTRALIA
www.unswpress.com.au

First published 2010

10 9 8 7 6 5 4 3 2 1

National Library of Australia
Cataloguing-in-Publication entry
Author: Lee, Robert S. (Robert Stuart), 1952–
Title: Transport: an Australian history/Robert Lee.
ISBN: 978 1 74223 213 3 (hbk.)
Notes: Includes index.
Bibliography.
Subjects: Transportation – Australia.
Transportation – Australia — History.
Australia – History.
Dewey Number: 388.0994

Design Di Quick
Printer Everbest, China

This book is printed on paper using fibre supplied from plantation or sustainably managed forests.

To my students

CONTENTS

'Morning commuters, 1938', Max Dupain's archetypal study of passengers alighting from the *Kubu* at Circular Quay. (Max Dupain, courtesy Jill White)

PREFACE AND ACKNOWLEDGMENTS

IT IS A PARADOX THAT Australians are intensely concerned with their mobility yet often seem to know little about how we came to be so mobile, nor have much understanding of the enormous investment of public monies that made possible, and maintains, our mobility. Too often we assume it is a given of national life. In their dealings with the electorate, governments often assume an ignorance of the history and significance of transport policy, which can lead to contempt and attempts to hoodwink the population. This book was written in Sydney at a time when New South Wales governments appeared to base their transport policies on the forgetfulness of the electorate and its willingness to tolerate neglect and, all too often, downright lies about transport policy. Important projects have been announced repeatedly, every time 'fully funded', and commonly deferred or abandoned. This observer found his attitudes about his government's repeated failures in transport planning move from bemusement through anger to rage, and his judgment of its performance from criticism to condemnation. It was an especially depressing experience because he had voted for it so many times.

Such a performance would be impossible if the electorate were well informed about transport policy and understood even a fraction of the issues. While the roles of transport and distance in Australian history are widely recognised, there has been no previous attempt to integrate the histories of different transport modes and different regions of the country. All transport modes articulate with each other in a host of ways. How governments allocate funds to transport infrastructure largely determines how people and goods move around the country; and there are always many choices. Arguments that such decisions are made on the basis of markets are specious, since every transport mode relies on public infrastructure and governments have the power to decide in which modes they will invest and in which they will not. Thus they affect, even determine, how people travel and goods move, and at what prices. While this book was being written, the New South Wales governments forever seemed to make the worst possible decisions on such matters, so it is a book born of rage. This is not a particularly admirable emotion, but thoughtful persons in Sydney contemplating their government's transport policy failings can be excused for feeling little else. It is the author's hope that this anger will not have been wasted, and that never again will governments be able to assume an ignorant electorate when it comes to transport policy.

The origins of this study are in a project the author undertook for the then Australian

Indooroopilly is a typical Australian suburb: every morning across the country millions of Australians pour into similar suburban railway stations. One chilly winter morning in 1966 the station assistant gave the 'right away' to the fireman at Indooroopilly. A few minutes earlier the platform had been crowded with Brisbane-bound commuters who had just seated themselves in new stainless steel cars ordered for electrification of Brisbane's suburban railways. That project had not yet been funded, so steam was still in charge in 1966. The locomotive is not as antique as it looks but a modern post-war machine – the apogee of the Australian suburban steam engine. (Eric Marggraf, QR Heritage)

INTRODUCTION

AUSTRALIAN ORIGINS, TRANSPORT AND THE INDUSTRIAL REVOLUTION

THINKING OF LOVE, he slung a pack on his shoulders and walked down the hill to Indooroopilly station in suburban Brisbane. As Aussie as could be, tanned with dyed sandy hair; his features hinted at the fact that he had been born in Seoul. A student with a part-time job, just 20 years old, he was on a mission, wearing his tightest tank top and loosest jeans, a combination he often found effective. Climbing the stairs to the platform, he swiped his TransLink *go* card and boarded the train. After a quick connection at Central, he was off on his journey, the train soaring on pylons above shopping centres, light industry and the swamps of Kedron Brook to the airport. He had booked his flight at the right price and checked in online, so soon he was taking off for Melbourne's Tullamarine Airport. Two hours later he had landed, ready to catch the express bus along the freeway to Southern Cross station. It was only a 20-minute ride to the new station, where he bought his two-hour MetCard and found his train to Camberwell. Here the person he had met in a chat room was waiting at a café, just as promised. After a chaste kiss, a cappuccino and a friand, they took the tram home (on the same ticket) and soon he would know if it had been worth the trouble.

But in reality there had been neither much trouble nor much expense. The whole trip – three trains on two gauges, a flight, a bus and a tram on a third gauge – had cost about what he earned in a day working in his uncle's Korean grocery shop, and the uncle was not a generous employer. He had breakfasted with his parents and was about to lunch with, well, he didn't really know, 1500 kilometres away.

A journey such as this – so spontaneous, so cheap, by so ordinary an Australian, and all for such a doubtful outcome – would have been inconceivable when he had been born, and he was a still very young man. It was made possible by a revolution in mobility propelled by linked computers, new infrastructure, integrated seamless ticketing (except in Sydney), and ever-improving and more economical transport technology. This journey, one of millions Australians make every day, shows that mobility is one of Australians' defining characteristics. People and goods move across distances both long and short with apparent ease and relative economy.

The continent's diversity of transport modes is enormous. Every modern type is represented, with the bizarre and humiliating exception of the high speed passenger trains which have done so much to transform intercity travel in most comparable countries. Superlatives, mostly positive, can be applied to many aspects of Australia's transport. This country, with its relatively small population but truly vast terrain, hosts one of the world's most intensive intercity air services (between Sydney and Melbourne); one of the world's greatest tramway systems (in Melbourne); the world's heaviest mineral trains (in Western Australia's Pilbara); and, less positively, one of the world's most dysfunctional and expensive public transport ticketing systems (in Sydney).[1]

The Albert Bridge at Indooroopilly soon after its rebuilding following the first bridge's failure in the 1893 floods. (Author postcard collection)

Australians have always been an intensely mobile people. The continent's isolation from the rest of the world has ensured that the ancestors of all Australians, including its indigenous population, came here as migrants from across the seas. Probably the most remarkable voyages people have ever made to Australia were the very first, as the Aborigines crossed the seas from Asia to their new home. They were the first human beings ever to cross the oceans to settle a new continent. We know nothing of their voyages other than that they happened about 50 000 years ago. Like all peoples, they had come out of humanity's cradle in Africa by foot. But whereas the rest of humanity was able to walk to its ultimate home, the Australian Aborigines had to sail across the watery depths of Wallace's Line to their destination.

What motivated them to cross the seas we will never know. They have lived in Australia for so long that their dreamtime legends contain no reference to their remote maritime past or seafaring adventures. These are full of stories of the land they made home, but not of their getting here. When they came from Asia to Australia the seas were lower than they now are, so Sumatra, Java and Borneo were part of the Asian mainland. New Guinea, mainland Australia and Tasmania were all one landmass. Their route was probably through the present eastern Indonesian islands of Sulawesi and

In 1920 photographer, filmmaker, adventurer and showman Frank Hurley (1885–1962) was travelling around Torres Strait filming *Pearls and Savages* when he captured this image echoing how the first Australians came to the continent. (Frank Hurley, National Library of Australia, NLA an23382195)

Halmahera to the western tip of New Guinea, thence by foot, settling the land as they walked all the way to Tasmania. The rising of the seas, ten to twelve thousand years ago, isolated them from the rest of humanity and the Tasmanians from the mainland.

Having reached Australia, the Aborigines became a people of the land, not of the sea. Nonetheless they did exploit the continent's seas and rivers, which they navigated for purposes of social exchange, commerce and fishing. In this, they were much the same as the peoples who followed them much later to the same continent. Aborigines lived on some offshore islands and frequently visited others. The Butchulla people of Fraser Island, the northernmost of the sand islands off the south Queensland coast, appear to have migrated to the island only in the last 5000 years, well after the rising of the seas, so clearly went there by boat. Fraser Island Aborigines traded with the mainland, especially in flint for tools, of which there was none on the island; and archaeological evidence suggests that this was imported from Cooroy, over a hundred kilometres to the south. During the winter fish run, mainland Aborigines seasonally migrated to Fraser Island for the plentiful food. As elsewhere in Australia, Aborigines' canoes were made from a large sheet of bark stripped from a eucalyptus tree, cut and shaped, and then sealed with a mixture of eucalyptus resin and wax. Trees stripped of bark for canoes survive on the Island.[2]

Tasmanian Aborigines also visited offshore islands, and a European observer recorded them visiting Maria Island off the east coast using logs rather than bark canoes as transport.[3] Kangaroo Island off the South Australian coast is a different case altogether and was inhabited by Aborigines from about 30 000 years ago until about 2000 years ago. However, island life could be hazardous for small numbers of Aborigines isolated from larger populations and the consequently larger gene pool on the mainland. They would have walked there originally but became isolated by the rising of the seas. We know nothing of the details, but inbreeding and limited resources presumably made human life unsustainable. Some may have made an escape to the mainland. It is a rare instance of humanity actually dying out in a country it colonised, probably because of inadequate transport.[4]

The isolation of Aboriginal Australia lasted until the 17th century, when Indonesian traders, mostly from south Sulawesi and generally known as Macassans (from the Dutch name of modern Makassar), began regular commercial traffic with what is now the Top End of the Northern Territory. Their trade with Arnhem Land is documented in Dutch sources from 1667 but may have begun much earlier. They came in sailing vessels called prahus, very similar to those which still trade in Indonesian waters, in search of the sea slug (also called *trepang* or *bêche de mer*) abundant in the shallow waters of the Arnhem Land coast. The Chinese prized dried sea slug as an aphrodisiac, probably because of its shape as much as anything else, so Australia's first overseas transport links and consequent integration into the world economy were part of the sex trade.[5]

While the Aborigines of the Top End traded and socialised with Asians, those on the eastern and southern coasts remained isolated until 1770 and their society unthreatened until 1788, when British colonisation began its inexorable transformation of almost everything in the country. At roughly the same time as the British moved into Australia, their own society was being transformed by the industrial revolution. As steam power was first applied to the problems of pumping water from the coal mines of Northumberland and Tyneside, and water power to the looms and mills of Lancashire, the first loads of convicts were sent across the globe to what would become Sydney. Indeed, the voyage of the First Fleet between 1786 and 1788 itself was characterised by the rational use of scientific knowledge for practical transport purposes. The great problems of navigation had been solved: its captains always knew exactly where they were, exactly where they were going, and how to harness the winds to get there. They also knew far more about maintaining the health of their crews and passengers at sea than had been the case even a couple of decades earlier. Scurvy was almost unknown on the first convict ships and, in general, the human cargo of the First Fleet arrived in Botany Bay in better shape than it left England. The death rate on board was astonishingly low.

Within a decade of the establishment of the settlement at Sydney, it began to acquire the rudiments of a civil society and a free economy. It could not and did not long remain a vast gaol. These changes meant the new colony had to develop its internal and external transport links and harness the latest technology for the production of wealth. Modern innovations were not long in coming. The first steam mill began operation beside Darling Harbour in 1813, just a year after the colony's first turnpike road from Sydney to Parramatta had opened. So, although New South Wales was the most remote of Britain's colonies and burdened with the unsavoury reputation of convictism, it quickly became integrated into the British-dominated global economic system.

The first sizeable export industry of New South Wales was based on whale products but, after the crossing of the Blue Mountains in 1813, the exploitation of the vast interior of the continent became possible, and a pastoral economy emerged. By 1850, Australia was one of the world's richest pastoral areas, and the wool its flocks produced enjoyed a reputation for being among the best in the world. This pastoral wealth required transport facilities, but these could be rudimentary, since wool was light in relation to its value, so could support the heavy costs of overland transport by bullock dray. Thus, at first transport could follow routes used for millennia by Aborigines, who had always traded small and valuable goods by foot. As society became more settled and the pastoral industry burgeoned, better transport technology was needed to cope with the traffic on offer. The ultimate solution was the railway.

Meanwhile, five more Australian colonies were established by 1860 with long maritime links between them. Each was dominated by a capital city which was also the largest port and commercial centre. Inland from each city was a large hinterland stretching far into the interior of the continent. Paradoxically, Australia's population was simultaneously both highly urbanised and widely dispersed. Combined with its enormous and often only marginally economically productive interior, this has given Australia its unique political and economic geography. Coupled with the Australian colonies' remoteness from England, this created, in Geoffrey Blainey's memorable phrase, the 'tyranny of distance' which has so dominated the patterns of investment, development, social exchange and political discourse throughout Australia's modern history.

Under these circumstances, it is not surprising that steamships were used in Australian waters as early as 1830, well before railway construction began. As with the first steam mill, this was remarkably early in the history of this technology, and points to the technologically progressive nature of early colonial Australia. Even in 1830, it was no convict backwater. Railway building began in Sydney in 1849, although the first lines were not opened until 1854 in Victoria and South Australia. Simultaneously with the beginnings of Australia's railway age came the gold rushes of 1851 and the origins of an enduring and stable European civilisation in Australia. Sydney and Melbourne suddenly became no longer mere settlements, but cities to rival similar places in the United States.

The Australian colonies embraced the new technology of the times with enthusiasm. In the second half of the 19th century Australians were using innovations such as telegraphs, telephones, cable and electric trams, and electric light practically as soon as they were invented. The establishment of subsidised mail steamship services between England and the Australian colonies in the 1850s brought regular and relatively safe passenger and postal communications across the globe. Then in 1872 the Overland Telegraph and its onward submarine cable connections through Asia and Europe brought almost instant if very expensive communication between Australia and the rest of the world. Gold gave a huge psychological as well as financial boost to Australia, culminating in the boom of the 1880s, when the basic infrastructure of its

Australia's first steam railway opened to Port Melbourne's Station Pier in 1854. This has always been a place where multiple transport modes meet: on one summer's day around 1900 a suburban train for Flinders Street, interstate and overseas liners, and a Port Phillip Bay excursion paddle steamer all wait for business while bathers cool off in the waters of Hobson's Bay. (Author postcard collection)

modern cities and railways as we know them today was put in place.

The depression of the 1890s ended the boom but spawned Federation and a growing idea of Australian nationality. However, transport patterns as they had developed over the previous half-century made little sense for a nation continent. Railways had been developed independently by each colony, with little regard for future connection. Three gauges were widely used, two of them practically identical in all technical respects, yet sufficiently different to be incompatible. Customs tariffs, differing rail gauges and manipulated freight rates all aimed to keep trade within colonies rather than encourage its spread across their boundaries. Only coastal and riverine shipping had a more national outlook, since much shipping activity cut across colonial boundaries.

Federation in 1901 brought a formal national identity and a national market. However, transport policy remained the responsibility of the individual colonies, henceforth known as states. This has remained the case ever since, although the role of the Commonwealth government in transport issues has grown. This applied partly to railways, since the Commonwealth built its own lines in South and Western Australia; even more so to roads, some of which were funded by the Commonwealth from as early as the 1920s; and almost entirely to civil aviation, which only developed after the Commonwealth was created.

In the 20th century, technology changed just as rapidly as it had in the 19th, although perhaps not with quite the same impact, since when the great leap was made from muscle and wind to steam power, subsequent leaps were not nearly as impressive. The motor age dawned with the new century and the car had a big impact on urban planning from as early as 1910, especially in Canberra. However, cars were not part of everyday life for most city Australians until after 1950, although they were important in the bush and for the urban rich by the 1920s. The adaption of cities to cars really occurred between 1950 and 1980.

During the 20th century new transport technologies came into being while the old technologies were refined and developed. Often, older technologies reached their apogee just as they were being displaced. Thus, Australia's finest interstate ships were built in the 1920s and 1930s, when railways (and even air travel) were taking much of their traffic. Forty years later, the best long-distance sleeping car trains were built in the 1960s, just at the dawn of the jet age, which would see them wither within two decades. Some forms of transport would disappear altogether, notably road transport by horse and bullock, while others were transformed. Sea and rail transport of freight became more specialised, concentrating on bulk shipments, while road transport took over a vast number of lighter transport tasks, and increasingly heavy transport tasks as well.

This development changed the appearance of the country's ports and railway stations, as once-busy centres handling thousands of small shipments gradually disappeared.

In a country of great distances like Australia, transport has always been crucial. Ever since Lachlan Macquarie, Governor of New South Wales from 1810 to 1821, governments have been proud to be judged by the quality of the roads (and later railways) they have built and managed. Transport issues often have dominated political discourse and led to the rise and fall of governments, recently and spectacularly in New South Wales in 2008 and 2009 when two premiers in succession each fell largely on the issue of funding urgently needed new suburban railways. Politicians have always prized transport portfolios for the access to patronage and policy development they bring. The careers of former Victorian Minister for Railways Robert Gordon Menzies and former New South Wales train driver Ben Chifley have demonstrated that an intimate knowledge of transport issues can take national politicians right to the top. This was partly because in Australia almost all significant transport infrastructure, and many transport operations as well, have been government creation, built for reasons of public utility and amenity at best, or pork-barrelling venality at worst.

There are major exceptions, notably in shipping and aviation, but Australia's transport history is largely the history of government enterprises. Most have been controlled by state governments, although municipalities have been significant, especially in the provision of urban public transport and in building roads and road bridges of local significance. The Commonwealth has dominated regulation of civil aviation, and at times its ownership as well; and become increasingly important in managing road and rail infrastructure. The most important corporate private initiatives have been in shipping and civil aviation, but even these have only thrived because of the government investment in port and airport facilities, and government subsidies disguised as postal contracts.

Most important railways were built and operated by a government, although there was significant private investment in mining railways. Shipping mostly has been in private hands and road freight transport has been overwhelmingly so, although operates on roads provided almost free by all levels of government. By contrast, railways have been burdened with the interest charges on the capital cost of their infrastructure as well as its continued maintenance, so state governments protected their investment in railways by regulating road freight, until this became technically and politically untenable around 1970. Bus transport has been mostly government or municipal within cities, and private in rural areas or over long distances. It is always easy, though, to find exceptions to these generalisations.

Early airlines were entirely in private hands, until the period of most dramatic growth in civil aviation between 1946 and 1990, when the largest airlines were owned by the Commonwealth. On the whole, though, the early private airlines survived and thrived for one reason alone – their lucrative postal contracts which in effect were government subsidies. Guinea Airways, operating in the unique situation of a colony with almost no roads, was the major exception. All major airports were owned by the Commonwealth. Since 1990 the aviation industry largely has been transferred into private hands. As well as these government and corporate enterprises there was and remains the small private initiative of many thousands of largely anonymous bullockies, cab drivers, drovers, and bus and truck operators.

This book brings together the story of these varied enterprises, and analyses how transport has developed in Australia to solve the human problem of moving people and goods around in the context of an expanding social and economic life. Australians in the cities and the bush have prized their mobility and the means

they use to attain it. These have been very diverse, from the saddle horse to the motor car; from the cheap and frequent tram at the corner to the weekly paddle steamer clunking by the river gums; from the intercolonial steamship and express train services (both of impressive speed and comfort) to the relative freedom of the skies offered by modern jet aircraft services. Transport of goods and people between widely dispersed locations is essential to the division of labour on which a modern economy is based, and is a central reality of the human experience in modern Australia. This book is its story.

The finest group of adjacent bridges in Australia spans the Brisbane River at Indooroopilly. On the left is the single span Walter Taylor road suspension bridge of 1936, the longest such bridge in Australia with its unique apartments in each tower. Next comes the railway two-span truss bridge opened in 1957 to supplement the 1895 two-span railway 'hogsback' Albert Bridge. Finally there is the 1998 Jack Pesch pedestrian and cycle bridge. (Author)

Sydney's hub of international and local transport at Circular Quay in 1931. P&O's RMS *Strathnaver* has not long completed her month-long maiden voyage from Southampton and will soon return, maintaining the tie that binds together the Empire. O and N class toast rack trams, already more than 20 years old, are heading out to the western suburbs, while newer taxis and cars already share the roadway with trams. The ranks of the flotilla of ferries crossing the harbour will be thinned when the great bridge nearing completion is opened the following year, but the half-hourly schedule of the Manly steamers (represented here by the 1922-built *Dee Why*) will continue to the present. (Ian Dunn collection)

Chapter 1

TIES THAT BIND

OVERSEAS SHIPPING

GLINTING IN THE bright Australian sun, the axe fell; the man screamed; blood spurted from the stump of his wrist. A severed hand quivered on the sand. A second scream, a second hand dropped; then the mutilated man was dragged to the gallows. The survivors cheered and jeered as mutineer, murderer, sadist, torturer and rapist Jeronimus Cornelisz danced a suffocating death at the end of a rope: a dose of his own medicine, lawful retribution at last. It was September 1629 and European civilisation, technology and justice had arrived in Australia.

SHIPPING IN AUSTRALIAN WATERS BEFORE 1788

THE FIRST TEMPORARY European settlement in Australia lasted from June to September 1629 on the Abrolhos Islands off the coast of Western Australia. The Dutch East Indies Company's flagship, the *Batavia*, had foundered on her maiden voyage from Amsterdam to the city after which she was named, modern Jakarta. The greed, mutiny, rape, murder, rescue and vengeance among her stranded crew were the horrors marking the beginning of Australia's integration into the modern world of commerce and trade. The ship had foundered there because the western coast of the continent lay close by the best route from the Cape of Good Hope in South Africa to the wealthy islands of what is today Indonesia. This archipelago was then the cynosure of world trade because of the spices it produced. These spices had become fetishes commanding enormous prices in Europe and the Arab world, wildly expensive because they were so exotic and so hard to procure.

Indonesia and Australia are very close but very different. For most of human history, Indonesia has been rich, Australia poor. Throughout the archipelago traders had found wealth for over a millennium: Indians and Chinese since the beginning of the Christian era; Arabs and Turks since the 8th century; Portuguese and Spaniards in the 16th century, and from 1602 the Dutch, who would go on to conquer almost the entire archipelago thereby creating the basis for the modern Indonesian state. It is inconceivable that not one of the merchant ships from so many parts of the world which sailed all the way to Timor (where there was sandalwood in abundance) never sailed the few hundred kilometres further to the coasts of Australia to see what was there.

However, these traders left neither records of their visits nor any cultural imprint on Australia, although their cultures, religions and blood deeply permeated much of the archipelago, making Indonesian society the rich and diverse phenomenon it is. By contrast, they left no trace of their probable visits to Australia, almost certainly because they were unimpressed with what they saw. For, in the words of the first description

The *Marquis Cornwallis* was built in India and named after the governor general, who had the misfortune to be the British general who surrendered to the United States at the end of the American War of Independence. In 1795 she brought a load of convicts to Sydney, but is seen here as painted by a Flemish artist near Calcutta in 1793. (FB Solvyns, State Library of New South Wales, SLNSW a928112h)

written of the continent in 1606, 'there was no good to be done there'. These were the dismal reflections of the Dutch East India Company's Willem Janszoon, the first of the company's captains sent to explore what lay to the south and east of Indonesia.

In the early 17th century the company's captains charted much of the coasts of northern, western and southern Australia, as well as Tasmania and New Zealand. It was rational exploration motivated by a relentless search for profit, which is after all what the Heeren XVII, the company's directors back in Amsterdam, were after. Since there appeared to be no opportunities for profit, all this exploration had few consequences other than scientific, and a sprinkling of Dutch names on the map, most significantly those of the most ambitious of the Dutch navigators, Abel Tasman, and his equally ambitious patron, Batavia Governor General Antonio van Diemen.

The Dutch East Indies Company kept immaculate records, so its voyages to Australia are the first of which we know any details. Almost certainly, though, they were not the first in the modern era. We know nothing of the voyages of anonymous Indian, Arab, Malay, Chinese and other Asian merchants to the Australian coast, other than that the voyages probably happened but had no consequences. There is the tantalising possibility of a visit by a Chinese official expedition in the early 15th century, at a time when China briefly considered a maritime and commercial future for itself, but the usually thorough Chinese archives are silent on the topic. Certainly they record the voyages of great 'treasure ships' commanded by the Muslim eunuch admiral Zheng He to Indonesia, India, the Persian Gulf and East Africa. A visit to northern Australia is credible, even probable, but there is no hard evidence of one.

There is oblique evidence for a Portuguese voyage along the Queensland coast in the first half of the 16th century. Maps dating from well before the time of the first documented Dutch voyages show this coast in some detail. Even their errors are predictable, resulting from the inability of navigators of this time to chart their longitude with any accuracy, as they lacked a reliable maritime chronometer. But no account of the voyage survives and, if it happened, as was probable, certainly it had no consequences.

Such a voyage was indeed possible, as the great advances in European shipping had occurred from the middle of the 15th century, above all in Portugal, and their first great fruits had been the extraordinary voyages of Christopher Columbus across the Atlantic in 1492 and of Vasco da Gama from Lisbon, around the Cape of Good Hope, to Calicut in India in 1497. Most importantly, both these navigators survived to return, so the routes they pioneered became commercial arteries. Europeans had the technology for blue-water navigation by 1500 and indeed one Spanish vessel sailed across the Pacific from South America to the Philippines as early as 1521. However, they were always looking for profit and so tended to follow in the wake of the mostly Asian merchants and sailors who had ploughed the seas before them with precisely the same motive – greed. But Australia, which appeared to produce no commodities worth trading, remained off their itineraries for centuries.

What Australia's apparent poverty meant was that the first European voyage of lasting significance was motivated not by profit but by scientific enquiry. The circumnavigation of the globe by the *Endeavour* under the command of Lieutenant James Cook between 1768 and 1770 was a voyage like none other before it. No vessel in these waters had ever carried passengers who were so talented and so well-educated; nor so thoughtful and well-connected. Nor had any previous voyage been funded so amply, and nor would any be so well documented. Unlike previous European visitors to Australia, the intellectually receptive and curious scientists and naturalists on board the *Endeavour* responded to the country and people with enthusiasm. For Cook, his most famous passenger Joseph Banks and their colleagues, eastern Australia was a place of wonder and excitement. Cook sailed after the development of the maritime chronometer, so always knew exactly where he was. Moreover, he had been chosen for the mission because he was Britain's finest cartographer. Naturally his maps were impeccable. When they returned to England, Cook and his passengers became celebrities feted by London society, and New South Wales, as he had named the continent's east coast, was all the rage.

Fifteen years later, the British government worked out something to do with the land about which Cook and Banks had been so keen. Because it was remote, because its inhabitants apparently were peaceful and unlikely to be too solicitous of any property rights, and because it was no longer a secret, New South Wales was chosen as the site for an improbable experiment. A new British society was to be founded there from the dregs of the old, its convicted criminals. In May 1787, 759 of them sailed in six vessels accompanied by three ships laden with stores and two naval vessels. Nine months later, on 26 January 1788, the first of them landed at the site of what would become Sydney.

EARLY SHIPPING IN NEW SOUTH WALES

NEW SOUTH WALES was conceived as a gaol and the subsidiary motives for its settlement were the provision of ship's supplies and security for the Admiralty and the English East India Company. Until 1813, this company, like its Dutch counterpart, had an official monopoly of all English trade with Asia (including Australia) and there was a host of regulations designed to prevent the new colony from getting into maritime enterprise. Early governors wanted to prevent convicts escaping, and in 1791 the first of them prohibited the building of vessels more than 14 feet (4.3 m) in length. This regulation was soon relaxed, but under the East India Company's monopoly, no vessel capable of trading with Asia or the South Seas could be built before 1813.[1] This was not a propitious beginning to what would become in many ways a maritime society.

Despite these prohibitions, very early it became evident that the new colony would need maritime transport. The terrain around Sydney was limited for agricultural purposes, but 23 kilometres up the Parramatta River there was rich pasturage and good soil. Parramatta became the colony's first agricultural centre, and as early as 1789 the government built the little *Rose Hill Packet*, colloquially known as *The Lump*, to connect the two settlements. The unlovely and unromantically named *Lump* rightly can be considered the beginnings of modern transport within Australia.

She was soon joined by other government vessels which, as the colony started to acquire a regular economic life, began operating a scheduled service, charging fares and freight. Private enterprise began when the emancipists (freed convicts) Henry Kable and James Underwood's 30-ton schooner *Endeavour* entered the trade in 1801. They were followed soon after by fellow emancipist Isaac Nichols, later to become the colony's first postmaster, who built and traded his 33-tonner *Governor Hunter* from 1805. Underwood was a talented shipbuilder, and built most of the colony's early vessels, including the first substantial vessel, the ship-rigged *King George* of nearly 200 tons, completed around 1805.[2]

As settlement extended to the even richer soils along the banks of the Hawkesbury, shipping services started running there, beginning in 1798. These involved a short voyage in open ocean from Sydney Harbour north to the mouth of the Hawkesbury, so in not much over a decade after Sydney was founded, the prohibition on seaward commerce had become obsolete. The sea voyage to the Hawkesbury was about three times as long as the land trip, but carried freight for about two-thirds the price. However, many Hawkesbury farmers used their own drays to take produce to Parramatta or Sydney, so the roads probably took more of the grain and other produce than the boats until steamers entered the trade in the 1840s.[3] This first Australian domestic blue-water navigation between Sydney and the Hawkesbury lasted until the early 20th century, despite availability of a good road from 1813 and a railway from 1864.

As early as the 1790s there was interest in exploiting the enormous number of fur seals and sperm whales found on the southeastern coast of New South Wales, around the Bass Strait islands and along the Tasmanian east coast. This bloody traffic was the basis of the early Australian shipbuilding and maritime industry in general, for there were enormous profits to be made out of whale oil (then the best lighting fuel in use) and seal fur. The early whalers and sealers were British, but soon American and French vessels began defying the British claims to a monopoly, and Sydney and Hobart's ships' chandlers were more than happy to cater to their needs. A domestic whaling industry eventually emerged, and the number of whaling ships operating out of Sydney increased from five in 1827 to 76 in 1835.[4] At this time about two-thirds of Australian shipping was engaged in whaling. Until around 1840 (when wool became king) whaling was the colony's most valuable industry and whale products its main export.[5] Meanwhile, other commodities also attracted maritime trade, such as cedar getting (initially on the Hunter, but later on other rivers north and south of Sydney) and carrying coal from Newcastle, beginning in 1804.

Coal was used both for domestic and industrial purposes. Sydney's first steam mill had opened as early as 1813, and in 1831 the first steamship arrived in Sydney. This was the 256-ton schooner-rigged paddle wheeler *Sophia Jane*, which, like all the early steamers, was an auxiliary steamer, using her paddle wheels only in unfavourable winds. In the same year Australia's first steamer the *William the Fourth* was built on a tributary of the Hunter near Newcastle. These auxiliary steamers were ideal for conditions on the coastal rivers of New South Wales, because they could exploit the wind at sea but use their (rather inefficient) engines effectively in the close confines of coastal rivers such as the Hawkesbury and Hunter. In 1839 Australia's first lasting steamship line, the Hunter River Steam Navigation Company, was established in Sydney with three imported iron auxiliary paddle steamers, rejoicing in the names of *Rose*, *Shamrock* and *Thistle*. As its name indicated, most of its trade was with Newcastle, but it also traded to the new and quickly thriving port of Melbourne.[6]

While coal had been mined around Newcastle since the early days of the colony, it was only around 1850 that mining became a major industry. The Australian Agricultural (or AA) Company had a legal monopoly over much of the Newcastle deposits. It prevented a rapid growth, since it favoured mining small quantities of coal to be sold at high prices. Even this trade, though, was sufficient to justify starting work on a tramway from its mines to the port of Newcastle as early as 1829. The great stimulus to coal mining at Newcastle was the California gold rush of 1849. No reliable source of coal was closer to San Francisco than Newcastle, so from 1850 American ships flooded into the port in search of fuel to power California's burgeoning energy needs. The AA monopoly was broken but neither mines, nor port, nor tramroads could cope with the demand.

Improving this situation was hard, since men as well as coals sailed across the Pacific on these ships, meaning that labour was scarce and expensive. The AA Company monopoly also had prevented the exploitation of coal deposits south of Sydney around Wollongong until the 1850s. Thereafter this also became an important shipping and mining district, as well as the main centre of the New South Wales dairy industry. There were intimate connections between all

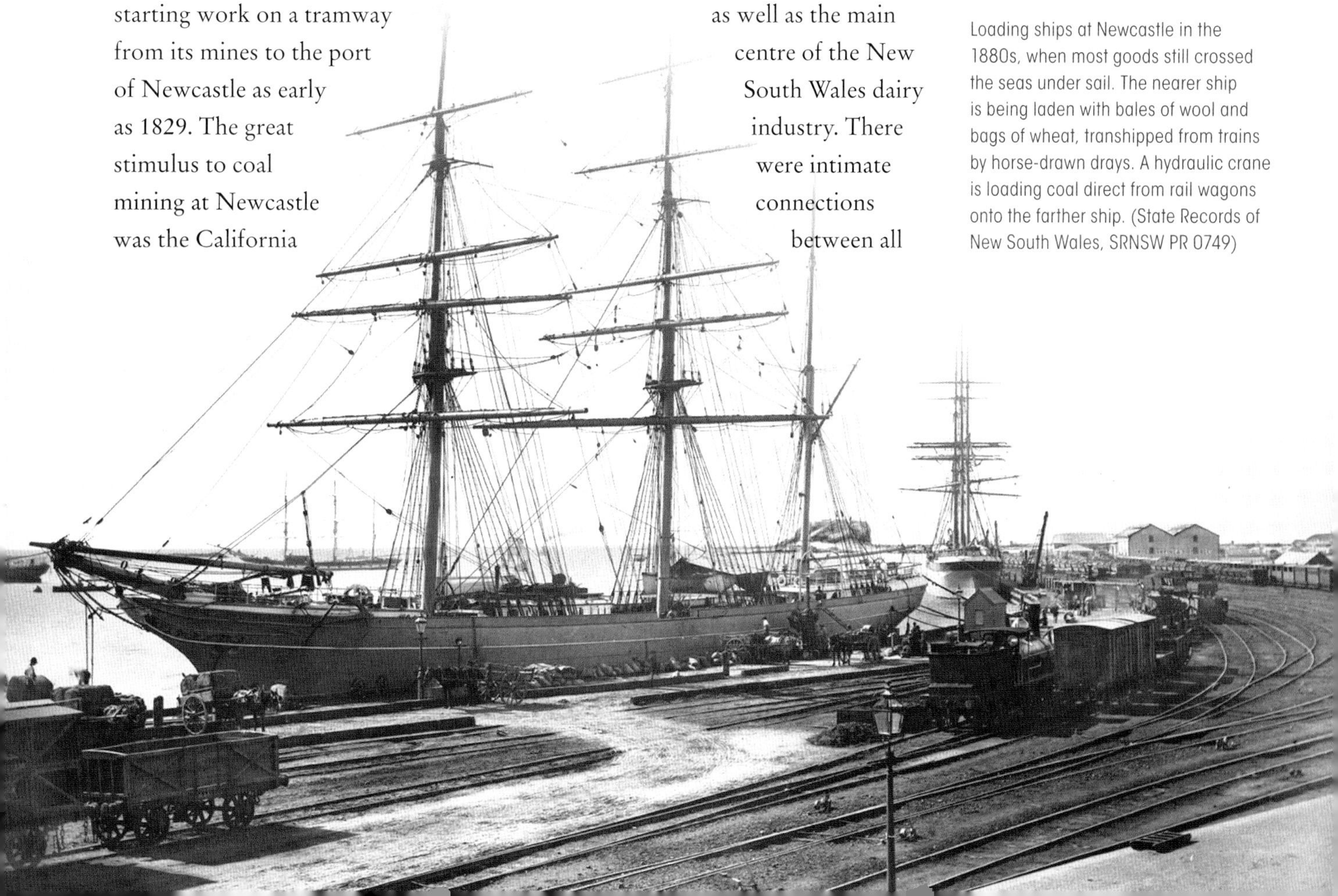

Loading ships at Newcastle in the 1880s, when most goods still crossed the seas under sail. The nearer ship is being laden with bales of wool and bags of wheat, transhipped from trains by horse-drawn drays. A hydraulic crane is loading coal direct from rail wagons onto the farther ship. (State Records of New South Wales, SRNSW PR 0749)

three industries, and, typically, Sydney entrepreneur TS Mort was at the centre of much of the activity, running refrigerated ships as well as dairies to provide their cargos as early as the 1870s.

The New South Wales Public Works Department Engineer in Chief for Harbours and Rivers, Edward Orpen (generally EO) Moriarty, had designed a scheme for Newcastle as a coal and general port as early as 1856, although at this stage rival coal companies were attempting to monopolise it as far as possible. From 1861 the government railway (NSWGR) was shipping coal to Newcastle, and it soon became more important than the colliery's tramways. In addition, by 1863 the policy of government ownership and operation of the coal-loading cranes at the port had triumphed. Moriarty installed an elaborate system of hydraulically powered coal loading cranes, powered from a central hydraulic power station, which survives to this day. He also had Newcastle Harbour dredged and breakwaters built to scour the mouth of the Hunter to give reliable access for the largest of ocean-going ships. The Hunter was the only New South Wales river on which this technique worked effectively, and the harbour works at Newcastle, still in use although updated, remain Moriarty's greatest legacy.

Newcastle became much more than a coal port after the 1860s. The reason for this was the extension of the Great Northern Railway into its hinterland. From the 1830s, the main port of the region had been Morpeth, the head of navigation for all practical purposes of the Hunter River. Morpeth, however, was twice the distance from the sea by river as it was by land. The sinuous river also meant that the new railway, opened from Newcastle to Maitland in 1857, bypassed Morpeth. Morpeth shipping interests were able to secure the construction of a branch railway from East Maitland to Morpeth in 1864. This was a very rare instance of a railway being built in New South Wales to serve a port other than Sydney or Newcastle. This railway, though, was a total failure. Shippers increasingly preferred to rail goods from the interior direct to the saltwater wharves at Newcastle. Moreover, as ships increased in size, Morpeth became increasingly inaccessible.

The inexorable decline of Morpeth as a port (and a railway terminus) was a product of equally inexorable improvements in railway and shipping technology. From 1889 wool from the New England region was being railed to Newcastle for direct export to Britain. This did not last long, however, for the opening of the great Hawkesbury River Bridge in the same year connected Sydney and Newcastle by rail. The NSWGR promptly introduced differential rates, under which goods from the northern part of the colony in effect were carried free from Maitland to Sydney. This was the final nail in the coffin of Morpeth as a port, although a fitful trade by small steamers lingered into the 1930s, and its useless railway limped on into the early 1950s. It also meant that Newcastle was reduced to a specialist coal port, rather than becoming the port of choice for the extensive territory to its north and west. Thus, in New South Wales railway rate policy deliberately and consciously centralised rail traffic on Sydney, preventing the development of rival ports.

Shipping could support surprising linkages between industries and create new patterns of trade. An early example was the smelting of copper ore mined in Australia's first ever mineral boom of the 1840s. The first copper mine was established at Kapunda in South Australia in 1844, and another larger one opened nearby at Burra the next year. Transportation of ore was difficult because the sea was 145 kilometres away. The ore needed smelting and local fuel supplies were limited – there is no coal and little timber in the region. The solution was expensive transport by cart to Adelaide (until the railway was completed) then shipment to Newcastle, thence shipping by rail to a smelter built especially to process the South Australian ore. The smelter, though, was beside the Newcastle coal mine, not the Burra or Kapunda copper mine, because Newcastle coal was closer to salt water than South Australian copper. Similarly, the rail links necessary for efficient operation could be built far more cheaply at Newcastle than in South Australia.

This early use of Newcastle's coal and maritime resources anticipated many such linkages created over the following century and more, including between Newcastle and Whyalla, South Australia, source after 1915 of much of the iron ore for Newcastle's steel industry established in that year. Once again, it was Newcastle's good harbour (by the standard of river harbours on the coast north of Sydney) and plentiful high-quality coal which made it the obvious choice for the first serious and lasting Australian foray into iron and steel making.

INTERCONTINENTAL MARITIME TRADE IN THE AGE OF SAIL

THE EUROPEAN SETTLEMENT of Australia had begun with the extraordinary voyage across the world of the First Fleet between 1786 and 1788. Such voyages, both by naval vessels and ships of the English East India Company, became the norm for the new colony's links with the outside world. Traditional sailing ships, little changed since those of the First Fleet and not much faster, continued to provide Australia's links with the outside world until the late 1840s. The abolition of the East India Company's monopoly in 1813 meant that these vessels belonged to many different owners. Some American vessels began to call at Australian ports, largely because American sailors were so active in the southern whale fishery and in sealing on the southern Australian coast. The opening of Chinese ports to legal Western trade following the First Opium War of 1839–42 made Sydney more important in world trade, because it could be a stage in round-the-world triangular voyages, typically from Europe or America to Australia, then on to China, and finally back to the home port.

By the 1850s, the clipper ship was setting the pace on the England–Australia run, with Melbourne as the ultimate destination. The clippers were named after their raking bow and were built for speed. Slim and elegant, they carried enormous quantities of sail and were driven hard in the high latitudes of the Great Circle route, which took them non-stop from English ports to Melbourne through Antarctic waters. Most timber clippers were built in the New England states of the USA, where there were ample supplies of timber and a strong maritime tradition. However, by the 1860s British-built iron clippers were dominating the trade. Among the most famous clipper ships of the time were the *Red Jacket*, the *Thermopylae* and the *Cutty Sark*. The *Red Jacket* established a record trans-Atlantic time of 13 days (which still stands for sailing vessels) on her maiden voyage from New York to Liverpool in January 1854, and then sailed to Melbourne in the then unprecedented time of 67 days non-stop. She returned to Liverpool via Cape Horn, once again non-stop, in 73 days.

Clipper ships continued to be competitive with steamers for many decades. The Glasgow-built iron clipper *Cutty Sark*, for instance, was not built until 1869 and was in more-or-less continuous service on the Australia run until 1894, generally completing her passage in between 67 and 85 days. Typical of many clippers, she often brought immigrants to Australia, then sailed to China with coal from Newcastle, returning to England with fresh China tea. Equally commonly, she would return directly from an Australian port laden with wool, often carrying loads of over 4000 bales. Australian ports she served included Melbourne, Sydney, Newcastle and Brisbane. Her exact contemporary and rival, the Aberdeen-built *Thermopylae*, sailed on her maiden voyage from Gravesend to Hobson's Bay, Melbourne, in 63 days. This was and remains the fastest passage by a sailing vessel on record. She then sailed in ballast to Newcastle, took on coal for Shanghai (which she reached in 31 days) and then sailed from Fouzhou (then spelt Foochow) to London in 91 days.[7]

The age of the clipper ship lasted a century, although after the 1860s they were mostly used for transporting goods. Bulky goods were their speciality, since they had no engines in their holds to prevent the loading of huge loads like logs for wharf piles. As early as the mid-1880s, steamers rather than sailing ships were taking much freight shipped over long distances, especially more valuable items.[8] However, right up until World War II, clipper ships were regular visitors to Australian ports, especially the South Australian wheat ports such as Port Lincoln, Wallaroo and Port Victoria, and also

On 17 April 1947 the *Pamir* became the last clipper ship to leave Sydney in commercial freight service with an unromantic load of cement bound for Wellington, New Zealand. The steam tug *Hero* towed her down the harbour and out through the heads. (Max Dupain, State Library of New South Wales PXD 596, vol 1, item 18, courtesy Jill White)

Newcastle, where they loaded coal. Clipper ships needed no fuel, and in their latter years they sailed mostly under the German or Finnish flag with very young, poorly paid crews. During the 1920s and 1930s this trade was already an anachronism and attracted attention for the 'grain races' between this dying breed of vessels. Aspiring novelists signed on as seamen and newsreel crews often filmed departures.

The last clipper ships in Australian waters were the *Pamir* and the *Passat*, built in Hamburg in 1905 and 1911. For much of their long lives they made regular voyages to Port Lincoln, Port Victoria and Sydney, always returning to Europe around Cape Horn. The *Pamir* was in New Zealand ownership as a prize during and after World War II and became the last clipper ship to leave Sydney when the tug *Hero* towed her through the Heads with a load of cement for Wellington on 17 April 1947. Both vessels left Port Victoria for the last time with loads of grain bound for Falmouth, England, on 28 May 1949. They were the last ever windjammer voyages from an Australian port.[9] The *Passat* was retired to serve as a youth hostel in Travemünde in Germany, where she still lies; while the *Pamir* foundered sailing from Buenos Aires to Hamburg in September 1957. Eighty men and boys drowned, their loss marking the end of the era of the clipper ship.

EARLY STEAMER SERVICES TO AUSTRALIA AND THE ENGLISH MAILS

ALTHOUGH THE FIRST steamship had arrived in Sydney as early as 1831, this date certainly did not mark the beginning of regular services by steam. For 20 years and more, steamers operated only close to ports while the free power of the wind continued to power vessels across the oceans. Simultaneously with the development of the clipper ship, though, was the emergence of another type of vessel based on similar principles. This was the fast auxiliary steamer – essentially a clipper ship with an auxiliary steam engine, which would be used only when winds were unfavourable. They were screw-powered vessels, since paddles could slow a ship and were vulnerable to damage in the wild seas of the high latitudes of the Southern Ocean where vessels on the Great Circle route made such spectacularly fast if uncomfortable progress under canvas.

Although their engines were neither powerful nor efficient, auxiliary steamers could make very fast times since they could sail under canvas at high speed and did not need to carry too much coal. Their speed was about 7 knots under steam and 11 knots under sail. On a typical voyage from England to Australia an auxiliary steamer's engine would be used for about 15 days on the 60-

day passage, mostly in the doldrums, the calm tropical waters of the mid-Atlantic. The heyday of the auxiliary steamer coincided with that of the clipper ship in the 1850s. Fares were always higher on auxiliary steamers, since they cost more to run and were faster, so the steamers tended to offer more luxurious accommodation. The finest of them, the *Royal Charter*, even had a piano on board for her passengers' amusement.

The great stimulus to the introduction of steamships on the England to Australia run was the Royal Mail contracts. The first commercial contract for the carriage of mail by sea had been signed in London in 1837 between the Post Office and the Peninsular Steam Navigation Company. It provided for a weekly steamer service between Falmouth and a number of Portuguese and Spanish ports. Previously mails had been carried either by the Admiralty (these were, after all, Royal Mails) or, east of Suez, more commonly by vessels of the British East India Company. In 1840 the Peninsular Steam Navigation Company was reconstituted by Royal Charter as the Peninsular and Oriental Steam Navigation Company (or simply P&O) and began a monthly mail service from England to Alexandria in Egypt. In 1842 P&O won the mail contract for steamer voyages between Suez and Calcutta, extended the following year to Singapore and Hong Kong. The company used Galle in Ceylon (now Sri Lanka) as the port where its services connected, although this was later changed to the city of Colombo. Initially transport of mails and passengers from Alexandria to Suez was by steamer on the Nile to Cairo and then by the company's 3000 camels across the desert, but the opening of Africa's first railways in 1854 from Alexandria to Cairo and in 1858 from Cairo to Suez, modernised this leg of the service.

Following the gold rush and the sudden commercial importance of the Australian colonies, the British government invited tenders for a mail steamer service to Australia. The plan was for it to operate as an adjunct to the China service to Hong Kong and Shanghai, connecting with the China steamers at Singapore. The ships were to run every two months, from Singapore to Sydney, stopping at King George's Sound (modern Albany), Adelaide and Melbourne. P&O predictably enough won the contract, and so sent their new steamer *Chusan*, named after an island off Shanghai indicating she had been intended for the China service, to Sydney instead. Thus, on 3 August 1852 the *Chusan* became the first steamer to bring mail to Australia, travelling on her maiden voyage via Cape Verde and the Cape of Good Hope. She then made the first regular mail steamer run to Singapore on the contracted route, taking six weeks. The run was shared by a similar vessel, the *Shanghai*.[10]

At Singapore, the steamers connected with another P&O steamer plying between Suez and Hong Kong. Transit across Egypt was by a mixture of rail, camel and horse, until the

completion of the railway from Alexandria to Suez in 1858, and then another P&O steamer completed the link between Alexandria and England. It was a slow route compared with the clippers or auxiliary steamers, but it was safer and more comfortable, since the entire voyage was made in friendly latitudes and stops were frequent, as indeed they had to be to take on coal. However, the 42-day five-stop voyage from Sydney to Singapore of the steamer *Chusan* in 1852, although faster than the contract time of 55 days, compared very poorly with the record 58-day non-stop passage of the auxiliary steamer *Royal Charter* from Melbourne to Cork in Ireland in 1859. There was one big difference though – the passengers on the *Chusan* all lived to enjoy their renown, whereas the *Royal Charter* foundered only days later with the loss of 383 passengers and crew, her weak steam engine unable to prevent her being blown onto rocks on the coast of North Wales. The tragedy destroyed much of the prestige of the auxiliary steamers and hastened the triumph of regular steam services for those who could afford them.[11]

However, despite all the enthusiasm the arrival of the *Chusan* had generated in Sydney, P&O soon found the service hopelessly uneconomic and withdrew it after just two years. It was still far quicker and much cheaper to reach Australia from England by clipper ship or auxiliary steamer non-stop by the Great Circle route. The British government called fresh tenders, and the successful bidder was the European and Australian Royal Mail Company, which made a complete break with traditional maritime routes to Australia and operated its service from Sydney to Panama via New Zealand and the Polynesian island of Rapa to Panama, from where passengers crossed the isthmus on the Panama Railroad, the world's first and shortest transcontinental railway. Connecting ships from Panama and Colón (on the Caribbean coast) enabled passengers and mail to reach San Francisco, US east coast ports and Europe.[12] Although the contract was for five years, the new route proved no more profitable than the old, and services ceased once again after just two years.

In 1858 a new contract was advertised, this time from Suez to the same Australian ports via Aden and Mauritius. P&O was the successful tenderer once again, and the service began, although it was rerouted from Mauritius to Galle in Ceylon after two years. Thereafter the service was permanent and, although there were variations in the exact route over the decades, continued in P&O's hands (shared after 1888 by the Orient Line which P&O eventually would absorb) until the 1960s. The 1858 contract provided for a transit time of 55 days from London to Sydney, which was the same as the contract time from Sydney to Singapore just six years earlier. This service was extremely complex: a steamer from London to Alexandria; then rail across Egypt to Port Said on the Red Sea; then a steamer to Galle in Ceylon, stopping at Aden and Bombay on the way. At Galle (later Colombo), the fulcrum of the whole enterprise, the Australian mails were separated from the China and Singapore mails, then shipped across the Indian Ocean to King George's Sound (later replaced by Fremantle as the Western Australian port), Adelaide, and Melbourne and Sydney.

The 30-year period after the arrival of the *Chusan* saw rapid improvements in maritime steam engine technology as well as in naval architecture. Steamers became bigger; steel hulls replaced iron; successively compound, triple expansion and even quadruple expansion engines meant that steam was used far more efficiently. Larger steamers carried many more passengers and were much safer as well as cheaper to operate. The economics inexorably came to favour steam over sail. The opening of the Suez Canal in 1869 did not have the impact on these services so often assumed, since passengers and mail could be transhipped by rail across Egypt cheaply and quickly. Indeed, P&O did not use the Canal until 1881, since the train was faster, not to mention cheaper than the astronomical fees the Suez Canal Company charged its users.

The Australian colonies were themselves subsidisers of mail steamers, since their post offices operated independently of the British mails. Thus, the New South Wales government even began operating its own mail service from Sydney to London from 1883. It contracted the Orient Steam Navigation Company to run the service,

SPEEDING THE ENGLIS

The transhipment of the English mails onto trains to complete their journeys, beginning with the service between Melbourne and Sydney, became more widespread with the opening of other Australian intercolonial railways. When the railway opened between Melbourne and Adelaide in 1887, Port Adelaide became the transhipment point for all the eastern colonies. Special mail trains ran from Largs Jetty or Outer Harbour (near Port Adelaide) to the Adelaide GPO. (Right, Author postcard collection)

These trains were arranged as soon as the lighthouse keeper at Cape Borda (on Kangaroo Island) sighted the steamer from Colombo and telegraphed Adelaide with news of the ship's imminent arrival. From Adelaide, a special mail train ran to Melbourne with the mails for Victoria, New South Wales and Queensland.[13] The Victorian Post Office sorted the Melbourne mails on board the train as soon as it cleared customs at Serviceton on the South Australia–Victoria frontier, so they could be delivered the day after their arrival in Adelaide.

From Melbourne, another Victorian special train carried the English mails on to Albury, where the New South Wales special took over for the overnight leg to Sydney, as fast as the locomotives could run.[14] By 1900, these trains were scheduled to run weekly, arriving very early in the morning so that the English mails could be delivered with the first mails of the day.

From Sydney, the special train ran north to Newcastle and on to Wallangarra for transhipment to a Queensland train for Brisbane and other Queensland destinations. Thus, a day after the mails arrived in Sydney, they reached Brisbane. Frank Hurley knew about this and went to Sydney station early one morning to photograph the weekly English mail train with its elegant D class locomotive just before departure for the Queensland border. (Below, Frank Hurley in Robert Mills collection) The transhipment of the English mails at Port Adelaide and the connecting special mail trains lasted until 1917, when completion of the Trans-Australia Railway enabled Fremantle to take up the role. From November 1921 a special train left Fremantle on Thursdays, when the mails normally arrived from England, with onward connections by special mail expresses to the eastern states, so the mail would not have to wait until the regular Saturday transcontinental expresses.[15]

AILS TO THEIR DESTINATIONS

specifying a transit time of 39 days from Melbourne to London. The mails went from Sydney to Melbourne by rail, both to save time and to provide revenue for the railways. This service began when the railway was completed from Sydney to Melbourne, and broke the P&O monopoly. This monopoly was never recovered, for from 1888 the British government's mail contracts were shared between the two lines as well.[16] During the 1880s the Queensland government also had its own mail contracts for a service from Brisbane and other Queensland ports to Singapore through the Torres Straits and stopping in Surabaya or Batavia. Contracted to the British India Steam Navigation Company, this was a hazardous route, abounding in reefs and cyclones. After the loss of the company's RMS *Quetta* and almost half her complement near Thursday Island in February 1890, Queenslanders learned to live with their geography which meant that they were the last Australian colony to receive the mails from England.

THE ERA OF THE OCEAN LINER

AFTER A PERIOD of experimentation and development, during the 1870s the passenger liner began to assume its modern appearance, with a straight (or nearly so) bow replacing the clipper bow of early steamers. Masts were gradually truncated and steamers began no longer to carry sail at all. Passenger decks above the hull, whose cabins had windows rather than portholes, began to appear and multiply, as conditions for first and second class passengers at least became positively luxurious. Typical of the new vessels were P&O's RMS *Assam* and RMS *Siam* of 1876 and 1877, the first vessels over 3000 tons regularly to serve Australian ports on the run from Galle to Sydney. The era of the ocean liner, sailing to schedules as regular and predictable as those on a railway, and POSH travel (Port Out, Starboard Home, to avoid sun on the cabin in the Red Sea) had arrived.

P&O's Australian services had begun as ancillary to those to India, Singapore and China but, in time, they became the line's most important. By the 1920s Sydney rather than Bombay was P&O's premier destination, and its best vessels were on the Australia rather than the India or China runs. This reflected the growing importance of Australia in the British Empire as a whole, and the growing wealth of the Australian middle

A P&O generic postcard from when the company's ships still had black hulls and names drawn from Asia and the Mediterranean. The ship could be any of the *Mongolia, Moldavia, Marmora, Macedonia* or *Mooltan*, all launched between 1903 and 1905. Shipping companies issued postcards to passengers for correspondence and as souvenirs and this is a fine example of early 20th century colour lithography from England. (Author postcard collection)

class, which was far more numerous than the relatively small population of civil and military officials and British businessmen who provided the bulk of the clientele on the ships to and from India, Singapore and China.

P&O did not have the field to itself, although, thanks to the mail contracts, it was first and was always the premier line. Alone among companies serving Australia, P&O never carried third class passengers. Its steamers were for first and second class passengers only, carried the Royal Mail, and offered their passengers the kind of colonialist pampering which their crews, recruited from across the British and Portuguese colonies of Asia (most of the available chefs and stewards were Goan), were well trained to provide. P&O's main competitor on the England–Australia run was the Orient Steam Navigation Company, established in 1878, which in its first year gave passengers in all three classes the option of travel on its new *Orient*, then the largest ship on the run. By the early 1880s between them the two companies offered a fortnightly service direct from London to Sydney, stopping en route at Malta, Suez, Aden, Colombo, Albany (later altered to Fremantle), Adelaide and Melbourne. By this time the India and China

One of the delights of the month-long voyages between Australia and England was the opportunity to indulge in all sorts of shipboard hijinks. The young man in drag was better known as aviator than shipmate, and certainly struck a more heroic pose in his flying kit. He is the future Sir Charles Kingsford Smith. (NLA vn3722854)

runs were quite separate, although connections were maintained at Colombo, then the world's busiest port. By the first decade of the 20th century both companies were building fleets of new large vessels of around the 10 000 ton mark, the P&O ships all having names beginning with M and the Orient liners names beginning with O.

While P&O did not carry immigrants to Australia, the Orient Line certainly did, and other companies were also active in the immigrant trade. The most important of these was the Blue Anchor Line, operating a fleet of vessels between England and Australia via the Cape of Good Hope to avoid the Suez Canal fees. Blue Anchor vessels had all-white crews, as required for immigrant ships under the British *Merchant Shipping Act*. Apparently only the wealthy had sufficient savoir-faire to enjoy the decadent luxuries of Asiatic service without being corrupted by the experience. In 1909 Blue Anchor's largest and finest ship, the *Waratah*, foundered off South Africa with the loss of over a thousand passengers and crew. It was the last major loss of a passenger ship on the Australia run. P&O, seeing an opportunity to get into the profitable immigrant trade without spoiling the snobbish reputation of its mail steamers, promptly bought Blue Anchor's remaining assets and set up the P&O Branch Line with them, continuing in the same trade, still via South Africa. This line operated until 1936 when P&O wound it up after the immigrant trade dwindled in the wake of the Great Depression.[17]

Meanwhile, a whole network of regular steamer services to and from Australia was established in the second half of the 19th century. The major European powers of France, Germany, and even Austria-Hungary for a few years before 1914, operated subsidised mail liners to Australian ports. The Japanese Mail Line, NYK, ran a similar service from Yokohama to Melbourne calling at Shanghai, Hong Kong, Brisbane and Sydney. This was cheap and popular because Japanese standards of service and safety were always very high. A number of American lines ran trans-Pacific services, notably the Matson Line, and these would last right up till the end of regular liner services to Australian ports around 1970.

Surabaya-based liners of the Dutch KPM (Royal Steam Packet Company) linked Australia with Singapore via ports in the Netherlands East Indies. After World War I, Italy replaced Austria-Hungary in offering regular services from Trieste to Sydney. Italian ships were always cheaper than English ones, and Trieste was a convenient port for destinations on the European continent, so, even before large-scale Italian migration to Australia, Italian ships were popular. The French mail vessels of Messageries Maritimes tended to be patronised by more sophisticated Australian travellers, but its Marseilles–Sydney route, with various branches to Saigon, Noumea and other French colonial ports, lasted from 1869 until 1981. Messageries Maritimes even boasted vessels exotically named (for the French) *Sydney*, *Melbourne* and *Yarra*, besides more predictable French colonial nomenclature, so it took its Australian business seriously.[18]

Standards on passenger liners continued to improve after World War I. P&O bought out the Orient Line in 1918, although management of the two companies remained separate for another 40 years. P&O already had taken over the British India Line in 1914 and aggressively established a virtual monopoly on British mail and passenger shipping to India, Australia and China. The rationalisation, combined with the need to make good the heavy losses of shipping during the war, meant that a whole new generation of larger, faster and more luxurious vessels went into service during the 1920s and 1930s. These included five new 20000-ton O class liners for the Orient Line, including the *Orontes* and *Otranto*, in the 1920s, and P&O's five magnificent all-white 'Strath' ships (with names like *Strathnaver*, *Strathavon* and *Strathaird*) which joined the run between 1931 and 1938. The two lines' services were co-ordinated, and regular weekly sailings were the norm. The weekly departures from Sydney in particular were real gala affairs, with pipe bands playing and thousands of coloured paper streamers linking those on board ship and those on shore until severed by the slow movement of the vessel from the wharf.

World War II brought an immediate end to regular line voyages because virtually all British and most Australian passenger vessels were put into military service as troop ships.

P&O's RMS *Strathnaver* slowly steams into the Suez Canal. This scene gave the artist the opportunity to include the exotic vessels and scenery of Egypt to entice passengers. Another publicity masterstroke is the inclusion in the background of a rival line's far less smart vessel awaiting admission to the Canal. The Suez Canal Company pilots always gave precedence to the P&O liners carrying the King Emperor's mails. (Author postcard collection)

During the war the great event in passenger shipping was the brief presence in Sydney of the two great Cunard liners RMS *Queen Elizabeth* and RMS *Queen Mary*. They had been built for the trans-Atlantic trade, and came to Australia to collect the second Australian Imperial Force to fight in Egypt. After the war, though, the first regular line voyage from England to Australia did not leave until February 1947. Aeroplanes already had replaced the liners for urgent passenger and mail transport.

Despite the ever-increasing importance of air transport for the carriage of mails and passengers whose status or wealth could justify the high fares, in the post-war period shipping services continued to be important, and liner services were developed and improved right up until the 1960s. Changes in the patterns of migration to Australia meant that new companies entered the trade. Lloyd Triestino was joined by two other Italian companies, Flotta Lauro and Sitmar; and Greek lines entered the Australia run for the first time, notably Chandris Lines. P&O-Orient Lines, as it became, also began operating more sailings via Panama.

The Greek and Italian lines had lower cost structures, which helped maintain their viability. They also had a more relaxed social environment on board than P&O, where in first class it seemed to many Australians that a viceroy of India was about to step on board years after there were no longer any viceroys to do so. The Greek lines and Sitmar tended to use secondhand vessels, but Flotta Lauro built a number of magnificent new vessels for the Australia run, including the *Galileo* and the *Angelina Lauro*. Sitmar's vessels had very un-Italian names like *Fairsea* and *Fairstar*, while Flotta Lauro and Lloyd Triestino (perhaps because of its former identity as Austro-Hungarian Lloyd) maintained a far more Italian image. Meanwhile, the English company Shaw Saville also continued in the immigrant trade, and even New Zealand vessels built for the England to New Zealand run via Panama were pressed into bringing hundreds of thousands of migrants to Australia from Mediterranean countries through the 1950s and 1960s.

The massive post-war migration thus gave deceptive and temporary buoyancy to passenger shipping between Europe and Australia in the 1950s and 1960s. The cheap fares migrant ships offered on the return run gave many young Australians an opportunity to visit Europe as working tourists, the first generation of Australians ever to enjoy this kind of intercontinental mobility. Across the Pacific, the American Matson Line's stylish ships *Mariposa* and *Monterey* continued to offer monthly sailings in cruise-like atmosphere right through the 1960s. Air transport remained expensive until 1970, both because aircraft were expensive to operate until the age of the Boeing 747 jumbo jet, and also because Australian aviation regulations were specifically designed to prevent the proliferation of cut-price charter air operations as had emerged in Europe during the 1960s. This assisted shipping companies, although clear evidence that the liners were doomed came when Chandris Lines began operating services from Australian ports to Singapore connecting with cheap charter flights for the rest of the journey to Europe.

Meanwhile, the premier services continued to be offered, as they had for a century, by P&O, which built a series of magnificent new vessels between 1948 and 1961 specifically for the Australia trade. These began with the elegant and fast RMS *Himalaya* of 1949 and culminated in two enormous vessels, the RMS *Oriana* of 1960 and the *Canberra* of 1961. At 41 915 and 45 170 tons respectively, these were the largest and fastest passenger and mail ships ever to visit Australia regularly. On her maiden voyage in December 1960 *Oriana* made the fastest ever passage to Australia of 27 days from Southampton to Sydney. It is unlikely ever to be bettered, for times were changing for P&O and for liner voyages in general. The British Empire

Station Pier at Port Melbourne in the twilight of the liner era in 1973. Three liners are in port, from left to right P&O's *Oronsay*; Chandris Lines' *Australis*, and Sitmar Lines' *Fairstar* (formerly TSS *Oxfordshire*). The days when three ships on intercontinental line voyages would be in Melbourne simultaneously were numbered. (Tony McIlwain)

RADIO
REFRIGERATORS
PENFOLDS
WINE
ORIANA

was fading fast, and the jet age was dawning. In 1954 P&O vessels called at Bombay and Colombo for the last time, and in 1970 the old China service to Singapore and Hong Kong was abandoned.

One bright spot was the introduction in 1961 of a service between Australia and Japan via Hong Kong and other Asian ports by P&O subsidiary the Eastern and Australian SN Company, or E&A. This used two new Belgian vessels made redundant by the sudden independence of the Congo, rechristened with the very traditional P&O names of *Cathay* and *Chitral*, but only lasted a decade. As the British Empire in Asia was wound up, Australia remained the focus of its passenger operations, but the line voyages were reduced in frequency until they became positioning voyages to move ships between the northern and southern summer cruising seasons. The closure of the Suez Canal by warfare in 1967 was a final blow for the line voyages. By the time the Canal was reopened seven years later, the jumbo jet era had arrived and, with it, the era of the regular scheduled ocean liner voyage had come to an end.[19]

The swansong of the liner era: P&O Orient's *Oriana* berthed at Sydney's new Overseas Terminal after her record-breaking maiden voyage in December 1960. The Cahill Expressway above Circular Quay railway station is also new. (Wolfgang Sievers, NLA an14156306-7)

PASSENGER TRANSPORT BY SEA AFTER THE LINER ERA

LARGE LINERS continued to service Australian ports, but were rarely on line voyages and no longer conveyed mail. Cruising was their new vocation, initially using vessels built for line service. However, from the 1980s the design of vessels changed, reflecting the reality that their passengers were holiday-makers rather than travellers; and that the onboard experience was more important than the destination, which was generally the port of embarkation in any case. Cruising has a social history of its own, not really part of the story of this book. However it has meant that vessels previously unimaginable in Australian waters now make regular visits. These include the massive and luxurious ships built to cater for the North American market cruising the Caribbean, and the last of the trans-Atlantic liners. None of these were or are more famous than the mighty Cunarders, which for over a century and a half have provided express and mail services between Southampton and New York. Prior to the 1980s the only Cunarders to visit an Australian port were the then new *Queen Elizabeth* and *Queen Mary*, which carried the Australian Eighth Division from Sydney to the Middle East in 1940. That was a result of the exigencies of war and was expected never to be repeated.

However, as air travel came to dominate the trans-Atlantic passenger and mail traffic as assuredly as it did the England to Australia market, the Cunarders began spending the northern winter cruising the world, including in the South Pacific. The new generation of Cunarders have become familiar visitors to Australian ports, above all Sydney, which most summers hosts the line's newer vessels, the *Queen Elizabeth 2*, decommissioned in 2008, *Queen Mary 2* and *Queen Victoria*. Their massive size, black hulls, white superstructures and red and black funnels are all in the North Atlantic tradition, but their function has changed and they now sail the world for the pleasure of their passengers rather than to take them anywhere in particular.

Pleasure, though, has not been the motive of many recent passengers arriving by sea. Millennia ago, the first Australians made hazardous voyages with a good chance of death to reach the continent from Asia. Like the Aborigines, modern peoples do the same thing, with the same risks, and for the same reason: a desire to escape parts of Asia where life had become intolerable to seek a better future in a new land. While the numbers of such travellers have been small, their profile has been high because of the risks involved, the deaths of so many, and the debatable legality of their voyages. Their vessels, although more robust than the Aborigines', were fragile diesel-powered fishing boats never intended for long voyages.

Cunard's *Queen Mary 2* moored at the naval wharf at Garden Island in Sydney in February 2007. This was the famous cruise liner's first visit to Sydney and coincided with the last of the *Queen Elizabeth 2*. The Arabic numerals indicate they are the second ships of that name, not the second queens. The occasion attracted enormous public interest and the crowds were huge. (Author)

These voyagers came to Australia in three waves, each following breakdowns of Asian societies. The first was from 1976 to 1980, following the communist victory in Vietnam; the second in 2001 as Iraq and Afghanistan descended into chaos; and the third in 2009, after the defeat of the Tamil insurgency in Sri Lanka. The arrival of the first Vietnamese refugees by boat in 1976 posed an unprecedented challenge for Australia. They became known as 'boat people', threatening the recently officially abandoned but still potent idea of White Australia. The Vietnamese set the precedent. Only a relative handful arrived by sea: about 2000 of the 94 000 refugees from Indochina granted residence in Australia in the 20 years after the fall of Saigon in 1975. The number of Vietnamese on each boat was small. For instance the *Thinh Vuong*, preserved in Darwin Museum as the 44th Vietnamese boat to arrive in Australia in June 1978, carried just nine passengers.

There were far larger numbers, mostly around 200, on bigger boats in 2001, reflecting a higher degree of organisation of the voyages, mostly using Indonesian vessels, to which the Australian Defence Force gave the extraordinary acronym SIEV (Suspected Illegal Entry Vessel). The two most crowded vessels in 2001 came to sensational if different ends. The 438 on board the *Palapa I* were rescued in distress by the Norwegian merchant vessel *Tampa* in 26 August 2001, provoking a political crisis in Australia about what to do with them. The 421 refugees who left Indonesia for Australia on an unnamed and grossly overcrowded 19.5-metre vessel on 18 October 2001 posed no such dilemma. It foundered a day later with the loss of 353 lives, one of the greatest maritime tragedies in Australian history. Initially identified as SIEV-8, it is known as SIEV-X because it never reached Australia. Four other similar vessels reached Australian islands that month.

The third wave from Sri Lanka in 2009 has confronted Australia with similar dilemmas about the vessels' passengers' status as both refugees and illegal entrants, although the numbers on each vessel have not been nearly as large as in 2001. Australian responses to arrivals of boat people since 1976 have ranged from calm acceptance to hysterical rejection. Except in 2001, governments have responded with measured attempts to balance humanity and security, appropriately enough since the number of people involved is so small and the risks they have taken so great.

So the sea remains a route to Australia well into the jet age. It is no longer the choice of most, but is the most luxurious and pampered way for those relaxing on cruise ships, the most hazardous and fatal for those desperate enough to attempt the voyage on a SIEV. The groups are extremes, but extremes define the whole: in the early 21st century Australia remains a land of fascination and attraction for those who approach its shores, no matter what their circumstances, as assuredly as it was for those first Aboriginal mariners 50 or so thousand years ago.

The vanished era of river transport in Australia. About 1925 the then new SS *Moongi* (left) was heading down the Clarence River from Grafton to Yamba when she passed the much smaller SS *Gladys Phelps* headed upstream near Ulmarra. In the background a vehicular ferry was waiting to make its next crossing. (Author collection)

Chapter 2

ALONG COASTS AND RIVERS

DOMESTIC SHIPPING AND PORTS

THE RIVER FLOWED slowly between the red gums towards an almost impossibly distant sea. Its silence had been interrupted on occasion by Aborigines hunting, fishing, fighting or celebrating; more recently by sheep grazing and more rarely by the lonely white men who shepherded them. Now the swoosh of paddles, the beat of the engine, the sonorous steam whistle, and the thud of axes cutting firewood had come to the river. First one, then another paddle steamer puffed upstream. Never before had the modern world intruded onto the river quite like this, suddenly transforming it into a commercial artery.

Commerce means competition and a race was on. Two captains had brought their vessels, one across the sea, the other hauled overland, to a river whose waters had never before felt the inexorable power of steam. They both hoped to win a prize and establish a profitable new maritime trade. Such had been the great aspiration of European humanity since the 15th century – the dream of maritime commercial monopoly for which so many had crossed the oceans and so many had died. It was a dream which had changed the world, made it one, and was remaking it in Europe's image. And now that dream had come to the interior of Australia.

It was August 1853 and the first two steamers to ply the Murray River met near Swan Hill. They had paddled up from its mouth, each hoping to pioneer the river's navigation and collect the South Australian government's £2000 prize for doing so. Both were rewarded, although Francis Cadell, aboard whose steamer was Lieutenant Governor Sir Henry Young, received the lion's share. The victory meant Cadell became the first shipping magnate on the river, although it brought him neither wealth nor renown: he would be murdered by the cook's mate of his schooner while trying to make a living recruiting pearlers in Indonesia. His body went to the bottom with his scuttled vessel.[1] He was always the opportunistic small-time mariner with an eye for the main chance.

A century later, two men were fishing off what they called the middle wall, an artificial stone structure dividing a vast estuary in two halves. The tide was almost full when the thump of a diesel engine announced the downstream progress of the North Coast Steam Navigation Company's MV *Wyrallah*. The middle wall was but one element of a huge system of hydraulic works for controlling the flow of the Clarence River to improve the navigation of the hazardous bar at its mouth. But all that work, paid for over decades by colonial and state governments, had been in vain: the *Wyrallah* would be the company's last vessel ever to cross the bar. Her cargo was meagre and included the company's books and archives from Grafton dating back almost a century. The two fishermen waved; a hoot from the *Wyrallah*'s siren returned their modest salute.[2] There was no other celebration: on 6 March 1954 the era of coastal shipping in northern New South Wales was coming to an end.

So the era of steam navigation along Australia's coasts and rivers lasted just a century. Even as these small vessels were establishing the links vital for an enduring European civilisation in much of the continent, their demise could be foreseen. The first railways were already being built when Cadell steamed up the Murray. By the time the *Wyrallah* left the Clarence for the last time a century later, railways covered the inhabited parts of the continent and were themselves being challenged for transport supremacy by cars, trucks and planes. Coastal and riverine shipping were destined never to dominate Australia's transport needs for long.

THE AGE OF COASTAL SHIPPING

BEFORE THE BUILDING of railways, ships were the main transport links between the Australian colonies and along their coasts. In the age of sail, most ships were owned by their captains or by relatively small syndicates. This situation lasted until the end of regular voyages by sailing ships around the time of World War II. Sailing ships were only used for carrying freight after about 1860, although they survived on such mundane duties for many decades. One of the last in service was the schooner *Huia*, which carried hardwood from Grafton on the north coast of New South Wales to New Zealand ports and softwoods in the other direction until about 1940. Sail could also be fast, and few vessels ever crossed the Tasman faster than the *Huia* in a gale.[3]

However, from the time steamships were introduced into Australian waters, companies began to dominate coastal trade. The early auxiliary steamers' engines, although very inefficient at first, gave them manoeuvrability – and hence safety – across the notoriously hazardous sand bars at the mouths of so many rivers along the eastern coastline, and the distances were relatively short, meaning they did not have to carry huge supplies of coal. At sea they relied on their sails. The Hunter River Steam Navigation Company of 1839 was the first of many such enterprises.

Benjamin Boyd (1803–51), a wealthy London entrepreneur, hoped to use steam power to establish Twofold Bay some 600 kilometres south of Sydney as a centre of maritime commerce. He lived in New South Wales for less than a decade, sailing out from England in 1842 in his own yacht and accompanied by three steamers to establish the trade. Twofold Bay was an excellent harbour, but had little in the way of a natural hinterland. Few roads, and no railways, would ever serve its immodestly named ports of Boyd Town and East Boyd. Even Boyd was forced to use Boyd Town as a place of transhipment, and had to build a wool store and shipyard in Sydney from where his goods

Typical of the small ships operated by the North Coast Steam Navigation Company between Sydney and the New South Wales northern rivers was the TSS *Yulgilbar* of 1907. The small vessel of just 799 tons gross served the Macleay River until sold in 1925. The Company's painting, issued as a postcard, shows her steaming into Sydney Harbour with North Head in the background. (Author collection)

were exported. Boyd's shipping, pastoral and banking empire proved to be transient, and by 1849 he was bankrupt. His death was as spectacular as his life – he disappeared and was probably eaten by cannibals on Guadalcanal in 1851 while attempting to establish a new commercial and political empire in Melanesia.[4]

Less spectacular and far less egotistical ventures proved more durable. In Tasmania there were two companies operating by the early 1850s, one in Launceston and the Tasmanian Steam Navigation Company based in Hobart. Sydney remained the centre of the industry, though, with the establishment of the Kiama Steam Navigation Company in 1854 and the Grafton Steam Navigation Company in 1857. These traded respectively to the coast south of Sydney and to the Clarence River port of Grafton, some 65 kilometres upstream from the mouth. Grafton and Lismore on the nearby Richmond River were the furthest inland saltwater vessels ever sailed on Australian rivers. The Kiama Company soon had a rival in the Illawarra Steam Navigation Company and the Grafton Company in the Clarence and New England Company. Through various amalgamations they settled down to become the North Coast Steam Navigation Company and the Illawarra and South Coast Steam Navigation Company.

These two companies dominated the trade north and south of Sydney until the 1920s, when a reasonable road opened along the south coast and a railway along the north coast. They survived this competition, though, and the North Coast Company was even able to compete with the train on speed with its two express liners, the first and second TSS *Wollongbar* steaming from Sydney to Byron

Bay faster than the mail train and carrying their passengers in rather more comfort. Coastal passenger traffic came to an end after Japan entered World War II, and the Japanese torpedoed the second *Wollongbar* off the New South Wales north coast in 1943 with the loss of all hands. After 1945 both companies were confronted with enormous wartime losses, greatly increased costs for new ships, and ever better and more efficient trains and trucks. They ceased services north from Sydney in 1954 and to the south in 1956, thereby ending one of Australia's oldest maritime traditions.

A similar service to those on the coasts north and south of Sydney existed between Adelaide and ports on South Australia's Spencer Gulf, of which Port Lincoln became the most important. Once again, there were no railways to take the traffic, nor would one ever be built, since the land route was far longer than that by sea. From 1882 this service was in the hands of the Adelaide Steamship Company. Its last ship in the trade, the passenger-cargo MV *Minnipa*, left Port Lincoln for the last time in 1960. A new roll-on roll-off vessel, MV *Troubridge*, maintained a freight service to Port Lincoln and Kangaroo Island until 1970, when the Port Lincoln service was abandoned: the *Troubridge* was sold to the South Australian government two years later, ending 90 years of coastal shipping services by the Adelaide Steamship Company, which was diversifying into practically every industry except shipping.[5]

The coastal rivers of New South Wales, and to a lesser extent Queensland, also had local services in their saltwater stretches. There were both passenger steamers, which also carried light freight and cream, as well as goods steamers, mostly small flat-bottom craft called droghers. Some of these passenger services were of quite a high quality; those on the Clarence River, for instance, featured large and comfortable steamers with similar amenities to the larger Sydney ferries. This was the largest and straightest of the coastal rivers, so was ideally suited to such operations, which were competitive with buses and lorries in the days before sealed roads became widespread.[6] The Mary River in Queensland had similar operations. In addition, from the Clarence northwards coastal rivers were used for the haulage of cut sugar cane from riverside farms to mills. These services mostly began in the 1860s and lasted until the 1970s.

During the 1850s and 1860s numerous shipping companies were established, creating a network of regular steam liner services connecting all the Australian colonies and Pacific ports. The major companies were the Adelaide Steamship Company (founded 1875); the Melbourne Steamship Company (founded 1884 and growing from a concern initially operating vessels on the Port Phillip Bay excursion traffic); Huddart, Parker Limited (founded in 1876 and also having its origins in the Port Phillip traffic, especially between Melbourne and Geelong); Howard

Smith and Company (another Melbourne company founded in 1854); the Australasian United Steam Navigation Company (formed in Brisbane in 1886 by a merger of the Queensland Steam Shipping Company and the Australasian Steam Navigation Company); McIlwraith, McEacharn Limited (founded in London in 1875 but not active in passenger shipping on the Australian coast until 1909); and the Union Steam Ship Company of New Zealand (founded in 1875 and very active in Australian interstate shipping following its purchase of the Tasmanian Steam Navigation Company in 1891). Huddart, Parker Limited and the Union Steam Ship Company of New Zealand established a jointly owned company in 1921, called Tasmanian Steamers Limited, specifically to operate services to Tasmania. Interestingly enough, not one of the major interstate shipping companies had its headquarters in Sydney, although several had workshops there.[7]

During the second half of the 19th century steamship technology was constantly improving, as boilers became more efficient and engines more complex. The big steps forward were in compounding, with the development of the double and then the triple expansion engine, which used the steam from the boiler three times at three different pressures. Then at the very beginning of the 20th century the first turbine steamers were introduced into Australian waters, lifting speed and efficiency another notch. As engines became more efficient, the auxiliary steamer became the pure steamer. After the 1870s few new steamers bothered to carry sail. The screw steamer also quickly replaced the paddle steamer. Australia's first screw steamer was built in 1851 in Melbourne, which was then

The Australasian United Steam Navigation's SS *Aramac* of 1889 was typical of the interstate steamers of the late 19th century. (Author postcard collection)

not yet the major port it would soon become. Named the SS *City of Melbourne*, she was soon sold to the Brisbane-based Australian Steam Navigation Company and so became the first screw steamer on both the Yarra and Brisbane Rivers.[8]

The great era of the Australian interstate coastal liner was the first three decades of the 20th century. By then such ships were large and comfortable. Thanks to the steam turbine, they were also quite fast. Turbines were first used in Australia on the Union Steam Ship Company's Dumbarton-built *Loongana* of 1904, which operated on the Bass Strait service at speeds of up to 20 knots. The Union Company also ordered the second turbine liner, the beautiful and speedy 5282-ton *Maheno* of 1905, whose wreck still lies on Fraser Island in Queensland. Probably the finest of the coastal liners was Messrs McIlwraith, McEacharn's Belfast-built 9424-ton TrSS *Katoomba* of 1913, which lasted on the Sydney–Fremantle run until 1941. Such liners could compete effectively with railways on speed and comfort, although the Post Office preferred to give the lucrative mail contracts to a railway wherever there was one operating. Thus, despite the Australasian United Steam Navigation Company's heavy investment in the TrSS *Bingera* of 1906, for the Brisbane to Townsville express service, the company lost the mail contract when the railway opened between those cities in 1923.[9]

Station pier at Port Melbourne with an interstate liner, many sailing ships and the train providing the connection to Flinders Street, about 1890. (Freedman collection)

The peak of the coastal shipping industry was in 1913 and 1914, when vessels with a total capacity of over 20 000 passengers made regular sailings around the Australian coast. In 1913 no fewer than five new passenger liners were delivered. The ships could offer comfortable services, which were competitive with rail in speed and far more comfortable, provided the weather was good. Journey times between Melbourne and Sydney or Brisbane and Sydney were typically around 36 hours, or two nights and a day. By comparison, it took about 30 hours from Sydney to Brisbane by train at the time on the inland route via Wallangarra, and passengers had to change trains at dawn and travel in unheated carriages over Australia's highest railway summit, where winter night-time temperatures were generally well below freezing. The ship – with its hot water baths, fine restaurants with orchestras and spacious cabins in first class – was an excellent option compared with the train, and generally cheaper as well. Most ships ran a regular run from Brisbane to Fremantle, stopping at all the mainland capitals on the way. With so many vessels in the trade, there was a sailing most days.

While the ships were more comfortable than the trains, they were not as safe, especially in tropical waters. The north Queensland run was especially hazardous, where there was the combination of frequent cyclones, which often reduced visibility to zero, and poorly charted reefs. In 1911 and 1912 the Adelaide Steamship Company lost two large liners (the SS *Yongala* and SS *Koombana*), together with their entire crews, mail, and complements of passengers without trace in cyclones in northern waters.[10] As the Queensland North Coast Railway was built in sections between Brisbane and Cairns, passenger and mail ship services were confined to providing the missing links between the railways parallel to the coast. The southern runs were far safer, and it was here that most ships were concentrated. Even in temperate waters, though, there were hazards, especially at the Rip at the entrance to Port Phillip Bay. Moreover, before the days of radio and radar, collisions could happen at any time, as for example when the North Coast Steam Navigation Company's little SS *Helen Nicoll* ran down the far larger Brisbane-bound passenger liner SS *Keilawarra* off Coffs Harbour in 1886 with the loss of 46 lives.

Interstate coastal shipping never regained its high point after World War I and the trade was mortally wounded by ship losses and cessation of regular services during World War II. Some passenger ships limped on through the 1950s, basically linking Sydney and Fremantle. By then, however, not only had transcontinental rail transport improved dramatically in both speed and comfort with dieselisation and air-conditioning, but air services had become much safer and cheaper as well. The last two interstate liners in service were McIlwraith, McEacharn's MV *Kanimbla* and the Adelaide Steamship Company's 10 000-

ton MV *Manoora*, both of which ceased their regular runs from Sydney to Fremantle in 1961. Both were truly luxurious 1930s liners with art deco details and every facility for passengers. Both had served as troop transports during World War II, and both were sold abroad in 1961, *Manoora* to China and *Kanimbla* to Indonesia.

Trans-Tasman passenger shipping operated as an extension of the Australian interstate services, most intensively between Sydney and Wellington, but also connecting other Australian and New Zealand ports. Most of the Australian coastal shipping companies were involved in the trans-Tasman trade at some stage, although the Union Steam Ship Company of New Zealand and Huddart, Parker Limited were the most active. The last vessel on the run was Huddart, Parker's 1932-built 9576-ton MV *Wanganella*. She last berthed in Sydney on arrival from Wellington on 25 July 1962, ending the era of company-owned Australian passenger shipping.[11]

Thus, by the 1960s, only government-subsidised services continued, notably the Western Australian Coastal Shipping Commission's run from Fremantle to Darwin via Kimberley ports, the Port Lincoln and Kangaroo Island services in South Australia, and the Bass Strait services linking Tasmania with the mainland. The Western Australian service dated from 1912 and had been an Australian pioneer of diesel ships with the MV *Kangaroo* of 1915. This was only the second diesel motor ship ever built in the United Kingdom. The commission was a state enterprise established by a Labour government, and filled much the same role as the railways in a part of the country where railway construction could not be justified.

Its ships had to cope with the extreme tide variations of the northwest, and often sat high and dry while moored at jetties at low tide. During the 1930s, the commission briefly operated a service connecting Fremantle and the northwest of Western Australia with Dutch East Indies ports and Singapore. However, improved roads and air services put the line out of business in the early 1970s. The second MV *Kangaroo*, built in Brisbane as late as 1962, was the final passenger-cargo vessel on the run. Her last voyage was in 1973, leaving only ships serving islands carrying passengers on regularly scheduled voyages.[12]

Although the completion of the Brisbane to Cairns railway in 1924 meant the end of most Queensland coastal shipping services, it was never extended north of Cairns. Moreover, Queensland's most northerly town is Thursday Island, which no railway or road could ever reach. The weekly Cairns to Thursday Island run of the MV *Trinity Bay* is the last survivor of Australia's once numerous passenger-cargo coastal shipping services. Its owner, Sea Swift, also provides freight services to a host of Torres Strait islands and other north Queensland ports with little or no road or rail access.

The most intensive domestic shipping services serve the largest Australian offshore

ABOVE A postcard produced in Melbourne about 1910 illustrates the interstate liners and Victorian trains of that period, when these were the only ways to travel around the country. (Author postcard collection)

BELOW During the last years of Australian National Line's Bass Strait ferry operations, TSMV *Empress of Australia* completes another crossing in 1983. (NAA Series A6180, Item K30/3/83/57)

island, Tasmania. Tasmanian Steamers withdrew from the trade in 1959, selling its most modern vessel, the 1934-built TSS *Taroona*. Only a government-owned company, the Australian National Line (ANL), was willing to step into the breach. The Commonwealth had set up ANL, at first called the Australian Coastal Shipping Board, in 1946 to revive coastal freight shipping services at a time when ships were in short supply and private companies were rightly sceptical of the future profitability of such services.

ANL introduced Australia's first roll-on roll-off car and truck carrying passenger ship, the Newcastle-built TSMV *Princess of Tasmania* on the Melbourne to Devonport run in 1959. The Commonwealth subsidised the

ship's construction by a state government-owned shipyard. The *Princess* was then the largest such vessel in the world and lasted in Bass Strait service until 1972. Her design was replicated on a larger scale with the TSMV *Empress of Australia*, built at Cockatoo Island, Sydney, which began operating between Sydney and Tasmanian ports in 1965. This was suspended in 1972 and the *Empress* replaced the *Princess* on the Bass Strait run. These vessels were basically carriers of cars and trucks and their drivers. Their design was clear evidence that, by the 1960s, passenger shipping could only survive in Australia where there were no roads or railways to carry the traffic.

Business was so brisk in the 1960s that in 1969 the Australian National Line introduced its third and largest roll-on roll-off vessel, the TSMV *Australian Trader*, into the trade. The 1970s were not so buoyant and by 1976 only the *Empress* remained. She lasted until ANL withdrew altogether in 1985. At this point the Commonwealth and Tasmanian governments co-operated in setting up the TT Line, owned by the Tasmanian Transport Commission, which would receive a direct Commonwealth subsidy for shipping cars and trucks across Bass Strait and only operate passenger carrying ferries. ANL sold the *Empress* to Greek owners, under whom she would lead a varied life before dramatically sinking off Singapore following a collision in 1991.

TT Line has operated five ferries, all built in Europe. The first, the *Abel Tasman*, began operations for the new company in 1985 after ten years of service in the Baltic Sea as the *Nils Holgersson*. Its other four ships have been named *Spirit of Tasmania*. Currently two of these, *Spirits of Tasmania I* and *II*, operate nightly services between Devonport and Melbourne, although in high season they run to faster schedules and do day sailings as well, effectively doubling capacity using the existing fleet, although using more oil per sailing. By the standards of previous ships for Australian domestic service, they are huge – at 29 338 tonnes and 194 metres in length – and fast, boasting a maximum service speed of 27 knots, albeit with high fuel consumption at such a speed. By comparison, the *Empress of Australia* was a 12 037 gross tonnage vessel, 443 feet (135 m) long with a maximum speed of 17 knots. *Spirit of Tasmania III* operated a service between Sydney and Devonport from 2004 to 2006, but it was not a commercial success. However, in the era of globalisation the vessel was sold back to a European buyer for more than her purchase price, so the experiment was not a financial disaster for the company.

Another TT Line experiment was using two Tasmanian designed and built wave-piercing catamarans on the Bass Strait run, named *DevilCat* and *SeaCat*. They offered a five-hour high-speed crossing but were only viable during the summer months because Bass Strait was just too rough for such vessels in winter. They also required a high power output and consequent high fuel use. They supplemented the first *Spirit of Tasmania* when it was the only conventional vessel on the run but, after the arrival of *Spirits of Tasmania I* and *II* in 2002, they were withdrawn because the new conventional vessels could handle peak capacity more economically. Meanwhile, ANL's freight services across Bass Strait were taken over in 1985 by Brambles Shipping, which in turn was acquired by Toll Shipping in 2002. It uses modern Korean-built roll-on roll-off vessels to offer a daily freight service between Melbourne and Burnie.

The route from Melbourne to northern Tasmanian ports is busier than it has ever been, but now largely operates as an extension of road transport. This reflects the situation in the North and Baltic Seas, between Japan and Korea, and between the north and south islands of New Zealand, where the transport geographies are similar. Only in such locations, where there really is no alternative, has sea transport survived for general traffic in the face of the increased productivity of road and rail modes.

HARBOUR WORKS

TWO OF AUSTRALIA'S first three ports, Sydney and Hobart, had such good natural harbours that they needed very little in the way of harbour works until vessels became much larger in the early 20th century. The same was not true of the third, Newcastle at the mouth of the Hunter River. The New South Wales coastal rivers north of Sydney have 'some of the worst bar entrances in the world'.[13] Most of them are a mass of changing channels in shoal-filled bays. A chart made one month might not be accurate the next, and channels change regularly, especially after floods.

The Hunter was the most benign of these rivers, although it too had a bar and its entrance was complicated by a steep rocky island called Nobby's. Australia's first harbour works began at Newcastle in 1813, including construction of Macquarie Pier and a breakwater to link Nobby's to the mainland, thus protecting the pier and fixing the channel, which was not completed until 1846.[14] About the same distance south of Sydney, landowners Hamilton Hume and Alexander Berry had assigned convicts to dig a new entrance to the (all too accurately named) Shoalhaven River in 1822. This was a short canal some 200 metres long across the beach and was a very rare example of private investment (albeit with free labour provided by the government) in a navigational improvement.

The dominant figures in building harbour works in 19th century Australia were EO Moriarty and Sir John Coode. Moriarty spent his entire career with the New South Wales Public Works Department in Sydney. The shape of Sydney and Newcastle's waterfronts is largely his work. He also began improving the navigability of the many rivers on the New South Wales north coast whose entrances were blocked or hampered by sand bars. Of these rivers, the Clarence and Richmond Rivers were the most important, although there was a sizeable trade on the Manning and Macleay Rivers as well, and even the smaller rivers were served by tiny ocean-going steamers manned by extremely plucky crews.[15] The history of navigation on these river entrances is littered with an extraordinarily large number of shipwrecks. Most (but not all) of these involved relatively little loss of life, since they were so near shore and occurred when everyone on board was cognisant of the risks of crossing the bar, hoping for the best but always ready for the worst.

Coode was an English hydraulic engineer who travelled extensively in Australia as a consultant in the 1880s and was widely considered the world's finest such engineer at the time. His works include the breakwater to Granite Island and its associated jetty at Victor Harbor in South Australia; the far

The waters of Shoal Bay, the estuary of the Clarence River, tamed by massive breakwaters built to the design of Sir John Coode. A ferry service across the bay was established as recently as 1986, viable because the distance is so much greater by road than by water. The ferry was built in 1939 as the MV *Stockton* for service between Stockton and Newcastle; became the *Birkenhead Explorer* operating on Sydney Harbour in 1982; and finally was renamed the *Harwood* in 1987 when bought to work across the mouth of the Clarence. (Yuki Kang)

The finger wharves at Sydney's Walsh Bay were very busy with shipping being loaded and unloaded traditionally by manual labour on this winter's day in the 1950s, as photographed from a helicopter by Frank Hurley. (Frank Hurley, NLA an23477947)

The *Wollongbar* aground off the beach at Byron Bay in 1921. The wreck became quite a centre of attention and there were even special trains run so that people could come and look at the sight. The wreck is still on the beach at Byron Bay and on a calm day it is easy to swim out and climb aboard. Apart from climbing on the wreck of the *Maheno* on Fraser Island (apparently no longer permitted, although the author did it years ago) it is the nearest anyone can get to boarding a coastal liner of the early 20th century, as none has been preserved. (Author collection)

grander Coode Canal and Victoria Dock at Melbourne; Fremantle's breakwaters and docks; and, most challenging of all, his enormously elaborate works to improve the navigability of the mouth of the Clarence River in northern New South Wales.[16] This last project began in 1893, based on Coode's plans of 1887, and construction only finished in 1973. Coode decided to overrule Moriarty's original plans for improving the navigation of this most important of all New South Wales north coast rivers. Back in the 1870s, Moriarty had attempted to fix the channel in the shifting sands of Shoal Bay to the south shore, but Coode developed a plan fixing the channel on the northern bank. This involved partially demolishing a breakwater already completed at Moriarty's behest.

Apart from the New South Wales coastal rivers, most Australian harbours have been either in natural harbours or open roads, where long jetties have been built on piles of turpentine timber out beyond the surf to take goods out to ships waiting moored beside them in the open sea. Jetties such as this have been built all over the country. Three of the most famous of the very many jetties of this kind were at Broome and Carnarvon in Western Australia and at Byron Bay in New South Wales. At both Carnarvon and Broome there were lengthy tramways built into the town from the jetties. Byron Bay's two jetties were the most easterly in Australia, and the first of these jetties was also the scene of one of the most dramatic and public, if least fatal, shipwrecks in Australian maritime history. This was in 1921 when the crack liner of the North Coast Steam Navigation Company, the magnificent 2005-ton TSS *Wollongbar*, was blown onto the beach by a sudden easterly gale while attempting to escape from the open port.[17]

Broome was famous for the extremely wide variation in tides, requiring an exceptionally high jetty to cope with the close to 10-metre variation between high and low water. During the early 20th century up to 300 pearling luggers operated out of Broome, with extremely cosmopolitan crews, including many Japanese, a lot of Malays and a sprinkling of islanders.

Australia's most important natural harbour, where there has not been any great need for works apart from occasional dredging and wharf construction, is Port Jackson at Sydney. Hobart is essentially similar, located like Sydney on a flooded river valley and so enabling the largest ships to come right into the city. Sydney's initial port facilities were concentrated around Circular Quay and remained there until the boom years of the 1880s. Thereafter, more and more of the harbour foreshores were used for shipping purposes. Most development was around Darling Harbour, which had direct rail access from as early as 1855. Circular Quay never had rail access, and increasingly became the berth for passenger liners, as cargo and mixed traffic vessels moved to the less picturesque but better served facilities of

Darling Harbour. However, wool continued to be loaded from wool stores around Circular Quay, and even new ones in Walsh Bay, well into the 20th century.

The great development of the late 19th century was the finger wharves resting on timber piles. No other port in the world had such a quantity of timber finger wharves as Sydney, nor wharves that required timber piles as deep. Piles of 43 and even 49 metres, cut from one tree, were commonplace on Sydney wharves. The first 20 years of the 20th century saw the construction of the timber finger wharves at Walsh Bay (the last such surviving complex in the world, built by the Sydney Harbour Trust in 1918); the enormous timber finger wharf at Woolloomooloo Bay (completed in 1916 and the longest timber building ever erected in the world); and the concrete wharves with railway sidings laid to shipside and complementary victualling store at Jones Bay, Pyrmont. The move into bulk grain shipping began during World War I, and in 1922 Australia's first and largest bulk silo complex was opened at Glebe Island as a joint NSWGR, Department of Agriculture and Sydney Harbour Trust project. The silos and concrete wharves with railways laid in them built in Sydney around 1920 anticipated many similar structures built in ports large and small around Australia. However, it would not be till the 1960s that the wheat bag was obsolete. Bulk wheat handling required trucks, silos in production areas, railway wagons, silos at ports and ships all designed specifically for the traffic, so the transition took many decades. Indeed it would scarcely be complete before the Glebe Island silos were closed and their functions transferred to Port Kembla.

Queensland ports have not demanded anything like the investment in breakwaters and harbour works required in New South Wales, because most of the coast is sheltered by the Great Barrier Reef. Even south of the reef, the Queensland coast is protected by large sand islands. Most Queensland ports merely required jetties to be built into the sea to a depth sufficient for the ships using the port. In some cases these jetties had to be very long. At Lucinda near Ingham the jetty completed in 1979 is no less than 5.8 kilometres long. Brisbane was particularly favoured with a broad and deep river debouching into the relatively sheltered waters of Moreton Bay. Brisbane shippers and wool merchants were able to build wharves, wool stores and warehouses very easily and cheaply along much of the river, especially its north bank downstream from the city in Teneriffe and New Farm. The largest ships moored at wharves further downstream at Pinkenba. After the 1880s these were served by rail. There were even coal loaders from the 1890s to the 1960s as close to the city as Woolloongabba on the south bank of the river.

Melbourne and Geelong too, have had the advantages of the protection of Port Phillip Bay. Melbourne's early port at South Melbourne was simply a pier jutting out into the bay, gradually expanded to carry the tracks of Australia's first steam railway from 1854. Station Pier, as it became known, still exists, although is much rebuilt and modified, and is now the Melbourne terminus of the daily ferries crossing Bass Strait to Devonport. For more than a century it was the major terminal for overseas passenger liners in Melbourne, and so was the point through which most migrants arrived in the city, in both its two major waves of immigration, between 1851 and 1890 and between 1947 and 1970. Melbourne, though, was a sufficiently important port to justify the investment in extensive facilities at the mouth of the Yarra during the boom years of the 1880s, including the Victoria Dock and Coode Canal. As in New South Wales, Sir John Coode was the designer of these facilites.

Adelaide, had a similar advantage to Melbourne, located on the smooth waters of the Gulf, and had jetties at places like Semaphore, Outer Harbour, Glenelg and Largs which, like Station Pier in Melbourne, simply ran straight out into the open sea. The initial wharf dating from 1840 was at Port Adelaide, but early in the 20th century a more complex network of wharves and connecting railways was built at Outer Harbour, opening in 1908. Fremantle required progressive construction of breakwaters and dredging to fix the channel into the mouth of the Swan River.[18]

Fremantle was still a small port at the turn of the 20th century. Loading facilities were limited, and shipboard cranes did most of the heavy lifting. Sandalwood was and remains a Western Australian speciality export commodity. (Author postcard collection)

The Macquarie lighthouse near Sydney's South Head by an unknown artist about 1820. (SLNSW a1528287)

Closely associated with ports were (and are) the navigational aids provided to assist ships safely to reach their destinations. Visibility around Australia's coasts is mostly good by world standards, although it is far from uniformly so. By contrast, the seas off Australia's coasts are very rough indeed by any standards, often with truly enormous swells. Throughout the 19th century and for much of the 20th century, lighthouses were the main way in which navigators were assisted to find their way at night. Australia's first lighthouse, the Macquarie Light, was designed by convict architect Francis Greenway and built a little south of Sydney Harbour's South Head between 1816 and 1818. Its location could and did confuse mariners unfamiliar with the entrance, most famously with the loss of the ship *Dunbar* with almost all aboard in 1854. In wild stormy conditions with poor visibility, her master erroneously and fatally thought the light marked South Head, and so sailed her straight onto the rocks between the light and the Heads. The light was not right at the Heads for the very good reason that the ground was far higher where it was built, but the tragedy demonstrated the hazards of such compromises. Lighthouses were built all over the Australian coastline during the 19th century. The first outside Sydney and Newcastle was built on the Derwent River near Hobart in 1833, and in the 1840s a series of lighthouses was built to mark the extremities of Bass Strait. During the 1850s lighthouses were erected on the Victorian and South Australian coasts, and eventually they identified most harbours and hazards to navigation. There was also some use of lightships to mark reefs in north Queensland.

After 1970 Australia's major ports were rebuilt and often relocated following the introduction of the shipping container. Traditionally wharves had been close to the heart of the major cities. Roads and railways around these wharves were often congested. The first international shipping containers reached Australia in 1969, prompting a revolution in the design of vessels and ports and a vast improvement in working conditions of stevedores. Previously, waterside workers had done a lot of manual handling of shipments, which were all of different sizes and weights. Shipping containers, in standard sizes of 6 and 12 metres, enabled a huge acceleration in ship turn-around time in port and the mechanisation of loading and unloading. Previously stevedores had been recruited largely for their muscles, and work was dependent on the number of vessels in a port. Many went to bed at night not knowing whether there would be work the next day or not.

Containerisation required far fewer workers, but better trained ones who worked in far more congenial conditions. Understandably, the tough conditions of the pre-containerisation waterfront had spawned some of Australia's most militant unions, and many of the industrial and political battles of the Cold War were fought on the wharves.

Stevedores loading ships the old way at Fremantle, where Frank Hurley captured this scene of bags of flour being handled in the 1950s. (Frank Hurley, NLA an23998662)

Ultimately, the issues arising from Cold War industrial politics on the pre-containerisation waterfront were not resolved until the great waterfront industrial dispute of 1998. By then both the Cold War and the era of hard manual labour on the waterfront were well and truly over. For all the bitterness it engendered, the dispute ended with a typical Australian compromise, which left the workforce unionised but conditions modernised to reflect the (by then not especially) new technology.

In Sydney, an entirely new location was developed for container traffic at Port Botany, opening in stages from 1979, while the eastern shore of Darling Harbour was also redeveloped as a relatively short-lived container terminal. The flight of industry from the city, the city's commercial and population growth, and improved road and rail transport meant that city waterfront land was no longer the best place for port facilities. In Brisbane and Melbourne the new container docks were built downstream from the old wharves, at Fisherman Island near the mouth of the Brisbane River and at a series of docks on the Yarra downstream from Coode's Victoria Dock.

Containerisation and the consequent closure of many inner-city wharves have provoked the greatest urban redevelopment projects Australia has ever seen. In Brisbane an opportunity was squandered when the Riverside Expressway was built on the site of many of the city's wharves, effectively cutting off much of the city from its waterfront, although the urban renewal as shipping has left New Farm and Teneriffe has been more impressive. Melbourne's Victoria Dock and Sydney's Darling Harbour have been redeveloped as residential, commercial and leisure precincts; and the same is planned for the now-closed container terminal on the eastern shore of Darling Harbour.

The second revolution in port facilities from the late 1960s was the development of new ports with bulk loading facilities catering to new mining industries. These involved automated conveyor belts conveying the mineral from rail hopper wagons (and trucks as well in the case of Port Kembla) direct to ships, avoiding the need for cranes. In some cases facilities were moved to new locations. Operations at Sydney's White Bay coal loader and grain terminal were wound down in the 1980s and transferred to Port Kembla. The rapid expansion of coal mining in central Queensland saw a host of new ports built primarily, but not exclusively, to handle export coal, all served by rail. The first bulk handling of coal in Queensland was at Gladstone in 1954, but expansion really began with the opening of Gladstone's Barney Point coal loader in 1967.

Since then, the transformation of central Queensland's ports has been astounding. No longer catering just for local shipping needs, they have been rebuilt and relocated to handle much of the coal which powers Asia's rapidly industrialising economies. New ports opened at Hay Point (1971), Dalrymple Bay (1983) and Abbot Point (1983).[19]

A typical provincial coastal port with rail access was Coffs Harbour in northern New South Wales. The North Coast Steam Navigation Company's SS *Cavanbar* had just arrived from Sydney and some lonely passengers already were walking up the jetty into town. Most were still milling around with friends and relatives. The little railway from Coffs Harbour to nearby Raleigh opened in 1915 and the 1901-built *Cavanbar* was sold to China in 1916, so the image can be dated with some precision. (Author postcard collection)

Newcastle had always been Australia's premier coal port and had, for the time, very advanced hydraulic cranes to move coal from rail wagons to ship way back in the 19th century. In 1976 the first (of now three) modern coal loaders was commissioned at Newcastle, enabling a huge increase in tonnage. At the same time bogie hopper rail wagons replaced the four-wheel timber inverted pyramid box wagons whose design had changed little in a century.

In Western Australia much the same thing happened with the development of the iron ore industry in the Pilbara. New ports opened at Dampier in 1966 and Port Hedland in 1969, the latter on the site of a former cattle port which had been served by an isolated and flimsy railway from 1913 to 1951. These ports are truly massive in scale and are Australia's busiest: in 2006–07 they handled 126 and 107 million tonnes respectively. One of the two big operators, Rio Tinto, is planning to expand capacity of its Pilbara ports to a total of 220 million tonnes each year.

By comparison, in Queensland Gladstone handled about 57 million tonnes in 2006–07 and Hay Point about 86 million tonnes. Port Kembla only exports about 13 million tonnes while Newcastle is eastern Australia's busiest minerals port, shipping over 90 million tonnes in 2008–09, overtaking Hay Point and up from 50 million tonnes in 1995, with substantial future growth planned. One big difference is that the New South Wales and Queensland ports are owned and operated by state government corporations, whereas the Pilbara iron ore ports (and the railways serving them) are owned and operated by the mining companies Fortescue Metals, Rio Tinto Australia and BHP Billiton.

The move into containers and bulk movement of commodities led to new styles of ships, the container ship and the bulk carrier. One of the latter was the bulk cement carrier *River Torrens*, built in 1977. In 2000 the ship was sold to an offshoot of Canadian Steamship Lines known as CSL Pacific Incorporated, was renamed *CSL Pacific*, and promptly became the centre of an industrial and legal dispute over crewing. Here she steams out of Sydney on a blustery afternoon in 2008. (John Lacey)

SHIPBUILDING AND REPAIR

AS WELL AS COMMERCIAL wharves, Australia's major ports – and some minor ones too – developed shipbuilding and repair facilities. The minor shipbuilding ports built small and medium-sized timber vessels until the 1940s when the last such business, at Tuncurry on the New South Wales north coast, went out of business. A small place like Huskisson on Jervis Bay even built ferries for Sydney Harbour in the first decades of the 20th century. World War II saw a brief revival of timber ship construction, since there were so many Japanese mines about, to which timber was relatively immune unless there was a direct hit (steel and iron ships attract magnetised mines).

The big shipbuilding and repair businesses, though, were in the capital cities, Newcastle and Maryborough. Australia had never been a builder of very large or sophisticated vessels, except for the navy and then almost entirely for political reasons. Large shipowners nearly always turned to Scottish or Ulster yards for their best vessels in the late 19th and early 20th centuries. Nonetheless, Australia's ports were the homes to a considerable shipbuilding industry. The primacy of Sydney in this industry was uncontested. Even the bulk of the pearling luggers for service in faraway Broome and Thursday Island were built on the shores of Berry's Bay and Lavender Bay in North Sydney.[20]

During the first 50 years of the 19th century, nearly all Australian ships were built of timber, most of them in small yards in Sydney and Hobart. After iron vessels, especially auxiliary steamers, became more common from the 1840s, these rudimentary practices were inadequate. The first iron foundry in Australia opened in Sydney in 1821 (on the corner of George and Market Streets) and by 1831 another foundry was able to undertake work as significant as rebuilding the steam engine of the *William the Fourth*.

By the 1840s there was a number of marine engineering works in Sydney, each capable of maintaining large early marine steam engines. The largest and most important was PN Russell's at the foot of Bathurst Street, and one of his main rivals, confusingly, was John Russell in Pyrmont, who completed a steamship with a locally made engine as early as 1838. In 1855 Australia's first dry dock, Mort's Dock at Balmain, was opened; followed in 1857 by the government-owned Fitzroy Dock on Cockatoo Island, initially intended for naval use. Both these were in Sydney, and by 1870 there were dry docks in most of Australia's major ports. Brisbane's Government Dock at South Brisbane opened in 1881.[21] Dry docks were essential to repair iron vessels and their machinery, especially steamers' screws.

By 1913 Mort's Dock had built 41 vessels, of which the largest was the 499-ton Manly ferry SS *Barrenjoey*. Mort's Dock built a second dock at Woolwich, on the northern side of Sydney Harbour a little upstream from Balmain, in the halcyon days of coastal shipping around 1900. This was the largest private dry dock built in Australia. The major Australian steamship companies maintained their own engineering works, to avoid the cost of repairing their vessels by outside contractors like Mort's Dock. The Australian Steam Navigation Company, for instance, had its engineering works at Pyrmont in Sydney, while the Adelaide Steamship Company maintained its vessels in its home port. None of these companies built their own vessels, indeed most ordered their coastal steamers from Britain, but the larger companies certainly preferred to undertake their own repairs if circumstances permitted it. The short-lived Melbourne Steam Shipping Company's workshop survived longer than its owners, becoming the Hobson's Bay Dock and Engineering Company. The Queensland Steam Shipping Company also had its own works on the Brisbane River, which later became the main works of the Australasian United Steam Navigation Company.

The most surprisingly located shipbuilder in Australia perhaps was Walkers Limited, who set up their dockyard some 33 kilometres

Sydney's Cockatoo Island in 1951 was a very busy place indeed, with seven large vessels at the island. Two destroyers and two frigates of the Royal Australian Navy are in dock for refits, while HMAS *Voyager* is under construction on the slipway. P&O's MV *Palana* is under repair. The giant floating crane *Titan* stands waiting for its next assignment. The dockyard's first priority was always naval work, although it undertook civilian contracts as well, just as nearby Garden Island does to the present. (Frank Hurley, NLA an23139983)

upstream on the Mary River near Maryborough, Queensland, as early as 1868. It built 13 vessels in the 1870s and 1880s, before ceasing shipbuilding until a revival brought on by the decision of the Hughes government to establish the Commonwealth Line in 1917. By 1923 Walkers had completed two of the four 6600-ton ships, far larger than anything they had built before or since, but the government was less than impressed by the slow progress. Shipbuilding continued on the Mary, although Walkers were always busier as general engineers, notably making locomotives for Queensland and Commonwealth Railways.[22]

Naval orders always played a large role in sustaining a shipbuilding industry in Australia. This was because Australian builders were never big enough to compete commercially with the yards of Glasgow and Belfast. During the early 1920s the Royal Australian Navy ordered 22 steel ships from the six Australian builders the government judged best able to produce large vessels. These were Cockatoo Island Works in Sydney; the New South Wales State Dockyard at Walsh Island in Newcastle; the Williamstown Dockyard in Melbourne; Poole and Steel in Adelaide; and Walkers Limited in Maryborough, Queensland. However, when the orders were complete, most had to close, or confine themselves to repairs. Cockatoo Island remained the most significant builder, eventually building more than 30 ships, both civilian and navy, between 1912 and its closure in 1990. There was also a brief revival of Williamstown's fortunes as a naval builder after World War II and the New South Wales State Dockyard at Walsh Island also undertook some major projects.

The most important ship repair facility in Australia, like the shipbuilding facility at Cockatoo Island, was a naval initiative. Garden Island in Sydney was home to the Royal Navy's Australia Station from 1857 until it was transferred to the new Royal Australian Navy in 1911. Anticipating war with Japan, and concerned about their ability to hold Singapore, the British and Australian governments decided in 1939 to build a dry dock at Garden Island capable of taking the largest ships afloat. Built between 1941 and 1945, the Captain Cook Dock, as it was known, was 1000 feet (305 m) long and 34 feet (10 m) deep. Associated with it was an enormous lathe capable of machining the largest ships' screw shafts, and a 250-ton crane. The whole project cost £10.5 million, or a little more than the Sydney Harbour Bridge. Although intended primarily for naval use (the first vessel docked was HMS *Illustrious* in February 1945), it has also been used for repairs to many civilian vessels.[23] The war years also saw the construction of the smaller Cairncross Dry Dock in Brisbane. At the same time, Brisbane began a new venture in shipbuilding, with the establishment of Evans Deakin slipway at Kangaroo Point using equipment and personnel from the construction of the Story Bridge.[24]

STEAMERS ON THE MURRAY–DARLING SYSTEM

INLAND NAVIGATION in Australia followed rather than preceded settlement, an almost unique situation in the annals of colonisation. The reason was that the squatters who wrested the interior of the continent from its Aboriginal inhabitants came from ports on its eastern (and later southern) coast while the rivers watering the interior flowed in the opposite direction westwards. They all eventually flow into the Murray, which debouches into Lake Alexandrina and thence over a treacherous bar into the Southern Ocean at Encounter Bay. Captain Charles Sturt resolved the early mystery of the westward-flowing rivers in 1829. However, since the mouth of the Murray was remote and not navigable for practical purposes, and in any case there was no settlement or port in the vicinity, his discoveries, despite their geographical and scientific interest, were of no immediate practical or economic use.

That situation changed after the establishment of the Province of South Australia in 1836. Navigation of the Murray seemed to offer the new colony bright economic prospects. Its first governor, John Hindmarsh, was a sailor who knew all about the realities of maritime commerce so proposed to move the capital from Adelaide to the mouth of the Murray, but lost this battle and was recalled. Nonetheless, the possibility of using the Murray as a highway into the pastoral interior continued to excite South Australian minds, so in 1850 the government offered a prize of £2000 each to the captains of the first two iron vessels to reach the junction of the Murray and Darling Rivers. These were rich pickings indeed for a plucky freshwater navigator, so soon the race was on.

River navigation began in February 1853, when a team of 20 bullocks hauled the 20-ton wooden paddle steamer *Mary Ann* from the Mount Lofty Ranges, where she was built, to the waters of the Murray near Mannum. This showed what animal transport could achieve, but the *Mary Ann* and other steamers following her could move far larger tonnages far more cheaply than animals, and at a tiny fraction of the investment needed for a railway. The *Mary Ann*'s master, William Randell, was unable to collect the prize on his first voyages, and soon he had a rival in the hunt, when in August 1853 Captain Francis Cadell brought the PS *Lady Augusta*, a wooden paddle steamer built in Sydney, successfully but hazardously across the Murray bar. Cadell was astute enough to negotiate an amendment to the prize conditions, allowing timber vessels to claim the reward. In fact, all steamers on the river in the period of its intense commercial navigation proved to be timber-hulled. The two rivals steamed up the Murray through the spring fresh of 1853, reaching the Victorian towns of Swan Hill and Echuca. The government

The wharf at Echuca in the 1870s. Neither the paddle steamers nor the wharf have changed much in the 130 years since. It is the locomotive, a Victorian Railways O class in original condition, which dates the image. (Freedman collection)

in Adelaide rewarded both for their efforts, and the era of commercial navigation of the Murray had begun.

Cadell established the River Murray Navigation Company, and soon the prosperous Adelaide entrepreneurs of the Elder family had set up the rival River Murray Company to operate fleets of steamers on the waterways. They were joined by independent owner-skippers in the competition for the trade, one of whom was Randell. A third major line, McCulloch and Company, was based in Echuca. Finally, in the 20th century Permewan, Wright and Company came to dominate the river trade out of Echuca. Ultimately nearly 200 vessels were built for the trade, which thrived between the mid-1850s and the 1890s. The basic design of the Murray paddle wheeler was developed early with Cadell and Randell's first experiments and scarcely changed. Powered by a simple steam engine (there were no experiments with triple expansion or compounding here) supplied with steam from a wood-fired boiler, nearly all were side-wheelers. There were a few stern-wheelers – the favoured vessel on the Mississippi and its confluents – in the trade, but the sinuous nature of the Murray better suited the more flexible side-wheelers. For the same reason, Murray steamers hauled their barges behind them, each with its own wheel and rudder, rather than push them as was the case on other rivers which did not meander with quite the same perversity as the Murray and its tributaries.

The early vessels had timber hulls, but by the late 19th century iron, which was far tougher for the vessels that all too often bounced along the bottom, was the favoured material. Many timber vessels were built locally, especially in Echuca, although some were brought from other places. The first two river steamers were built in, improbably enough, Mount Lofty, and, rather more predictably, Sydney. Most of the iron vessels were built in Sydney and steamed around the coast in fair weather. About half of all iron vessels built in Sydney before 1914 were for the Murray and Darling Rivers, so vessels for the inland rivers made a significant contribution to Sydney's shipbuilding industry.[25]

Shipyards where river steamers were maintained were located at the major river ports. William Randell, for instance, had a floating dry dock at his base at Mannum which remained in commercial service until 1927 and still exists. At Echuca there was a dry dock built into the bank, and at many river ports there were small engineering works and slipways capable of maintaining the hulls, boilers and engines of the steamers.

Between 1855 and 1859 the practical limits of the trade were established in a series of adventurous voyages, taking vessels up the Murray to Albury; the Murrumbidgee to Gundagai; and the Darling and its tributaries as far as Walgett, near the Queensland border. Walgett is more than 1600 kilometres upstream from where the Darling joins the Murray, so this was riverine transport on a long-distance scale indeed. Not that it much impressed one 1880s visitor, who described it as 'a mere collection of huts on a scorched and sandy plain'.[26]

The trade was dependent on water levels in the rivers, and these were highly variable. In flood seasons, navigation was possible even along the tributaries of the Darling into Queensland, and the flat-bottom steamers would even head out across flooded plains with supplies and collect wool (at a price) from isolated flood-bound properties. In 1890 the PS *Brewarrina* became the first and only inland steamer to reach Mungindi in Queensland, and so become the only vessel ever to navigate the rivers of all four colonies of eastern Australia.[27] By contrast, in drought most of the Darling and Murrumbidgee Rivers were scarcely navigable at all, and even on the Murray navigation was only possible downstream from Echuca with absolute certainty. In most seasons, water was reliable for at least a few months of the year as far as Bourke on the Darling; Hay on the Murrumbidgee; and Albury on the Murray. This reliable water in spring was all that was really needed, since the most important traffic in these regions was wool outbound (which was shorn in spring, when waters were at their highest) and stores inbound.

Places like Bourke, Menindee and Wilcannia on the Darling; Balranald, Hay, Narrandera and Wagga Wagga on the Murrumbidgee; and Wentworth, Mildura, Swan Hill and Echuca on the Murray, all became important inland ports with facilities such as customs houses and bond stores. Sometimes the steamers ventured up the Goulburn River in Victoria as far as Shepparton, only 150 kilometres from Melbourne. The river steamers were far more efficient than the teams they replaced for long distances, although most squatters still relied on horse or bullock teams (occasionally even camel teams) to link their runs with the nearest wharf. Steamers could also bring fodder for the teams, so the whole transport task became more efficient and regular, except when droughts were really severe, as they were in the late 1860s. Reliable navigation of the Murray also stimulated new industries, notably fruit growing, which could also rely on water from the river for irrigation, beginning at Mildura in 1887.

South Australia soon addressed the problems with the mouth of the Murray by building a horse tramway from Goolwa, on Lake Alexandrina, to the blue waters of the Southern Ocean at Port Elliot. This was Australia's first public railway, as discussed in chapter 4, and meant that the Murray at last had a commercial mouth, even if it was one of iron rails rather than navigable water. Goolwa became for a time Australia's busiest riverine port, but its domination did not last long.

The paddle steamer *JC Arnold* loading bales of wool onto its barge at Bourke, New South Wales, in the 1920s. (Ian Dunn collection)

In 1864 the Victorian Railways reached Echuca, which suddenly became the entire basin's major entrepôt. Echuca was only 250 kilometres or seven hours from Melbourne by the trains of the time. The opening of the railway to Echuca changed the shape of the river trade dramatically. No longer did most of the steamers from the Darling and Murrumbidgee paddle down the Murray to South Australia; but instead turned upstream for Echuca. Echuca became Victoria's second busiest port in terms of the number of vessels cleared, although Geelong handled heavier tonnages. Victoria built an enormous wharf at Echuca, which kept expanding with the trade until it was nearly a kilometre long, on which were laid railway tracks connecting directly with the saltwater wharves in Melbourne. Goolwa and its tramway went into decline as they lost the upper Murray and Murrumbidgee trade to Echuca. In 1878 the railway from Adelaide at last reached the Murray at Morgan, which thereafter became the preferred point of transhipment for such river traffic as flowed into South Australia. Morgan was able to compete effectively with Echuca for the Darling and lower Murray trade, and a large wharf (which still exists and was the largest on the South Australian section of the river) was built there.

The real challenge to the supremacy of the rivers as a means of transport in inland New South Wales, however, came from the New South Wales Government Railways, which in the 1880s at last reached the navigable waters of the inland rivers, first at Wagga Wagga, and later at Albury, Narrandera and Hay. Finally in 1887 the rails reached Bourke. The transfer of traffic to the railways was not immediate. Rail freight was more expensive than river freight, although on the railways there was little insurance to pay whereas insurance premiums were high on the riskier river steamers, which were forever catching fire or being marooned by dry weather. However, river steamers continued to take goods beyond the railheads. So rail connection in some ways was actually good business for the steamers, which, for instance, after 1887 began taking all sorts of traffic in both directions to and from Bourke. The NSWGR offered discounts for long-distance traffic, which certainly encouraged shippers in inland New South Wales to send their goods to Sydney by rail rather than anywhere else, but often steamers were still required to get these goods to the railheads.

River traffic continued to be fairly buoyant into the 20th century. However, after 1900 more branch railways were built into the Riverina, and roads were always improving, enabling first horse teams and then trucks to oust the slow and ponderous bullocks. Trucks would soon oust the paddle steamers as well. The unreliability of the Murray's flow was the main burden under which the steamer had to labour. This was even more true of the Darling, although the Murrumbidgee was more reliable in the spring when the snows melted on the Australian Alps to feed it. The colonies found it impossible to work out a scheme for improving the Murray's navigability, even though an intercolonial conference resolved to do so as early as 1863.

The problem was that improvements to river navigation, while they might improve transport for New South Wales pastoralists, would reduce the revenues of the New South Wales and Victorian Railways. It was not until 1917, well after Federation, that the states signed the Murray River Waters Agreement and established the Murray River Commission. The commission began works on a system of weirs and locks whose aim was to create a channel with a reliable depth of 1.8 metres all year from Morgan to Mildura. This would avoid the need to haul steamers over sandbanks and mudflats by winch when waters were low. During the 1920s and 1930s the Murray River Commission worked hard on this project, however it was all too late. Indeed, most river traffic on the South Australian section of the river by then was gravel crushed to build the weirs and locks. The Murray River Commission used a huge stern-wheeler, the PS *Captain Sturt*, to push its gravel barges from quarry to worksites.[28]

These works on the Murray tended to make it resemble the canals of Europe and North America, but there have never been any canals built for inland shipping in Australia. There are two reasons for this. First, Australia was opened up for modern exploitation and settlement after the invention of the railway, which almost always was a better transport option than a canal. Second, canals required large supplies of water, especially if locks were involved. Australia is generally deficient in water supplies, and those parts of the country which are well watered are those least suited to canal construction.

Even the locks and weirs on the Murray were completed too late to maintain the river trade's dominance. Moreover, they had been built as much with a view to enabling the use of the river's waters for irrigation as to assist the steamers. In this they succeeded admirably, although at an environmental cost in terms of wetlands degradation, but the era of long-distance transport of wool from New South Wales stations to Morgan or Echuca was well and truly over. Nonetheless, some commercial traffic on the river continued into World War II, especially around Echuca, where steamer-based gangs would cut timber on the banks and then rail it from Echuca to Melbourne. By the late 1940s there were hardly any boats left in the trade. Flooding in 1956 caused a brief and final revival of a trade dead for nearly 40 years, when the PS *Success* collected loads of wool from sheep stations along the Darling cut off by floodwaters. However, the few steamers left soon found carrying passengers as tourists paid better than any freight offering. With this new traffic the river trade has survived and thrives, mostly still using paddle steamers built during its halcyon days of a century and more ago. Moreover, just as in the 1860s, the great rivals for contemporary tourist traffic on the Murray remain Goolwa and Echuca.[29]

For the first century and a half of Australia's modern history, the horse was Australians' first choice for personal transport. Various breeds were used, although in much of Australia the cheapest horses were 'nags' of no great distinction in breeding. The Clydesdales hauling these travellers' wagon appear better bred than their saddle horses. The pony truck wagon, whose front wheels were on a pivot with a rigid shaft through which traction was delivered from the animals to the wagon, was a versatile and long-lasting design, as long as roads were adequate. Frank Hurley saw these horses and wagon being used for personal transport in central Queensland in the 1920s, at which time such scenes were coming to an end. (Frank Hurley, NLA an23242751)

Chapter 3

BY TRACK AND ROAD

WHEN MUSCLES MOVED AUSTRALIA

HE WAS AN OLD MAN and a very cranky one, on board a ship he detested, far from the pastoral interior he loved, where for decades he had roamed purposefully and acquisitively on his two-wheel buggy or horseback. Sea spray was not for him, for he loved mammalian effusions – sweat, blood and the slimy fluids of reproduction – even more than he loved ale and wine. He had been as fecund as the rams, bulls and stallions of his vast pastoral holdings across western New South Wales and Queensland, fathering 11 children at his Bathurst home. Unlike so many of his generation, the scent of burning coal mingled with steam and hot oil on burnished steel, the olfactory sensation of the steamship and the train, failed to move him.

James Rutherford was dying and knew it. His life had been rich and varied. Before leaving New York for Melbourne at 20 he travelled the United States and British North America from Iowa to New Brunswick, leaving behind a trail of blood. He had made, lost and remade fortunes to become the leading shareholder and guiding spirit of Cobb and Co, moving the company out of Victoria and into New South Wales and Queensland, expanding its operations beyond the coaching for which it was famous into the pastoral industry.

Now aged 84, he was returning from the company's property Davenport Downs near Longreach, where he had been camping out with one of his sons supervising the muster. He wanted to return to Bathurst in his buggy across that vast interior he loved and which Cobb and Co had dominated, but his health was failing. He reluctantly agreed to return by steamer. He had the wealth but no inclination to be a pioneering motorist, and never used a car. They rode to Townsville and boarded the ship, but he was so sick the captain insisted he disembark at Mackay where he soon died, far from the coaching routes and vast spreads which had made his wealth and gave him such happiness as his restless and querulous soul allowed. His body was returned to Bathurst by ship and train. It was September 1911: the era of coaching would scarcely outlast his death.[1]

BEASTS OF BURDEN

FOR THE FIRST 66 years of British colonisation in Australia, human and animal muscles powered its land transport. Early New South Wales was not much different from a slave colony, since the vast majority of its inhabitants were not there by choice, were unpaid, and had to do whatever work their masters ordered. This included working as beasts of burden, so human beings were modern Australia's first pack animals. However, this being a British colony, there were legal as well as physical limits to what convicts could be expected to do. Convicts were not totally deprived of civic rights. It was certainly a cruel judicial system, but cruelty had its legal limits, and was

Tom Roberts, *Bailed up*, 1895, 1927, oil on canvas, 134.5 x 182.8cm, purchased 1933, Art Gallery of New South Wales. Tom Roberts painted *Bailed Up* from life on the Glen Innes–Inverell road in 1895. By then the days of bushranging were well and truly over and the railway through to Wallangarra carried most of the traffic. The secondary mail routes from Glen Innes to Inverell and Grafton remained in Cobb and Co's hands until motor services took over in 1913, and Roberts hired one of these coaches as his model. Service frequencies have not changed much in more than a century: in 2010 CountryLink motor coaches run three times a week between Grafton and Moree via Glenn Innes and Inverell. While the hold-up aspect was contrived and nostalgic even when it was painted, as a representation of the coaching age it is accurate, indeed peerless, richly deserving its fame and popularity.

administered systematically to recidivists rather than indiscriminately to the bulk of the convict population. By 1800, when the new colony was a functioning economic unit with a significant market economy, convict labour, both used by the government and assigned to private farmers and other entrepreneurs, was part of a regular if eccentric economic system. By then, as convicts' sentences expired, there was also a free labour market beside the slave labour of convicts.

Convicts carry loads like working animals while their gaolers look on in this 1823 aquatint of Sydney published in London. (Robert Havell, NLA an5575513)

Thus, the convict system in its purest form, and the accompanying notion of New South Wales as a vast gaol, did not last long. Convictism would remain part of the economic and social scene until the 1840s in New South Wales, and rather later in Tasmania and Western Australia; but from the beginning of the 19th century it existed beside a free economy, in which individuals made their own decisions about how to make money, improve their lives, and move themselves and their property around. Convictism, like all slave systems, was not especially efficient, but it did enable early colonial governments to build infrastructure on a scale which would have been inconceivable without free labour, including the surprisingly good main road from Hobart to Launceston.

Convicts were used for transport purposes in early colonial New South Wales, as is apparent from early paintings of Sydney, which feature convicts hauling and carrying considerable loads. However, animals almost always were more efficient in such roles than human beings; so such activities did not endure for long. They were the result of a shortage of animals and co-existed with notions of punishment, but were not a lasting solution to the transport needs of the new colony. Human power for transport lasted longer where convicts were numerous; their punishment was severe; and animals were limited in numbers. This was the situation in Van Diemen's Land right down to the 1840s.

Port Arthur was established in 1832 as a place of secondary transportation, where men were incarcerated who had committed crimes – or who had been unmanageable – while already under sentence of transportation to Australia. Beasts of burden were never used at Port Arthur, and convicts served all its land transport needs. These included moving the logs and stones for the construction of the establishment itself, the ruins of which remain to this day. Port Arthur had a terrible reputation for cruelty captured so evocatively in Marcus Clarke's *For the Term of his Natural Life*. From a transport perspective, Port Arthur's really eccentric feature was a most unusual tramway. Some 6 kilometres long and dating from the beginnings of the gaol, it ran from Taranna, the small port where vessels arrived from Hobart, to Long Bay. It was almost dead straight. Convicts pushed carts along its wooden rails, leaping onto the back of carts on downhill stretches. This tramway lasted about 30 years, until the closure of the gaol.[2]

The first convicts and their gaolers brought with them to New South Wales seven cattle and seven horses, all obtained from the Cape Colony, then a Dutch settlement in South Africa. They flourished, despite the escape of the first herd of cattle which was found a few years later to have thrived and multiplied at the place called in honour of their discovery Cowpastures, then deep in unexplored terrain some 65 kilometres southwest of Sydney. Cattle came from India and the Cape, as did horses, although some Thoroughbreds even were imported direct from England. By 1800 there were 203 horses and 1044 cattle in New South Wales.[3]

Most of the horses were of high quality, even this early, and the cult of the horse was already established. Horses were scarce and expensive, so were used as saddle horses by officers and the growing class of landowners to differentiate themselves from the convicts, emancipists and marines who remained as the colony's first pedestrians, a means of transit they shared with the Aboriginal population. The Australian saddle horse, a mixture of Arab and Thoroughbred, with less speed but more strength than an English Thoroughbred, was already an established breed as early as 1800. Sydney's fine climate and the manifest enthusiasm of its early inhabitants for horse breeding, riding and racing meant these horses thrived. Saddle horses were also used for light harness work, such as drawing carriages, sulkies and buggies.

In early colonial New South Wales there was precious little harness work for horses, because there were so few carriages,

The convict powered tramway at Port Arthur, seen in an 1852 view, might be considered monstrous, but human beings have been used as motive power on many light railways in many countries. (Unknown artist from Edward Searle's album of photographs, c 1911, NLA vn4556428)

or roads that carriages could use for that matter. After 1810 this began to change, and Governor Macquarie set the new tone by going about town – and even into the country – in a splendid carriage drawn by four horses, an unprecedented equipage for Australia. He had convicts build stables for Government House's equine residents on such an extravagant and pretentious scale that they now serve as Sydney's Conservatorium of Music. Soon coaching and medium-weight harness horses such as the Cleveland Bay were being imported and bred, as road development and wider settlement around Sydney occurred. These horses were bred to haul wagons and coaches at moderate speed. They lacked the finesse of the earlier Arab-Thoroughbred crossbreeds and generally were unsuitable for use as saddle horses. Heavier breeds of draught horses such as the Clydesdales and Shires came later to Australia, since the poor roads meant that bullocks were better suited for heavy haulage.

Bullocks bred in Australia were a mixture of English and Indian types. Their early importation was deprecated by officials back in England as an extravagance, but by 1820 bullock teams were established as the Australian draught animals *par excellence*. They would remain so well into the railway age, and bullock teams continued to work in the timber industry, where roads were poor or non-existent, into the 1960s. Draught horses would have a role carting around cities, and in those rural areas where there were decent roads, but in most of southeastern Australia it was either the bullock or the railway which carted goods until the last decades of the 19th century. Draught horses were about 30 percent more powerful than bullocks, but required higher quality and more expensive feed. Horses also cost much more. Bullocks were cheaper, more robust, and their fodder was free until settlement became denser after the 1860s.

Thereafter bullockies engaged in almost constant struggle with farmers and pastoralists in their efforts to graze their beasts and avoid the cost of fodder – once bullockies had to feed their animals, the economics swung rapidly in favour of horse or camel teams. Bullocks had superior grip on uneven and soft surfaces than horses, but went lame more easily than shod horses on made roads. The bullock team, then, was motive power for the frontier or beyond the reach of made roads. So far as can be ascertained, Australia's last working commercial bullocks were in forests near Gosford, New South Wales, during the 1960s. This is less than 100 kilometres from Sydney and anything but the frontier, so, in specialised situations, bullock teams were remarkably competitive with more modern power such as horses, trains and trucks.

The commonly sized team of 16 bullocks hauling timber along a temporary tramway on the bed of the Barron River near Cairns, north Queensland. Long after bullock teams ceased being used on public roads they worked carrying timber from forest to mill, although their use on tramways like this was rare. (Author postcard collection)

Bullock teams still worked on the Atherton Tableland in north Queensland towards the end of World War II, but were attracting photographers' attention as increasingly rare relics from the past. (Frank Hurley, NLA an23289353)

Draught horses began to replace bullocks from as early as the 1830s. Importation of draught breeds, road building, and the increasingly ready availability of fodder were the main factors behind the shift. Given a decent road and adequate fodder, horses could cart a heavier load faster and cheaper than bullocks, especially as horse prices fell during the 19th century with their growing numbers. From the 1830s, the Hawkesbury area out of Sydney shipped fodder to the capital, which helped in the rapid shift from bullocks to horses around Sydney. Much the same thing happened almost from the beginning of Melbourne's history. The coming of railways and river steamers also helped the change. Hay, oats and other types of horse fodder are relatively light, and rail rates for their carriage were quite low. For many years the largest building at Sydney station was the hay shed, where fuel for the city's horses was handled. Similarly, the North Coast Steam Navigation Company shipped enormous quantities of cheap maize from the fertile farming valleys of the New South Wales north coast to feed the city's horses.

In the productive interior of the continent watered by the Murray–Darling river system, trains and steamers also helped with the change from bullocks to horses. River steamers could only operate for six months of the year on the upper reaches of the rivers. This made speed important, and horses were faster and more reliable than bullocks. If the spring's shearing missed the last river steamer before summer's heat made the river unnavigable, it was a serious matter indeed. Missing a river steamer in December could mean ruin, since the wool might not be shipped till the following August. Steamers and railways also made distribution of fodder far easier. McCulloch and Company, for instance, made Echuca on the Murray the centre of their fodder distribution network, sending bags of Victorian grains there by rail, then shipping them by steamer throughout the river basin across the west of New South Wales to feed the horses which carried the wool to the wharves. The horse teams would often return to the remote stations with their own fodder as a significant element of the backloading freight.[4]

This operation began with the arrival of the Victorian Railways in Echuca in 1864. The spread of the telegraph through the west of New South Wales in the 1860s and 1870s similarly helped the process of the dislocation of the bullock teams. Steamer arrival dates, movements of freshets along the rivers, shearing dates and fodder prices could all be telegraphed across the interior, enabling a far more efficient transport

A camel train in central Australia about 1920. The Afghan camel driver heads the array while his presumably satisfied customers pose for the occasion. The photographer, the Reverend John Flynn, used this image in his illustrated lectures on outback life to raise funds for the Australian Inland Mission. (John Flynn, NLA an24283844)

operation of the valuable fleeces from the shearing sheds to the wool sales of Melbourne and Geelong and thence for shipment to the world. By the 1860s this involved multiple modes – horse teams from sheep station to the river (sometimes camel teams to the Darling), river steamers to Echuca, trains to the shores of Port Phillip Bay, and finally the clipper ships which would sail round Cape Horn to Europe, where the fleeces would be transformed into clothing.

This was a far cry from the bullock wagon carting the bales direct from the shearing sheds to the port. Despite the increasing prevalence of horse teams and the spread of railways and river steamers, the bullockies could still compete, especially when work was short and they were willing to cut costs. On one celebrated occasion in the 1890s bullock teams suddenly reappeared on the streets of Sydney with loads of wool from the northwest of the colony, claiming they had delivered the load cheaper (although far slower) than the railway. No doubt they had too, since the squatters had employed them, and it is true that in the 19th century rail freight rates for wool were very expensive, but this quixotic attempt to revive the days of the bullockies' domination of the trade was not repeated.

There were experiments with donkeys and mules as pack and draught animals in Van Diemen's Land about 1820 and on the Australian Agricultural Company's estates north of Newcastle in New South Wales in the 1840s. Despite their apparent abilities to combine the best aspects of their rivals – the power of horses, the ability to traverse rough ground of bullocks, and the tolerance of dry conditions of camels – they never caught on in Australia. Donkey and mule teams did enjoy some success in mining and pastoral enterprises in the drier parts of Queensland and Western Australia in the period from 1890 to 1920, but in such regions the camel became the preferred draught animal.[5]

The use of camels as animals for the exploration of the dry interior of the continent was proposed as early as 1827, but the first were not imported until the 1840s. The Burke and Wills Expedition of 1860–61, which was the first to cross the continent from south to north, used camels as pack animals, although sufficiently ineffectively for all but one of its human members to perish in the attempt. This disaster did little to endear the camel to the Australian popular imagination, and it was Burke's horse, Billy (who was devoured in the course of the venture), not his camels, who became the four-legged hero of the affair to the public. In fact, the camel proved to be the beast which enabled the economic conquest of central Australia. One of the expeditions which set out looking for the tragic Burke and Wills, leaving from Adelaide under John McKinley in 1862, found that camels were in fact very useful in the interior of the continent. Indeed McKinley, without the loss of a single man and with modest funding, achieved what Burke had died attempting and his success started something of a camel craze.

This began with the importation of 122 camels from Karachi in India (now in Pakistan) by the South Australian entrepreneur and grazier, Sir Thomas Elder, in 1866. From 1854 to 1889 more than 1000 camels were imported into Australia, all of them from India. They thrived and bred well in Australia's interior, where there was generally some water but equally generally not enough for horses or bullocks to work effectively. Camels were used both as pack and draught animals, predominantly the former. Generally they would work in a string of from 20 to 30 pack animals, linked by ropes from nose to tail. Each camel would carry between 80 to 270 kilograms, or two bales of wool, one on each side. As commercial carriers, camels proved themselves in the construction of the Overland Telegraph Line between 1870 and 1872. This was a South Australian project, and South Australia always remained the main centre of camel use. Casualties among horses and bullocks on this project were enormous, and the successful use of camels was the start of their widespread usage.

With Elder's first camels back in 1866 came their handlers. They mostly came from India's Northwest Frontier Province and from Baluchistan, both abutting on Afghanistan, and so were generally called Afghans. The 'Ghans', as they became known, had no monopoly as camel handlers, but they remained an important element in the business throughout. Indian cameleers were nearly all Muslims, which excluded them from most social life in inland Australia, which tended to revolve around the consumption of copious amounts of beer or rum.[6] This distinctive cultural difference contributed to the general lack of integration of the camel as a beast of burden into the Australian popular imagination or psyche. The role of Afghans in attacking a holiday excursion train near Broken Hill in 1915 further alienated them from much of the population. They did this out of loyalty to the Caliph of Islam, the Ottoman Emperor, then at war with the British Empire, and paid for their zeal with their lives. Moreover, in a country where the horse was so highly prized, the alien camel, like the alien cameleer, was always held in some contempt. Bullockies, just like horsemen, hated camels, since they were able to undercut bullock rates in marginal country like much of western New South Wales and Queensland, and even into the Wimmera district of Victoria. Patsy Adam-Smith could recall camels laden with bags of salt coming to a remote Victorian railhead near Mildura as late as the 1920s.[7]

Despised or not, the camels were essential where water supplies were low. Stronger than horses or bullocks; able to go for up to eight days (about 130 miles or over 200 kilometres) without water, compared with three for a horse; and not all that much slower than horses (and faster than bullocks), camels turned travel in Australia's outback from exploring into exploitation. Oodnadatta, terminus for 30 years of the railway stretching north from Port Augusta into the heart of the continent, became Australia's great camel centre, from where the camel trains left for Alice Springs and throughout the Northern Territory. Camels were the main beasts of burden on the major infrastructure projects in the outback between 1870 and 1930, including the Overland Telegraph (1870–72), the Canning Stock Route in Western Australia (1908–1910), the Trans-Australia Railway (1912–17), and the Oodnadatta-Alice Springs Railway (1927–29).[8] In the case of the two railway projects, of course, they were carrying the sleepers and rails which would help consign them to a future as picturesque irrelevancies, but for 60 years the despised camel was the main transport motive power throughout much of the Australian continent.

From 1788 to 1930 over 5200 horses were imported into Australia, 80 percent of them from Britain, with the rest coming mostly from the United States, India and Arabia. This gave the country a fine breeding stock which, coupled with natural increase, produced a large horse population. The quality of this horse population was highly variable. There were some excellent horses, but a lot of breeding experiments were failures and produced 'nags', ill-formed horses not really suitable for any work in particular. In 1870, expert opinion considered 55 percent of harness horses in New South Wales to be of low quality; and only 20 percent of saddle horses to be good, meaning of sound Arab or Thoroughbred extraction. These were poor figures, and were improved with culling and more scientific breeding thereafter. The horse population of New South Wales was about 10 000 in 1829, 251 000 in 1850 and 661 800 at its peak in 1920. There was about one horse for every two people. Victoria's population, where horse quality was highest and breeding the most scientific, peaked in 1913 at 562 000, while Queensland had become Australia's largest horse breeding state with more horses than people when the peak population of 741 024 was reached in 1920.[9]

By the mid-19th century, Australia's horses were sufficiently numerous and of sufficient quality to be exported, mostly to India where they were highly regarded for cavalry and civilian use as both light harness and robust saddle horses. There had emerged a distinctively Australian breed, heavier and with more stamina than the Arab or Thoroughbred, but suitable for similar work. In India, these horses were, and still are, called 'Walers' (since they came from New South Wales). They showed that, within a century, a distinctively Australian equine solution to transport problems had been produced, with applicability beyond the shores of the continent.

ROADS AND BRIDGES IN THE PRE-MOTOR AGE

FOR THE FIRST 20 years of its existence, New South Wales hardly had any real roads. Such commercial traffic as there was went by boat along the Parramatta or Hawkesbury Rivers, while other transport was by saddle horse or dray along bush tracks. That changed after 1810 with the arrival of Governor Lachlan Macquarie, who had the personality, drive, budget, skills and technical experts to implement Australia's first ever sustained public works program. Within months of his arrival in Sydney, he called tenders for the building and operation of a turnpike road, 32 feet (10 m) wide and funded by tolls, from Sydney to Parramatta. This opened by October 1812, and was Australia's first real road. Tolls were not cheap, ranging from twopence a head for driven cattle to 10 pence for a dray drawn by up to four horses or bullocks, to an expensive 3 shillings for a four-horse carriage. The next year the turnpike was extended to Windsor, where the tollhouse survives, and soon after to Liverpool. Macquarie also quickly had built slightly lower-standard carriage roads beyond these points, especially into the Hawkesbury district, and from Parramatta to the Nepean River at Emu Ford, now Penrith. These roads had no tolls and were expected to be able to take a carriage in safety if not comfort during reasonable weather. They were better than tracks, and did have some permanent structures such as bridges and earthworks, but were by no means all-weather smooth roads like the turnpikes.

The greatest of the carriage roads was built by a team of 50 convicts under William Cox in just seven months during 1814. It went from Emu Plains across the Blue Mountains to the banks of the Macquarie River at Bathurst, following literally in the footsteps of the explorers who had been the first Europeans to make the journey the previous year. It was about 160 kilometres long, and its relatively poor quality can be gauged from the fact that its first user, none other than Lachlan Macquarie himself, took five days to travel its length. It was the most important road yet built in Australia, and has claims to be the single most significant piece of transport infrastructure ever built in Australia, for this was the road which opened the vast interior of Australia to the modern world. Henceforth, New South Wales no longer would be a small colony timorously clinging to the sea, a suitable depot for the reception of convicts with marginal security value, but little else. Now it would be a rich and growing country, a truly valuable acquisition for the British Empire.

Cox's road crossed a summit of over 1000 metres, and climbed escarpments higher and steeper than any road built before in Australia, or indeed for another 50 years after. It was a remarkable achievement with

Convicts working on the new road descending Victoria Pass on the western escarpment of the Blue Mountains, which opened in October 1832. This was built under the direction of Thomas Mitchell and was an improvement on the earlier routes dating from 1814. It is still in use as the Great Western Highway. (Charles Rodius, NLA an6332110)

a lasting impact. The most difficult part of the road was the western descent from the Blue Mountains at Mount York. The gradient here was 1 in 4 (or 25 percent in American terms), far too steep for normal traffic to use. Drays required an extra team (or two) of bullocks to help them up the slope, and dragged logs behind them to help with braking on the descent. All but the most confident or foolhardy riders dismounted and walked their horses down the slope. At the foot of the hill, the town of Hartley grew up to serve the needs of the road's users. It was a slow route for bullock drays, which did well to cover more than 11 kilometres a day. In these circumstances, only wool, with its very high value relative to its weight, could stand the expense of cartage costs.

Cox's precipitous descent of Mount York has been rebuilt many times, yet it remains the most direct route from Australia's first European settlement into the interior of the continent. The first replacement was cut by Lieutenant William Lawson in 1824 and remains intact if unused, known as Lawson's Long Alley. Over the next few years, Archibald Bell and Hamilton Hume cut a new, even more arduous road from Richmond to Hartley via Bell. Completed in 1827 it was, and still is, known as Bell's Line of Road. Then in 1832, Surveyor General Major Thomas Mitchell, who had come to the position in 1827 with a determination to build quality roads as his memorial, cut the Victoria Pass – the descent is still in use, with its magnificent convict-hewn rock embankments and Mitchell's Bridge, the first of a series designed by David Lennox. Finally, between 1912 and 1935 there was the easiest graded road cut through the site. Sinuous and dangerous, it was known as Berghofer's Pass and was built to enable early motor traffic to cross the range. These successive descents of Mount York, together with the two railway descents (the Great Zig Zag of 1869 and the Ten Tunnels route of 1910) a few kilometres to the north, together constitute a remarkably intact record of human ingenuity's wrestling with this extraordinarily difficult terrain.

By 1822, just after Macquarie had left for Scotland, there were 276 miles (444 km) of made road in New South Wales, compared to none when he had arrived. By 1830, there were about 800 kilometres of stone-paved roads in New South Wales, on which coaches and carriages could operate safely and reliably in most weathers. There were thousands more kilometres of tracks suitable for bullock drays or saddle horses deep into the interior.[10] Mitchell had a deliberate policy of building high-quality stone-paved roads on the three major radial routes from Sydney: west following Cox's line (which he substantially improved) to Bathurst; south to Goulburn; and north to the Hunter Valley. On the western road, his most notable work, apart from the Victoria Pass, was the replacement of the Lapstone zigzag on the eastern escarpment with a new, more easily graded road modestly christened Mitchell's Pass. This road involved the construction of a large stone bridge. At the time, Mitchell feared that the expertise to build such a bridge in the colony did not exist. Happily, though, the very talented Scottish stonemason, David Lennox, had just migrated. Lennox had been a contractor for the greatest road builder Britain had yet seen, Thomas Telford, and won the contract, and the result was the magnificent stone arch bridge bearing his name and standing to this day. The liberal-minded Governor Bourke rode over Lennox's new bridge in 1833.

Lennox built other bridges for Mitchell, including three near Sydney: Church Street across the Parramatta River; Parramatta Road across Duck River; and, most adventurously of all, the long (110 feet or 33 metres), shallow arch over Prospect Creek at Lansdowne on the Liverpool Road. All three still carry heavy modern traffic.[11] One of Mitchell's failures as a road builder is perhaps his greatest memorial. This is the Great North Road, built by convict labour from Sydney to the Hunter Valley between 1825 and 1833. Some 164 miles (264 km) long, its major features were the sharp climbs to and from Wiseman's Ferry, where it crossed the Hawkesbury River. The northern ascent, for instance, cut by a team of 550 convicts over nearly three years from 1829 to 1831, included stone retaining walls some 12 metres high and no fewer than 43 stone box viaducts.

The road was a total commercial failure, as only a few adventurous riders chose to use it. Hunter River producers found it far easier to ship through the port of Newcastle, an easy trip across fairly level terrain, rather than use

Mitchell's road to Sydney. It would not be until the completion of the Hawkesbury River railway bridge in 1889 that significant traffic from the Hunter would be carried overland to Sydney, and then of course by rail not road. The result was that the road fell into disuse. So high was its quality, though, that it remains intact, a surprising relic from the era of convict road building, and the only substantial 19th century road in Australia to survive in its original form. Commercial failure has ensured its remarkable preservation.

As squatters spread out beyond areas officially recognised for settlement, they were obliged to create their own roads. This saw the construction of a few private roads (or at least tracks) especially in southern New South Wales, where Benjamin Boyd had tracks cut in the 1840s from his base on Twofold Bay into the high country of the Monaro where he had a number of sheep stations. Other graziers co-operated to cut the so-called wool road, from Braidwood near the future site of Canberra to the sea at Jervis Bay at much the same time.

Apart from the three main roads into the interior from Sydney, during the 19th century most roads in southern Australia were in poor condition during winter. The most notable exception was the high road from Hobart to Launceston, entirely stone paved with the labour of thousands of otherwise unemployed convicts. This fine road was perhaps the most lasting positive result of the peculiar economic system of convictism, where investment did not need to take into account labour costs.[12] It included the fine stone bridge at Ross, finished by convict labour in 1836, and made possible the growth of the Tasmanian Midlands, which lacked navigable rivers, as a wealthy pastoral district. The Ross bridge, and its similarly convict-built predecessor at Richmond, completed in 1823, are the oldest surviving bridges of any size in Australia. However, they lack the engineering audacity and large spans of Lennox's bridges.

At the time of Victoria's separation from New South Wales in 1851, it was still primarily a pastoral district, so needed little in the way of made roads. Bullock drays and wagons could traverse the mostly easy terrain from the shearing sheds to its main ports of Melbourne, Geelong, Warrnambool and Portland. The discovery of gold in the same year as separation made good roads essential, but there was little technical expertise or administrative infrastructure to do the job. Fortunately, though, gold meant that there was plenty of money around, although, less happily for road builders, labour and materials were in short supply and available only at highly inflated prices. David Lennox, responsible for some of the finest stone road bridges around Sydney, was recruited to Melbourne and promptly set about building the new colony's first good roads. They were desperately needed. The first coach service began to Ballarat in October 1851, but had to be replaced by packhorses when the wet weather came in the winter of 1852.

From 1853, the colony's roads were the responsibility of the Victorian Central Road Board, which in its brief existence built good, all-weather roads to the goldfields, as well as a number of roads around Melbourne. Very briefly, Victoria had Australia's best roads. However, after 1857, when Victorian Railways began operations and the private companies building Victoria's main railways failed, it became clear that the government would need to fund railway construction. Naturally enough, railways were considered more urgent than roads, since they were far better solutions to transport problems with the technology available at the time. The result was a gradual neglect of Victoria's roads, which lasted until well after the establishment of the Victorian Country Roads Board in 1913. Roads became the responsibility of municipal authorities, which were always underfunded and saw no point in building or maintaining roads for any other than local purposes. After about 1880 this could be justified since no colony invested more lavishly than Victoria in its railways or came anywhere near attempting to provide rail services to almost its entire population.

The result, though, was that Victorian roads in the late 19th and early 20th century were some of the worst in Australia, despite its density of population. Nowhere was this clearer than at the crossings of the Murray River, where the bridges were paid for half each by the New South Wales and Victorian governments. They were all built to New South Wales designs, since there was no substantial corps with road bridge engineering expertise in Victoria. On the New South Wales bank of the Murray the colonial government built well-engineered approaches. In contrast, local municipalities were left to do the job on the southern bank, and there were cases of bridges opening without any approaches at all on the Victorian side.

In South Australia, as in Victoria, there was not as much to do in the way of road bridge building compared with New South Wales, simply because there were far fewer rivers and in any case the pastoral and agricultural areas were much nearer the coast and so served by its cheap railways. South Australia, though, was the only place in Australia that laminated timber arches were used with any success, and Australia's last such bridge survives there at Angle Vale near Gawler. Some similar examples were built for railway use in New South Wales from the 1860s to the 1880s, but all had been replaced by the 1920s. South Australia's most important road bridge was the large iron girder bridge over the Murray River. Built between 1873 and 1879, it was considered such a wonder that the town which grew up around it became known simply as Murray Bridge. Bridges were largely the work of the South Australian Main and District Roads Board, established in 1849, rather than the municipalities, but it confined itself to building the few bridges the colony really needed, since the dry climate meant that natural roads served coach traffic adequately most of the year. South Australia's interior presented few challenges to road builders (until the arid far north of the colony was reached) and its early roads, both those cut to serve the copper industry at Burra and elsewhere from the 1840s, and those cut to encourage agriculture, required no bridges or other large structures.

In Queensland, most roads still had natural surfaces, and there was greater emphasis on building many kilometres of light and very cheap narrow-gauge railway. The outback, though, had few railways. The 1889 *Picturesque Atlas of Australia* found much to praise in Cobb and Co's coach services there, but was sarcastic about Queensland's roads:

> The bush-roads are not the smallest part of the piquant treat of coach travelling. The deep ruts cut by teams travelling with heavy loads of wool or stores are regular pitfalls. The banks of the creeks and gullies are steep and stony and few have bridges. In flood-time they are dangerous in the extreme. The country is for the most part flat, but over the ranges the descents are precipitous, even neck-breaking, and the roads often mere tracks. In dry weather the sand smothers the traveller with dust, in wet weather the black soil becomes an impassable bog.[13]

Western Australia had better roads, not so much because the population justified it but because there were otherwise unemployed

There is a concentration of Public Works Department (PWD) composite timber and iron bridges in coastal northern New South Wales. This was a district to which the railway came late, so before 1920 most government expenditure on transport infrastructure was on roads, bridges and facilities for shipping.

Harvey Dare designed the opening McFarlane Bridge at Maclean (far right), which features counterweight tracks on curves of six different radii. It opened in 1906. Dare built no fewer than eight such bridges across navigable streams. The two-span timber truss bridge with a central cast iron pier over Sportsmans Creek at Lawrence (below) was also the work of Harvey Dare. Opened in 1911, although built on piers dating from 1885, it is typical

NEW SOUTH WAL

of about 400 timber truss bridges built to evolving designs throughout the state, of which about 80 survive.

The Bawden Bridge across the Orara River (above left) was designed by William Bennett and opened on Easter Monday 1874 'amidst shouting

OAD BRIDGES

and other demonstrations of joy'. The cast iron piers and wrought iron lattice girders were made at Mort's Foundry in Balmain in Sydney then shipped by steamer and wagon to the isolated site, where they were assembled and riveted. The smaller approach spans, as on many road and railway bridges in New South Wales (and Queensland too), are simple timber beams on timber piers.

Bridges such as these gave the New South Wales Public Works Department (NSWPWD) its incomparable worldwide reputation as a great builder of economical road bridges, mostly but not entirely in timber. All three are still in service after more than a century and, since traffic on them is light, may well remain so for another. All photographs are recent, dating from 2010. (Author)

convicts there later than in the eastern colonies to build them at negligible cost. The most important road ran from Perth to Albany, Western Australia's most important port and a coaling station for steamers plying between Europe and eastern Australia. Entirely convict built, it was not heavily used. In the mid-1880s it enjoyed a fortnightly mail coach service, which covered the distance of 261 miles (420 km) in about 50 hours, although on one occasion when the Governor was travelling it was completed in 23 hours. Even this convict-built road could be so boggy in winter that passengers had to get out to help push the coach out of the mud. Little wonder that once steamer services between Perth and Albany began few passengers bothered any longer with the mail coach.[14]

In the late colonial period, New South Wales had better roads than any other Australian colony, and needed to. In Victoria, railways were built to every inhabited corner of the colony in the 1880s (and to some uninhabited ones too). By contrast, New South Wales built a simple system of main railway lines, leaving local transport needs to road or river transport and coastal transport to steamers. In the long run, this would be good business for the railways of New South Wales, which were the best financial performers in the country; but it imposed the need for considerable investment in the colony's roads and bridges. Moreover, New South Wales has many large coastal and inland rivers, and thousands of substantial creeks. Put simply, there were a lot of rivers to cross there, especially compared with South Australia, Western Australia and Tasmania. In addition, in New South Wales it was the colonial government which was obliged to build and maintain these roads and bridges, because only a tenth of New South Wales was incorporated into municipalities until the local government reforms of 1906. By contrast, virtually all of Victoria had been incorporated into shires and municipalities, many of them with slender resources, and these had the responsibility of building and maintaining such works. This meant that, in New South Wales, road bridge designs came out of the large and professional drafting office of the Public Works Department in Sydney, whereas, in Victoria especially, bridges were often the work of untrained contractors.

The scale of road investment in New South Wales can be gauged from figures which show that almost as much was spent on roads as on railways during the period of the great railway boom. In the half century from 1857 to 1906, the New South Wales government spent a total of £72 505 241 on transport, divided as follows:

Railways £32 054 853
Tramways £2 294 854
Roads and Bridges £23 837 410
Harbours and Rivers £14 318 124 [15]

This pattern of expenditure reveals the continuing importance of road transport in the railway age. New South Wales had a clearly articulated and thought through road transport policy, established in the 1850s when

Ben Hay Martindale was Commissioner for Inland Communications, which included both roads and railways. His aim was to build three main roads to decent standards from Sydney west to Wellington, southwest to the Murray at Albury, and north from Newcastle to Tamworth. These aims were enshrined in the *Main Roads Management Act* of 1858.[16] Elsewhere, the government would provide bridges and other essential works to make 'natural' roads more easily used by bullock teams. In reality this was an extension to the now defined and truncated borders of New South Wales of the scheme Macquarie had begun back in the second decade of the 19th century.

For much of the second half of the 19th century, the New South Wales Commissioner for Roads was William Bennett. He followed Martindale's general principles, and also found funds to build a few remarkable roads of his own, including the Glen Innes to Grafton road, intended basically for bullock wagons to use to reach a port, yet boasting such features as a tunnel cut through sheer rock and the 1874 iron lattice girder bridge over the Orara River. No other colony would even contemplate such features on such a remote road, and its enduring quality is one of many testimonies to the seriousness of the late 19th century New South Wales road-building program. New South Wales even built a very large American-style Whipple steel truss bridge for road use across the Shoalhaven River at Nowra as early as 1879. This was an amazing structure for what was then merely a local road, and it is still in use for the heaviest highway traffic. Once again, it is a stunning example of New South Wales primacy in bridge construction in Australia at this time.

Indeed, it would not be an exaggeration to assert that in Australian road bridge construction right up until after World War II, it was a case of New South Wales first, Queensland second (on the strength of the Indooroopilly and Story Bridges across the Brisbane River), and the rest nowhere. Any one of dozens of bridges of this era still existing in New South Wales would be considered remarkable if it was in any other state. Even the NSWGR got into the act of erecting adventurous road bridges, building a Schweidler iron truss with a single span of no less than a clear 135 feet (41.2 m) for a road across the railway yard at Bathurst in 1888.[17] It is still in service. While the Nowra and Bathurst truss bridges were extraordinary enough as early examples of metal road bridges, the outstanding feature of New South Wales road bridges at this time was the work done with timber. New South Wales had plentiful supplies of ironbark and turpentine, just about the best bridge-building timbers in the world. It also had a Public Works Department with a commitment to building quality roads and bridges throughout the colony, with a budget sufficient to do a lot of such building, but not so generous as to allow for extravagances. The result was the design and construction of timber bridges unequalled in the world. A recent study explains why Victoria never built timber bridges on anything like the scale or to the quality of New South Wales, concluding that 'by 1900, the most efficient timber-truss bridges being built anywhere in the world were in New South Wales.'[18]

A total of 422 timber truss road bridges were built in New South Wales between 1860 and 1936, a wealth of such bridges unparalleled elsewhere on the planet. Of these 82 survive. They fall into five basic types, from the Old Public Works Department design, based in English precedents, through the local developments each named after NSWPWD engineers. In chronological order these are McDonald, Allan, De Burgh and Dare trusses.[19] Indeed it is remarkable that NSWPWD engineers of this period have timber truss designs named after them, internationally recognised as such. The work of PWD engineers in developing timber road bridges was aided by Professor William Henry Warren, who had come to Sydney as an engineer in 1881 and in 1884 became the first Challis Professor of Engineering at the University of Sydney. He worked and wrote extensively on timber bridge construction, giving a solid academic and theoretical base to the practical task of spanning the colony's all too numerous rivers and creeks economically and enduringly. John Whitton and EO Moriarty, the PWD engineers in charge of railways and harbours respectively, also designed some truly remarkable timber structures, so there was in Sydney an expertise in timber engineering of a depth which matched the natural resources of the forests of New South Wales.[20] Bennett and Whitton were inclined to be conservative and favoured British over American bridge-building technology, although not in too doctrinaire a way: after all the Shoalhaven road bridge and Hawkesbury railway bridge – both distinctively American designs – were built under their direction. Both retired in 1890, with enormous achievements to their credit, but their successors unquestionably were more innovative and adventurous.

Some of the timber bridges of this era were opening bridges, including a number over the Murray (half paid for by Victoria, but entirely Sydney designed, including Swan Hill, Tooleybuc and Barham) and others on coastal rivers, such as the McFarlane Bridge on the south arm of the Clarence at Maclean. There is a particularly dense concentration of timber truss bridges around Maitland, including the two surviving early PWD-style bridges, an opening bridge at Hinton and a long truss bridge at Morpeth. This is a rich agricultural district which, in classic New South Wales style, was served by just one main line of railway with only one short branch (to Morpeth, reluctantly built by the railways because a shipping company pressured them into it), as well as a few colliery lines. Most traffic was carried by river or road, whereas in Victoria a comparable district would not have had a navigable river, scarcely any trafficable roads, but a reasonably dense network of branch line railways.

The outstanding timber bridge in Australia, though, and one of the world's finest timber bridges, is Percy Allan's Pyrmont Bridge in Sydney. This is a long bridge of 1635 feet (500 m) divided into 90-foot (27-m) timber Allan truss spans. In its centre is a swing span, which opens to allow shipping to pass. This was the first electrically powered opening span in the world, and Allan used ordinary Sydney electric tram motors and control equipment to do the job, so that they could easily be repaired or replaced. Opening in 1902, it astounded expert opinion around the world with the speed of its operation and 'the phenomenally low cost' of its openings. A technically identical but shorter opening bridge was opened to Allan's design at Glebe Island (only a kilometre away on the other side of the Pyrmont Peninsula) the following year. Both of these two bridges survive, evidence in the heart of Sydney of New South Wales world leadership in timber road bridge technology at the dawn of the 20th century.[21]

FREIGHT VEHICLES IN COLONIAL AUSTRALIA

SURPRISINGLY EARLY in its transport history, Australia developed vehicles peculiar to its conditions. In general, Australian goods vehicles were heavier than their European progenitors. The first was the dray, a two-wheel cart based on the very first wheeled vehicles used by humanity – the two-wheel ox-carts of ancient Mesopotamia. Australian drays were based on the Scotch cart, and were essentially a box mounted on a single axle. Local development soon went in two directions: first into a light dray used for farm and general light haulage work, and drawn by a single draught horse in the shafts (although many were sufficiently light for harness horses to be used); and second into a heavier dray hauled by teams of between four and ten horses or (more commonly) bullocks, arranged in pairs on either side of a pole. The latter, also called the pole dray, was the pioneer vehicle of Australian inland transport, and could carry reasonably heavy loads over unmade roads for long distances. Braking was its greatest weakness, a serious issue on the colony's first road into the interior over the Blue Mountains. Such desperate remedies as dragging a log behind the dray downhill to provide braking power were all too common.

The pole dray was soon superseded around Sydney and Melbourne by four-wheel wagons

George W Lambert, *Across the black soil plains*, 1899, oil on canvas, 91.6 x 305.5cm, purchased 1899, Art Gallery of New South Wales. George Lambert's vivid painting of a team hauling a giant Australian flat-top wagon with some difficulty across the level but sodden black soil plains of northwestern New South Wales. Lambert lived in Warren in the early 1890s and his painting depicted bales of wool being carted to the railhead at Nevertire. The Nevertire to Warren railway opened in 1898, ending such scenes.

of various designs. However, wherever there were no made roads, the dray's flexible design remained in favour for moving stores out to remote properties and hauling the bales of wool back. A typical pole dray could carry more than 2 tons, or about 12 bales of wool. Although rare in settled districts after the 1840s, these drays remained common where there were no roads until the end of the 19th century, especially in outback Queensland. The light dray was more versatile and has remained in use virtually unmodified in design to the present. Wherever light loads of up to a ton needed to be carried relatively short distances, this was an extremely economic form of transport. If there was a horse around not otherwise gainfully employed, it was virtually free. As such the pole dray was much favoured by small farmers well into the 20th century, and is still competitive with motor transport on properties where there are horses.

From the 1820s, four-wheel wagons replaced drays wherever there was the semblance of a road. These required a road, since they lacked the dray's ability to make sharp turns over obstacles such as stumps, logs and rocks. Developed from the English box wagon, they were heavier in construction and used the stronger and denser Australian hardwoods. They were tough vehicles. Their great disadvantage was their inability to make sharp turns, a serious issue in Sydney's narrow dockside streets as much as in the bush. The solution was the development of the pony truck. The front pair of wheels,

placed outside the box on a rigid axle on early wagons, was replaced by a swivelling pony truck. The poles through which traction from the animals hauling the wagon was applied to the vehicle were attached to the pony truck. This was a more complicated design, and required sound iron fastenings, but it permitted sharp turns to be made. It was also inherently more fragile, because of the increased number of moving parts, and so was better suited to operations where roads were adequate. It also required higher skill levels to maintain, because of its crucial ironmongery. That said, it was a much more efficient design, and became general in more settled areas than the old design with fixed external front wheels. By the 1850s, once again in places where roads were better, these vehicles were being fitted with springs. Such vehicles were nearly always worked by draught horses rather than bullocks, since, if the conditions existed for such relatively sophisticated vehicles, they also existed for horses to be more efficient than bullocks. The size of these pony truck wagons varied enormously, from one or two horse delivery wagons used in city streets (in the case of one Sydney stationer until the 1990s) up to 8-ton capacity wagons worked by teams of twelve horses.

During the 1880s, there were two major innovations in wagon design. First was the introduction of the light American Conestoga wagon, the vehicle with which the American West was won. This suited hawkers and drovers, because it was cheap and light, but had limited applications in the Australian pastoral and agricultural industries. More importantly, and uniquely Australian, was the development of the giant flat-top wagon. These carried loads which in most places would have justified the building of a railway. The point was, though, that Australian sheep stations produced only one, extremely valuable, crop a year, not enough to justify a railway. This wool had to be transported to the nearest navigable water or railway station as quickly as possible, not because it spoilt (wool lasted for years in storage or transit) but so the grazier could sell it at the spring sales and so maintain his cash flow.

The giant flat-top wagon, worked by teams of up to 30 horses or bullocks, was ideal for moving the fleeces. These required space to operate, since the leading animals were more than 30 metres from the swivel-pin, the all-important piece of ironmongery through which traction was transmitted to the wagon. It was more than 6 metres long with front wheels 1.5 metres and back wheels 2 metres in diameter. These carried loads up to an extraordinary 32 tons, or almost as much as a modern articulated truck. Wool and wheat were the main commodities they carried, although their enormous size meant they were also well suited to lighter goods such as chaff and hay, the all-important fuel for their equine motive power. From the 1880s to the 1930s, these giant wagons delivered the riches of Australia's interior to the wharves along the Murray, Darling and Murrumbidgee Rivers, and to railway stations from Hay to Cloncurry. The extremely spacious layouts of many New South Wales and Queensland inland railway stations were designed with these wagons in mind. They were never seen in the coastal cities, where they would have been unmanageable. Many survived to be replaced by World War II surplus ex-army trucks, and so represented the ultimate development of the muscle-powered vehicle in Australia.[22]

PERSONAL AND PASSENGER TRANSPORT IN THE AGE OF THE HORSE

PEDESTRIANISM WAS and has remained the most basic of all personal transport options, although even as early as 1810, freed convicts were putting all their spare money into buying horses, as much to prove that they no longer needed to walk (like convicts) but rode (like gentlemen) as because they needed one. Owning a horse was as much about status as transport, and so it has remained till the present, although car ownership has largely, but not entirely, replaced horse ownership as a means of social cachet. Of course, few people had greater psychological need to prove their status and respectability than former convicts or their offspring, so the Australian obsession with saddle horse ownership had deep roots in the mind and the soul.

At the dawn of the motor age, the buggy was a cheap means of personal transport. It was light and economical to build, easily maintained, and only required one horse. Provided distances were short and hills not too steep, a saddle horse or 'hack' (mixed breed of no distinction) could be put to work between the shafts. Comfort was limited and passengers could not expect much warmth in the snow of the Adelaide Hills. (Author postcard collection)

Of course, a saddle horse was also extremely useful. A journey takes only a fifth the time on horseback as on foot, and the rider has the sense of command and authority which height and speed bring. With just a saddle horse and a packhorse for supplies, a single rider could cover enormous distances. Not until the introduction of the bicycle in the 1890s was there any rival to the saddle horse for fast personal transport. A horse was not that cheap. For most of the 19th century, a good saddle horse cost about £15, saddlery about £2, shoes up to another £2 each year, and feed (if kept in the city) £20 a year. This was when decent wages were around £50 to £100 a year. Obviously the economics of horse ownership were always more favourable for farmers and graziers and their employees than for urban dwellers, since feed was free in good seasons. Most horses, because of their cost, were expected to work, even if the work was simply carrying their master to work. Until the early 20th century, saddle horses were widely used for personal urban transport by middle class men in Sydney and, more especially, Melbourne, where the horse cult was (and in some ways remains, albeit confined now to racetracks and their environs) virtually a fetish.

While the saddle horse was the main means of personal transport, from the early 19th century the very rich and those with a social point to make drove carriages. Until about 1815, this was an expensive way to be pretentious, since the carriages were imported and rather fragile, and roads so poor that the carriages required constant repairs. With road development under Macquarie, and the simultaneous growth of a more affluent society, this began to change, and carriages were imported in larger numbers. Most were used by people who wished to make a statement about themselves, although public carriage transport began as early as 1805, when William Robert began Australia's first land public transport service, a 'stage wagon' which ran from Sydney to the Hawkesbury. This took 16 hours and cost 7 shillings and sixpence, which were substantial investments of time and money. The service did not thrive because a saddle horse could always do the trip faster, cheaper and, given the primitive roads, more comfortably too. William Highland revived much the same route with a weekly service between Sydney and the two Hawkesbury towns of Richmond and Windsor in 1814.

A true stagecoach system on the English model, with quality carriages and regular staging of horses, was not introduced until 1819, when services began between Sydney and Parramatta and between Hobart and Launceston. These were then the only two decent roads in Australia. Then in 1820 William Watsford began a twice-daily service between Sydney and Parramatta, a route his coaches would dominate until he closed the service with the opening of the railway in 1855. By 1823 Watsford's coaching services had been extended to Penrith and Windsor; and in 1824 other operators began services from Sydney to Parramatta, Windsor, Liverpool, Penrith and Bathurst. What is astonishing about these early services of the 1820s is how closely subsequent railways followed the same routes, and indeed the way in which rail services nearly two centuries later mirror these very first coach services.

Watsford's main competitors were Ireland and Richards, who by 1834 were running services from Sydney to Goulburn and Bathurst (exactly the routes planned for the Sydney Railway Company a couple of decades later). They used nine imported coaches worked by four-horse teams changed every 16 to 24 kilometres. We know a lot about their enterprise because they went spectacularly bankrupt in 1834 and their entire business was valued and auctioned. Their collapse prompted the government to begin land transport regulation with the *Stage Carriage Act* of 1835, setting fares and rates, and awarding mail contracts. These contracts were the basis of profitable coaching companies throughout the coaching era. Services were known as the Mail, a terminology that was transferred to the trains which replaced them on the busier routes after the 1850s and survived until Australia's last mail trains, the North Mail, South Mail and Western Mail, ran out of Sydney in 1988. Once again, the continuity of transport arrangements between early colonial and modern New South Wales is striking indeed.

The styles of coaches used varied considerably. On the better roads near Sydney and between Hobart and Launceston, where there was sufficient mail and passenger traffic to justify daily services, English coaches were used, typically costing £200 each with as much again for their sets of harnesses. From the 1830s, the horses used were mostly Cleveland Bays, an English breed developed specifically for harness work. They combined speed with endurance, at a cost of strength. Four Cleveland Bays formed a typical team to haul the quite light coaches. By the 1830s, English coaches were being modified for colonial conditions, basically by strengthening their springs. Coaching services were over made roads, not bush tracks, and, by the 1840s in New South Wales and Tasmania at least, these roads, while often the subject of complaint, were far from primitive, and featured extensive earthworks and fine stone bridges. Hence, modified English coaches were appropriate to these tasks.

The coaches stopped every 15 kilometres or so at coaching inns to change horses, and colonial travel had begun to resemble that back in England. The mail coaches were colourful and impressive, nearly always painted red with yellow lining and black ironmongery, lettered in gold 'VR' (Victoria Regina) and 'Royal Mail'. Much the same livery would be used later in the century by nearly all Australian railways for their passenger coaches. They had a driver and a guard (once again the railways would later use the same terminology), who would sound a bugle when entering towns and villages, and had charge of the mail. Travel was reasonably fast where roads were decent, typically covering about 100 kilometres a day, even over mountainous terrain such as between Sydney and Bathurst, which was done in two days with one overnight stop.[23] This distance of 100 kilometres became typical of that between towns in much of rural Australia, as coaching inns developed into townships.

As essential to the coaching age of Australian transport as the service station is to the motor age was the coaching inn, where horse teams were changed and passengers enjoyed refreshment or repose. Many examples survive around the country. This one at Nymboida, New South Wales, dates from late in the coaching era, 1905, although proprietor Russell Crowe's Harley Davidson is definitely early 21st century. (Author)

In the more remote areas, light horse carts (with accommodation for the odd passenger or two who for some reason did not want to go on horseback) covered the mail contracts. By the mid-1840s, the coaching business was sufficiently mature for a weekly coach service to be established between Sydney and Melbourne, although its primary function was to carry mails and some passengers between intermediate places on the route, rather than through traffic. Coastal steamers would remain the fastest and most comfortable way of travelling between the two cities until their direct rail connection, and remained competitive with rail well after that.

The era of English-style coaching lasted until the 1850s, when there was a sudden shift to American practices. The innovators were the founders of what was soon known as Cobb and Co, destined to become Australia's greatest (and last) coaching company. The four partners in the enterprise, Freeman Cobb, John Peck, James Swanton and John Lamber, were all Americans attracted to Melbourne by the promise of the Victorian goldfields. Like so many others, they decided that doing what they knew best in a boom economy had better and surer prospects than digging for the elusive metal. In their case, this was the coaching business, and they brought with them distinctively American techniques and styles. In 1853 they began operations on the busiest route in the country, from Sandridge (Port Melbourne) to Melbourne. They dominated the traffic for a year until Australia's first steam railway opened over the same terrain.

Cobb and Co introduced the American Concord coach to Australia, so called because it was first built in Concord, Massachusetts. The principle of the Concord coach was that sprung suspension was replaced by leather straps (called thoroughbraces) on which the entire body was suspended. This made for a smoother ride on rough roads, although the ride was not as good as a sprung coach on a paved or well-metalled road. Passengers in a Concord coach often felt a sensation of seasickness, because of the coach body's free swaying motion, supported as it was only by the very flexible thoroughbraces. In fact, a combination of braces and springs, as later developed by Cobb and Co, gave the best ride. Cobb and Co soon developed a distinctively Australian design, lower, squarer and more open (since Australia's climate was much milder) than the American stagecoach on which it had been based. Thus, in coaching as in so much else in Australia, the ideal practice proved to be a compromise between British and North American notions, with a few colonial innovations (notably wide open unglazed windows) added.

In 1854, as the railway took over their business in Melbourne, Cobb and Co moved into the equally lucrative traffic to the goldfields, establishing routes linking Melbourne with Castlemaine and Bendigo, and Geelong with Ballarat. As with the first New South Wales coaching routes, these

Even before the motor age a big country town like Toowoomba, Queensland, could be a busy place. Saddle horses and a variety of horse-drawn vehicles crammed the streets to such an extent that parking, even back in 1890, was an issue. (Author postcard collection)

anticipated Victoria's first mainline railways. By then, the roads to the diggings had been improved dramatically from a few years before, and the coach services were reliable and efficient, and could even reach their destination in a single day from Melbourne. With characteristic marketing flair, they called their services the American Telegraph Line, a name which captured all that was new and speedy in the 1850s. On the route from Geelong to Ballarat, traffic was so intense that they built a special coach accommodating 90 passengers and drawn by a team of no fewer than 16 horses. This they modestly christened the *Leviathan*.

By 1862, when the railways opened to Ballarat and Bendigo thereby depriving Cobb and Co of their heaviest traffic, the original partners had made their fortunes and sold out. The new owners, a consortium led by James Rutherford, retained the name but changed the philosophy. Railway building compelled them to look further afield than the rich pickings around the Victorian diggings. As early as 1861 Rutherford moved Cobb and Co's headquarters north to Bathurst. It would be another decade before the rails would reach Bathurst from Sydney, so the company's future was far more assured there. Soon after, it began operations in Queensland. It first operated between Ipswich and Brisbane (which were not linked by rail until 1875), and from the railhead west of Ipswich up the range to Toowoomba. When the railway along this route was completed, the emphasis of Cobb and Co's Queensland operations moved to the interior, linking Toowoomba with Warwick, Dalby, Roma and the Condamine. Under Rutherford's direction, Cobb and Co never attempted to compete with railways, but tailored their services to act as feeders to the new inland railway termini. This ensured friendly relations with the colonial governments, which, after all, were investing huge sums in railways and had no desire to succour competitors. These relations in turn led to Cobb and Co winning nearly all the colonial mail contracts. These formed a reliable revenue base on which to run the coach services. So dominant was Cobb and Co in the coaching business that one writer has claimed that 'the story of coaching in Australia is essentially the story of Cobb and Co'.[24]

As railways were extended, Cobb and Co's operations moved west and north. Rutherford set up coach-building works in Bathurst and later in Brisbane and Charleville, a long way from the company's Melbourne origins. Its Victorian operations wound down rapidly in the 1880s, as a railway network was built covering virtually all that colony. In New South Wales and Queensland, though, where railway networks were never as dense, coaching would remain important well into the motor age. Rutherford opened the Charleville works in response to the peculiar conditions in which the company found itself. Its routes increasingly were confined to the outback, where the climate was generally very dry. Timbers tended to crack when exposed to such dry conditions, so he built coaches in Charleville so that timbers could be cured in the dry inland air and so be less susceptible to cracking.[25] It was an attention to detail typical of the company, a characteristic it shared with Australia's better shipping companies and railways.

The period from 1870 to 1900 were the halcyon days of Cobb and Co's operations in the interior of New South Wales and Queensland. In 1870 it was harnessing 6000 horses every day and its coaches were running 45 000 kilometres a week. As settlement moved further into the interior and population increased rapidly, its business kept expanding. As one route was closed by the opening of a new railway, another – deeper in the interior – would start. Its services could be fast, although not especially cheap. For instance, in 1880 Cobb and Co's coach from the Victorian railway station at Geelong to Mortlake took just 13 hours to cover the 92 miles (148 km). The fare was an even pound, three days' labour for an unskilled worker, so coach services were not for the poor.

Mail contracts included the carriage of gold from the diggings to the capital, and transport of banknotes and coins on behalf of banks. This meant that Cobb and Co's coaches could be rich pickings indeed for bushrangers. The company's guards were armed, and, when bushrangers were active, coaches were often accompanied by troops of mounted police. The interior of Australia was never quite as wild as the American Wild West, because the colonial authorities moved in very quickly to establish courthouses, police stations, gaols and the general coercive apparatus of the state as soon as there was a significant population which needed policing. Not one Cobb and Co driver was ever killed by a bushranger, although a few did have shots fired at them in anger. The most lucrative robbery under arms of a Cobb and Co coach was early in the company's history, when in 1861 Frank Gardiner's gang robbed the Forbes to Orange coach in New South Wales of some £12 000 in gold and banknotes. Perhaps more typical of the hazards of a bushranger's life was the confession of William Green, who in 1851 complained that his robbery of the Melbourne to Port Fairy mail coach had yielded far more love letters than valuables.[26]

Coach travel, clearly, was neither as safe nor as comfortable nor as cheap as train travel, but Cobb and Co did have a good safety record and its drivers were impressive men. The first drivers were Americans, but soon most were locals. They had a reputation for being extremely trustworthy, reliable, a touch autocratic, and with the understandable vice of being inclined to flirt – in a chivalrous way – with unaccompanied female passengers. Accidents were more common in the early days, when the coaches operated in more mountainous districts. In their later years, plying outback routes across the plains, they were extremely safe and reliable.

Horses were less inclined to break down than motor vehicles in the vast expanses of the outback, where farriers and blacksmiths were numerous but motor mechanics rare. For this reason, Cobb and Co's coaching services lasted well into the motor age. The company, lacking the entrepreneurial drive of its early days, did not move into motor transport, and was wound up in 1924 after the teams hauled its last coach from Surat near Roma to the railhead at Yuleba. It was a significant event, although perhaps Cobb and Co's historian has exaggerated a little in claiming that its coaches made in Charleville and used on its last services were 'the last and most successful of man's attempts to ally his own ingenuity with the strength of the horse to produce an ideal vehicle for conditions encountered in virgin country'.[27]

Cobb and Co's coaching services ceased at much the same time as the last horse bus services in Brisbane and Sydney. Horses continued to be used to haul hansom cabs about Australia's cities for another decade, but in the 1920s the era of horse-powered passenger transport came to an end. The motor vehicle, not the railway, replaced the last generation of coaches in the outback.

DROVING

OF ALL THE pre-mechanised forms of transport, none seems more basic than droving. This is the deceptively simple-looking business of drovers on horseback driving flocks of sheep or herds of cattle to market. In fact, though, droving was a complicated business, with economics all of its own and surprising legal and infrastructure requirements.

Droving skills began with the European settlement of the interior of New South Wales in the 1820s. Squatters and their small staff of a few overseers and stockmen (often assigned convicts in the first couple of decades, but increasingly free labour) would drive cattle from settled districts onto virgin pastures, which they would then occupy. This was called overlanding, and was the crucible in which European Australians learned their bushcraft skills. By 1860, all the good land in southeastern Australia had been taken, and the squatters were no longer illegal occupants of 'empty' land, but had become the wealthy pseudo-landed gentry of Australia. Overlanding, though, continued in the harsher conditions of the more remote parts of the country.

Paradoxically, it was the disaster of the Burke and Wills Expedition of 1860–61 which provided the stimulus to the exploitation of these remote regions. It quickly became evident that Burke and Wills had died as a result of incompetence, not because the country was so hostile as to be fatal. In the following 30 years, cattle stations were established right through western Queensland, the Northern Territory and the Kimberley district of Western Australia. Deserts there were, but there was also plenty of adequate grazing country, and the overlanding skills learned in the early squatting days of the 1820s and 1830s were applied to the far larger distances of the remote north. A typical feat of this era was Nat Buchanan's droving of 900 bullocks from Wave Hill station in the Northern Territory to Murchison in Western Australia, a distance of almost 3000 kilometres, in 1892. This was overlanding and droving on a grand scale indeed.[28]

During the 1870s the great droving routes were established in an arc across the north of the continent. These linked the Kimberleys in Western Australia, the cattle country of the Northern Territory and the Gulf Country of Queensland with the western railheads of the Queensland and New South Wales Railways, the northern railheads of the South Australian Railways and even the northernmost branches of the Victorian Railways. By the 1920s about 40 000 head of cattle a year were being driven from the Northern Territory into western Queensland, so this was a busy route. A branch track, one of the most arduous of all, left far western Queensland along the route of Eyre Creek to the South Australian railhead of Oodnadatta. This was the famous

A Cobb and Co mail coach in southwestern Queensland, from a postcard published by Kerry in Sydney about 1900. The 'Australian mail coach' lasted into the 1920s in these parts, and its advantages over motor transport in country where roads were poor and rainfall occasionally intense are obvious in this image of a coach crossing a flooded river. (Author postcard collection)

Birdsville Track, which, skirting Lake Eyre and passing through the driest cattle stations in Australia, had surprising significance as a commercial stock route. This was because it had access to good bore water and served the southwest corner of Queensland, which was very remote from the nearest Queensland and New South Wales railheads.

The Port Augusta to Oodnadatta railway was significant in the development of a cattle industry in the only spasmodically well-watered centre of the continent. From the vast area stretching from Alice Springs to Birdsville large numbers of cattle were driven to Oodnadatta (or later Marree) until the railway was opened through to Alice Springs in 1929. For instance, in 1907 about 50 000 head of cattle and 300 000 head of sheep were driven from the Northern Territory to Oodnadatta for railing south to supply the South Australian market.[29] This was a peak year, as sheep did not last long in central Australia. The average number of cattle driven to Oodnadatta on the Birdsville Track was 19 000 per year from 1910 to 1924, while an average of 11 300 came each year over the same period from the Alice Springs region.[30]

Similar to the Birdsville Track, and perhaps even more arduous, was the Strzelecki Track along the course of Strzelecki Creek in the far north of South Australia. Except after heavy rain, this creek is dry, but it has a number of natural permanent waterholes along its course. From the 1870s it became an important route for driving cattle between Farina railway station (formerly Government Gums and the railhead for Port Augusta) and the centre of the continent. It ceased to be used after the extension of the railway from Marree to Alice Springs in the late 1920s. Both the Strzelecki and Birdsville Tracks followed routes used for millennia by Aboriginal people to travel through the arid country.

The heartland of the droving industry was western Queensland and New South Wales. Stock routes led from Queensland south through Hungerford on the New South Wales–Queensland border to Bourke and further south to Hay, Deniliquin and Echuca. Bourke and Hay were not much more than 24 hours by cattle train from Sydney, and Echuca and Deniliquin only a day trip from Melbourne. As droving destinations, they were clearly superior to Oodnadatta, for instance, which a drover reached along the formidable Birdsville Track, only to leave the cattle at the railhead for a long, slow and expensive ride by narrow-gauge train to Port Augusta. As a market and a port, Port Augusta could hardly compete with Sydney or Melbourne. Nor could the Birdsville Track compete with the well-watered and well-maintained New South Wales stock routes, except for the isolated cattle stations in Queensland's extreme southwest.

Not all droving routes were through rough country. There was an important route along the northern bank of the Murray through Wentworth linking New South Wales and South Australia. This was well watered and extensively used, even well into the railway age, since the route by train was indirect and required transhipment between trains operating on tracks of different gauges. Since the two colonies were affected by different weather systems, there could be drought in one and plenty in the other, so large numbers of cattle were driven along this route.

Between 1857 and 1907, the New South Wales government spent no less than £1 700 000 on water supplies for stock routes. To put this huge figure in context, this was almost as much as the £2 294 854 spent in the same period on building Sydney's and Newcastle's tram systems, including electrification.[31] This massive New South Wales investment in stock routes ensured that state's domination of the meat trade, allied as it was with a network of mainline railways which carried stock (or refrigerated meat, for there were abattoirs at Bourke and the NSWGR was a pioneer of refrigerated rail wagons) the long distances from places like Bourke and Hay to Sydney at discounted rates. Droving then, was a trade allied with modern transport and formed part of a complementary network of linkages between this most primitive form of cattle movement and the most modern transport the world then offered.

The New South Wales expenditure on ensuring water on stock routes was a wise investment. Not only did it produce profitable traffic for the New South Wales Railways, it also increased the general productivity of the country, for droving could be a hazardous business, and during drought heavy stock losses were common. This investment was sanctioned by the *Public Watering Places Act* of 1884, itself a response to an 1880 report which had found that, of the eighteen stock routes in the colony, only seven were well watered, nine fairly watered and two poorly watered. By 1900 there was permanent water along 1400 miles (2255 km) of New South Wales stock routes, and similar (although not as ambitious) programs were under way in South Australia, the Northern Territory and Queensland.[32] These included the provision of adequate water supplies, drawing on the underground reservoirs of the Great Artesian Basin, along the Birdsville Track.

Droving remained a favoured method of moving stock well into the 20th century, largely because there were very few north–south railways in the inland, and this was the flow of most cattle. It has been estimated that in 1920 some 1.3 million cattle and 7.95 million sheep were being driven along stock routes at some time during the year.[33] Moreover, rail charges for cattle were not cheap, and droving could be competitive in price, especially in good seasons when feed and water were abundant. Even rail travel itself was an extension of droving, as the railway administrations provided

The drover cracked the whip to bring an errant steer back into the mob of cattle he was driving to Alice Springs in 1954. From the Alice the cattle would be railed to markets in South Australia, as recorded a few days later by the same photographer on p 112. (Neil Murray, NLA vn4589710)

accommodation for drovers on cattle trains. The drover, not railway officials, was responsible for watering and otherwise caring for the cattle while they were on the train.

Not all traffic on stock routes comprised cattle and sheep destined for market. Stock were moved between different parts of the country to avoid drought and take advantage of surplus pasture when there were shortages elsewhere. Because the northern two-thirds of Australia (roughly north of a line drawn from Sydney to Oodnadatta) is monsoonal and enjoys summer rain while the southern third (roughly south of Sydney) has winter rainfall, there can be drought in some parts of the country and plenty elsewhere. Occasionally cattle and sheep from the Port Augusta region of South Australia were driven up to feed on the Birdsville Track, when monsoonal rains brought rare rich pasture to the country north of Oodnadatta, while the usually far better watered Gulf region of South Australia languished in drought. The diversity of weather patterns affecting Australia, and the fact that the centre of the continent mostly (but certainly not always) misses out on rain coming from whichever direction, had much to do with determining the use of Australia's remotest stock routes in the interior.

One of the last great stock routes to be established (and one of the least ever used) was also the longest. This was the extra-ordinary Canning Stock Route, which linked Halls Creek, a remote and tiny town in Western Australia's tropical Kimberley district, with Wiluna, an equally tiny town about 190 kilometres from the railhead of Meekatharra, the furthest point into the northwest of the state reached by the tracks of the Western Australian Government Railway (WAGR). This was a distance of about 1800 kilometres, across some of the most arid country on the continent, including the Great Sandy Desert, the Little Sandy Desert, the Gibson Desert and the Tanami Desert.

The Canning Stock Route was pioneered in response to the 1898 prohibition by the WA government on the Kimberley cattle farmers shipping their cattle to abattoirs elsewhere in the colony. The reason was the infestation of cattle herds there with a tick imported from Java with some of the stock. The tick thrived in the humid conditions of the sea voyage to market, but died in dry conditions. Taking the cattle overland to Meekatharra seemed to be a solution. In 1906 Alfred Canning and a party of eight, supported by 22 camels, surveyed the route and, with the help of local Aborigines, found supplies of surface and artesian water on the way. Between 1908 and 1910 the track was built, the main works being the establishment of 51 watering points, mostly wells, about 25 kilometres apart. This required a work party of 31 men and 70 camels.

The Canning was never much of a success and only ever carried a relative handful of cattle. It was just too long and too rigorous for drovers to use it with any good prospects of a commercial return. Described as

'unquestionably the loneliest, most difficult and dangerous stock route in Australia', it is scarcely surprising that its use never met early expectations.[34] It was very rare for more than two mobs a year to use the track. The stock routes leading east into the Northern Territory, with railheads for Darwin, or beyond to railheads in western Queensland and New South Wales were always far more attractive than the Canning to Kimberley graziers. By 1929 it had fallen into disrepair, although in 1930 its wells were rebuilt in an attempt to revive trade, and the railway was even extended all the way to Wiluna in response to a brief minor gold rush to the town.

Its wells were derelict again by 1942, when once again they were repaired in case the Canning were needed as an evacuation route from a possible Japanese invasion of the northwest. It was not, and the last cattle were driven south in 1958. One of the most interesting features of the Canning was that it was the last part of Australia where there was active and occasionally violent Aboriginal resistance to European exploitation of the land. During its construction there were spears thrown and shots fired, with fatal results to both sides. Tension between local Aborigines and drovers (many of whom were also Aborigines, but more integrated into the modern economic and social system) was a

From 1 January 1913, just a year after James Rutherford died, Cobb and Co lost the contract to carry the mail between Grafton and Glen Innes. At that time the post office sent mail from Sydney to Grafton by train to Glenn Innes then by coach because it preferred the reliability of rail and coach transport to the hazards of the steamers. The last mail coach and the first motor lorry to make the run posed outside Grafton post office on the day one transport mode faded and another became dominant. (NAA C4078, N7255/2)

A cattle train leaving Alice Springs in 1954. Droving had a symbiotic relationship with railways, since drovers generally accompanied cattle from the pastoral station to the railway station, whence they went to the port or abattoir by train. Road transport of cattle would bring an end to this relationship. (Neil Murray, National Archives of Australia, NAA Series A1200, Item L17450)

long-lived characteristic, certainly increasing its hazards.

Droving, the most elemental of all means of animal transport, lasted longer than any other form of muscle-powered transport in Australia. This was because it was reasonably priced and was an effective way of moving cattle and sheep along routes where there was no railway. State investment in watering facilities meant that, in all but the very worst seasons, it was a secure trade, certainly a romantic one, and even a pleasurable one for those who enjoyed horses and camping. This could even be true on the Birdsville Track, since most droving took place in the cooler months, although it was never true of the Canning. Sydney solicitor AB Paterson certainly thought so when he observed that 'the drover's life has pleasures that the townsfolk never know', while lamenting 'the fiendish rattle of the tramways and the buses' outside his Sydney office.[35] But he always was one to romanticise the bush.

Large-scale building of developmental roads in the remote inland only began in the

1950s, so it was not until then that trucks acquired the ability to move loads of a size and at a speed previously only seen on rail. With this development, droving at last began to drift into obsolescence, more than 30 years after the horse was displaced by the motor vehicle for most transport tasks in the more settled parts of the country.

The Birdsville Track became in the 1930s one of the pioneering outback roads, with a regular mail service by truck beginning in 1936. Large trucks, though, required good roads to be economical, as at that time transport costs by truck were twice those of rail and six times those of droving. What the trucks did offer though, was extremely rapid and direct transport. For, even if a truck travelled only marginally faster than a train, the real difference was in loading and unloading and transferring cattle to the railhead. Trucking enabled cattle and sheep to be moved large distances in a couple of days, certainly at a high cost, but a cost which could be justified by giving the producer maximum access to the best pasture and best prices.

By contrast, the old system of droving to a railhead (where rail cattle wagons had to be booked in advance and demurrage paid daily on wagons if the drover was late) committed the pastoralist to an early decision as to what would happen to his cattle. The old system of using droving and railways came to an end during the 1960s and 1970s. An era ended when boss drover Eric Oldfield rode on horseback driving a mob of cattle into Marree's railway stockyards for the last time in 1972.[36] The railway is now closed beyond the coalmines at Leigh Creek and the Birdsville Track has become an adventure playground for four-wheel-drive enthusiasts. Road trains on development roads move the pastoralists' cattle to markets and, in the outback at least, the droving days are over.

Droving survives, though, as a profession and an economic practice. One short-sighted New South Wales government may have destroyed its patrimony in closing Sydney's tramways, but none has been foolish enough to sell off its stock routes, although some have been tempted. While droving cattle and sheep on these routes is no longer the best transport option, it certainly remains a way of obtaining feed in drought, and the New South Wales stock routes continue to host many mobs of cattle and sheep together with their drovers. Their nickname though, the 'long paddock', indicates they are more useful to contemporary pastoralists for their fodder than their transport function.

Australia's first railway workshops of any substance were at Williamstown near Melbourne. In 1866 its staff were erecting the B and O class locomotives imported from England to work the country's first great mainlines to Bendigo and Ballarat. O class engine 21, lower right, had just entered service. (Freedman collection)

Chapter 4

THE GREAT INNOVATION

AUSTRALIA'S FIRST RAILWAYS TO 1873

HIS COMPANIONS WERE all dead. Half crazed by the loneliness of the outback and hardly able to talk, his 'every action and look showed the extreme debility to which his sufferings had reduced him'. A mob, 'which, although numbering a few decent people, was to a large extent composed of people and dirty boys who did not know in the least what was due', was shouting, demanding a few words from the pitiful and confused survivor. It was 25 November 1861 and John King had returned to Melbourne from the Gulf of Carpentaria after fourteen months exploring, starving and being cared for by Aborigines. He was the first man to have crossed the Australian continent and live to tell the tale: the other members of the great expedition, including its leaders, Robert O'Hara Burke and William John Wills, had starved to death in the attempt.

The explorers had left Melbourne on horseback, their gear loaded onto 27 camels but, in the year since, travel had changed and King returned mundanely on 'the six o'clock train from Woodend'. A journalist noted that 'an union-jack attached to the engine announced that it brought King'. At Spencer Street station he was 'hustled and shoved' out of the carriage, a modern traveller confronted with a modern crowd.[1] In late 1861, the flawed heroism of the explorer already seemed an anachronism, confronted by the steam-powered efficiency of the railway. After so much drama and pathos, this most famous and tragic expedition in the history of Australian exploration ended with a punctual, comfortable and routine train trip over a brand new railway.

The manner of King's return said much about how the iron tentacles of civilisation were reaching into the continent's sometimes fatal interior. Less than a year later, while he was opening the railway from Woodend to Bendigo, Victorian Governor Sir Henry Barkly expansively predicted a transcontinental railway laid in King's footsteps:

> It was not too much to imagine that [the Bendigo to Echuca extension] would be followed by a further extension … to the far north, and all the fine country which had been opened up by the undaunted courage of Burke … It scarcely needed a fervid imagination … to picture the iron horse careering across the continent to the city of Burke on the shores of the Gulf of Carpentaria.[2]

Barkly's vision was fulfilled in general if not in detail, since railways were built by colonial governments and confined to their own territories. So it would not be a Victorian railway which would stretch out towards the tropical waters of the Gulf, but Queensland ones. These were built largely through the drive of Queensland Premier Sir Thomas McIlwraith who, as a young railway engineer, had been at Bendigo to hear Barkly's 1862 prophesy. By 1889 the Sydney poet Henry Lawson could assert that,

> The mighty bush with iron rails
> Is tethered to the world.[3]

THE ORIGINS OF AUSTRALIA'S RAILWAY AGE

NO TECHNOLOGY transformed economies and human interaction across the globe in the 19th century more than the railway. The railway age had begun modestly enough, with the gradual improvement of tramroads connecting coalmines to ports in northeastern England with the progressive introduction of iron rails and steam power. The Stockton and Darlington Railway, completed in 1825, was the first to use this technology to transport general goods traffic and passengers (initially in their own road coaches mounted on rail wagons). Then in 1830 the first modern railway opened between Liverpool and Manchester. This was conceived from the beginning as a total transportation system, carrying a wide range of goods as well as passengers in different classes of accommodation in scheduled trains exclusively run by the Liverpool and Manchester Railway Company The railway age had arrived.

The Liverpool and Manchester Railway was a stupendous technological, social and financial success. Ever since, the railway has been humanity's first and best choice for resolving transport bottlenecks. The spread of the railway was rapid. Within a few years all the advanced countries of western Europe and the United States were building railways. Management models differed widely, from strict state control to a total reliance on private capital. Technological progress was rapid, as vast sums of capital were invested in this most profitable and potent of innovations. Remarkably early, railways were built in colonies and other economically underdeveloped countries far from Europe. The first was in Cuba in 1837. However, the powerhouse of railway development remained western Europe and North America, and above all England, where the great railway boom of 1846 laid the foundations of the world's first truly national system, funded entirely by private capital. The crash which followed the boom meant that shareholders' expectations of their investments were not always realised, and the novel concept of the hitherto highly profitable railway as a potential financial disaster also dated from this decade.

The British railway boom of the mid-1840s saw many ambitious companies promoted whose prospectuses suggested that rails might soon span the globe. There was even a Calais, Constantinople and Calcutta Railway to tempt the unwary investor. In this buoyant atmosphere, railways were proposed in the Australian colonies. The boom's collapse meant that none of these schemes ever amounted to anything, but the seeds of an idea were sown. These germinated in the foundation of the Sydney Railway Company (SRC), Australia's first, in 1848. Capitalised at

Sydney's 1872 terminal station photographed in the 1880s. Workers are maintaining the steam tram tracks in the foreground and the original station already has been surrounded by additional platforms to accommodate the rapidly growing rail traffic. (Author postcard collection)

£100 000, it aimed to build railways to connect the port and capital of Sydney with the colony's two main inland towns of Bathurst and Goulburn. These towns, strategically located on the Great Dividing Range, commanded the dray traffic from the pastoral districts of the interior. The wool, which passed through them bound for the sea and export, and the stores, which passed the other way, were expected to be the railway's main traffic.

It would be seven years before the SRC's line was opened, and then it extended from Sydney only as far as Parramatta, just 23 kilometres. Even this achievement was ruinously expensive for the company, and so much of the £550 000 required for the project (equivalent to nearly £40 000 per mile) was invested by the colonial government that it took over the SRC just before the line opened. Thus was born the New South Wales Government Railways (NSWGR), destined to become Australia's mightiest corporation for the much of the 19th and 20th centuries.[4]

Simultaneously, the New South Wales government took over the colony's other railway project, the Hunter River Railway Company, which was building a line from the coal port of Newcastle to Maitland. This line, opened in 1857, became the NSWGR's Great Northern Railway. However, it was not the first railway in the district, as the Australian Agricultural Company had built a horse tramway as early as 1831 to connect its coalmines with wharves on the Hunter River. This had been Australia's first railway, although its traffic was confined to the single commodity of coal. Thus, the emergence of railways in Australia was a close copy of their development in northeastern England, where horse-operated coal tramways had anticipated the railway age by close to a century. A second such horse tramway began operating in Newcastle in 1850, and it was converted to steam traction in 1857. By the mid-1850s there were three separate colliery railways in and around Newcastle, which thus has claims to be recognised as the true cradle of Australia's railway industry.[5]

However, unlike the lines from Sydney and Melbourne, Newcastle's railways were (and to some extent remain) industrial railways. These are railways developed as ancillary to another industry, whose needs they serve exclusively or very nearly so. Over the following 150 years, such railways have been developed throughout the country in association with industries such as mining, sugar cultivation, logging, metallurgy, and cement manufacturing. In general they are owned by the parent industry and so often were called 'private railways', to distinguish them from the mostly (but not entirely) government owned mainline and common carrier railways. However, in some parts of Australia, the distinction between industrial railways and common carrier railways has been a fine one. This was particularly true of the Newcastle-Maitland area of New South Wales and on Tasmania's west coast where railways built by mining companies carried passengers and general freight on regularly scheduled trains.

During the seven years of the SRC's existence, the railway age spread rapidly around the globe, as the first lines in similar countries such as Argentina, India, Canada, Chile and Brazil opened in the early 1850s. Nor was New South Wales alone among the Australian colonies in developing railways. Both Victoria and South Australia opened their first lines a year before New South Wales. For, whereas the SRC had always envisaged its lines penetrating deep into the colony, the promoters of the first steam railway actually to open in Australia – from Melbourne to Port Melbourne – were far more modest in their aspirations. There can be little doubt that this modesty had much to do with its success. Melbourne, unlike Sydney, was not situated on navigable water. Its port was some 4 kilometres distant on the waters of Hobson's Bay. The discovery of gold in Victoria rapidly transformed the colony from a rural backwater into the most dynamic and wealthy of all the Australian colonies. Gold, found in sufficient quantities in New South Wales to cause the inflation and labour shortages which so plagued the SRC but in insufficient quantities to stimulate the extraordinary growth it induced in Melbourne, was a hindrance to railway construction out of Sydney. By contrast, in Victoria it was a stimulant.

While vague and impractical railway schemes had been floated in the Port Phillip district in the 1840s (it was not separated from New South Wales to form the new colony of Victoria until 1851), it was the gold-induced boom following the discoveries of that very same year which made railways not only viable but also necessary. There were two great transport bottlenecks, which only railways could unplug. First (and more modestly and profitably) was between Melbourne and its port. Second was from the ports of Melbourne and Geelong to the goldfields at Bendigo and Ballarat. During 1852, following the passing of one of the Victorian parliament's first Acts authorising railway construction by private capital, no fewer than eight companies were promoted, of which three were approved but only one succeeded in completing and operating a railway.

This was the Melbourne and Hobson's Bay Railway Company, formed in August 1852 and capitalised at £100 000. For a 2¼-mile (3.6-km) line across level terrain, this was a far more generous capitalisation than the SRC. Even it, though, was compelled to double its capital to complete the line. Nonetheless, it was built far more quickly than the Sydney to Parramatta line that had been begun so much earlier. Indeed, so quickly was it completed that the locomotives ordered from England had not yet arrived, so it opened on 12 September 1854 with two home-built machines (one a goods truck with a pile-driver engine adapted to power it) as its motive power. It was an instant financial success because its fares were high and traffic dense. A half-hourly passenger service was operated from the beginning, compared with the initial four trains a day between Sydney and Parramatta. The success of the Hobson's Bay Company prompted other capitalists

A Tait train, named after the Victorian Railways chief commissioner who ordered them but deferred electrification, crosses the Yarra River bound for Port Melbourne in 1972. This was the route of Australia's first steam railway opened in September 1854. In the background is Flinders Street station. The four-track iron girder bridge was locally built and dates from the 1880s. The bridge is no longer in railway use and most of the route is now operated by trams. (Tony McIlwain)

to invest in railway schemes in the eastern suburbs of Melbourne. Nowhere else in Australia was there such a concentration of privately owned railways.

South Australia's first experiments with railways were yet more modest. The colony lacked the pastoral or mineral resources of Victoria and New South Wales, but its first railway certainly was conceived with an eye on its neighbours' wealth. The mouth of the Murray was in South Australia, and this river and its tributaries were becoming important transport routes through the pastoral districts. The South Australian government was trying to attract the trade from the vast area of eastern Australia watered by the Murray and its tributaries to Adelaide. The problem was that the river's mouth was unnavigable. A short railway connecting the river with an ocean port seemed to be the solution. Since the traffic was more theoretical than real, and resources limited, this was built as a horse tramway with very light rails. It opened as Australia's first, very humble, common-carrier railway in May 1854. It was only 7 miles (11 km) long and traversed the easy terrain between Goolwa on Lake Alexandrina and Port Elliot on the Southern Ocean. The line was extended to a superior ocean port at Victor Harbor (always thus spelt by South Australian Railways) in 1864 and northwards through agricultural country to Strathalbyn in 1866. These extensions made it Australia's largest horse-powered railway.[6]

Australia's first public railway was South Australia's horse-operated line connecting the Murray at Goolwa with the open sea. Opened in 1854, most of it was converted to steam operation 30 years later. However, a fragment in Victor Harbor remained horse operated, linking the town with Granite Island across a breakwater. It still operates as a tourist attraction. This view dates from about 1940, when tourism already was its main function. (Author postcard collection)

THE GAUGE MUDDLE

THUS, DURING THE YEARS 1854 and 1855 the first railways opened in the three major colonies. Sparsely populated Tasmania and Western Australia would have to wait until the 1870s, while Queensland was then still part of New South Wales. The three railways were very different and reflected in many ways the colonies themselves. The New South Wales railway was easily the most ambitious, traversed by far the hardest terrain, but had endured the hardest political and financial struggles, ending up as a government enterprise by accident rather than design. The Victorian line was relatively modest in conception but met a pressing transport need, was profitable immediately and remained privately owned. The South Australian line was extremely modest and had to be built by the government because no investor would consider such a scheme.

The railways also differed from each other in gauge. Misunderstandings and blunders led to New South Wales building its railways to one gauge and Victoria and South Australia to another. The ideal gauge for a railway was a matter of intense debate between engineers at this time. The standard gauge of 4ft 8½in (1435 mm) had emerged in northeastern England in the 1820s because that was the gauge of the tramroads built over the previous century to serve coalmines. It is a peculiar measurement, probably arising from the fact that the rails were laid 5 feet (1524 mm) apart measured across their outside faces, thereby creating what became the standard gauge between the rails' inner faces. During the 1830s and 1840s many engineers believed this gauge was too narrow for mainline railways and so experimented with larger gauges, most notably IK Brunel's 7ft ¼in (2140 mm) gauge to which the English Great Western Railway was built. However, by the 1850s, the standard gauge clearly was dominant in most countries where railways already had been built. In countries that were just beginning their railways, though, there was a preference for broader gauges, most commonly 5ft 6in (1676 mm), widely used in the Iberian peninsular, Latin America, Canada and India. A similar gauge of 5ft 3in (1600 mm) was adopted in Ireland and Brazil.

When the SRC was incorporated in 1848, the Colonial Secretary, Lord Grey, specified that all Australian railways should be built to standard gauge. However, the SRC's tumultuous history included the frequent replacement of its chief engineer. One of these, Francis Sheilds, advised the company to change to the Irish gauge because, he argued (with some justice), expert opinion at the time believed this to be the technical ideal. The company accepted his advice, requested permission for the change from London, which concurred, meanwhile advising the other Australian colonies of the change. Thus, the South Australian and Victorian schemes, then still at the planning stage, were developed to a gauge of 5ft 3in. However, another change of chief engineer in Sydney brought contrary advice and the SRC's hapless directors, totally ignorant of technical matters, obliged their senior employee by reverting to standard gauge.

By this time the other colonies were ordering equipment and the die was cast. So Australia's first railways came to be built to two different gauges, both quite similar, neither of which offered the least technical or economic advantage over the other. John Whitton, Australia's dominant railway engineer of the 19th century, was appointed Engineer-in-Chief of the NSWGR in 1856 and immediately advised conversion of the then still infant railway to the Irish gauge, but his political masters demurred at even this modest expense. They were unable to envisage intercolonial traffic ever developing. Whitton's defeat (one of his few) on this issue meant that the gauge problem would remain to plague Australian railway development across three centuries.[7]

A decade later, when Queensland came to build its first railway, it chose to do so to a narrow gauge of 3ft 6in (1067 mm). This was a rational enough decision, since there were some economies of building railways to such a narrow gauge, especially if traffic was expected to be light. These economies were often exaggerated by proponents of narrow-gauge railways, of whom the English engineer Robert Fairlie was the most influential. Certainly, money saved in construction costs was lost in more expensive operational costs once traffic grew. Western Australia and southern Tasmania followed the Queensland example for precisely the same reason of economy of construction. So, less rationally, did South Australia for some of its secondary lines in the 1870s.

Chelmer is now a Brisbane suburb but was out in the bush when the Queensland Railway's 3ft 6in gauge Intercolonial Express posed there in the early 1890s. The train was headed for the break of gauge on the border at Wallangarra, where it would connect with the standard gauge New South Wales train to Sydney. The locomotive A12 No 261 was an American import. (QR Heritage)

PATTERNS OF RAILWAY POLICY TO THE EARLY 1870s

THE FIRST 20 YEARS of railway development in Australia were characterised by very different patterns in each of the four colonies involved. Victoria, easily the richest and most dynamic colony at this time, rapidly implemented a grand plan which then took some digesting. New South Wales, confronted with the most challenging terrain and longest distances, struggled hard to build railways to Whitton's plans even though his political masters all too often challenged them. Queensland built a spectacular line remarkably quickly but to low standards; while in South Australia railway development was ad hoc and tentative. There was one common element in all four colonies' railway strategy: each aimed to build railways to attract the trade of their neighbours' pastoral districts to their own ports and capitals. In this contest Melbourne was the clear early winner.

The Victorian policy of building railways to a government plan using private capital, on the model of the successful Melbourne and Hobson's Bay Railway Company, rapidly collapsed. Three main railways were envisaged: from Melbourne northwards to the goldfields city of Bendigo thence onwards to the Murray River at Echuca; from the port of Geelong to the other major goldfields centre of Ballarat; and between the two ports of Melbourne and Geelong. Private enterprise only succeeded in building the last of these railways, which traversed the easiest terrain. This was also the first main line to be opened, in 1857. Companies building the other two lines failed, the government taking over their works and the Melbourne and Geelong Company as well, thus forming Victorian Railways.

The Ballarat and Bendigo lines required heavy earthworks, tunnels and notable bridges, although ultimately the potential traffic and profits were far greater, since marine competition was not an issue as it was between Melbourne and Geelong. The two goldfields railways were built to the highest standards of English main lines, with double track throughout, relatively easy grades, generous curvature, splendid bluestone stations, and three magnificent bridges. These were the bluestone viaduct at Malmsbury and the iron viaducts on stone piers at Taradale and across the Moorabool River near Geelong. The first two were on the Bendigo line. The last was 1000 feet (300 m) long and 115 feet (35 m) high. Its completion in 1862 enabled trains to run through from Melbourne to Ballarat, then Australia's fourth largest city. The Great Northern Railway was opened to Bendigo in the same year, taking rails across the Great Dividing Range for the first time. It was extended (as a single track line) across flat country to reach Echuca on the Murray in 1864.

Once the rails had reached the Murray, Melbourne was assured at least of the temporary economic domination of the rich pastoral districts of southwestern New South Wales. For this was the famous 'meeting of the whistles' where the trains from Melbourne met the paddle steamers on the Murray, which serviced the vast basin drained by the navigable waters of the Murray, Murrumbidgee and Darling Rivers. For a time Echuca became Victoria's second busiest and Australia's fourth busiest port, its traffic exceeded only by Melbourne, Sydney and Newcastle. Thus, Victoria's aims were achieved quickly and effectively, and her relatively short railways secured for Melbourne the trade of much of the interior of New South Wales. But there was a price to pay, for these had been very expensive railways. The first 255 miles (410 km) of Victoria's railways, completed in 1864, had cost no less than £34 000 per mile, including the very easy lines from Melbourne to Geelong and from Bendigo to Echuca. Of all railways built in Australia in the 19th century, only the pioneering line from Sydney to Parramatta cost (marginally) more per mile. While the railways were profitable enough, the enormous investment they required was more than even booming Victoria's finances could digest with ease. Their completion was followed by a grand pause, when no new railways were opened for almost a decade.[8]

Seen from Sydney, Victoria's problem was a nice one to have. For in 1864, when Victorian metals reached the Murray, New South Wales's two main lines running south and west from Sydney were stalled at the banks of the Nepean River, about 60 kilometres from Sydney. The Murray was still nearly 600 kilometres from the railhead, the Darling nearly 800 kilometres. Moreover, the prospects for further extension were marginal because beyond the Nepean lay the steep escarpments of the Blue Mountains. So desperate was the situation that many (including the last really powerful governor of the colony, Sir William Denison) argued that future extensions should be built as horse-operated light tramways laid along the roads. Some reputable authorities even suggested that it was downright impossible to build a railway across the mountain barrier. Whitton destroyed both arguments in his usual categorical manner, pointing out that horses might be capable of hauling traffic across level ground, but would be quite ineffective over mountains, and that steam railways could indeed be built to Goulburn and Bathurst for about a third the cost of the Victorian lines.

Whitton's arguments won the day, partly because electors in the interior demanded railways, and partly because Sydney's mercantile community was unable to sit by and watch much of its income flow south of the Murray to Melbourne. Thus the Nepean was crossed in 1863 by two iron bridges at Menangle and Penrith, which were far and away the most expensive structures ever built in the colony, and from 1865 the rails began to climb the mountains. They reached Goulburn and Bowenfels (near Lithgow) in 1869 and the banks of the Macquarie River opposite Bathurst in 1873. Over the same period, the Great Northern Railway was extended up the Hunter Valley and by then had reached Murrurundi. Thus, the NSWGR at last had achieved the aims of the SRC, exactly 25 years after the company's foundation.

Whitton's two transmontane railways were extraordinary achievements, especially in view of the rough terrain they conquered and how little they cost. The contrast with the Victorian goldfields railways could not be greater. Whitton's lines were built with the strictest economy he could tolerate. Grades were extremely steep, indeed at the absolute limit of locomotives of the period. The average grade, for instance, of the western line over the 80 kilometres from the Nepean to its summit of 1114 metres at Clarence was 1 in 50. This was the same as the few short steepest pitches on the Bendigo line. By way of contrast, the summit where the Bendigo line crossed the Great Divide was just 580 metres. There were sustained climbs on both Whitton's transmontane railways of 1 in 30. The sharpest curves were as tight as 8 chains (160 m) radius compared with 60 chains (1200 m) in Victoria (with a couple of exceptions in stations). The New South Wales lines were single track throughout and the smaller stations were simple timber buildings, although Whitton insisted on brick and stone

Goulburn station in the New South Wales southern highlands, shortly after the railway from Sydney reached there in 1869. The goods train is typical of the period and the 17 class locomotive a product of Robert Stephenson and Company of Newcastle-upon-Tyne. (SRNSW H 541103)

The Great Zig Zag near Lithgow as depicted in the *Illustrated Australian News* of 20 May 1871. (Author collection)

for the few major towns. Even the terminal stations at Goulburn and Bathurst were very modest affairs compared with the imposing structures at Geelong, Ballarat and Bendigo.

Most remarkable of all were the two zigzags by which the western line climbed the eastern and descended the western escarpments of the Blue Mountains. These involved reversing trains twice to climb up the face of the sandstone escarpments. Whitton used enormous sandstone viaducts to cross the ravines which scarred the mountainsides. These were dramatic ensembles of bridges and cuttings, tunnels and embankments, all cut through a wild, inhospitable landscape. Moreover, the most expensive contract, for the 15 miles (24 km) near Lithgow including the larger of the two zigzags, cost under £22 000 per mile. There is no doubt that New South Wales acquired its main lines at bargain prices, although the cost ever since has been expensive operation and slow trains.

Even that, though, was too much for many in New South Wales public life. Thus, when the transmontane railways were completed, the debate of a decade earlier on whether they should be extended or not was replayed on a larger stage. Once again, horse tramways had their advocates, as did narrow-gauge railways. Once again, there was a pause in New South Wales railway construction.[9]

The enthusiasm in some quarters in New South Wales for narrow-gauge extensions arose from the success of Queensland in building Australia's first narrow-gauge railway in the mid-1860s. This was highly innovative technology for the time. Queensland was a new colony, established in 1859 by the simple expedient of excising the northern part of New South Wales. This had occurred at the request of its relatively few white inhabitants, dominated by rich graziers. These men were alarmed at the democratic and progressive tendencies then emerging in

Sydney politics. Having secured their own colony, they were anxious to intensify its economic exploitation and increase its white population. Railway building seemed to meet both *desiderata* and so was a top priority.

The government appointed a Chief Engineer, Abram Fitzgibbon, who was given the task of building a railway from Ipswich, the head of navigation on the Brisbane River, to Toowoomba, the largest town in the rich pastoral district of the Darling Downs. There was no gentle climb to the Darling Downs: the railway would involve a steep ascent of the eastern escarpment of the Great Dividing Range. Fitzgibbon reported in 1863 that the project was feasible, and recommended the use of sharp curves and a narrow gauge of 3ft 6in to reduce costs. Only in Norway was such a gauge being used, where it had been pioneered in 1862. The large English contractors, Peto, Brassey and Betts, were engaged to build the line.

Its first section, on easy terrain from Ipswich to Bigge's Camp (now Grandchester), opened on 31 July 1865. It is now the world's oldest surviving 'medium gauge' (3ft, metre, or 3ft 6in) railway. The 92-kilometre extension to Toowoomba opened on 1 May 1867 and climbed from an elevation of 143 metres at Helidon to 612 metres at Harlaxton near Toowoomba. Fully two-thirds of those 43 kilometres were in cuttings and there were 47 bridges, nine tunnels and 126 curves, 49 of which would be of just 5 chains (100 m) radius. Many of the bridges were composite structures with iron girders resting on timber piers. The ruling gradient was the only relatively easy aspect of the line: it was kept to 1 in 50. No railway quite like this had ever been built before. The Toowoomba Range Railway was thus the precedent for many such lightly constructed and sinuous narrow-gauge mountain railways all over the world.

Moreover, the speed of its construction was dazzling compared with the New South Wales western line. The latter's construction had begun in 1850, and the rails did not reach the Great Zig Zag, approximately the same distance from Sydney as Toowoomba is from Brisbane, until nineteen years later. From approval to opening, the Ipswich to Toowoomba line was completed in just over three years. Admittedly its engineering standards were much lower than those on which Whitton insisted, let alone those of the magnificent Victorian main lines, but its completion did illustrate what could be done building railways with low engineering standards and high operational expenses if budgets were tight and traffic light.[10] The irony was that a narrow gauge was not an essential element of cheap railway construction, the gauge difference contributing very little to the economy of the project.

In South Australia, there were two quite distinct fields of railway endeavour. The first was the construction of the horse-operated 'Southern Tramways' at the mouth of the Murray. The second was the more conventional project to connect Adelaide and its

wharves at Port Adelaide with a steam railway, opening in April 1856, five years after work had begun. A short extension north of Adelaide opened the next year, and by 1868 this had reached Kapunda. The gauge of both the Adelaide railways and the southern tramways was 5ft 3in, as the colonies had agreed.

By about 1870 the pioneering age of Australian railway history was over. Prosperous Victoria's, indeed, had ended as early as 1864. New South Wales had built railways across some of the hardest terrain in the continent in an effort to maintain economic control over Sydney's hinterland. Queensland, with its small population and limited resources, had used contractors to build a remarkable mountain railway extremely quickly, using the new technology of the narrow gauge. The South Australian achievement was more modest, for no railways had yet been built there over difficult terrain, but the railway clearly was established as part of the colony's economic and social life. In all colonies, though, there was some confusion as to future policy, and hard decisions remained about using railways to solve their transport problems.

Queensland Railways' first line from Ipswich to Toowoomba, completed in 1867, was not extended into Brisbane for almost a decade. Its most significant feature was the Albert Bridge, named after the Prince Consort, which opened on 5 July 1876. This photograph was taken a few days earlier when it was being tested. Its 160-foot (48.8-m) wrought iron hog-back main span was quite an achievement for the colony, but the piers proved inadequate when the Brisbane River flooded in February 1893. It collapsed and was replaced with the present bridge with two main spans. (QR Heritage)

The Hawkesbury River Bridge of 1889 linked the Sydney and Newcastle systems. The terrain around the bridge was almost as difficult as the river itself for the engineers building the railway. The location was and remains isolated and Frank Hurley risked his life to photograph a P class locomotive on a Sydney to Newcastle train coming off the bridge and into a cutting. If a train had come from the other direction, he would have had nowhere to go. The image dates from about 1908. (Frank Hurley, NLA an 23477933)

Chapter 5

STEAM AND STEEL

THE RAILWAY AGE, 1874–1920

IT WAS AN AWAY game for Hughenden, B zone premiers of the North Queensland Rugby League. Their opponents were Mt Isa, 588 kilometres away, but that was not a problem. The club secretary sauntered down to the railway station and booked a train: six carriages, a locomotive and a dining car for £250 (roughly $25 000 in 2010 values), a slight discount on commercial rates. Local grocers and butchers donated supplies, including half a bullock; a supply of ale ('strictly reserved for service with meals') was got in; and Greek café proprietor Nick Bounader donated his services as chef. The great weekend came. Every seat on the train was sold with tickets at 28 shillings and meals at 2 shillings and sixpence (about $140 and $12 in contemporary values). The football team and two girls' basketball teams (thereby establishing a certain ratio well before the Beach Boys sang about it), together with their supporters left Hughenden on Saturday at 2.30pm, arriving at Mt Isa at 8.15am on Sunday. When the dining car stove ran out of fuel, the train stopped so the footballers could cut scrub to keep it burning. After the games and some jollification, they left Mt Isa late Sunday night to reach home, tired, victorious and happy, about 3pm on Monday.

Teams in north Queensland made long train trips like this every other weekend right through the winter. Hughenden's captain coach, North Queensland international Ron O'Connell, travelled over 10 000 kilometres by train in a season.[1] Many sporting teams in rural Australia similarly relied on chartered trains to maintain their competitions throughout the railway age. In Victoria there were even hunt club carriages especially designed and built for hunters and their horses. However, these Hughenden players and supporters were among the last: it was 1950 and such jaunts soon ended with society's rapid motorisation. But for 80 years from the 1870s the steel rails and the people who ran the trains on them were the sinews which bound Australian society together: it was truly a railway age.

THE GREAT GLOBAL RAILWAY BOOM

AROUND 1873 RAILWAY development in Australia seemed stalled. No new lines had opened in Victoria for nearly a decade, and in New South Wales there were serious doubts about the colony's ability to fund any railway extensions beyond the current termini of Goulburn and Bathurst. In fact, though, Australia was poised on the brink of its great railway boom. The late 1870s and 1880s were the period when Australia's railway system reached maturity. In New South Wales and Victoria, a few lines became the basis of two extensive networks; something similar happened on a smaller scale in South Australia; in Queensland, small railway systems blossomed along its enormous coastal region; while even the sparsely populated and impecunious colonies of Tasmania and Western Australia opened their first lines. The statistical trends were always upwards. The New South Wales figures were typical: in the ten years between 1878 and 1888 the NSWGR's mileage more than trebled from 688 to 2398 (from 1107 to 3859 km); its passenger traffic quadrupled from 3 705 510 to 14 881 604; and goods traffic more than doubled from 1 625 886 to 3 485 839 tons.[2]

This railway boom was part of a wider boom in the Australian colonies in general. On a global scale, it was the heyday of European imperialism, the time of the scramble for Africa and the grabbing of large chunks of southeast Asia and the Pacific by advanced Western countries, the United Kingdom digesting the lion's share. All this was powered by a capital-rich Europe looking for investments which were highly profitable or secure, preferably both. Colonies, where there were often government guarantees on investment, were favoured destinations for this capital. Railways, which seemed to symbolise all that was modern and civilising, won similar favour. Through the jungles of Asia and Africa; across the rainless deserts of North Africa and the frozen wastes of Siberia; to the summits of the Andes and deep into the interior of the wildest parts of Latin America, plucky and ingenious engineers laid their ribbons of steel, mostly funded with European capital.

In the 1880s the Australian railway boom was in full swing. Timothy Coghlan, who as New South Wales statistician was part of the action, commented that 'from 1884 onward Governmental expenditure became a riot, limited in its violence only by the amount of accommodation available in London'.[3] Much the same thing happened in India, Canada and Argentina. In all three cases, British capital flooded into the countries and laid the foundations of impressive railway systems. The exact details of financing and management differed. In Australia, almost all railways were built by colonial governments with government-guaranteed bonds sold in London. These guarantees were predicated both on the anticipated profits of the railways and continuing colonial land sales. Land sales were the main source of government revenue in the Australian colonies, and railways easily the largest government investments.

There were considerable differences between railway policies in each Australian colony. In New South Wales and Victoria there was a clear overall plan to build railway systems centred on the capital cities of Sydney and Melbourne. Both colonies' politics were dominated by a prosperous urban mercantile class, and railway policy reflected that reality. One significant detail difference between them was that Victoria built urban railways in a way which New South Wales did not. In Queensland, railway policy was more decentralised. This was a colony dominated by pastoral interests, although miners and farmers were

By 1890 the basic structures of the railway systems in southeastern Australia were in place. In New South Wales, where initial construction had been more economical than Victoria, it was time to begin renewals and upgrades, including duplication of main lines, new bridges and heavier locomotives. In May 1907 NSWGR officials tested the new double-track truss bridge across the Nepean River at Penrith with four of the heavy T class locomotives which were then being built to haul the railway's burgeoning freight traffic. The original 1865 bridge is (and remains to this day) on the right. (SRNSW D 510463)

also influential. They were spread over an enormous area and served by numerous ports along an extremely long coastline. Many small, lightly constructed lines were built from these ports into their hinterlands. These hinterlands were sometimes dominated by agriculture (especially cane growing near the coast), sometimes by mining, and sometimes by the pastoral industry. At one time there were as many as ten separate and unconnected small railway systems in Queensland.

By contrast there was only ever one system in Victoria (except for suburban lines) and never more than two in New South Wales. South Australia had elements of both the Queensland and Victorian models, but the latter soon triumphed. In Tasmania there was bipolar railway development centred on both Launceston and Hobart (in that order). In Western Australia, the last colony to build railways, development was based at first on the need to serve the extractive industries of mining and logging. Soon after, though, a network based on Perth and its port of Fremantle emerged, although it was never as self-consciously centralising as in Victoria and New South Wales.

In most of Australia the long railway boom came to an abrupt end in 1890. The immediate cause was the default of an Argentine loan and consequent collapse of the England banking house of Baring Brothers. By then, though, the boom in domestic spending had reached an end anyway. The Melbourne land boom (and the less spectacular housing booms in other colonial capitals) had subsided by 1890 and the value of urban real estate began to fall. Wool prices too were falling, affecting the entire economy. The situation was worst in Victoria, while Western Australia and Tasmania's west coast were exceptions, enjoying mining and railway booms in the 1890s while most of Australia was stagnating.

THE RAILWAY BOOM IN LATE COLONIAL AUSTRALIA

THE RAILWAY BOOM of the 1870s and 1880s flowered most luxuriantly in Victoria, but was also a very healthy plant in New South Wales. Total overseas investment (mostly from Britain) in the four major Australian colonies was around £33.6 million between 1876 and 1880; £70 million from 1881 to 1885; and £100 million from 1886 to 1890. More than half of the £100 million arriving in the peak years of the boom went to Victoria.[4] Growth took off in all the colonies around 1874. Indeed the change in mood between 1872 and 1875 was remarkable. There was a sudden spurt of optimism expressed in high levels of investment in railways. In New South Wales, for instance, there was still discussion of horse tramways for the main line from Goulburn to the Murray as late as 1873. By 1875 it was clear that even the steam railways being built were inadequate for the traffic on offer. Until 1885, most of the investment was prudent, often overdue. The same could not be said of the last five years of the boom, when many railways of marginal utility and no prospects of commercial success were built, especially in Victoria.

VICTORIA

No colony had a better railway system than Victoria, nor one that had been built more quickly or more extravagantly. However, the grand pause in construction that followed the opening of the Murray Railway to Echuca in 1864 lasted the best part of a decade as the colony digested the financial consequences of its investment. Planning for extensions began in 1869, but in very different circumstances from those of the golden decade of the 1850s. Engineer-in-Chief Thomas Higinbotham was asked to plan future extensions at 'minimum cost' and for a 'maximum speed of 15 miles per hour' with stations 'of the cheapest kind possible'.[5] The three routes anticipated were westwards towards Hamilton, the main centre of Victoria's rich Western Districts; northeast to the Murray; and eastwards to Sale in Gippsland.

Two great controversies raged over Victorian railway policy in the early 1870s. The

first concerned the gauge of future extensions; the second the route of the main line to Hamilton. Narrow-gauge railways were a worldwide fad around 1870, and Victoria was not immune from the dangerously infectious fashion. There were few places, though, where narrow gauge offered so little by way of advantages, since the terrain for all Victoria's projected lines was about as benign as could

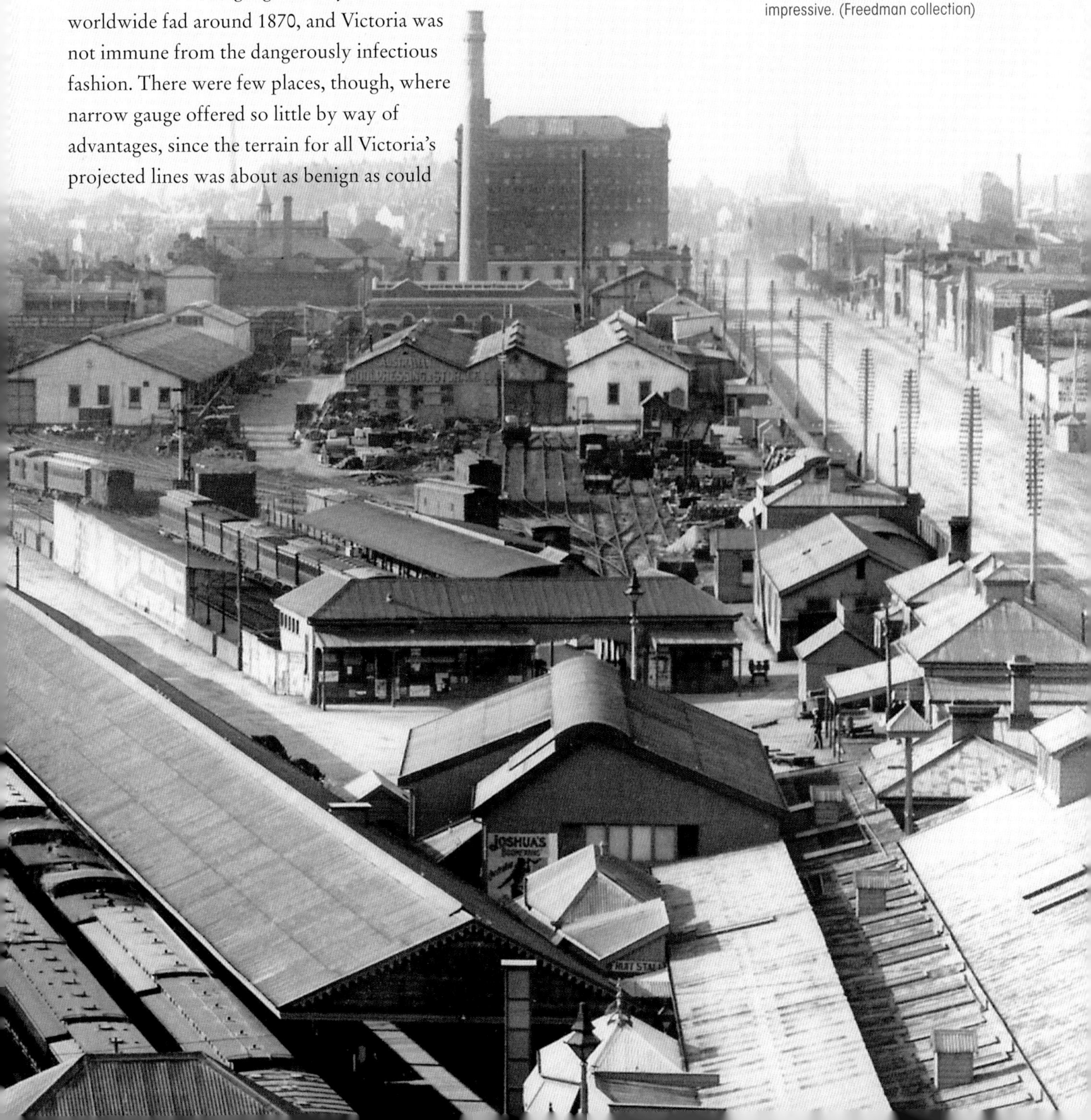

In the 1880s Melbourne's Spencer Street was Australia's busiest long-distance railway station, although its 'temporary' station buildings were anything but impressive. (Freedman collection)

Victorian Railways generally built its 19th century structures more solidly than the other colonies. Melbourne goods sheds, adjacent to Spencer Street station (below), and Bendigo locomotive depot (above) are examples of the Victorian determination to build to impress and to last. The presence of British (left) and North American (right) style locomotives at Bendigo is typical of most Australian railways at the beginning of the 20th century. (Freedman collection)

be. Narrow gauge achieved its economies with sharp curves and smaller cuttings and embankments, and so was best suited to mountainous country where light traffic was anticipated. Higinbotham successfully argued against those who wanted the northeastern line built to a gauge of 3ft 6in.

His strong and forthright leadership on this issue prevented Victoria making the same disastrous mistake as South Australia would at precisely the same time. So, when contracts were let for the building of the northeastern line from the suburban terminus of Essendon to the Murray at Wodonga, they specified a 5ft 3in gauge line, as Higinbotham had wanted, although the stations and other structures were to be far less imposing than on Victoria's earlier railways. Since the route over the Great Dividing Range to Seymour was comparatively easy, and was a railway builder's dream across the plains beyond, this economy of construction was no lasting impediment to the line's quality. It opened in 1873, and was extended across the Murray as a joint New South Wales–Victorian project ten years later to permit through rail travel between Sydney and Melbourne, with a change of trains for the break of gauge at either Albury or Wodonga. Higinbotham's alignment, although economical, was such that the line was and remains one of the straightest and fastest railways in Australia.

Equally contentious as the gauge issue was the route of a railway to the Western Districts, the 'Australia Felix' whose fine pastures had made Victoria a viable entity before the discoveries of gold. In 1870 Higinbotham proposed four different routes to Hamilton, each drawn in a different colour on the map accompanying his report. Thus began the famous 'battle of the coloured lines' in which supporters of various routes loudly denounced the rivals and all sorts of ephemeral political alliances were concocted in attempts to secure parliamentary backing for one route or another. Higinbotham argued strongly for the Pink Line (the others were black, green and blue) and ultimately won the day. This line ran westwards from Ballarat to Ararat, then turning southwest to Hamilton. It opened to Ararat in 1875 and on to Hamilton and Portland in 1877. Meanwhile, proponents of other routes were mollified by the completion of a loop line from Castlemaine (on the Bendigo line) to Ballarat via Maryborough in 1875.

The third important Victorian line built in the 1870s was the Gippsland line from Oakleigh (in southeastern Melbourne) to Sale, opened in stages during 1877 and 1878. Bizarrely enough, services between Oakleigh and Melbourne were provided by road coaches, because railways in southeastern Melbourne were owned not by Victorian Railways but by the Melbourne and Hobson's Bay United Railway Company. When the government purchased the company in 1879, it immediately built a connection from the former company line at South Yarra to Oakleigh. Higinbotham, unaware that nationalisation would soon take place, planned an 'Outer Circle' government line to Oakleigh to link the Gippsland line with the rest of the government system without trespassing on the company's lucrative suburban territory.

Thus, by the end of the 1870s, Victoria's main line network was nearing completion. The only really important lines not yet built were the direct line from Melbourne to Ballarat, completed in 1889; and the Intercolonial Railway from Ararat to the South Australian border at Serviceton. This opened to Horsham in 1879 but was not completed until 1887, essentially because its South Australian section was not even begun until 1883. A blow of the late 1870s was Victorian Railways' loss of its talented and effective Engineer-in-Chief, Thomas Higinbotham, in circumstances which had absolutely nothing to do with his professional competence or political judgment.

Higinbotham was, after John Whitton, the dominant figure in Australian railway engineering in the 19th century. It is true that he had more resources than Whitton, and easier terrain over which to build his railways. Hence his task was easier than Whitton's and as a result Victoria was able to build its railways to a higher quality than New South Wales. Like Whitton, he was courageous and forthright in dealing with political interference in what he regarded as 'his' railway and, also like Whitton, he successfully resisted proponents of narrow-gauge railways and the introduction of an internal break of gauge in Victoria. Higinbotham was summarily dismissed on 'Black Wednesday', 8 January 1878. His fate was shared by 136 other senior officials and judges, dismissed because the government had run out of funds due to a deadlock between the Legislative Assembly and the Legislative Council over Appropriation Bills. While some officials later were reinstated, Higinbotham was not.

Thus, just as Victorian Railways entered their most manic phase of expansion, Higinbotham was no longer around to provide the sound technical and commercial advice and astute management he had offered over the previous 20 years. For the 1880s were boom years for Victoria in general and for its railways in particular. Much of the boom was speculative, especially in urban real estate, but there was real, solid and sustained growth in the colony's population and economic activity. Victoria's heavily protected industries thrived during these years, building, among other things, nearly all the colony's locomotives and other railway equipment. This was in sharp contrast with New South Wales, the only other colony with the potential for such industrial production, where, true to its free trade principles, most railway equipment continued to be imported from Britain. During the decade 1883–92 Victoria's railway system grew from 1355 to 2903 miles (2181 to 4672 km), an average of 155 miles (250 km) per annum. By contrast, during the previous decade it had grown at

A Victorian Railways DD class locomotive built at Melbourne's Newport Workshops in the canadian red livery of the first two decades of the 20th century. The scene is typical of Melbourne suburban railways. (Author postcard collection)

an average of 104 miles (167 km) each year and annual growth in the following decade of depression would be only 42 miles (67 km). Growth would peak again in the 1913–22 decade when its annual average reached 69 miles (111 km), mostly light and cheap wheat lines in the state's northwest. By 1930, all of Victoria, except its alpine and semi-desert regions, was within 8 miles (13 km) of a railway station.[6]

The frenzy of the 1880s culminated in the notorious 'Octopus Act' of 12 December 1884, which authorised no fewer than 66 new railways. If constructed, these would have given Victoria a railway density out of all proportion to its population, productivity or potential rail traffic. The crash of 1890 brought an abrupt end to the riot of spending on railways, and to much else besides. The 1880s boom in Victoria was far wilder than the boom in other colonies, and the depression consequently far deeper. Melbourne's urban property values declined by 60 percent in four years and the city even lost population in the 1890s, and surrendered its status as Australia's largest city to Sydney. New South Wales, with its open economy and more restrained expenditure in the 1880s, experienced a far less severe depression than did Victoria.

Victorian railway construction limped on in the 1890s, as previously authorised projects were completed. When it resumed at the turn of the century, it is significant that the first new lines were extremely light, cheap railways built to a gauge of 2ft 6in (762 mm). These four lines were all closed in the 1950s and 1960s, although the busiest of them (from Upper Ferntree Gully to Gembrook) subsequently was partly converted to broad gauge and electrified, and partly restored as a tourist railway. This, the famous Puffing Billy, has become one of the world's busiest tourist railways, carrying around 250 000 passengers per annum, a happy outcome which its promoters of the 1890s, who were thinking primarily of its potential potato traffic, could never have foreseen.

The final bitter coda to the boom years was the dismissal in 1892 and subsequent ruin of Chairman of Commissioners Richard Speight. He had been appointed from the Midland Railway in England in 1884, and had presided over the extravagances of the boom years. He was savagely attacked by *The Age* for his role in the boom, and then asked by Railways Minister William Shiels to reduce expenditure and increase income. Unable to do this, he was dismissed and then sued David Syme, *The Age*'s proprietor, for libel. The verdicts in the cases were inconclusive, but Speight was a ruined man, financially and personally. Victoria's extravagant 19th century railway program thus claimed its second victim.

NEW SOUTH WALES

Of all the Australian colonies, New South Wales had the least ambitious and most affordable railway policy, unsurprisingly producing easily the best financial results. It was also a railway which had clear aims from the very beginning. By the early 1870s, the aims of the Sydney Railway Company had been achieved, as Whitton's transmontane railways had reached Goulburn and Bathurst. The new aims were extension of the three main lines to their natural termini – south to the Murray at Albury, west to a point as yet undetermined on the Darling, and north to the Queensland border. Over the next 15 years, these aims would be achieved. In dramatic contrast with Victoria, though, there would be very little filling in of the network. Indeed, throughout that period, not a single mile of track was laid within 200 kilometres of Sydney. This single-mindedness in completing the three main lines proved to be the great strength of New South Wales railway policy.

The main personality behind this coherence of policy was John Whitton, Engineer-in-Chief from 1856 to 1890. His continuity in office was unique in Australia's colonial railway history and gave him a measure of authority which even Higinbotham could not approach. Although he did not always get his way and had his rivals and critics, Whitton was a commanding figure who dominated policy. His first great challenge after completion of the transmontane railways came from his deputy JH Thomas, who wanted to build the extensions beyond the then termini as narrow-gauge light railways. The struggle was bitter, but Whitton won the day, and in 1873 funds were voted for standard-gauge extensions, albeit to lower specifications than Whitton wanted. Indeed, the great problem with all Whitton's main lines was that he

Spectacular scenery means engineering challenges, and there were plenty of both on the coastal railways north and south of Sydney. Beyond Stanwell Park the Wollongong line ran right on the coastal escarpment. Frank Hurley was there when one of the 191 members of the P class, which handled most New South Wales passenger trains at the time, was working a train through this section. Hurley has painted the coaches in the 1920 tuscan red and russet livery, so the postcard was sold after then, although he may have taken the photograph a decade or more earlier. (Frank Hurley, author postcard collection)

was forced to build them to lower standards than he wanted. The consequence has been that they have needed constant upgrading and rebuilding ever since, and have remained inadequate for the traffic they carry. Light loads, inefficient operation and slow speeds have been the lasting legacy of the inadequate funds Whitton was given to build the NSWGR's major railways.

All three of the New South Wales main lines were built over difficult terrain, so to avoid sinuous, steeply graded alignments would have meant heavy expenditure of the kind Victoria made on its goldfields railways between 1857 and 1862. Such funds were never available in colonial New South Wales. The northern line to the Queensland border at Wallangarra, for instance, climbed to Australia's highest railway summit of 1376 metres near Ben Lomond. All Whitton's railways also included notable bridges, some stone, some iron and some timber.

Despite the often hostile terrain, construction over the long distances of New South Wales proceeded relatively quickly. Once the lines had descended the western side of the Great Dividing Range, the challenges were those of bridging great rivers rather than climbing mountains. The Murrumbidgee at Wagga Wagga, for instance, required a bridge 7900 feet (2408 m) in length. Whitton's railways eventually reached their termini of Albury in the south in 1881, Bourke on the Darling in 1885, and Wallangarra on the Queensland border in 1888. During the 1880s the first branches were constructed, as well as coastal lines to compete with shipping near Sydney. The first branch line in the interior opened from Junee to Hay in 1881 and 1882. Soon there was a handful of others – but only a handful, compared with the octopus-like spread of railways across Victoria. The New South Wales branches (and main lines too) were, of course, far longer than their Victorian counterparts, or indeed than any railways elsewhere in Australia at this time.

Whitton's commanding contribution to Australia's railway development was crowned by the two coastal railways north and south from Sydney, to Newcastle and Wollongong and beyond respectively. Built between 1882 and 1889, these involved tunnels and bridges on a scale never before seen in Australia. The Sydney–Newcastle railway was the first built in New South Wales as a double-track line since the Sydney–Parramatta railway in 1855 and included both the longest tunnel and the biggest railway bridge in Australia. The latter, the Hawkesbury River Bridge, was especially significant as it marks the introduction of the American-style truss bridge into Australia. More than a century later, these structures remain the second largest in each category.[7] Whitton retired in 1890 just as the railway boom ended, having held the top job on the NSWGR since 1856.[8]

The 1880s were boom years in New South Wales as in Victoria; there was even a New South Wales equivalent of Victoria's 'Octopus Act' of 1884. This was premier George Dibbs' 1884 railway policy, which proposed to build 18 railways with a total length of 1197 miles (1926 km) at a cost of £14 688 808. Only two of the 18 were built at the time, for within a year it was clear that the optimism of 1884 was exaggerated. Thus, New South Wales was spared the worst of Victoria's extravagances. Nonetheless, the expansion in mileage was impressive. At the beginning of 1870 there were just 318 miles (512 km) of railway in the colony. Over the decade to 1879 this increased by 416 miles (670 km), or by an average of 42 miles (68 km) per annum. Over the following decade, 1880–89, there were 1437 miles (2313 km) opened, at an average annual rate of 147 miles (237 km).[9] This compared with an annual average for the roughly comparable period in Victoria of 155 miles (250 km). The New South Wales mileage, though, mostly comprised the completion of the long main lines to their natural termini; the two coastal railways north and south of Sydney; and a small number of very long branches in the interior. All these were useful railways, and most remain open to this day (Wallangarra is the most important exception), compared with the hundreds of kilometres of uneconomic, now mostly abandoned, short branches in Victoria.

The most significant challenge to the centralising policy of New South Wales railway construction came from the north coast region, where there were a number of ports aspiring to a direct connection with the interior. The oldest and most important of these was Grafton, but it had its rivals such as Lismore, Byron Bay and Coffs Harbour. From the 1880s to the 1940s, a number of schemes for such railways were mooted, and even at times achieved parliamentary approval. However, four factors meant that none was ever built. First was the hostility of the Railway Commissioners, for whom such a line would compete with the northern line to Wallangarra. Second was the rivalry between the various north coast ports, which thus were unable to present a united front. Third was the apathy or even hostility of the rest of the colony (including Sydney) to such a scheme, even including the interior districts to be served by such a line, which were generally perfectly happy with a direct rail link to Newcastle and Sydney. Fourth was the toughness of the terrain, which would have made the railway one of the most expensive ever built in Australia.

A Grafton–Glen Innes line, for instance, was included in the Dibbs 1884 railway policy, but ultimately his rival Henry Parkes worked out a compromise whereby a railway was built instead from the Tweed to the Clarence Rivers, connecting the rival ports with their immediate hinterlands. Its first section opened in 1894, centred on Byron Bay. Ultimately, this became the NSWGR's fourth main line, connecting Maitland (near Newcastle) with the Tweed River on the far north coast. Built from both ends and in isolated sections at times, it was not completed until 1923. Even then there remained a crossing of the Clarence River at Grafton by train ferry until the completion of Grafton's magnificent double-deck opening bascule bridge in 1932. In 1930, a Commonwealth-funded extension from Kyogle to South Brisbane, as discussed below, made possible through travel between Sydney and Brisbane by the coastal route. The result

Newcastle in 1886 was already a busy rail terminal even though there were not yet any trains through to Sydney. The customs house tower dominates the scene. (Ian Dunn collection)

was the gradual strangling of coastal shipping on the New South Wales north coast, culminating in the winding up of the North Coast Steam Navigation Company in 1954.[10]

The North Coast line was easily the most significant rural railway development in New South Wales of the first three decades of the 20th century. Most lines built in this period were branches serving the wheat and wool country of the interior, and were of little wider commercial or social significance. Most met real enough needs, though, and a surprising proportion of them remains open, at least seasonally. The most important had a wider purpose and took the NSWGR's tracks through to Broken Hill in 1927. However, this railway was unable to change the reality that most of Broken Hill's mineral production continued to take the shorter South Australian route to salt water at Port Pirie rather than the longer New South Wales route to Sydney or Newcastle. In the first half of the 20th century, though, the really important investment in railways in New South Wales was in and around Sydney.

QUEENSLAND

More than any other colony, Queensland had a deliberate policy of decentralised railway construction. All its railways were built to rather low engineering standards and to the same narrow gauge of 3ft 6in. This pattern of railway development was the result of its enormously long coastline and the political significance of its provincial port cities. The first line, from Ipswich to Toowoomba, soon was extended east to Brisbane and by 1880 as far west as Roma with a southwestern branch that would reach the New South Wales border at Wallangarra in 1887. By 1881 there were four other isolated railways serving pastoral, agricultural or mining districts from their nearest ports. These were based on the ports of Townsville, Rockhampton, Bundaberg and Maryborough.

By the end of the century there were no fewer than ten isolated Queensland railways. Some, such as the Central Railway based on Rockhampton and the Great Northern Railway based on Townsville, became extensive networks with a relatively dense traffic. The Central Railway would even include a branch line with a rack inserted between the rails to assist traction on the heaviest grades, similar to the Mt Lyell Railway in Tasmania, to reach the mines at Mount Morgan. Others, like the Mackay Railway, were more modest affairs serving agricultural districts, in this case a rich sugar-producing district. Mineral lines tended to be transient, including the northernmost line from Cooktown to the now-forgotten mining town of Laura. A number of lines were destined for an early linking into the ultimate coastal railway, including the isolated line nearest Brisbane, the 1881 Maryborough to Gympie line, whose fate was an early connection through to Brisbane.

The North Coast Railway was Queensland's last main line, and was not completed through from Brisbane to Cairns until 1924. The through route from Brisbane to Cairns enabled the introduction of the *Sunshine Express*, whose journey of 1043 miles (1678 km) was one of the longest narrow-gauge journeys possible anywhere in the world.[11] The reason for the late completion of the Queensland North Coast Railway was precisely the same as that for its counterpart in New South Wales: coastal steamers adequately handled the traffic until the 1920s.

The most spectacular of Queensland's isolated railways was the Cairns Railway, built over five years between 1886 and 1891. The Atherton Tablelands, sitting atop an escarpment behind the coastal plain of far north Queensland, had rich mineral and agricultural potential, if the extreme difficulties of access up the wild rainforest escarpment could be resolved. Initial controversy surrounded the choice of a port, with Port Douglas, Cairns and Innisfail all making strong claims. Ultimately the government decided to follow expert advice and make Cairns the terminus, which is the only reason Cairns rather than some other place has become the leading city of northern Australia. The climb through the Barron Valley from Redlynch to Kuranda, from an elevation of 78 feet (24 m) to 1073 feet (327 m) in a little over 15 miles (24 km), was extremely arduous. Works included 15 tunnels and the steel bridge over

Queensland Railways were built economically as a series of light railways, with curious results once they were connected. There was no plan to have the main line from Brisbane to Cairns run through Denison Street in Rockhampton, but that is what happened. In September 1972 there were still local commuter trains operating around Rockhampton, and this was one of them. (Tony McIlwain)

the Barron Falls, where trains pass through the waterfall in the wet season.

One of the most unusual, unquestionably the most isolated, and certainly the strangest survival of the era of isolated Queensland railways was the Normanton to Croydon line. Built between 1889 and 1891, this 93-mile (150-km) line connected the Gulf of Carpentaria port of Normanton with the gold rush town of Croydon. It was laid with steel sleepers pressed directly into the muddy topsoil, without any ballast, the idea being that floodwaters would wash over the line without damaging it, as would have been the case with a conventional ballasted railway. The theory worked, and the railway has required remarkably little maintenance as a result. The cost is uneven track and very rough riding. However, such is its longevity that the railway survived the end of mining at Croydon in 1907 and has continued until the present with just one train a week. It is the last survivor of the light, isolated Queensland port-to-interior railways.

While the Queensland Railways were built to low engineering standards, they were

Queensland Railways' bridge over Stoney Creek Falls on the ascent from Cairns to Kuranda, from a postcard published in the early 1900s soon after the railway's completion. Engine 217 was one of Queensland Railways' light, versatile and efficient PB15 class, of which 233 were built, mostly in Queensland, between 1900 and 1926. They were the second most numerous type of locomotive (after the NSWGR's T class) in Australian railway history. (Frank Hurley, author postcard collection) appropriate to the needs of the colony. They were cheap to build. The most expensive section was the 15-mile climb to Kuranda on the Cairns railway, which cost roughly £19 000 per mile. Low standards, though, meant high operational costs, slow service speeds, and light and hence not very powerful locomotives. As long as Queensland remained relatively undeveloped compared to the southern colonies, this was an acceptable trade-off. Queensland was able to build at modest cost the largest (if far from the most intensively worked) railway system in Australia. The Queensland Railways were not really deficient until exposed to the stress of the Pacific War between 1941 and 1945, when it became clear that their light standards were as inadequate for the defence of the country as they were for intense economic development. The result has been that no Australian railways were more extensively rebuilt in the second half of the 20th century than Queensland's.

There was one attempt at building a great transcontinental line deep into the interior of Queensland by the McIlwraith government in 1883. He proposed to fund it on the land-grant principle and allow an English company to build it in return for substantial land grants. This system would be used with some success in Western Australia, but never worked elsewhere, and McIlwraith's government fell in the attempt. The proposed land-grant railway would connect Roma (and hence Brisbane) with the far northwest and, ultimately, with a new port at Point Parker on the Gulf of Carpentaria. The railway's initial financial prospects were bleak, hence the need for land-grant funding, although as a national project it had great significance. Its failure was an interesting illustration of the fundamentally parochial pressures that drove railway policy in Queensland, and indeed in the other Australian colonies as well.[12]

SOUTH AUSTRALIA

South Australia's railway history is the least coherent of any of the mainland colonies (although South Australia styled itself a 'province', not a colony). For, despite being the location of Australia's first minerals boom following the discovery of copper at Kapunda in 1843, South Australia always lacked both the rich pastoral or agricultural districts and the sequence of mineral discoveries which did so much to drive the growth of New South Wales, Victoria and Queensland in the second half of the 19th century. Even the favourable geography for railway construction of much of the province worked against the development of a coherent railway policy. Its flat agricultural regions were close to the sheltered coasts of its two gulfs, so cheap horse-operated tramways going to nowhere in particular in the interior from jetties on the gulfs could meet real transport needs.

The first of these, running into the interior from Port Wakefield at the head of the Gulf St Vincent, opened in 1870. On the advice of William Hanson, then Railway Manager, it was built experimentally to the Queensland gauge of 3ft 6in, since it was never expected to join the 5ft 3in gauge lines near Adelaide. Hanson resigned after the tramway was authorised but before construction began. His successor, HC Mais, a former engineer of the Sydney Railway Company, advised against introducing a second gauge into South Australia, but the provincial parliament, impressed with the alleged economies of narrow gauge, absurdly and stupidly overrode its technical expert on the matter. In fact, by 1880 the tramway had been extended into a network linking Port Wakefield; the pastoral interior; the copper towns of Kadina, Moonta and Wallaroo on Spencer Gulf; and Adelaide (with a break of gauge at Hamley Bridge, which in 1880 became the first of South Australia's far too many break-of-gauge stations). From 1876, steam locomotives replaced horses. Two other narrow-gauge lines were also in service, one further north based on Port Pirie and another in the southeast based on Mount Gambier.

Thus, in less than a decade, Hanson's entire foolish rationale for introducing narrow gauge and horse working had been overthrown by the natural development of the colony. The new railways carried goods and passengers more economically than the coaches and drays they replaced, but the difference in speed was not as dramatic as it had been in the eastern colonies. The journey time on Cobb and Co's coach between Adelaide and Kadina was 12 hours. By comparison, the same trip of 185 kilometres by two mixed trains, including the change from broad to narrow gauge at Hamley Bridge, took some seven hours and 12 minutes in 1886.[13]

The narrow-gauge railways in northern South Australia continued to expand under the stimulus of mineral and pastoral development. There were two important main lines built in the 1880s. First was what began as the Port Augusta and Government Gums Railway. At the ceremony to begin construction of the line at Port Augusta in January 1878, Governor Sir William Jervois expansively observed that the railway would not just serve the province's pastoral northern interior, but ultimately reach Port Darwin and so provide connections with India, Java, Siam and China. This was just eight years after the first tenuous horse tramways had opened in the district. The line opened to Quorn in 1879, taking tracks through the Pichi Richi Pass into the north, and was extended in stages to reach Oodnadatta in 1891. It was extended to Alice Springs in 1929 (by which time it had become part of Commonwealth Railways) and there the rails ended until the final extension to Darwin opened in 2004.

The second important line connected Port Pirie with Broken Hill in far western New South Wales. Opened in 1888, this line allowed the development of Broken Hill's rich silver, lead and zinc deposits, and virtually created the town of Port Pirie, where the smelters for the new mines were located. The short distance within New South Wales from the border to

Broken Hill was built and operated by the Silverton Tramway Company. There were three other significant elements to the South Australian narrow-gauge system. These were the grain and mineral lines of the Eyre Peninsula, centred on Port Lincoln; the southeastern lines around Mount Gambier; and the Palmerston (later Darwin) railway in the Northern Territory, which under South Australian management would run as far south as Pine Creek.

As the narrow-gauge system expanded, the problems of a dual-gauge system became ever more acute. Moreover, in 1912 the Commonwealth decided to build the transcontinental railway from Port Augusta to Western Australia to standard gauge. Eventually, by a state-Commonwealth agreement, the South Australian broad-gauge line was extended northwest to Port Pirie and the Commonwealth Railways' transcontinental standard-gauge line was extended south from Port Augusta, and to

South Australia's Intercolonial Railway completed in 1887 involved crossing the Adelaide Hills. From the beginning it carried Australia's first through train from capital to capital, called the Intercolonial Express for many years before being named the *Overland* in 1926. Two of William Thow's R class of the late 1880s were required to work this train over the hills about 1910. (Author postcard collection)

Port Pirie in 1937. This at last eliminated the circuitous narrow-gauge link between Adelaide and Port Augusta.

The expansion of the broad-gauge network around Adelaide was more straightforward than the building of the narrow-gauge lines. There were three main aims: to reach the rich mining town of Burra from Adelaide; to connect the Murray at Morgan with Adelaide; and to build the Intercolonial Railway to link with the Victorian Railways. The first two were achieved in 1870 and 1878, although traffic in both cases was disappointing: Morgan was no Echuca and Burra no Ballarat. The Intercolonial Railway was a more complex scheme, both politically and technically, and there was considerable debate as to the best route southeast from Adelaide. The line, which involved ascending and descending the Adelaide Hills and a bridge across the Murray, was opened in stages between 1883 and 1887. A branch between Mount Barker and Strathalbyn opened in 1884 to connect the Intercolonial Railway with the pioneering southern tramways, which were soon converted from horse to steam operation. Thus, after 30 years, the most important country horse tramway in Australia came to an end. With the completion of the Intercolonial Railway, the 'classic system' of the South Australian Railways was virtually complete. However, such had been the confusion, incoherence and downright stupidity of the province's railway policy that, as a state in the new Commonwealth, its railways would be rebuilt, their gauges changed and their uses redefined far more than was the case elsewhere in Australia.

TASMANIA

Like South Australia's, Tasmania's early railway history was complex and beset by political and technological confusion. Tasmania initially relied on private enterprise to build its railways. The first was the Launceston and Western Railway, authorised in 1865. The Tasmanian government refused to contribute funds and insisted that its guarantee of a return to investors be met by those who would benefit from the railway. A poll of landowners along its route in 1865 resulted in a vote of 2259 in favour of the guarantee and 545 against. Construction began in 1868, following an elaborate ceremony to commemorate the turning of the first sod by the Duke of Edinburgh, the most distinguished royal visitor Australia had seen. The line, built to Victoria's 5ft 3in gauge, opened between Launceston and Deloraine, a distance of 45 miles (72 km), three years later in February 1871. Secondhand construction engines from Victoria provided most of the motive power.

Nineteen months later the company was bankrupt and the line closed for six weeks until the government took it over. It then set about collecting the funds to cover the railway's losses from landowners, most of whom lived in Launceston. This led to one of the most serious outbreaks of civil unrest in Australia's history, as the government sent in the bailiffs to confiscate the goods of landowners who refused to pay. There were riots and damage to property. The Launceston police were unable to maintain order, and other civil servants refused to support the government or be sworn in as special constables because they considered its behaviour unconscionable. This prompted the government to send 35 heavily armed Territorial Police from Hobart to quell what was in danger of becoming an uprising. It even threatened to send a gunboat to bombard Launceston if resistance became too fierce. The Launceston *Examiner*'s anti-government rhetoric was so violent that the attorney general sued it (unsuccessfully) for libel. Ultimately the funds were recovered,

Even in 1919 there were faster ways of getting around Tasmania than the mixed trains of the Tasmanian Government Railways. Motorbike and sidecar look on while a Manchester-built Beyer, Peacock 4-4-0 locomotive hauls goods and passengers over the River Leven at Ulverstone in 1919. (H King, author collection)

but at enormous cost and in a way that nearly led to the splitting of the colony. A change of government in 1874 led to the abandonment of the hated railway levy, and civil disturbances came to an end. It is little wonder that property taxes have been little used to subsidise railways in Australia.

At the very moment the Launceston and Western Railway opened, the Hobart government was negotiating a contract with English capitalists for the construction of a line from Hobart to Launceston. Signed in August 1871, before the full extent of the Launceston company's woes was apparent, it provided for the building of the line subject to a government guarantee on capital of 5 percent. This was not further devolved to landowners, which further incensed Launceston opinion, since Hobart's railway was to be guaranteed by the government while Launceston's had to be guaranteed by local landowners. Work on the Tasmanian Main Line, at it was known, began in 1873, and the railway was built to the 3ft 6in gauge, as had just become fashionable. Its construction was riven by controversy over routings and allegations of engineering incompetence, but nonetheless it opened through to Evandale near Launceston in March 1876 where it met the tracks of the Launceston and Western at Australia's first (of far too many) break-of-gauge station.

Relations between the Tasmanian Main Line Company and the government were always acrimonious and frequently litigious. Ultimately the government bought the line in 1890. By this time it already had built branches from both the Tasmanian Main Line and the Launceston and Western. The most important of these was the Deloraine to Devonport line, opened in 1885 as a 3ft 6in gauge line. This left the Launceston and Western as a short length of broad-gauge line connecting two narrow-gauge ones. The solution was obvious, and in August 1888 its conversion to narrow gauge was completed. Thus, by 1890 the 3ft 6in gauge Tasmanian Government Railways (TGR) dominated the railway scene in the colony.

This newfound unity did not last long, for the copper boom on Tasmania's wild and inaccessible west coast soon prompted a rash of railway construction there by mining companies, railway promoters and the government itself. In the 1890s construction was so intense and the rival claims of various railway companies' prospectuses so extravagant that it was described as the West Coast Railway Wars. The Van Diemen's Land Company had built the first, a 3ft gauge, wooden-rail horse tramway running southwards for 44 miles (71 km) from Emu Bay (Burnie) to its mines near Waratah. Converted to a 3ft 6in gauge steam railway with steel rails in 1884, this line was bought by the Emu Bay Railway Company in 1897. The new owners raised capital in Melbourne to extend the line southwards to Zeehan, where they hoped to tap the riches of the new Mt Lyell mining district.

The extension opened in 1900, but there were already other players in the district, notably the TGR's line from Strachan (the port on Macquarie Harbour) to Zeehan and Dundas, which had opened in 1891. The most remarkable of the lines in the area, though, was the Mount Lyell Mining and Railway Company's main line from Queenstown, location of its rich copper mines and smelters, to the navigable waters of Macquarie Harbour at Strachan. Opening in 1896, it was so steep as to be built as a rack railway to the Abt system. This system, invented by Roman Abt, involves a third rack rail being laid between the running rails, into which a cog on the locomotive can bite to increase traction on very steep grades, It was one of only three such public railways ever built in Australia, the others being the almost contemporary Mount Morgan line in Queensland and the very much later electrified passenger Skitube line in New South Wales's Snowy Mountains. Thus was created a through but very circuitous rail route from Hobart to Queenstown, by the Tasmanian Main Line (after 1890 TGR) track to Evandale; then over the former Launceston and Western (by then TGR) trackage to Deloraine; then over the TGR's own line to Burnie; then by the Emu Bay Railway to Zeehan; over the TGR once again to Strahan; and finally by the Mt Lyell's Abt railway into Queenstown.

For variety of owners and confusion of purpose, there was nothing in Australia quite to rival the situation on Tasmania's west coast. Two other railways on the west coast copper belt were particularly notable. The TGR's 2ft gauge North East Dundas Tramway was famous as the line for which the world's first Garratt articulated locomotives were built in 1911, and was also one of the most scenic lines ever built in Australia. For extravagance, uselessness and lack of longevity, though, the North Mount Lyell Mining and Railway Company's railway was in a class of its own. This was a rival of the Mount Lyell Railway, and opened in 1900 from near Queenstown to a new port on Macquarie Harbour at Kelly's Basin. Its 33 miles (53 km) cost £316 638.[14] Although easier to operate than the Mount Lyell Abt railway, it was unable to win much traffic, and its design and management were inept. In 1903 the North Lyell enterprise was bought by its rival, the Mount Lyell Mining and Railway Company, which promptly closed the entire line after just three years' operation. This brought an abrupt end to the ebullient era of the West Coast Railway Wars. Thereafter stability reigned, until the lines started to close during the Depression of the 1930s. By the 1960s all had disappeared except for the Emu Bay Railway Company's line.

WESTERN AUSTRALIA

In railway development, as in much else, Western Australia was a case apart. Until the 1890s it was the least populated and developed Australian colony. Its first railway was a 12 mile (19 km) line built to carry timber from logging camps to the navigable waters of Geographe Bay near Busselton in the colony's southwest. Its first locomotive was built not in England but at the Victoria Foundry in Ballarat. Obsolete and underpowered when built, this fragile machine inaugurated rail transport in Western Australia in mid-1871. It established the 3ft 6in gauge as the colony's standard, and was the precedent for a number of other timber tramways built in the southwest over the rest of the decade.

The first government railway, and the nucleus of the later Western Australian Government Railways (WAGR), was built for specialised traffic far from the colony's capital. In 1874, work began on the government's line from the port of Geraldton to the lead and copper deposits of Northampton. Although only 33 miles (53 km) long, construction took five years, and traffic was never especially brisk. Just as the Northampton line opened, work began on the first stage of the Eastern Railway, from the colony's main port of Fremantle through the capital Perth to York, then the colony's main agricultural centre. The first stages of this line (opened in 1881) were easy enough, but its completion by 1885 involved the ascent of the western escarpment of the Darling Range. This was built according to the ideas of JH Thomas, who had come to Perth following his defeat at the hands of John Whitton in New South Wales. Here he had the opportunity to put into place his ideas on light railways.

Western Australia's operations included local trains in and around Perth. Here one brings a weekend crowd to South Beach at Fremantle. (Author postcard collection)

Predictably, his main line was inadequate for the traffic and needed rebuilding after ten years.

The Eastern Railway's completion began an era of rapid expansion with a characteristic unique to Western Australia – the construction of two main lines by private capital under the land-grant principle. The eastern colonies were highly dependent on land sales revenue, so were unwilling to give away land to capitalists in order to have railways built. McIlwraith's attempt to do so in Queensland in 1883 foundered on the opposition of the squatters, for whom cheap pastoral leases were sacrosanct. However, with its apparent enormous land resources and small population, the Western Australian government saw matters rather differently, and in 1886 signed two contracts with English syndicates for the construction of railways in return for land grants along their routes. These were the Midland Railway, running north from Midland near Perth to Walkaway near Geraldton; and the Great Southern Railway, running south from Beverley near York to Albany. They were opened in 1894 and 1889 respectively. The Midland remained in private hands until 1964, but the government, its funds buoyed by the gold rush, bought the Great Southern in 1896 for fully a million pounds.

During the 1890s Western Australia's economy boomed following gold discoveries near Kalgoorlie. The WAGR built the colony's last two main lines in these buoyant times, from near Perth to Bunbury (opened in 1893) and the eastwards extension of the Eastern Railway, known as the Eastern Goldfields Railway. This was completed through to Kalgoorlie in 1896. For a time Kalgoorlie was so busy that its suburban train service was more intense than that between Perth and Fremantle. As the Eastern Goldfields Railway was being completed, the original Eastern Railway was improved by duplication from Fremantle to Midland and construction of a deviation on an easier alignment of the ascent of the Darling escarpment. The engineer of these works was the brilliant and energetic CY O'Connor, who had replaced the adventurous if less competent Thomas in 1892.

Thus, by 1897 the skeleton of the Western Australian railway system was complete. It was a rational, well-conceived and efficiently operated railway system, and would remain so throughout its history. Over the following 20 years mileage increased rapidly, but most of the new lines were lightly trafficked agricultural branches. Growth of traffic on the main lines, though, was spectacular. Between 1895 and 1915 the WAGR's goods tonnage increased nearly ten times (from 255 839 to 2 454 021 tons) and its passenger traffic by almost 20 times (from 1 022 248 to 18 635 327).[15]

FEDERATION AND TRANSCONTINENTAL RAILWAYS

AS IN ALL AUSTRALIAN colonies, railways were a big political issue in the West in the late 19th century, but typically they took rather a different form. Federation was firmly on the political agenda of the Australian colonies in the 1890s, and there was rather less enthusiasm for it in Western Australia than elsewhere, especially as the other colonies (above all Victoria) were in depression while the West was booming. Western Australia's premier, Sir John Forrest, was a believer in Federation, but was well aware that his views were not shared by most of the population. He astutely used the promise of construction of a railway linking east and west as a bargaining tool in the Federation debate, and managed to secure a promise of its building as a condition of Western Australia's adherence to the new Commonwealth in 1901. Forrest knew the magnitude of the task, as he had cut his teeth as an explorer and twice walked across the vast Nullarbor Plain.

As part of the federal settlement, railways were left in the hands of the states. This was in contrast with the situation in Canada, India and South Africa, the three countries whose administration most closely matched Australia's. In all three cases, the central governments always have had responsibility for railway policy. Australia's unique situation in this regard was the result of the reality that the vast bulk of its railways were owned and operated by the colonial (from 1901 state) governments. They were also built to different and often incompatible technical standards, of which gauge was the most important but by no means the only one. Federation may have brought an immediate end to the customs houses at border stations such as Albury, Serviceton and Wallangarra, but to little else. The railways' administrations did agree to common technical standards on matters such the loading gauge (the clearance of structures from the track which determines the size of rolling stock) as early as 1906. However, this only affected future construction and was not a commitment to any rebuilding to common standards.

Even in the case of the transcontinental railway, the promise Forrest had extracted from other colonies' representatives was not a commitment, and it was not until 1911 that the Commonwealth government, then in the hands of a centralising Labour government, authorised construction. The conservative Forrest was in opposition, but was the Bill's greatest parliamentary supporter. The Commonwealth Railways were set up to do the job under Engineer-in-Chief Henry Deane, recently retired from the same position in New South Wales where he had been understudy to John Whitton back in the 1880s. Deane, although far from young, was progressive and energetic. Prime minister Andrew Fisher turned the first sod at Port Augusta, the railway's eastern terminus in South Australia, in February 1912, just two months after the authorising Act was passed, and Deane, together with his successor and first Commonwealth Railways Commissioner Norris Bell, built the railway 1051 miles (1691 km) across the desert in just five years. The railway was built as a standard-gauge line, even though it connected two 3ft 6in gauge railways. In this sense, it contributed to the gauge muddle, but in selecting the standard gauge in 1911 the Commonwealth set the norm to which Australia's railways eventually would begin to conform in the second half of the 20th century.

Transcontinental expresses began operating, with much fanfare, in October 1917. Construction was not without its hazards, industrial disputes and shortages of materials, for the railway was built through the most desperate days of World War I, and so to rather austere standards. This austerity did not extend to its passenger cars, which were equipped with showers (for first class passengers anyway) and a piano in the lounge from as early as 1918. At last the continent could be crossed by rail, and the journey only took five days, despite the need to change trains on account of gauge differences no less than eight times between Brisbane and Perth. Through freight traffic, though, would remain insignificant until the 1960s.

The Commonwealth Railway's workshops and operations headquarters were established at its eastern terminus of Port Augusta, although the business headquarters remained in the then national capital of Melbourne. Deane had hoped to use internal combustion locomotives (either petrol or diesel) because of the absence of coal and assured water along the route. Indeed, more than a fifth

Commonwealth Railways' Transcontinental Express began running between Port Augusta and Kalgoorlie in 1917, traversing the longest straight track in the world across the treeless Nullarbor Plain. Operations with steam locomotives were always difficult in such isolated and dry conditions and were coming to an end when the express was photographed far out in the desert in 1949. (Cliff Bottomley, NAA Series A1200 Item L12215)

of all traffic on the railway would be coal and water for its steam locomotives. Use of diesel traction would have made the Commonwealth Railways a real world pioneer, but tight budgets and engineering conservatism stymied his plans. Standard New South Wales steam locomotives were ordered for the railway and operated until 1951.

Just before the Commonwealth decided to build the transcontinental railway, it had got involved in the railway business as a subsidiser, if not yet as an owner and operator. Following the transfer of the Northern Territory to the Commonwealth in 1907, two South Australian 3ft 6in gauge railways similarly were transferred from 1 January 1911. These were the Darwin to Pine Creek railway and the Port Augusta to Oodnadatta railway. Neither was an especially thriving business – losses on the Oodnadatta line in the first decade of the 20th century were around £80 000 per year – but they did form the two extremities of the proposed north–south transcontinental railway. They remained operated by the South Australian Railways until 1926, although the Commonwealth government covered the deficits. Thus, from 1926 Commonwealth Railways, like the South Australian Railways, became a two-gauge operation, although the two gauges were different from that of most of the state system.

Under the terms of acquiring the Northern Territory, the Commonwealth undertook to 'construct or cause to be constructed a railway in South Australia proper, from any point on the Port Augusta railway to a point on the northern boundary line of South Australia proper, to connect

Commonwealth Railways' narrow-gauge line to Alice Springs was completed in 1929 and remained in use until replaced by a standard-gauge railway in 1980. It was built cheaply and a trip on the old narrow-gauge *Ghan*, seen here leaving Alice Springs in 1968, was always slow and, especially after rain, often an adventure. Since there was no sealed road between South Australia and Alice Springs at the time, patronage was buoyant despite these difficulties. (NAA Series A1500 Item K19354)

with that part of the Transcontinental Railway to be built in the Northern Territory southwards to the northern boundary of South Australia proper'. The expectation was that this north–south railway would be constructed sooner rather than later. Even the program for the turning of the first sod of the east–west railway described it as 'one of the two Transcontinental Railways, the construction of which is to be deferred for the present'. Maps of the time suggested that the future fast route from Sydney to London would be by train to Darwin, steamer to Port Arthur in Manchuria, thence by train across Siberia.[16]

It never happened. The Commonwealth honoured its promise in part with the extension of the Oodnadatta line to Alice Springs between 1927 and 1929, a line it rebuilt to standard gauge on a different route in the mid-1970s. At the same time, though, it closed the North Australia Railway, as the line stretching south from Darwin had become known. Contracts for the extension from Alice Springs to Darwin (including the rebuilding of the North Australia Railway to a different gauge) would not be signed until 2001, by which time the railway would no longer have anything like the impact on travel or trade patterns it would have had 80 years or so earlier. One consequence of the transcontinental railway planning and construction was that the tiny South Australian railway town of Quorn became bizarrely significant. For this was where the north–south and east–west routes intersected. One brave soul forecast in 1909 that 'At some future time Quorn will be the most important railway station in the whole of Australia.' It never was, although the South Australian Railways did erect a new and imposing station there in 1915 in deference to its anticipated status. The dream of Quorn becoming an antipodean Chicago may never have been realised, but it was an important railway centre through the busiest years of the Port Augusta to Alice Springs railway from 1942 to 1945. Even General Douglas MacArthur trod its dusty platform on the penultimate leg of his epic escape from Japanese-besieged Corregidor in Manila Bay to Melbourne in 1942.

The Commonwealth's forays into the railway business included two other railways, both built before the shocks of World War II which would transform forever Australian transport policy. First was the little branch from Queanbeyan to the national capital site of Canberra, opened in 1914, which would always be operated by the NSWGR despite its Commonwealth ownership. Second, and far more significant, was the last section of the direct coastal route between Sydney and Brisbane, opened with Commonwealth funding assistance in 1930. This line, from Kyogle in northern New South Wales to South Brisbane, had for 70 years the unusual status of being partly owned by the NSWGR, partly by QR, but operated throughout by the NSWGR although with QR employees on the Queensland section. Not only that, the dividing point between the two owners was in the middle of a tunnel under the MacPherson Ranges which form the border. Its construction cut six hours from the longer, two-gauge route via Wallangarra, which also had involved the climb over Australia's highest railway summit. This railway, the first of the many uniform-gauge intercapital lines built with Commonwealth financial assistance after World War II, was also a significant engineering feat, climbing to the subtropical rainforest-covered range at the border on an alignment which included Australia's first spiral, where the track redoubled on itself to gain altitude.[17]

WORKSHOPS AND ROLLING STOCK ON AUSTRALIAN RAILWAYS

THE BOOM YEARS forced all Australia's railways to upgrade their initially modest maintenance facilities, obliging them to become mature industrial enterprises with extensive infrastructure to support their transport functions. Australia was then not yet industrialised, and this meant that the railways became pioneers of modern heavy industry throughout the country. They were, to use an apposite metaphor, the locomotives which hauled the train of Australian industrialisation. It must be admitted that it was a very short train, even at the end of the 19th century when, for instance, the NSWGR employed more workers than the colony's entire private manufacturing industry. Moreover, a significant proportion of that industry was devoted to the manufacture of railway carriages and wagons. However, the great railway workshops of the 1880s laid the foundations of the future industrialisation of the country, which really got under way during World War I. It was in them that metallurgy, forging, machining, and assembly first were practised on a large scale in colonial Australia.

Large railway workshops were built for all Australia's government railways in the 20 or so years from the mid-1880s. Locations included Ipswich near Brisbane, Townsville, Islington near Adelaide, Midland near Perth, and Launceston. The two most impressive workshops were built in Sydney and Melbourne during the mid-1880s at Eveleigh and Newport. Their functions were rather different. For two reasons Eveleigh was the more spectacular ensemble of the two. First, it included the large running sheds where locomotives working trains out of Sydney were serviced, whereas in Melbourne the locomotive depot was located closer to the city than Newport, at North Melbourne. Secondly, there were a number of smaller railway workshops established in Victoria at locations such as Ballarat and Bendigo, as part of a policy of decentralisation. By contrast, in New South Wales centralisation was the key – even the Newcastle workshops were scaled down after the 1889 opening of the Hawkesbury River Bridge linking the northern and southern New South Wales systems. Thus, Eveleigh was the most expansively conceived and lavishly equipped of all the colonial railway workshops, although Newport had one important function which Eveleigh did not.

Locomotive construction at Victorian Railways' Newport Workshops about 1910. (Freedman collection)

This was the construction of locomotives, because Victoria and New South Wales followed very different policies in locomotive procurement. From the mid-1870s Victoria was protectionist. This was an unusual and paradoxical situation, given that the British Empire was based on the principle of free trade and did not hesitate to wage war on recalcitrant kingdoms (even large and powerful ones like China) whose policies deviated too much from this principle. In the name of colonial self-government, though, Victoria was able to get away with protectionism, and orders for the railways, easily the most important single customer for heavy industry on the colony, naturally enough were subject to this policy.

Thus, sustained local locomotive building for the Victorian Railways began as early as 1871 when Victorian Railways built its first locomotive at its Williamstown shops (the precursor of Newport). Then in 1873 Phoenix Foundry of Ballarat delivered the first of about 350 machines it would build for VR over the next 30 years. Thereafter, few locomotives were imported into Victoria until the late 1940s. South Australia too, increasingly tied economically to Victoria, followed protectionist policies. New South Wales, however, remained rigorously free trade until Federation. This meant that, apart from a handful of experiments, all its locomotives were imported until after Federation, when New South Wales was forced to adopt protectionist policies. The majority came from one builder, Beyer, Peacock and Company of Manchester. In fact, throughout Beyer, Peacock's 110-year history, the NSWGR was its biggest customer.

The local workshops (especially Eveleigh and Newport), the skill-base they developed, and the drafting office of Beyer, Peacock in Manchester, became the basis of a recognisably Australian school of locomotive design by the end of the 19th century. The leading early figure in this school was William Thow, successively locomotive superintendent in Adelaide during the 1880s and then Chief Mechanical Engineer in Sydney from 1890 to 1911. Thow developed his R class 4-6-0 locomotive at Adelaide. Subsequently refined with a lot of assistance from Beyer, Peacock, this was transformed into the New South Wales P class, also a 4-6-0, the first example of which was completed in Manchester in 1891. This was a very successful machine, of which 191 eventually were built for service in New South Wales and a further 26 for Commonwealth Railways' transcontinental railway. Victorian Railways developed designs from 'pattern engines' supplied by Kitson's of Leeds but in 1902 introduced its indigenous D^D class, another 4-6-0.

Thow also introduced a moderately heavy 2-8-0 goods locomotive in New South Wales, the T class of 1896, which he claimed combined the best features of recently imported British and American machines. This was the first locomotive entirely designed in Australia and was so successful that, together with its more refined sisters of the TF and K class, more than 600 were built not just for New South Wales but also for Commonwealth Railways and for British Army operations on Belgian railways during World War I. By contrast, in Victoria the English 0-6-0 type remained the standard goods engine long after it had been superseded in New South Wales. However, Victoria opted for larger goods locomotives after World War I (the C, N and X classes) rather than refining existing designs, as Thow's successor, EE Lucy, did in New South Wales. Thus, the great leap forward in goods locomotive power occurred later in Victoria than New South Wales, but was more profound.

As passenger types developed, Lucy led the way with his NN class of 1914. His Victorian counterpart, Alf Smith's slightly earlier A^2 class initially was less imposing, but was subsequently refined into an effective machine. These were typically Australian locomotives, both 4-6-0s, rather larger overall than their British counterparts, somewhat smaller than what was then being built in the United States. Their overall conception was rather American, but nearly all the design details were British. Most of these machines lasted until well after World War II (and in New South Wales into the 1970s), which is evidence of the quality of the designs Thow and Smith developed.

Queensland too developed excellent and economical indigenous designs at Ipswich. They necessarily were light, so technically unadventurous, but one (the C17) was good enough to be chosen by Commonwealth Railways as its standard narrow-gauge design. The other narrow-gauge networks in Tasmania, South Australia and Western Australia lacked capacity for local design and innovation. In general the locomotives on these railways were built (largely by Beyer, Peacock) to much the same designs as their counterparts working on similar British-run railways in Africa, Asia and Latin America. Australian railways, though, were important customers, and Beyer, Peacock undertook much of the refinement of its narrow-gauge 2-6-0 locomotive with inclined cylinders for its Australian customers.

Australia's and the world's first Garratt articulated locomotive works past Montezuma Falls on the Tasmanian Government Railways' 2ft gauge North East Dundas Tramway in 1924. The pioneering and very influential locomotive was built by Beyer, Peacock and Company in Manchester in 1911 and still exists, operating on the Welsh Highland Railway. (H King, author collection)

A further important innovation on Australian railways was the development of the Garratt locomotive. The design and development of the Garratt was entirely undertaken in Britain, specifically in Beyer, Peacock's drafting office in Manchester using the ideas of HW Garratt. Australian railways were the first customers for this articulated design which ultimately came to represent the pinnacle of steam power for relatively lightly laid railways, above all in Australia and Africa, but also in parts of Asia and Latin America. Beyer, Peacock built the first experimental Garratt for Tasmania in 1911, and Tasmania and Western Australia were the first two important customers for the design. Ultimately, every Australian state railway ordered Garratt locomotives on a large scale, except Victoria, which only ever had two, and those only on its narrow-gauge lines. The vast majority of these were built in Manchester to Beyer, Peacock's designs, although there was an indigenous design developed and built locally during World War II. Designing Garratts, though, was a highly specialised art, and these local Garratts, the products of emergency wartime conditions, were about the worst specimens of the genre ever built.

Steam locomotives were the most visible and technically advanced items of rolling stock. However, passenger cars and goods wagons were equally significant and also developed in distinctively Australian ways. Nearly all such equipment was made in the colony where it operated. This was the case even in free trade New South Wales, since local manufacturers could compete on price and quality with importers because of the high quality and cheap price of Australian timber. Once again, Australian rolling stock tended to be characterised by a mixture of British and American influences. New South Wales used American-style end-platform suburban cars, Victoria British-style side-loading cars, and South Australia and Queensland a mixture of both.

For long-distance traffic all colonies used a mixture of British and American styles. There was a fair amount of copying of imported cars and wagons by all colonial railways. Rolling stock was largely built by private companies and the rolling stock industry was one of the most important components of late colonial Australian manufacturing. Henry Lawson, for instance, found a job in Sydney as a painter of new passenger cars at Hudson Brothers' plant at Granville. Related to rolling stock was the question of how trains were braked. Australian railways adopted higher braking standards than British railways in the late 19th and early 20th centuries, the larger systems fairly quickly applying Westinghouse air brakes (or vacuum brakes in Western Australia and Tasmania) to all passenger and most goods stock. By contrast, British railways remained stuck in the era of non-braked goods trains well into the 1960s.

RAILWAYS AND INDUSTRIAL POLITICS

THE GREAT RAILWAY WORKSHOPS were social as well as technical institutions. They had important roles in the development of technical education and training, in the emergence of trade unions, and in the origins of the Australian Labor Party. Railway Institutes, established in all states around 1900, extended the railways' educational and social roles to towns throughout the nation. The first two great waves of industrial unrest in Australia, in 1890 and 1917, both affected the workshops. In 1890, the strikes began in the bush and the railways were among the last industry to be affected. However, out of this wave of industrial activity came the beginnings of parliamentary representation of railway workers, the first being William Schey, who represented the Eveleigh workers in the New South Wales parliament. Schey's judgment was poor and he had a nasty streak, but his victory in the 1891 election marked the beginnings of a new phase in the complex relationship between the railways and their government owners. Henceforth, railway workers would have a voice in colonial (later state) parliaments, with all that implied. All railway workshops were nurseries for Labour politicians, and no fewer than 24 state and federal Labour (after 1922 spelt Labor) politicians worked at Eveleigh early in their careers.

The 1917 strike was on another level altogether. Coming as it did in the most desperate months of World War I, it reflected and created many cleavages in Australian society. The immediate issue was the introduction into New South Wales railway and tramway workshops of the American Taylor system of scientific management involving timed job-cards. However, the conduct of the war, and especially Irish Australians' growing hostility towards a war in support of an empire which seemed to be ravaging Ireland, were important background issues. Among the leaders of the strike was Joe Cahill, an Irish Catholic Labourite notorious as the future premier of New South Wales guilty of closing Sydney's tram system.

Despite the massive support of workers for the strike – almost all the wages staff at Eveleigh was on strike for at least the first couple of weeks – it was defeated as the weeks drifted by and hunger and evictions descended on the railway suburbs. Unions were deregistered, and the strikers dismissed. Long-term strikers ultimately were accepted back with loss of seniority. Among the victims was the Bathurst engine driver Ben Chifley, who became first an organiser, then a politician, and nearly 30 years later Prime Minister as a result of his experiences. The strike lasted 82 days and about 70 000 workers, or 14 percent of the state's workforce, was on strike for at least some of that period. The failure of the strike was largely because it was not just about job-cards. Many workers supported the war effort and, while

Workers who refused to participate or returned to work early in the great New South Wales rail strike of August 1917 were characterised either as 'scabs' or 'loyal', depending on the outlook of the person describing them. A group of them, naturally described in the official record as 'loyal', poses at Eveleigh carriage workshops in Sydney on 19 August 1917. (SRNSW R459 247)

willing to participate in a short strike on a straight industrial issue, were unenthusiastic about its wider political agenda. This included many union organisers, who were sometimes among the more languid participants.

Victoria did not have the same levels of industrial militancy as New South Wales, and indeed there was only one strike in the history of its railways before 1945. This was the 1903 engine drivers' strike, which lasted only a week and was insufficiently supported to prevent many trains running. Its main result was that unions were recognised by the railway's management for the first time, more than a decade after the New South Wales management accorded them this status. Elsewhere in Australia railway unionism was not as significant a factor in the changing landscape of late colonial and early federal politics.

AUSTRALIA'S RAILWAYS ABOUT 1920

THUS, BY THE 1920s, Australia's classic colonial-based railway network was in place. The completion of the New South Wales and Queensland North Coast lines (from Maitland to Murwillumbah and from Brisbane to Cairns respectively), and the New South Wales line from Parkes to Broken Hill in 1923, 1924 and 1927, marked the end of this phase. Railway workshops were important social, technical, educational and industrial enterprises. A distinctively Australian school of railway engineering, both mechanical and civil, had emerged; and railway engineers dominated engineering professional bodies and engineering education. Rails linked all major centres – and a great many very minor ones as well – to ports, but railways remained colonial rather than national in conception. Interstate links existed, but interstate traffic was sparse and confined to the upper end of the passenger market. Most interstate freight still went by ship, and interstate shipping also remained competitive for passenger traffic.

However, by the 1920s the shape of the future was becoming discernible. Already lightly trafficked rural branch lines began closing. More positively, electrification of suburban railways was a reality in Melbourne from 1919 and from 1926 in Sydney. Commonwealth Railways already had begun operations on its transcontinental railway in 1917 on the standard gauge, and before the end of the decade the Commonwealth would fund a second standard-gauge interstate link – the completion of the direct coastal line from Sydney to Brisbane. So, as the colonially conceived railways reached their maturity, their transformation to focus on long-distance interstate and intense urban traffic was beginning.

Nowhere in Australia has ever excelled Woolloongabba in Brisbane for diversity of transport modes. In 1965 a Queensland Railways PB15 class locomotive was climbing from Woolloongabba locomotive depot up to South Brisbane before taking out a south-side suburban train. The Balmoral tram was a standard 1938 vintage Brisbane City Council four-motor car while the trolley bus was working route 24 crossing the Story bridge. It was one of the first 30 imported from Wolverhampton in England in 1950. Toyota was then a new car maker in Australia and was advertising aggressively, but very few people thought it would have much of an impact, let alone become the dominant force in the Australian motor industry by the end of the century. The Ford Falcon, white with whitewall tyres, represents the family car of choice of the era. (James McCarthy)

Chapter 6

THE MAKING OF CITIES:

URBAN TRANSPORT TO THE 1950s

THE SWORDSMAN RUSHED on horseback past the startled throng and slashed the ribbon, declaring the great bridge across Sydney Harbour open 'on behalf of the respectable citizens of New South Wales'. He was promptly arrested, the ribbon retied, and the premier, with commendable coolness, cut it again, declaring the bridge open, this second time for 'the people of New South Wales'. It was Saturday, 19 March 1932 and the equestrian's gripe was that a member of the royal family should have performed the job. More significantly, though, the crowd was the largest ever assembled in Australia before or since and virtually everyone there travelled by train or tram. The real issue was not royalty, but the far more important if prosaic one of paying for the facilities the vast crowd used that day. Premier JT Lang had presided over a massive investment, roughly £30 million, in Sydney's urban transport, electrifying and rebuilding its railways to increase their capacity, building the city underground railway, and crowning all with the bridge to unite the city. The loans to pay for this had been subscribed in London, their repayment predicated on the increased profits the electrified suburban railways would generate. But the Great Depression and new transport technology had intervened: train traffic was down not up; profits evaporated; unregulated private buses picked the eyes out of the most lucrative urban transport markets.

Regulation of private buses to support railway and tramway profitability had created resentful former bus proprietors, many of whom rushed to join the New Guard, the anti-government paramilitary group of which the horseman, eastern suburbs antique dealer Francis De Groot, was so conspicuous a member. Lang was desperate enough to consider a moratorium on loan repayments which, in the eyes of 'the respectable citizens of New South Wales', was perilously close to default. Six weeks later the governor dismissed the premier because he suspected Lang's measures to meet the financial crisis were illegal.

The real problem was that New South Wales could not afford its 1920s investment in Sydney's urban transport, but nor could it afford not to make that investment as the city's liveability depended on it. The notoriously prickly Lang paid the political price, but the issue was far bigger than Lang. The year 1932 has cast a huge shadow over Sydney's urban transport ever since, and no subsequent government has been willing to make the necessary investments to cope with ongoing growth, so scarified have they been by the fate of the second Lang government.

Moreover, making those investments has become harder since the 1920s. Suburban railways no longer generate the profits to repay investment in them; and, despite all the improvements in productivity, construction costs have risen: £30 million is roughly the equivalent of $6 billion in 2010 values, but today $6 billion would only pay for a fraction of the works completed in the 1920s. How to pay for much needed investment in urban transport for Australia's cities was in 1932 and remains today one of the greatest social, economic and political issues in the land.

PATTERNS OF URBAN GROWTH

UNTIL THE 1850s Australia's cities were small and their transport needs met cheaply by human and animal power. None extended beyond today's central business districts. Many empty lots remained even within Melbourne's central grid. Sydney was denser, and had genuine slums. However, its only urban inhabitants who lived outside the city proper were the rich, whose villas dotted the foreshore east of the city and north of the harbour, and semi-rural areas southwest of the city. Similar villa districts, not quite suburbs but hardly rural, had developed in all Australia's larger cities by the 1850s. The owners of these properties came to the city by private carriage or on horseback. Workers, however, virtually all lived within walking distance of their place of employment. In 1850, the working class suburb did not yet exist in Australia.

At that time cities were the least important they would ever be in Australian history. Sydney had held 51 percent of the colony's population in 1800, but this had fallen to just 28 percent by 1851, when its population was about 50 000. Thereafter its proportion began to increase, reaching 36 percent in 1901, and rising continuously ever since.[1] This unimportance of the city (and in 1851 Sydney was the only real city in Australia) relative to the rest of the country was a product of the domination of the pastoral and whaling industries in the Australian economy in the first half of the 19th century.

All that changed with gold. For, although the goldfields were in the countryside, they stimulated urbanisation enormously. The early goldfields were not that far from the capital cities, especially in Victoria; much of their productivity was spent on urban investment; and they spawned cities of their own. The city most dramatically affected by gold was Melbourne, whose 1851 population of about 20 000 increased by more than 800 percent in a decade to over 170 000 in 1861. Sydney was growing quickly too, but suddenly Melbourne was twice its size. Both cities continued to add population at much the same rate until Melbourne became a city of half a million in 1891. In the last decade of the century, Sydney caught up and, in the first couple of years of the 20th century, overtook Melbourne. By the 1920s their populations had doubled again to about a million, and by the 1950s had reached two million.

Other Australian cities grew rapidly too, Adelaide increasing steadily over the half century between 1851 and 1901 from 20 000 to 160 000. Brisbane and Perth were tiny towns in the 1850s, but each had a growth spurt driven by gold rushes in their respective hinterlands. Brisbane's was in the 1880s, when its population leapt from under 30 000 to over 100 000. Perth's was in the next decade, when it suddenly went from a village of 5000 to a small but busy city of 60 000. Meanwhile, in the 1870s Ballarat was the fourth largest city in Australia. Only Hobart remained stagnant, hardly growing from the days back in the 1840s when it had held Australia's second largest urban population, most of whom were convicts not there by choice.[2]

Thus, the pattern of future urbanisation in Australia was established by 1900. In Sydney and Melbourne there were two large cities, roughly similar in size, of global cultural and economic significance. Next in importance came three provincial capitals, also around the same size each, in Adelaide, Brisbane and Perth (although in 1901 Adelaide was still twice the size of rapidly growing Perth). Finally, there was the rest of Australia, where there were two main types of provincial cities. There were ports, whose growth tended to be stable. Examples include Hobart, Launceston, Portland, Geelong, Newcastle, Mackay, Townsville and Cairns. Then there were fluctuating cities driven by mineral booms in

Brisbane's second Victoria Bridge, opened in 1874, had horse tramlines laid across it in 1885 and is seen here in 1890, when Brisbane was Australia's fastest growing city. (Author collection)

non-ferrous metals such as Ballarat, Bendigo, Broken Hill, Charters Towers and Kalgoorlie. Newcastle was both a port and a mining centre, but its growth was driven by the more mundane mineral of coal, and hence was more measured than that of the flashy gold or silver cities. Some ports later became centres of minerals processing including Newcastle, Wollongong-Port Kembla, Burnie, Whyalla and Port Pirie.

Transport largely determined the patterns of urban growth. Port cities thrived if they had both good navigable water and the best railway route into their hinterlands. If they did not, they stagnated. Thus, Cairns became a city because it had the easiest railway route into the interior of north Queensland, whereas Bowen, Innisfail and Port Douglas stagnated because they did not. The interesting case of Grafton – ambitiously laid out on precisely the same street plan as Melbourne, and with similar expectations for its growth – is slightly different. Like Melbourne, its site was determined by the fact that it was the head of navigation for ocean-going vessels of the

By the early 20th century, Melbourne's Yarra River was already crossed by numerous bridges, much as the more technically challenging Brisbane River would be a century later. The finest was and remains the Princes Bridge, designed by John Grainger, father of composer Percy Grainger, and completed in 1888. Work on the great Flinders Street station, which commenced in 1905, was not yet evident, although the card was sent one hot day in January 1908. (Author postcard collection)

Melbourne and Grafton had similar expectations for their futures, but turned out very differently. Much smaller Grafton could boast a fleet of modern buses by 1938 while Melbourne developed its tram system. Pre-war (right) and post-war versions of Melbourne's drop-centre W class trams cross Collins Street near the terminus of the Elizabeth Street lines in 1972. Above all looms the clock tower of Flinders Street station. (John Forbes and Tony McIlwain)

1830s into a promising pastoral district.

Grafton had a sustained spurt of growth as the leading port of northern New South Wales in the days of bullock carts taking the wool of New England to the coast (roughly from 1840 to 1885), but construction of the railway from Newcastle into the northern interior of New South Wales in the 1880s condemned Grafton to drift into merely local significance as a port. Changing transport technology could determine which cities would grow and which would not, resulting in very different futures for what in the 1840s had been the similar towns of Melbourne and Grafton. Brisbane, with its richer hinterland and better access to the sea, became the leading port city of northern New South Wales, despite Grafton's more propitious beginnings as a centre of commerce rather than a depot for recalcitrant convicts. Separation of Queensland in 1859 added political impetus to Brisbane's growth.

Cities' growth after 1860 was mostly in new suburbs, requiring new transport technologies. Supply of transport created demand for travel (an inversion of classical economic thinking) and with it suburbanisation. Economic growth too was partly driven by transport technology. The relationship between the copper boom of the 1880s and 1890s, electricity, and trams is obvious. Similarly, the shipping, railway and mining industries were all mutually interdependent and acted as stimuli for industrialisation and urbanisation. Ballarat was based on gold but was also the terminus of one of Victoria's first railways. The railway stimulated the industrialisation of the city, which became the major centre of locomotive construction in Australia, mostly at the Phoenix Foundry, where more than 350 locomotives were built between 1873 and 1904. As mining became more industrialised, it too required steam machinery, much of which was built in Ballarat. Thus, the railway sustained the continued growth and industrialisation of what had begun as a mining city. Within the bigger

COBURG
20
ESSENDON
52
SUTTONS
HOTEL
LONDON
AUSTRALIAN WATCHING
30 4061
Made tough for Australia
Olympic TYRES
DUFOR
engine valves
928
283

cities, railway maintenance and manufacturing was also a spur to suburban growth, especially around the railway workshops in Redfern in Sydney and Williamstown (later Newport) in Melbourne. The railway industry was also important for urban and industrial growth in Launceston, Newcastle, Ipswich and Townsville.

WATER TRANSPORT IN AUSTRALIAN CITIES

AS THE CITIES GREW, traditional transport became stretched and inadequate. The development of steam ferries meant the two cities most dependent on water for their transport, Sydney and Brisbane, were able to defer large-scale investment in urban transport. Both cities expanded along their harbour and river frontages. Ferrying passengers around Sydney Harbour by steamboat was significant from the 1830s. Ferries were also part of Melbourne's urban transport scene, connecting Williamstown and the city. This, however, was also the route of one of Victoria's first railways, so Melbourne never developed the intensive ferry services of Sydney and Brisbane.

What did develop uniquely in Melbourne was excursion traffic on Port Phillip Bay. This had its origins in shipping between Melbourne and Geelong, which declined after the railway opened between the two cities in 1857. Owners diverted their vessels into running weekend excursions to destinations around the bay such as Queenscliff and Sorrento, and later built new large steamers especially for the trade. This was how the Manly ferry service developed in Sydney Harbour, but Port Phillip was much larger and the distances too long for commuting. By the time the motor age arrived, the cost of replacing these fine steamers could not be justified and the trade faded into oblivion, but for half a century from the 1880s to the 1930s Port Phillip hosted Australia's finest excursion steamers.[3]

The great growth in ferry transport was in the 1880s. By then Brisbane had a series of ferries crossing the river, privately owned but operated on a lease basis for the City Corporation.[4] Perth, which developed into a city rather later than the eastern capitals, also had a small ferry operation across the Swan River, owned by the state government from 1912. Not quite an urban ferry service, but not really ocean shipping either, were the ferries plying from Fremantle to Rottnest Island. This was, and remains, primarily an excursion trade.

In Sydney a host of new ferry companies was established in the late 1870s and 1880s, beginning with the Port Jackson Steam Boat Company in 1877 and the North Shore Steam Ferry Company in 1878. The former operated the service to Manly. The opening of an irregular steam ferry service from Sydney in 1855 had begun the career of Manly,

isolated by road until 1924, as a Sydney dormitory suburb. Reorganised several times and absorbing its rivals, it became the Port Jackson and Manly Steamship Company in 1917, and operated a fleet of double-ended mini-liners, mostly built by Mort's Dock, although its last three most luxurious vessels were imported from Scotland. Its elegant Brunswick green ferries, adorned with varnished teak upper decks and tall white immaculately painted funnels capped in black, were renowned for their high standards of catering and remarkable speed; they became potent symbols of the city, running every 30 minutes on schedules that have scarcely changed in over a century. Manly's hinterland was developed by a government-built tram system radiating from Manly wharf. The opening of the Spit Bridge in 1924, ending Manly's isolation by road, followed by the introduction of government bus services across this bridge in 1932, marked the beginning of the end of profitability for the Manly ferries, and the service was taken over by the state government in 1974. The service remains, but the cachet of the Port Jackson Company's days has gone.[5]

In the early 20th century Sydney Ferries Limited adorned its ferries in a smart chocolate and ivory livery, later replaced with a more serviceable light green, cream and red. Then as now Mosman Bay enjoyed a service every 30 minutes. The SS (later MV) *Kanangra* was a regular for over 70 years and is now part of the Sydney Heritage Fleet. (Author postcard collection)

The North Shore Ferry Company ultimately absorbed most of the other large Sydney ferry companies (of which the Balmain and Parramatta Companies were the most important), becoming Sydney Ferries Limited in 1900. Many of the inner routes it served were abandoned during the first decades of the 20th century in the face of competition from trams, but the big blow for Sydney Ferries came with the opening of the Harbour Bridge in March 1932. From over 50 million in 1927, patronage fell to 20 million in 1933. The government took over the company in 1951 when it was almost bankrupt.

For most of the 20th century the distinctive Sydney 'inner harbour' ferry (to distinguish them from the outer or Manly ferries) was Sydney Ferries' light green double-ender. Both companies slowly replaced the steam engines in their vessels with diesels between 1930 and 1970. The Parramatta ferry service, which had remained independent, closed in 1943, together with the steam tramway the ferry company had operated since its incorporation in 1888 to connect Parramatta wharf and the town. It was truly the end of an era, because the Sydney to Parramatta boat service had been the first regular public transport in Australia at the end of the 18th century. This also meant the closure of Australia's last steam tramline.[6]

THE ORIGINS OF URBAN PUBLIC TRANSPORT

BACK ON LAND, Australia's cities were primarily walking cities, at least so far as the working person was concerned, until the 1880s. The rich came from their villas to their offices in horse-drawn vehicles with exotic names, landau or brougham, victoria or buggy, depending on their status and needs of the day; although some businessmen remained resolute equestrians, including the man who was the public voice and greatest power-broker of boom-time Melbourne, David Syme, proprietor of *The Age*. In 1881 the English visitor, Richard Twopeny, was struck by 'the extraordinary number of horsemen' in the streets of central Melbourne.[7] Throughout the 19th century, roads and streets in Australian cities were generally poor, deep in mud when wet and dusty when dry. 'Ill-kept', 'wretched', 'muddy' and 'dusty' were the adjectives Twopeny used repeatedly to describe Sydney's streets.[8]

Early macadamised roads were no great success, and the best surfaces were expensive bluestone blocks used to pave some of Melbourne's streets and the hardwood blocks used first in Sydney in 1880, and then elsewhere, including Melbourne and Adelaide. By 1900 both Sydney and Melbourne had laid over 40 hectares of hardwood block roadway.[9] King William

Street was Adelaide's first thoroughfare to be wood-blocked, using Western Australian jarrah, in 1908. The cost was so high and aroused such controversy that there was a minor political and constitutional crisis, with electoral reform mooted as a result of the city council's inability to obtain funds for the scheme. Ultimately the blocks were fitted as part of the rebuilding of the street's tramways for electric traction.[10] Hardwood blocks proved remarkably durable, resilient and effective as a road surface, and blocks were still in place in many Sydney streets well after World War II, and survive in a few places into the 21st century.[11]

Public transport in the streets of Sydney and Melbourne began in the mid-1840s, a time of depression when there were many carriages offered cheaply for sale and many unemployed. The latter found work driving the former for public hire. During the 1850s, the 'jingle' a one-horse, single-axle cart with a pair of seats back-to-back became Melbourne's favoured means of public transport, partly running on fixed routes, partly available for hire, as remains common with small vehicles in

The apogee of the Sydney double-ended ferry was reached with the SS *South Steyne*, built in Scotland in 1938. This postcard was issued by the Port Jackson and Manly Steamship Company to celebrate her entry into service. The artist was probably English and was certainly unfamiliar with Sydney Harbour. There is no lighthouse on North Head and the vessel is steaming in open ocean towards Wollongong. (Author postcard collection) southeast Asia to the present. The jingle was superseded in the 1870s by the six-passenger one-horse wagonette, 'light boxes on wheels, covered with oil-cloth, which can be rolled up in a few seconds if the weather is warm'.[12] Most of the drivers were Irish and fares on regular runs were as low as threepence.[13] This seems to have been the standard urban transport fare, as it also applied on many tram systems and for hansom cabs. As a proportion of earnings, the fare was then about 3 percent of an unskilled worker's daily wage compared with about half that today. In the 1860s the hansom cab, a one-horse enclosed vehicle for private hire, and the horse bus, began replacing the wagonette.

Horse buses varied in size and power from two- to four-horse vehicles, and could carry up to 40 passengers. It was the horse bus which pioneered the concept of the regularly scheduled service into the suburbs and so made possible the commuter. Horse bus companies operated in all of Australia's major cities by the late 1870s. In New South Wales the *Public Vehicle Regulation Act* of 1873 established the Metropolitan Transport Commissioners, whose job it was to supervise road transport. Their records survive, providing an accurate picture of the extent of the horse bus industry in Sydney at least. The Melbourne Omnibus Company, established in 1869, operated Melbourne's horse buses and would later reconstitute itself to take on building the city's cable trams as well. They excited Twopeny's admiration:

> Nowhere do omnibuses drive a more thriving trade than in Melbourne, and they deserve it, for they are fast, clean, roomy, and well managed. The price of labour makes conductors too expensive a luxury, and passengers have to put their fare – in most cases threepence – into a little glass box close to the driver's seat.[14]

Owner-drivers initially operated most horse buses, but there was a rapid tendency to monopoly, especially in Melbourne and Sydney. This was not universal: there were 15 horse bus operators in Brisbane in 1891, but only one of any significance in Sydney. Together with a handful of smaller companies, this inaccurately named Sydney Tramway and Omnibus Company (it never owned or operated a tramway) operated 64 routes in and around Sydney. Many of these routes were virtually identical to the bus routes of more than a century later. Service frequencies also have remained stable to this day, at about every five minutes on the more popular routes down to every 20 minutes for the less important. Horse buses ran to what were then rural localities such as Belmore, Hornsby and Ryde, although generally only a few times a day and they carried mail as well as passengers. There were also extensive horse bus services acting as feeders to suburban railway stations, especially in Melbourne.[15] Horse buses lasted longer than might be expected: there were still 40 in Brisbane in 1919; while in Sydney there were 240 in 1901 but only 12 left in 1920, the last year they appear in the statistics.[16]

TRAMS IN AUSTRALIAN CITIES

HORSE BUSES' DOMINATION of city transport did not last long. Transport technology changed more rapidly in the late 19th century than at any time before or since. The crucial innovation which suddenly made the very large city possible was the humble tram. Except for Melbourne (ironically, because it is the only Australian city to retain a large tram system), whose growth was train-driven, Australia's sprawling suburbs were the handmaidens of the tramline. In a dizzyingly short time, Australia's trams progressed from horse, through steam and cable, to electric traction. Cities large and small, and even some quite small towns, invested in the new technology. Some cities used a mixture of traction or moved from one system to another. Sydney used all four. Australia's first tramway was a horse-powered line from Sydney's inconvenient railway station to Circular Quay along Pitt Street which opened in 1861. Unloved by the NSWGR which reluctantly had built it, it was no great success, because its rails, dangerously for other traffic, were not recessed into the street and because its frequencies could not compete with horse buses. It was pulled up in 1867.

Only two Australian cities developed horse tramways on a significant scale. These were Adelaide, the flattest city in Australia, and, surprisingly, hilly Brisbane. Adelaide was the pioneer of the lasting Australian tram system, with the first horse line opening in King William Street in 1878. Soon there were nine companies operating about a hundred trams across the city and making possible its suburbanisation beyond the parklands ringing the city proper. The lines remained horse-powered until after the city council took them over in 1907 and vested them in its Municipal Tramways Trust, which quickly rebuilt and electrified the entire system from 1908. Adelaide, Australia's first city to have horse trams, was also its last.[17] In provincial South Australia, a horse tram service for holiday-makers began at Victor Harbor in 1894 and was not abandoned until 1954. It was revived in 1986 and still operates, one of the very few in the world.

In Brisbane, the Metropolitan Tramway and Investment Company opened its first horse line from Woolloongabba across the Victoria Bridge spanning the Brisbane River to Breakfast Creek in 1885. This was soon extended, but the company failed in 1893 and its assets were taken over by the British-financed Brisbane Tramways Company. The new owners began electrification and extension of the system from 1897, but in 1922 the company was nationalised, being vested in Brisbane City Council from 1925. In this way, Brisbane's early tramway history closely followed Adelaide's, although the transition to public ownership was more ideological, based on the Queensland Labor Party's faith in nationalisation hardened in a bitter tram strike of 1913.

There were horse tram operations on the fringes of Sydney and Melbourne during the late 19th century, but these were independent from the main tramway systems of those cities. The first horse trams in Melbourne were on a line built by land speculators to entice buyers to the sale of the Fairfield subdivision in 1884. It lasted only six years, and closed when the land boom turned into a crash in 1890. Other similar lines operated beyond the reach of Melbourne's cable trams, most of which survived to be electrified during World War I. In Sydney, there was short-lived use of horse traction on two government lines (at St Peters and Manly) where traffic did not justify the use of steam trams.

The big revolution of around 1880 was the advent of mechanical traction in city streets. Sydney and Melbourne led the way, but adopted very different technologies. In both cases, though, the technology and prototypes came from the USA. Trams returned to Sydney's streets in 1879, although this time broad Elizabeth Street rather than narrow Pitt Street was the chosen thoroughfare. Its aim was to shift the crowds from Sydney's inconvenient railway station on the city's fringe to the International Exhibition in the Domain. Four steam-tram motors, in effect small, enclosed railway locomotives, were imported from Baldwin in Philadelphia, together with some cross-bench trailers. The line was an enormous success and moved huge crowds. Just over two million passengers caught the tram in its first full year of operation. The line was soon extended into a system covering the eastern, southwestern and inner western suburbs, and by 1890 was carrying 60 million passengers a year, worked by a total of 122 steam motors, most built locally.

One of Sydney's first steam trams in Elizabeth Street soon after the line's opening in 1879. The upper level of the double-deck trailers did not last long. The NSWGR then preferred fast loading to stretching capacity. (SRNSW B281477)

Impressive as they were, Sydney's steam trams were dirty, noisy and more than a little dangerous, since they were often real trains of up to three trailers and a motor hurtling down city streets. They were also alarmingly fast at times. Indeed fast running – or 'shooting through like a Bondi tram', as the Sydney saying still current 50 years after the last trams ran puts it – was to remain a characteristic of Sydney trams throughout their life. In 1923 a group of visiting English experts found that Sydney's trams (by then electrified) were the fastest in the British Empire by far. Speeds of up to 80 kilometres an hour were attained on the longish flat stretches in reservation in Oxford Street and out to Randwick and beyond to La Perouse. In contrast to the municipal or privately owned tramways of other colonies, Sydney's trams were built, owned and operated by the NSWGR, and so had a remarkably railway-like quality.

Because of their connection to the NSWGR, wherever possible, the engineers of Sydney's tramways laid the tracks off streets in separate reservations. These reservations included the dramatic descents through deep sandstone cuttings to salt water at Coogee, Bronte, Bondi, Watson's Bay and Balmoral. No other tram system in the world had anything even slightly comparable. In steam days its termini even had stationmasters. Indeed, especially in the city's eastern suburbs, the trams were the cheaper substitute for the railway that was needed but not completed until 1979. The off-road reservations out in the suburbs contrasted with the extremely crowded city streets the trams shared with road traffic in the city centre.

While Sydney relied on its wild and exciting steam motors, at least for the first 20 years of its tramway operations, Melbourne opted for a more sedate and safer system. In 1883 the Victorian parliament authorised the Melbourne Tramway and Omnibus Company to install cable trams and operate them on a 32-year lease. The company's principals included Francis Boardman Clapp, who had spent some time in the United States and whose son would later be Victorian Railways' Chairman of Commissioners. The first line opened along Flinders Street and out to the Yarra River bridge at Richmond in November 1885. Trams were drawn along the streets by a subterranean cable powered by a steam engine at a winding house. The cable moved at a steady 12 miles per hour (20 km/h). By the end of the decade Melbourne had the world's largest network of cable trams, some 72 kilometres in length and carrying about 50 million passengers a year.

One wit observed that in Melbourne's inner northern suburbs trams operated down every street and not a few lanes. Others praised their silence and 'swan-like' motion. Service frequencies were impressive, with trams every minute in the city and every five minutes on the suburban runs. Fares were a penny in the city and threepence out into the suburbs, comparable with Sydney's flat fares of threepence cash or twopence by prepaid ticket and, in terms of spending power, only a little more than today's fares. The cable trams were immensely profitable, returning a dividend in the late 1880s of 20 percent. By 1890 its ten-shilling shares were trading at £9 each, which meant that the stock-market valuation of the company was an absurd £8 500 000, more than four times the cost of the network. The inevitable crash came soon after, and profits fell dramatically too, as many of those who still had jobs chose to walk to work to save their threepence. Tramway workers' wages were cut by a third by 1893, prompting formation of a union and the beginnings of a very long tradition of worker militancy on Melbourne's trams.[18]

In the 1890s Melbourne cable trams looked infinitely more modern than the horse-drawn vehicles which, apart from elegantly attired pedestrians, were then the only other traffic in Collins Street. Fashionable ladies obviously enjoyed a turn of speed in the open cable car where the grip man worked his magic with the levers connecting the tram with the continuous cable beneath the street (Author postcard collection)

Cable trams were effective, but capital costs were high and could only be justified where traffic was dense, as in inner Melbourne. At the time of their introduction, Melbourne was the second city in the world to have a cable tram, after San Francisco, where the first line had opened in 1873. Their great advantage in that city was their ability to climb steep grades, since the trams were quite independent of their motive power. For that reason, San Francisco now has the world's last, as well as having had the world's first, significant cable tram network. Melbourne's cable system, unusually but not uniquely, was

Pitt Street in Sydney has always been synonymous with crowds and there were plenty of people about this busy afternoon around 1908. Paper boys were hawking the news while richer schoolboys posed for photographer Frank Hurley. How many of these boys lay dead in France within a decade? (Frank Hurley, author postcard collection)

built on fairly flat terrain – Denver, Colorado, whose topography and population were generally similar to Melbourne's, also built an extensive cable system. The only other Australian city to use cable trams was, briefly, Sydney where, on the model of San Francisco, two cable lines were built where the terrain was too steep to permit steam operations. These were the North Sydney and Edgecliff lines, opened in 1886 and 1894 respectively.

The real future of tram operation, though, lay in electric traction. Werner von Siemens built the world's first electric tram in Lichterfelde near Berlin in 1881. Eight years later Australia's first electric tramway opened at Doncaster in outer eastern Melbourne. Like the pioneering Melbourne horse tram, it was a land speculator's marketing tool, and closed in 1896. In 1890, the NSWGR Commissioners experimentally electrified a short branch line in the eastern suburbs. They were sufficiently pleased with the results to transfer the equipment to the new line they built beyond the terminus of the North Sydney cable line to Mosman. This opened in 1893, and thus became Australia's first permanent electric line, surviving until the general closures of 1958. Almost simultaneously a short, narrow-gauge electric tramway opened under private ownership in Hobart. This was extended into a modest system with three main lines, acquired by the municipality in 1907. Its defining characteristic was double-deck cars, common in England but rare in Australia. The Hobart system lasted until 1960 and a small system also operated in Launceston from 1911 to 1952.

Electrification of Sydney's main tram network began in 1899 with the building of the George Street electric lines, and was completed by 1908. With electrification came considerable extensions to the network and the building of tramlines along all four of the city's north–south thoroughfares to cope with the density of traffic. Steam trams continued to operate on some peripheral lines, the last government line (from Kogarah to San Souci) closing in 1937. The impact of electrification and continued urbanisation on passenger statistics was dramatic. Patronage more than trebled in the first decade, from 63 to 190 million passengers between 1900 and 1910, and reaching 308 million in 1920. By then the system was basically complete at about 291 kilometres, including the isolated systems in North Sydney, Manly, Enfield, Rockdale and Kogarah.

Sydney's tramways always had a close relationship with its leisure facilities. The two most important of these were Sydney Cricket Ground, served by an extensive network of loops and sidings; and Randwick Racecourse, where there was a tram station capable of moving the largest crowds ever assembling in Australia at that time in 30 minutes. The tram station at Randwick Racecourse had a series of platforms with access by footbridges, and was larger than all but a handful of railway stations in Australia. It remains substantially intact, although now only used by buses serving the comparatively tiny crowds now bothering to go to the track. Weekend traffic to beaches was also enormous.

After 1920, only a few extensions would be built before closures began in 1939. The most important and spectacular of these was opened in 1932 over the Sydney Harbour Bridge and into the terminus at Wynyard in the city, located in a tunnel. On the northern approach to the Harbour Bridge the tram tracks crossed the world's largest trams-only bridge. Approaches to the harbour were always interesting on Sydney's tramways, from the lines through the bush at the Zoo, Watson's Bay and Balmoral; to the counterweight cable car at Balmain; to the amazing Fort Macquarie Depot on what is now the site of Sydney Opera House, the only mock-Tudor, quasi gothic-revival, balustraded and turreted tramshed in the world.

With features like this, Sydney unquestionably possessed the most interesting, varied and spectacular tram system anywhere on the planet. It had no rivals, anywhere. It was, and would remain, the second largest system in the British Empire (after London) and one of the largest in the world. It was also extremely intensively worked, with about 1500 cars in service at any one time when mature. Patronage peaked in 1945 at the extraordinary level of 405 million. Throughout the first half of the 20th century, there was an average of more than one tram journey per day made by every man and woman, infant and child in the city. It is doubtful if any city in the world used its trams with more enthusiasm than Sydney.

It was a similar story on a smaller scale in Brisbane, which also had a very efficient and massively patronised electric tram system. Its mileage peaked as late as 1952 at 68 (109 km) and ridership in the same year as Sydney at 160 million in 1944–45. For a city of half a million people, this was a remarkable figure. Following the successful introduction of electric trams in Sydney and Hobart in 1893, and then Brisbane in 1897, most Australian cities turned to this technology.

The two Victorian goldfields cities of Ballarat and Bendigo had begun tram operations in 1887 and 1890 respectively. Ballarat used conventional horse trams, but Bendigo experimented with battery-powered electric trams. The company collapsed after a year and the tramway was sold to new owners who ordered steam motors like those operating in Sydney from Baldwin. These at least were reliable, but the 1890s depression affected revenue and it was sold again in 1899 to the British-based Electric Supply Company of Victoria. It completed electrification of the line and extended it into a modest but efficient system of 15 kilometres. It then took over the Ballarat horse tramways, which it also electrified in 1905 and extended into a 22-kilometre system. Finally it built a smaller system in Geelong, which opened in 1912. The State Electricity Commission of Victoria took over the three systems in 1934 when it acquired the electricity generation business. It kept the unprofitable provincial tramways operating with some reluctance, buying secondhand Adelaide and Melbourne trams to improve services but always wanting to abandon them as soon as possible. Geelong was the first to go in 1956, but spirited public opposition and affection for the trams in Bendigo and Ballarat (and the fact that both are very fickle marginal political seats, which no government dare alienate) meant they kept their trams until 1971 and 1972 respectively. They survived long enough for significant proportions to be retained for heritage purposes which in Bendigo includes the depot and main line through the heart of the city.

Across the continent, tramway development began later in Western Australia and in Perth electric traction was used from the beginning. A British company, Perth Electric Tramways Limited, opened the first line in 1899. By 1913, when it was nationalised and put under the control of the Government Railways, this had become

The end of the line for Ballarat's quaint trams in the winter of 1971. The conductor will not have to swing the trolley pole around the old four-wheel car at each terminus for much longer. (Tony McIlwain)

a 37-kilometre system. Passenger numbers rose from 11 million in 1915–16 to 35 million in 1933, and trackage peaked in 1941 at 68 kilometres. Meanwhile, separate systems were built in Fremantle, Kalgoorlie and in the tiny mining town of Leonora, in the outback 240 kilometres northwest of Kalgoorlie. In Fremantle, the Fremantle Municipal Tramways and Electric Lighting Board, formed on local municipal initiative, undertook both electricity generation and tramway construction. The system opened in 1905 and 1906, with patronage peaking at 9 million in 1943. However, the tramways were only occasionally profitable after 1930, and when the State Electricity Commission took over the city's power supply in 1952 it promptly closed the system, without much public protest.

Out in the eastern goldfields were Australia's most isolated tramways. Kalgoorlie had a lavish electric tramway, as befitted a gold rush town with ambitions. The Kalgoorlie Electric Tramways Limited opened its first line

Perth was a small but growing city in the first few years of the 20th century. The new trams of Perth Electric Tramways Limited share Hay Street with horse-drawn carts and the very latest thing, a motor car. (Author postcard collection)

in 1902 and two years later had extended it into a system some 14 kilometres long linking Kalgoorlie and the nearby mining town of Boulder. Even before completion, though, the company sold some of its larger cars to Perth because its ambitions outran the traffic on offer. The system limped on under private ownership until 1949 when the Eastern Goldfields Transport Board acquired it. In an unlikely twist of events, Kalgoorlie had Australia's last privately owned tram system. The Transport Board, though, ran only peak-hour and miners' special services, and closed the system in 1952.

For eight years from 1908, the tiny town of Leonora was graced by a short electric tramline worked with just one car. It was rough operating a tram in the outback, and the greatest hazards were not always natural: in 1911 some boys placed four plugs of gelignite on the tracks to see what might happen. The tram only just survived its brush with high explosives, only to close when the power station burned down in 1916. A converted truck ran along the tracks to provide a desultory service for another five years after that, ending the bizarre career of the Leonora tram.

In 1905 places as diverse as Ballarat, Launceston and Kalgoorlie might have had electric trams, but Australia's second largest city and temporary national capital, Melbourne, did not. This was because cable trams, even though obsolete by then, continued to do their job so well. Melbourne's two first permanent electric lines opened from the cable tram terminus at Alexander Bridge into the northwestern suburbs in 1906, built by a British company, the North Melbourne Electric Tramway and Lighting Company. In the same year, Victorian Railways opened what it described as an 'electric street railway' from St Kilda station along Port Phillip Bay to Brighton.

Melbourne's first electric trams set the precedent for a large number of electric tramways built over the following 20 or so years, all connecting with the cable trams' outer termini and taking tramlines into a new ring of suburbs. All except the first two were built and operated by local municipal tramways trusts. There were four of these trusts, all owned by groups of local councils. There were the Prahran and Malvern Tramways Trust; the Hawthorn Tramways Trust; the Fitzroy, Northcote and Preston Tramways Trust; and the Melbourne, Brunswick and Coburg Tramways Trust. The two remaining horse tramways were electrified in 1915 and 1916. Except for the Hawthorn Tramways Trust's line built through unremunerative parkland to its terminus on the edge of the city at Princes Bridge, none of these trust lines was able to penetrate the dense cable network and approach the city centre.

Thus, central Melbourne remained the preserve of the cable trams until after the amalgamation of all Melbourne's tramlines (except the VR line south from St Kilda) under the Melbourne and Metropolitan Tramways Board (M&MTB) in 1920. This immediately became Australia's second largest tramway operator after the NSWGR's tramway division, although the M&MTB, initially at least, was a far from unified system, since it comprised a core of cable routes with five unconnected electric systems on its fringes. The cable trams had passed into the hands of the state government in 1916, when the company's 32-year concession had expired, and the creation of the M&MTB was the government's way of managing its new acquisition.

Steam trams may have been obsolete by the early 20th century, but they were cheap and simple. For this reason the NSWGR built steam-tram systems in three New South Wales provincial cities, Newcastle (1887), Broken Hill (1902) and Maitland (1909). Electrification of the Sydney system meant that rolling stock essentially was free. Broken Hill was (apart from Leonora) the most isolated tram system in the country. All its equipment had to be shipped from

Sydney to Port Pirie and then conveyed on rail freight wagons to Broken Hill. The Broken Hill and Maitland systems closed in 1926, unable to compete with motor buses.

Newcastle's was more robust and survived to be electrified progressively from 1923, although its steam extremities closed in 1930 without ever having wires strung over their tracks. Ultimately, all of Newcastle's 38-kilometre system closed by 1950. While the mighty and profitable NSWGR could afford to flirt with loss-making provincial tramways to satisfy its political masters, the same was not true of the other provincial operator of steam trams, Rockhampton City Council. In 1908 it bravely ordered four steam-powered four-wheel units from Valentin Purrey in Bordeaux. This was new technology at the time – and French at that – and Rockhampton was one of very few cities anywhere to make it work. Operations began in 1909 and lasted for 30 years, continually under municipal ownership. One of the trams, the last of its type in the world, survives at Rockhampton's Archer Park Station Museum.

AUSTRALIAN ELECTRIC TRAMCAR DESIGN

IN THE PERIOD from 1900 to 1935, there developed a distinctively Australia school of tramcar design. Early trams were imported mostly from the USA, with a few coming from England (mainly in Tasmania). Most early cars followed American precedents, and the California combination car was the most widely used design. This was a half-open, half-saloon car, a design appropriate to the Australian and Californian climates. The first cars were four-wheelers, but by 1900 eight-wheel bogie cars were more common. While some Australian systems continued to follow American tramcar design development, and build enclosed bogie saloon cars with doors at each end of the type almost universal in North American cities by about 1910, the larger Australian systems soon went their own way.

In Sydney, local development centred on the cross-bench, side-loading car, commonly (and not always affectionately) called the toastrack tram. This design was used for excursion traffic in many cities around the world, especially those with warmer climates, but only in Sydney and Rio de Janeiro (among the world's more substantial tram systems) did it become the standard tramcar type. The reason was simple – no other design accommodated so many seated passengers or

Hobart was the only Australian city to operate double-deck trams for a long period. Max Dupain was unable to resist the temptation to photograph such an oddity when he visited Hobart in 1947. (Max Dupain, NAA Series A1200 Item L9532)

could load and unload them more quickly; and Sydney's was a spectacularly crowded tramway system. Fortunately for Sydney's tram passengers, the climate is relatively warm for eight months of the years, because passengers in toastrack trams were always more-or-less exposed to the elements. The idea of the toastrack tram came from the first steam-tram trailers imported from Philadelphia in 1879, whose lower deck had this design. Early toastrack electric trams were four-wheelers, but in 1901 the first of the 96 seventy-passenger N class cars was delivered; followed in 1907 by the first of no fewer than 626 eighty-passenger O class cars; and in 1921 by the first of 258 P class cars. The O class was the most numerous class of tram in Australia – and one of the most numerous in the world – and throughout the 1910–60 period was a true Sydney icon.

Melbourne, Brisbane and Adelaide, where the pressure of numbers was not so great, all developed versions of the drop-centre bogie car during the 1920s. This featured two enclosed saloons (with the luxury of padded seats in the southern cities, although not in sticky Brisbane) above the bogies at each end, with a lower section with open doors and more austere seating in the centre. This accommodated smokers and short-distance travellers, and the drop in the centre meant that passengers did not need to climb flights of steps to enter the car. The M&MTB's W class design, first introduced in 1923, was the classic of the genre, conceived to replace the mass of diverse designs the M&MTB inherited from its constituent parts. The most numerous was the W2 design, first built in 1927,

Sydney toastrack and corridor trams at Neutral Bay Wharf in 1956. This line, with its steep grades, was the last regular haunt of four-wheel trams like K class car 1296. The R1 class car behind was new but destined for a short life. On the left is a glimpse of the Port Jackson and Manly Steamship Company's workshop. (Noel Reed)

which lasted in service for 60 years. The W series as a whole (variants W1 through to W7) numbered nearly 800 units, built between 1923 and 1956. The post-war cars featured such refinements as all-padded seats and automatic doors. Later examples are still in service in Melbourne.

Brisbane, like Melbourne, became a unified system in the early 1920s and immediately developed its own drop-centre car, the 400 series, a more open, tropical version of the type, sultrily flaunting its toastrack heritage in its open drop-centre section. The first was built in 1923, the same year as the first Melbourne W class. This was superseded in 1938 by the streamlined FM car, which at last brought padded seats to the northern capital. Adelaide introduced its F type drop-centre car in the early 1920s, although reverted to the American saloon design for its last series, the H class of 1929, introduced specifically for the Glenelg line which was converted from railway to tramway operation at that time.

While Perth and Hobart continued to build American-type saloon cars, and Hobart even kept its English-style double-deck cars, the triumph of the drop-centre design was confirmed when Sydney joined the ranks of their operators in 1933. Although not used on the busiest services, Sydney's new R class cars were much more comfortable than their toastrack predecessors. Coming later than the Ws, 400s and Fs on which they were based, they were also more sophisticated and had high standards of design aesthetics. It is doubtful that a more beautiful tram than a Sydney R class ever has been built. A total of 195 were delivered during 1933–35, their sleek lines and comfort symbolising the city's determination to rid itself of the Depression. How could anyone be depressed riding in an R car? A further 155 were built to the slightly modified R1 design (with a truncated central drop section but more padded seats) in two batches up to 1953.

THE DECLINE OF AUSTRALIA'S TRAMWAYS

AUSTRALIA'S TRAMWAYS were nurturing the seeds of decay and death even as they reached their zenith. As early as the 1920s, serious threats were emerging. Trams never had a monopoly on urban transport. Horse buses had been able to compete effectively with trams in Sydney and Brisbane, and in Melbourne suburban railways always competed for the same passengers. The NSWGR even briefly experimented with steam buses itself, and during 1905 and 1906 ran two steam bus services, most importantly from Darlinghurst to Potts Point through King's Cross, already the most densely populated part of Australia. However, during the 1920s, a new threat emerged. This was not yet the private car, but the privately owned motor bus.

Kalgoorlie's tram depot with crews in 1947.
(J Fitzpatrick, NAA Series A1200 Item L8386)

In most Australian cities, buses did not compete directly with trams, because the bodies responsible for regulating city transport also operated the trams. The great exception was Sydney, where the NSWGR owned the trams. Here, private bus competition was unregulated and exploded in the 1920s. In 1915 there were just 15 motor buses in Sydney, rising to 149 in 1920 and 612 in 1929.[19] There were almost half as many private buses as there were tramcars. These buses competed overtly with trams, often running just ahead of them to poach their passengers. What was especially galling for the NSWGR was the fact that it was paying for the maintenance of the road surface between tramlines; and in much of suburban Sydney that meant the entire paved section of roads. So the competing buses were running on roads maintained by the tramway operator.

In Melbourne, the situation was more positive. The M&MTB began a gradual process of closing the cable tram system and replacing it with electric tramways. These extended the former municipal trust and private lines into the city, eliminating the need for longer-distance Melbourne tram passengers to change at the interfaces of the cable and electric networks. First to be converted were the Swanston Street and Flinders Street lines in 1926 and 1927 respectively. The process continued through the 1920s and 1930s until the last cable lines, in Bourke Street and running into the northern suburbs, closed in 1940. In each case the former cable lines were lifted and new electric lines were laid set in concrete. This meant that, during the late 1920s and 1930s, Melbourne's entire inner-city tram network was completely renewed. The exception was the Bourke Street cable lines, which were not replaced with electric trams but with buses. This was not the result of deliberate policy, but was caused by wartime steel shortages.

Meanwhile, all Australian states had seen the creation of motorists' associations by the 1920s. A national motorists' body, the National Roads Association, was established in Sydney in 1920, but was unable to operate effectively throughout Australia. In 1923 it was reconstituted as the National Roads and Motorists' Association (NRMA) which, despite its name, only operated in New South Wales. It was a lobby group from the beginning, a function which the older Royal Automobile Clubs of Victoria and Queensland (RACV and RACQ, established in 1903 and 1905 respectively) also embraced. These organisations were hostile to trams, and urged governments to replace trams with buses at every opportunity. Illogically, they portrayed trams as the prime cause of congestion, rather than as the only means of moving sufficiently large numbers of people along streets to assuage congestion. It was certainly true that there was severe tram congestion in Sydney, but this was because more people were using the trams than the system could handle. In Elizabeth Street, trams ran at an average frequency of every 19 seconds in the 1930s, and most services were operated by coupled pairs of toastrack cars seating a total of 160 passengers. King Street, operated by modern R class cars after 1934, was almost as busy. The assertion that buses could reduce congestion on this scale was ludicrous, but frequently made. The only solution was the construction of a railway (or two) into the eastern suburbs.

The crisis in Sydney came to a head during the second tumultuous premiership of John Thomas Lang. He was determined to smash the private bus operators to restore tramway finances. This he did very effectively by legislation, but there were political and administrative prices to pay. Politically, the bus operators were the backbone of the New Guard, which agitated against Lang's government; administratively, Lang had to separate the tramways from the NSWGR in 1930. After a series of transient managements, the trams came under the control of a Department of Road Transport and Tramways in 1933, the Department of Government Transport (DGT) from 1952. This organisation was not exactly hostile to trams – after all it ordered the R class immediately it was created – but its focus was rather different from the old NSWGR management: the trams had lost their railway ally. Thereafter, the NSWGR strongly supported completing Bradfield's Eastern Suburbs Railway, which it believed would win the enormous tram revenue of that area back into its coffers. Meanwhile, the government's first bus services began late in 1932, linking St Leonard's station and Manly Wharf. It was soon supplementing tram services with a range of motor bus operations, especially in the eastern suburbs.

The new technology of the trolley bus also attracted the interest of the new department. This was a vehicle with the electrics of a tram but the body and suspension of a bus. The 1930s were the decade of the trolley bus craze in England, where many tramway systems were replaced by trolley buses. These used the power generation and distribution systems of the tramways they replaced, and also enabled tramway maintenance skills to be used. They were a compromise between retention and abandonment of tram systems. Australia's first trolley buses began operating in East Perth in October 1933 and Sydney's first operation opened in January 1934. This was from Sydney Town Hall to King's Cross and Potts Point in the city's eastern suburbs, effectively duplicating and relieving pressure on the over-patronised King Street and William Street tram services. Part of the route also followed the experimental steam bus route of 1905. It also served Australia's first suburbs of residential flat buildings, as the elegant mansions of the 1830s were demolished to make way for what was for Australia the radical innovation of apartment living.

The pioneering lines in Perth and Sydney soon were followed by others in Adelaide, Hobart and Launceston. In Tasmania the trolley buses supplemented rather than replaced tram services. In Adelaide the city and Port Adelaide had separate, unconnected tram systems. But in 1935 trolley buses replaced trams in Port Adelaide, and began running through to Adelaide itself. This was the first general closure of a tramway system in Australia. Brisbane came to the trolley bus party rather late in the day. Not until 1951 did its first trolley bus line open, once again supplementing rather than replacing trams. Trolley buses never operated in Melbourne. In 1937 the last government steam tramline in Sydney, from Kogarah station to Sans Souci on Botany Bay, was replaced by trolley buses. Planned as the first such substitution, it turned out to be the last as well as the first. Trolley bus operations received a fillip from a most unusual source in 1937, when Leyland in England built 70 trolley buses for Canton (or Guangzhou), China. The Sino-Japanese War prevented their delivery and they were offered to Australian buyers at bargain prices. 'Cantons', as they were known, went to Adelaide, Perth and Hobart.

The trolley bus craze was short-lived, in Australia as in England. Sydney, where the expectations of trolley buses had been the highest, soon found that diesel buses could do much the same job more effectively and cheaper. The Potts Point line was closed in 1948 (12 years before the trams they were supposed to replace), and the Sans Souci lines in 1959. Adelaide lost its trolley buses soon after, while they lingered in the Tasmanian cities until 1968 and in Perth and Brisbane until 1969.

The second general closure of electric tramways in Australia (after Port Adelaide) occurred in Sydney in September 1939, when the entire Manly system was closed. It reopened in 1941, when wartime fuel shortages began to bite, but it was only a reprieve. The larger Australian cities all commissioned overseas consultants to report on their transport problems in the post-war period. Their function was to justify tram closures in the face of popular opposition. Few policy decisions in Australian history have been as ill-considered, venal or irrational. Sydney was first off the mark with the Sinclair report of 1948, which recommended the closure of the entire tram system. NSWDGT Commissioner Alfred Arthur Shoebridge favoured a policy of closing outer tramlines and replacing them with a more diffused bus network with one-man crews, but retaining an inner core on dense routes. He was overruled politically, so presided over the destruction of one of the world's greatest transport systems.

Shoebridge's consolidation policy saw the closure in the late 1940s and early 1950s of the isolated networks (except for the North Sydney lines) and some of the longer, less densely used lines of the main system. More positively, deliveries of R1

class cars continued and some of the main lines, especially in the eastern suburbs and north shore, were re-laid in mass concrete roadways. Thus, in parts at least, Sydney's tramways were being modernised just as their political masters, under pressure from the NRMA, were preparing to close them. It is a paradox that tramways often are regarded as a poor man's form of transport, but that the most heavily used lines in both Sydney and Melbourne have been in places like Mosman, Woollahra, Rose Bay and Coogee; Toorak, Kew and South Yarra – the richest suburbs in Australia. Indeed the first significant public protests at an Australian tram closure occurred in 1950 when the line through Vaucluse to Watson's Bay – two of the most expensive places to buy a house in the entire country – was converted to bus operation. So intense were these protests that the line was reopened after six months.

World War II did not have much impact on Australians' mobility in its first year and Sydney's Kings Cross was as busy as ever. Cars and taxis, some new all-metal vehicles, others showing their age, jostle for space with two new R1 class corridor trams and an electric trolley bus headed out to Sydney's 'flatland' of Potts Point. In 1940 these were the most modern urban street transport in Australia. (Author postcard collection)

Hats and gloves were still *de rigueur* for ladies going into town in Brisbane in January 1962. The passengers boarding the four-motor tram in Queen Street included the author, the nine-year-old blond boy with his family. (Stuart Lee, author collection)

Fortitude Valley in Brisbane was a busy place in peak hour in 1951. The sheer numbers of tram passengers were the big issue. While the roads look congested, in fact one tram could easily accommodate every person in every motor vehicle in this picture. On the left are examples of the two main types of drop centre cars used in Brisbane, the 1923 vintage 400 series on the extreme left and then one of the FM (four-motor) series introduced in 1938. (John Oxley Library 64409r)

It was a final flutter for the tram system, however, especially since the New South Wales Premier, John Joseph (Joe) Cahill, was no friend of the trams. General closures took place in stages between 1957 and 1961. The Pitt and Castlereagh Street lines closed first. The overhead was removed immediately after the last tram passed, and the tracks were tarred over the next morning, to prevent a reintroduction of tram services if the replacement bus services were a failure. There were no great difficulties on this occasion, as the southwestern lines they carried passed through the narrow confines of King Street, Newtown, and were far from Sydney's busiest. It was a different story when the next major closure occurred – of the North Sydney lines including the Harbour Bridge in June 1958. There was chaos and the beginnings of the north shore traffic snarl that lasted until the opening of the Warringah Freeway ten years later. The western (George Street) lines closed in November 1958 and the busiest of all, the eastern lines, in three stages in 1960 and 1961. Sydney's last trams – to Maroubra Beach and La Perouse – ran on 25 February 1961.

It was a similar story in Brisbane. Once again it was a Labor government which drove the policy, in this case the Brisbane City Council under Lord Mayor Clem Jones. Jones' vision was of a city where every working man could own a car. The trams, with their reliable and regular ten-minutely services throughout the inner suburbs, were an obstacle to this vision. However, much of Brisbane's tram trackage had been set in concrete during the 1950s, and its fleet was comparatively modern. Virtually all off-peak services were handled by the modern FM cars, all built since 1938, supplemented in peak hours by older drop-centre cars dating from 1923. Conveniently for Jones' plans, Brisbane's Paddington tram depot burnt to the ground in September 1962, destroying 65 trams and providing the excuse for the closure of four routes that Christmas. No-one was ever charged with arson and the truth about the fire remains a matter of speculation. The tramway workshops built eight new trams in 1963 and 1964 using parts recovered from the fire. These were the 'Phoenix' cars; arisen from the ashes; Australia's last new trams for 20 years; and the last of the classic distinctively Australian drop-centre design ever built.

The Phoenix cars, though, were at best a symbol of defiance, and Jones got what he wanted in 1965 when a group of North American consultants recommended closure of the tram system, a major reduction in train services, and the construction of freeways. Queensland government funding for roads in the city was made contingent on the closure of the tramways, so a new Victoria Bridge, linking Brisbane and South Brisbane, was designed without tramlines, and this sealed the system's fate. The Victoria Bridge, over which Brisbane's first horse tramway had been laid back in 1885, was at the heart

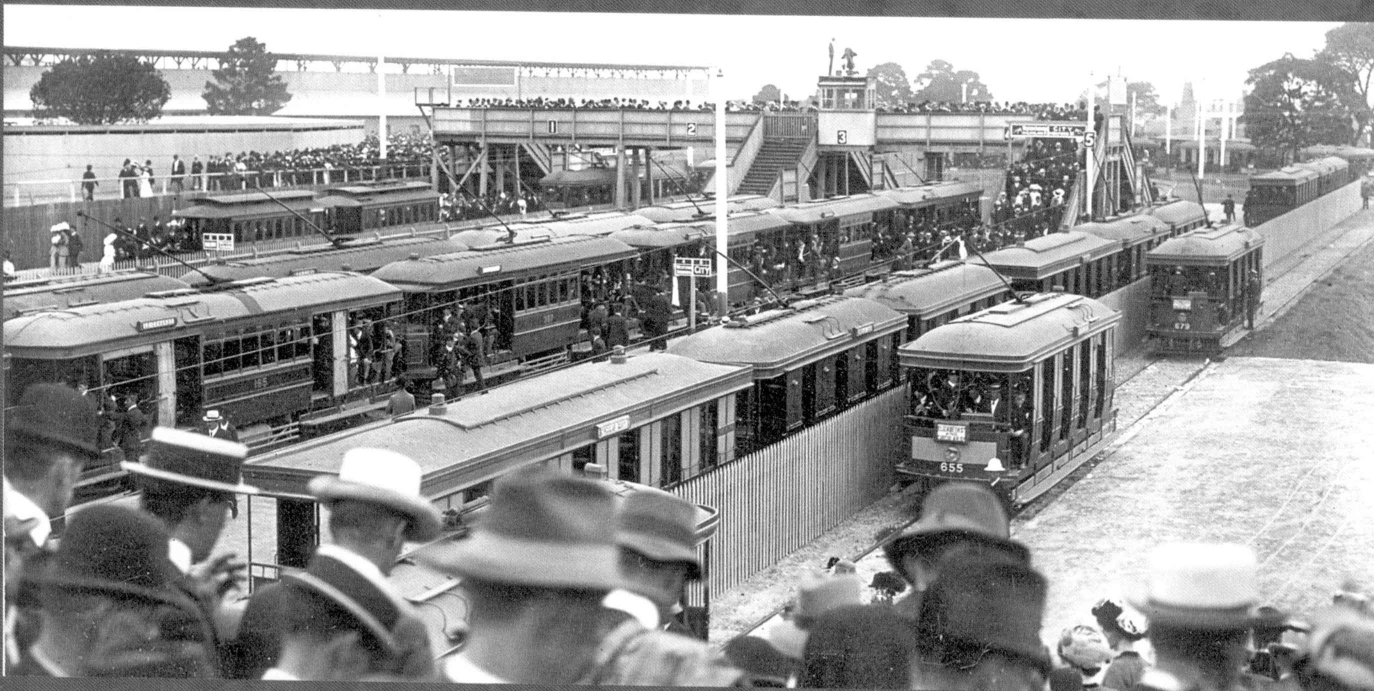

SYDNEY'S EXTRAORDINARY TRAMWAYS

Sydney's tram system was one of the wonders of the world, deeply embedded in the city's collective consciousness. Patrick White once reflected in London that among the few things which defined Australia in his memory were 'the ham sandwiches of the New South Wales Railways' and 'the maze of tram tracks behind Circular Quay'. This (right below) was what he recalled and celebrated, the magnificent sight of one of the world's densest concentrations of tram movements, as it was when Paddy was a boy in the 1920s. O class cars, of which there were then over 600 in service, dominated the scene. (Ian Dunn collection)

While Circular Quay was the system's hub, tram traffic to leisure facilities was always dense. Punters head home from Randwick Racecourse's extraordinary tram station about 1908 (above). Former steam-tram trailers are towed by pairs of electric E class trams on the second track from the photographer. On the next track are examples of the L class California combination cars. This enormous traffic would be more efficiently handled by train. It was true of the area around Randwick Racecourse and the University of New South Wales in 1910 and it is even truer a century later. With typical lassitude, no New South Wales government has yet got around to building the much-needed railway, despite planning and announcing one every decade or so. (Ian Dunn collection)

Built for the electrification of the western suburbs lines and the new electric line along George Street opened in 1899, Fort Macquarie Tram Depot on Bennelong Point (right above) was designed in mock-Tudor style to recall the fort previously on the site, now occupied by the Sydney Opera House. This view dates from the 1920s. (SRNSW B281283)

MANLY
BEACH.

of the system. All Brisbane's remaining tram and trolley bus routes were closed in 1968 and 1969. Closures were preceded by service reductions, in a fraudulent attempt to demonstrate that the replacement bus services were better. Despite this, there were citywide protests and a campaign against closure funded by public donation, products of a fruitless enthusiasm for retaining the trams. The era of people power had not yet come: rulers ruled, trams went.

Events turned out very differently in Melbourne, largely because of the strong leadership provided by M&MTB Chairman from 1949 to 1970, Sir Robert Risson. Melbourne lacked the difficult topography of Sydney and Brisbane, which meant its tramway system, while not as spectacular, was easier to operate. Melbourne's wide, straight streets helped tram operations, which in many cases effectively could be separated from motor traffic. This meant that buses, with their need to move in and out of the curb, often would hinder car traffic more than trams. Melbourne also had set nearly all its tramlines in concrete when the cable trams were replaced, and nearly all its trams in the 1950s were relatively modern enclosed drop-centre cars of the various W classes. It is true that Brisbane shared many of these characteristics, and that even Sydney was on the way to renewing its tramways at the same time. In Risson, though, Melbourne's trams had a strong, intelligent and passionate defender.

Risson argued that a tram would always attract greater patronage than a bus on the

Melbourne's Princes Bridge station in 1886 with a typical suburban train of the period. The tracks on the left lead to the adjacent Flinders Street station. (Freedman collection)

same route. He was right, and proved the point when he restored trams to Bourke Street in 1956. This was the year before Sydney's first big closure, yet Risson secured funding for the rebuilding of a significant part of the Melbourne system as an Olympics project. The buses (which had operated since the last cable tram had run in 1940) were replaced by Risson's new W6 and W7 trams, to the delight of their passengers but to the excoriation of sections of the press and the RACV. It was a decisive blow in favour of continuity of tram operation in Melbourne, and the system never has been seriously threatened since. The only significant closures of Melbourne tramlines were three short lines in Footscray, abandoned in 1962.

In the smaller cities, policy followed Sydney and Brisbane, although it was difficult to justify continued tram operation in Perth, with many single-track routes needing duplication and rebuilding to cope with modern traffic conditions. In Adelaide, with its wide streets and good fleet, bus replacement was less easily justified, but it was largely uncontested. Adelaide had a shortage of trams in the 1950s. Since new buses were cheaper than trams and traffic was nowhere near as intense as in Sydney, Brisbane and Melbourne, tramway abandonment was relatively uncontroversial. Adelaide also kept its newest trams and its fastest and most efficient tramline, which had been converted from the railway to Glenelg in 1929. Its retention meant that Adelaide's tramway closures did not provoke the enduring bitterness, even hatred, towards the perpetrators common in Sydney and even more in Brisbane, where the trams lasted long enough for people to be acutely aware of the value of what was being taken from them. Adelaide's and Perth's last trams (except for the Glenelg line) both ran in 1958.

BUILDING AUSTRALIA'S SUBURBAN RAILWAYS

AUSTRALIA'S FIRST STEAM railway was a suburban line, running trains every half hour from Melbourne to Port Melbourne from the day of its opening in 1854. Half-hourly train services have been part of Australian suburban life ever since. Although Sydney's first railway opened to Parramatta a year later, it was a very different sort of an enterprise, striking into the interior of a continent, and envisaged no suburban traffic. Its trains ran only four times a day and its Sydney station was sufficiently far from the city centre to be useless for commuter traffic. This pattern would continue until the 1890s. In Melbourne, an extensive suburban system, mostly in private hands, would be built over the next 40 years. In Sydney the first purely suburban railway from Sydenham to Belmore would not be built until as late as 1896, and the city's station would remain on its fringe, a tram, cab or bus ride away from where most potential passengers worked, until as late as 1926.

By 1861 four private companies had built separate lines out of Melbourne into its suburbs, using three separate city termini – Flinders Street (for the Brighton and St Kilda lines); Princes Bridge (for the Richmond, Hawthorn and Prahran lines) and Spencer Street (for the Williamstown and Essendon lines). The Spencer Street lines were soon nationalised, while the other two were amalgamated in 1865 as the Melbourne and Hobson's Bay United Railway Company (M&HBURCo), whose network ultimately comprised five lines from Melbourne to Port Melbourne, St Kilda, Hawthorn and Brighton Beach. The M&HBURCo's two city termini were convenient to the business heart of Melbourne. It also enjoyed flat terrain over which to build its lines cheaply so was a successful enterprise, returning a steady 7.5 percent. Ultimately, though, its directors decided to sell the company to the colonial government, but the company was in sufficiently good shape for it to indulge in protracted haggling over the price. Eventually it was transferred on 1 July 1878.

The 1880s saw an orgy of railway building in Melbourne's eastern suburbs, whose system reached its peak in 1891. Some lines were speculative. One railway was traversed by just one train before closure, and the greatest symbol of the entire wasteful orgy was the extraordinary Outer Circle line to Oakleigh. This was completed in 1890 to a scheme predating the government's purchase of the M&HBURCo. When first mooted it would have the advantage of connecting VR's isolated Gippsland line to the rest of the government's railways, but by the time it was built it was completely useless, meandering through Melbourne's northeastern suburbs contrary to all the flows of traffic. Services ceased after just three years. While some of the 1880s investment in suburban railways around Melbourne was wasteful, even corrupt, most of it was useful and the network laid down, even if ahead of its time, has meant that the city has had a good radial suburban railway system, bringing quite remote suburbs close to the city. Equally useful was the connection on viaducts between the two city termini of Flinders Street and Spencer Street, opened in 1891. Princes Bridge and Flinders Street had been connected back in the days of the M&HBURCo.[20]

Meanwhile in Sydney, there was only very slow growth of suburban services along the main line to Parramatta, as places like Stanmore and Burwood became suburbs of substantial villas. By 1880 Sydney at last had a half-hourly service along the main line as far as Homebush, some 8 miles (13 km) from the inconveniently located Sydney station. The North Shore line (opening to the harbour side at Milson's Point in 1893) conveyed significant suburban traffic from the beginning, but was only built because parliament thought it would be a shorter route for country produce from the north to Sydney Harbour, a role it never fulfilled. Up until the 1880s train fares were expensive and rail commuting was the preserve of the middle class. The first workmen's weekly tickets were introduced in Sydney in 1881 and in Melbourne in 1882, and suddenly the second class compartments of suburban trains became crowded with the kind of people who had never before been able to travel such long distances to work. It was a spur to further suburbanisation and marked the beginnings of the Australian phenomenon of suburban sprawl.

By the early 1880s the wealth of Melbourne was concentrated in its suburbs, where there were thousands of large houses and tens of thousands of comfortable villas. After describing the affluence of these suburbs, which was on a scale unknown in England, one perceptive visitor discussed the importance of the railways built by the M&HBURCo to their development:

> All these suburbs are connected with the town by railway. A quarter of an hour will bring you ten miles to Brighton, and twelve minutes will take you to St Kilda, the most fashionable watering place. Within ten minutes by rail are the inland suburbs, Toorak, South Yarra and Kew, all three very fashionable; Balaklava, Elsternwick and Windsor, outgrowths of St Kilda, also fashionable; Hawthorn, which is budding well; Richmond, adjacent to East Melbourne, and middle class; and Emerald Hill and Albert Park with a working class population. Adjoining the city itself are North Melbourne, Fitzroy, Carlton, Hotham and East Melbourne, all except the last inhabited by the working classes ... Nearly everybody who can lives in the suburbs, and the excellence of the railway system enables them to extend much farther away from the city than in Adelaide or Sydney.[21]

Train services were nowhere near as good on the main lines near Sydney, except to Homebush. For instance, when the railway opened from Strathfield to Hornsby in 1884, which would be very much a suburban line at a similar distance from Melbourne, it rejoiced in just two trains a day. In short, Melbourne was a train city and Sydney was a tram city, the exact reverse of the situation a century later. Part of the reason was the poor location of Sydney's station, and there were repeated attempts in the second half of the 19th century to build a new terminal somewhere closer to the city.

Sydney and Melbourne were the two Australian cities where the relationship between railway construction policy and urbanisation was clearest. However, railways also had an impact on the process of urbanisation (and suburbanisation) in smaller cities. Even cities as small as Perth and Hobart have had their patterns of growth affected by railways: in Perth, suburban development ran along the axis from Fremantle to Guilford, the route of the eastern railway into the interior; while in Hobart there was similar ribbon development along the route of the Tasmanian Mainline Railway north of the city parallel to the Derwent. Brisbane is an interesting case, for railways were late coming to the city but important in determining its shape. The first railway in Brisbane was not opened until 1875, fully ten years after the first Queensland line had opened in the interior of the colony. The following year the original line (whose eastern terminus was Ipswich) was connected to Brisbane. During the 1880s branch lines were built north of the river to the docks at Pinkenba, Sandgate on Moreton Bay, Dayboro and Caboolture; while a separate system was created centred on South Brisbane. For a full century, passengers from south of the river would need to cross Victoria Bridge by tram to reach the city. The South Brisbane system comprised two main lines, a shorter line east to the shores of Moreton Bay at Manly and Cleveland; and a longer one to the coast at Southport, opened in 1889 and extended to the New South Wales border at Tweed Heads in 1903. The Brisbane railway system as built in the 1880s was to remain remarkably unchanged for the best part of another century.

In Adelaide, even flatter than Melbourne, suburban railways were easily and cheaply built, and the typical Adelaide suburban railway of the late 19th century was a very flimsy affair, often running along streets and not conveying a very serious traffic by the standards of Melbourne or Sydney. The Semaphore, Grange and Glenelg lines were typical examples of such railways. Like Sydney, but for almost exactly the opposite reason, Adelaide was essentially a tram city in the 1880s and 1890s, and remained so for longer than Sydney.

While transport was being mechanised in the later 19th century, the horse still commanded enormous respect and enthusiasm in Australia. Those who no longer worked with horses or could afford to own one, could always bet on them and watch them perform at the races. The turf was late colonial Australia's most popular form of leisure, and in Melbourne the railway had an important role in the logistics of getting punters there. This was in stark contrast with Sydney, none of whose racecourses was served by rail until the Belmore line was extended to Canterbury, and where an elaborate steam-tram station was constructed to serve the most important track at Randwick and less elaborate ones to serve the other racetracks scattered through the eastern suburbs. By the 1920s, the crowds being moved by tram from Randwick would rival those moved by train from Flemington. So intense was Randwick's traffic that side-loading cars would move through the racecourse platforms without stopping as punters scrambled aboard. The trams then travelled through the inner eastern suburbs on their own tracks, separated from the rest of the regular routes. As with the Melbourne punters' trains, only return tickets were sold for these trams, ensuring that unlucky or desperate punters would at least have a ride home.

In the Melbourne of the 1880s, Twopeny was struck by what seemed to him the extraordinary efficiency of VR's services to the Victoria Racing Club track at Flemington, which he saw as a model that English railways and turf clubs could well emulate:

> On race-days trains run out from Melbourne every ten minutes; and as you can buy your train and race ticket beforehand in town, you need never be jostled or hurried. Everything works as if by machinery. It would really pay the [London and] South Western [Railway's] officials to take a lesson at the Spencer Street Station next Cup-day, to prevent the annual scramble at Waterloo every Ascot meeting.[22]

The race crowds VR handled, even in the 1880s, were astounding. In 1881 greater Melbourne's population was about 280 000, but no fewer than 100 000 were at Flemington for the running of the Melbourne Cup in the Exhibition year of 1880. This was more than a third of the city's entire population and most travelled by train. Normal attendances on Cup day were between 60 000 and 80 000. This was an enormous number to move, and VR did it efficiently enough to excite the admiration of an observer as experienced and critical as Twopeny.

ELECTRIFICATION OF AUSTRALIA'S SUBURBAN RAILWAYS

IN THE EARLY 20th century, Melbourne easily had the best public transport in Australia, and far-and-away the best suburban trains. Its transport mix was reflected in the almost equal numbers using its trams and trains: in 1907, for instance, both modes carried about 60 million passengers. By comparison, in Sydney, with a similar population but few suburban railways, in 1908 the trams carried 147.7 million and the suburban trains just 41.4 million.[23]

By the beginning of the 20th century, the technology existed for railway electrification, which had clear environmental and operational advantages over steam traction for a busy and intensive service. The initiative for electrification came in Melbourne from two parliamentary committees which investigated its prospects in 1898 and 1903. The first rejected the idea, while the second suggested further research. The Chairman of Commissioners from 1903 to 1910 was Thomas Tait, previously operations manager on the Canadian Grand Trunk Railway and a man determined to modernise. Tait was sent to Europe and North America in 1907 specifically charged to examine electrification and to assess the relative

Post-World War II modernisation of Melbourne's electric rail transport is evident in this view of the viaduct over Spencer Street in 1972. Post-war W class trams head out over the Yarra River while a 1950s steel Harris train (named after the then chief commissioner) passes beneath the semaphore signals between Flinders Street and Spencer Street stations. (Tony McIlwain)

merits of the technology in use. While overseas, Tait met Charles Hesterman Merz, consulting engineer on electrification to the English North Eastern Railway, and commissioned him to do a report on the options for railway electrification in Melbourne.

Merz believed that Melbourne, with its 298 miles (480 km) of suburban railway carrying 59 477 123 passengers with a train mileage of 2 772 669 in 1907, could support the estimated cost of £2 227 050. However, he pointed out that operating costs would be lower and that, even though train mileage would increase, so would patronage. However, Tait and his brother commissioners, while they accepted the technical aspects of Merz's report, rejected its financial argument, preferring to acquire more D^{DE} class 4-6-2 tank locomotives. These were designed for ready conversion to tender locomotives if electrification ever occurred. Even the moderniser Tait concluded that steam was more economical.

Despite the commissioners' attitude, the politicians were still keen on electrification. In late 1910 the government appointed a Metropolitan Traffic Commission, which recommended immediate electrification. Merz was commissioned to prepare a second report. Now in partnership as Merz and McLelland, they presented their report in 1912. Merz pointed out that technology had improved rapidly, and that the financial situation had improved. He now advised use of 1500 volt DC overhead current collection by pantograph. This was truly radical, for not one such system existed anywhere in the world. Melbourne appeared destined to have the world's first, because the Victorian parliament approved the scheme and authorised the expenditure in December 1912. Merz promptly returned to England (via Bombay, now Mumbai, where he would install an electric railway system virtually identical to Melbourne's) and began ordering equipment for the conversion of 400 steam-hauled carriages to electric motorcars. Locally, the largest task was construction of the power station at Newport and erection of the overhead. Merz and the commissioners had envisaged the introduction of automatic signalling accompanying electrification, but in fact little was accomplished. No new railways were built, and the other major capital work of the time, the construction of the new 11-platform Flinders Street station, had been completed in 1910.

Construction began in earnest in December 1913. It was a large project involving the electrification of some 240 route kilometres. It had been hoped to operate the first electric services in June 1915, but wartime conditions led to delays, both in the supply of equipment from England and because some specifications were changed as technology improved. Electric operations began in Melbourne on 28 May 1919. It was just early enough in the history of the introduction of the motorcar in Australia for the impact to be considerable. Suburban patronage was 96 797 783 in 1917–18, the last year of all-steam operation, but rose by 63.4 percent over just six years to 158 194 558 in 1923–24. The commissioners boasted in their annual report that Melbourne then had the largest electrified suburban service in the world that had been converted from steam, powered by the greatest power station in the southern hemisphere. What they did not boast about was the fact that the electrification project had not been accompanied by any other works. The trains, track, stations and signalling remained as they had in the days of steam. This had made the scheme a relatively cheap one, but also meant that its limitations would soon become apparent.[24]

In Sydney, railway electrification was not so much the answer to the problems of congestion on the steam railways, as it was in Melbourne, but to tram congestion. This meant that, very differently from Melbourne, suburban railway electrification would be accompanied by the construction of new railways and one of the world's most spectacular railway bridges (which would also carry a roadway). By 1919 the tram system was mature and traffic reflected this: there were 253.9 million journeys by tram that year, compared with only 89.5 million by suburban train. Even the ferries, in this most maritime of cities, carried only 35.3 million. The train's documented share of Sydney's public transport load was only 23.6 percent, in reality less, since there were horse and motor buses (for whose traffic no statistics exist) in the city as well.[25] By then Sydney's tram traffic in the morning peaks frequently approached gridlock in the city, as tram after tram from the suburbs, especially the Eastern Suburbs, poured into its narrow streets. This occurred even though motor traffic was still insignificant.

The transition from steam to electric suburban trains in Sydney was slow, beginning in 1926 and not completed until 1969. In February 1954 steam and electric trains were taking tens of thousands of school children home from Redfern station after they had visited the city to see Queen Elizabeth II pass by in a motorcade. (SRNSW H 540167)

Moreover, Sydney's splendid new station, opened in 1906, was only a few hundred metres nearer the city centre than the old. It did have the advantages of being well planned, spacious and having excellent facilities for passengers to transfer to trams running to the city, but it was still not a city station. Indeed its construction on that site was a deliberate decision to postpone the building of a railway into the city. This decision proved wise, given that bringing steam trains into the heart of the city would create as many urban problems as it would solve. As electric railway technology improved rapidly in the first decades of the 20th century, it became clear that electrified underground railways would be the solution.

In these circumstances, expert and popular opinion concurred: Sydney needed a city and suburban railway to prevent it choking under the weight of its own traffic. The problem was getting a parliament dominated by rural interests to vote funds for one. It was to be a long process. The Railway's Engineer-in-Chief, Henry Deane, had proposed underground and submarine electric tramways – in reality light rail – as early as 1895. By 1905 electric railway technology had improved sufficiently for Deane, then about to retire, to advise electrification of existing railways. Charles Merz's 1907–08 report into railway electrification in Melbourne was avidly read in Sydney, and all interested parties drew the lessons from it they wished. Thus the NSWGR Commissioners, conservative and determined to maintain profitability, noted Merz's conclusions that electrification would certainly entail greater expenses but not necessarily proportionately increased revenue and profits.

The political response in Sydney was the establishment of the Royal Commission on City Improvements in May 1908. The first recommendation was 'the immediate introduction of a system of underground electric railways'. It also advised the construction of the metropolitan goods lines, as proposed by the railway commissioners, which would separate the freight traffic to Sydney Harbour from passenger trains. At this point, the first ever Labour government in New South Wales was elected in 1910. Urban problems were a more pressing issue for the new administration than its rural-dominated predecessors. At the urging of the railway commissioners, the new government was able immediately to start work on the metropolitan goods line and the widening of the entrance to Sydney yard. These moves would also benefit country producers, so appropriation passed through the conservative-dominated Legislative Council without difficulty. The goods lines, used by the trams of Sydney light rail since 1998, were completed in 1922. It would be a different story for the city railway.

The Labour government referred the city railway and harbour crossing issues to the Parliamentary Committee on Public Works. The star witness was a brilliant Public Works

Department engineer, Queensland-born Dr John Job Crew Bradfield. He advised abandonment of plans for a submarine harbour tunnel, and the erection of a single-span bridge across the harbour. Together with an underground rail loop under the city, the bridge would connect the railways on the north and south side of the harbour. He also envisaged another rail loop, partly underground, into the densely populated eastern suburbs. The government adopted Bradfield's recommendations and appointed him in 1912 to head a new department with the ambitious title of Sydney Harbour Bridge and City Transit. Bradfield rallied the railway commissioners to his opinions, since by then they too believed that electrification was essential. Thus, a City Railway Bill embracing parts of Bradfield's scheme (but not including the bridge) passed through the Legislative Assembly in October 1913, only to be rejected in the Legislative Council, dominated by conservative politicians representing rural interests, a week later.

Bradfield and the government were undaunted, and used political defeat as an opportunity to refine their thoughts further. In 1914 Bradfield visited the United States and Europe, returning just after the war broke out. Bradfield was most impressed with what he saw in New York, and much of what he recommended reflected New York practice, including the need for all-steel, wide-bodied electric trains. Bradfield's report became law in a new *City Railway Act* of October 1915, which provided for electrification of existing suburban railways, and construction of an underground city loop as well as two new railways, an Eastern Suburbs Railway and a Western Suburbs Railway. Construction began immediately but was suspended in May 1917 as the war became ever more desperate and an ever-greater drain on resources. Despite this, the railway commissioners pressed on with widening track centres, cutting back platforms and tunnels, installing automatic signalling, and ordering 196 new wide suburban passenger cars (still timber bodied, but with steel underframes and automatic couplings between cars) capable of conversion to electric operation.

Work on the city railway recommenced in February 1922. Intense political pressure with elections due in March, the completion of the metropolitan goods lines, and the commencement of electric train services in Melbourne appeared to be the main stimuli. Labor lost the election – it lost the 'u' in its name the same year in a flurry of spelling reform – but work continued uninterrupted throughout the politically turbulent 1920s. The scale of the work was huge. It included two separate underground railways, one double-track, the other of four tracks, from Central station into the city. On these railways were four underground stations: one with two platforms; one with four; and two each with six platforms on two levels; as well as a new suburban electric station beside the existing Sydney Central station. One of these underground railways would emerge from its tunnels at the northern end of the city and leap over Sydney Harbour on Bradfield's stupendous steel arch railway bridge – the largest arch railway bridge in the world. This was ambition on a grand scale, and there was a touch of megalomania to Bradfield's personality, a fact for which Sydney can be grateful.

The bridge and city railway Acts passed despite virulent opposition from the Country Party, whose leader described them as 'a blot on the Statute Book'.[26] The works also included the so-called flying junctions, which enabled a train to move from any one line to another between Central and Redfern without crossing a line in the opposing direction; four new electric carsheds; a dedicated workshop at Chullora and a new power station and the distribution network for the DC power. When these works are added to the loading gauge-widening, quadruplication

Building the Sydney underground railway through Hyde Park in November 1925. The platforms of St James station are clearly evident. A year later it would be open for traffic: they worked fast in the 1920s. (Ian Dunn collection)

(in places sextuplication) and resignalling of the railways around Sydney, it would be no exaggeration to say that the system was rebuilt in the eight years leading up to the operation of the first electric trains in March 1926. The first stage of the underground opened without ceremony to Museum and St James stations on 20 December 1926. It was the second in the world outside Europe and North America; the first, light rail in style, having opened in Buenos Aires in 1913.

Bradfield's steel cars began to arrive in 1925, the first 150 being delivered from Leeds Forge in England, the remaining 438 built locally. Finally, in 1924, after Labor had been returned to office, the contracts were let for the construction of the Sydney Harbour Bridge as conceived by Bradfield. Once commenced, work could not be suspended, despite two changes of government and vehement opposition in the bush to this alleged extravagance. So, the bridge was completed in March 1932, at a time of unprecedented economic and political chaos in New South Wales. With the bridge's opening, the first wave of electrification of Sydney's suburban railways was completed. There is no more impressive piece of infrastructure in Australia than the Sydney Harbour Bridge, and no place which more eloquently symbolises the nation's aspirations and ambitions.

To Bradfield's disappointment, the final stage in his city loop, connecting St James and Wynyard stations by way of Circular Quay, was not built at the time and nor were his Warringah and Eastern Suburbs Railways. The postponement of the Warringah Railway had the advantage of enabling its tracks on the bridge to be used to take the north shore trams into the city. Despite these disappointments, the ensemble of the bridge, electrified suburban railways and the city underground as planned and executed by Bradfield have been an enormous success. New lines and extensions of electrification have been added roughly every decade since. Eventually in 1956 the loop line through to Circular Quay was opened, achieving a dream already a century old. In addition, two new suburban lines opened in the 1930s, to East Hills and Cronulla. The Eastern Suburbs Railway eventually opened in 1979 (although diverted to run through King's Cross instead of beneath Oxford Street as Bradfield had envisaged), 18 years after the trams it had been conceived to replace had been withdrawn. Its construction was the most protracted of any of Sydney's railways, work having begun in 1917. Mainline electrification began in 1956, with the electrification of the railway across the Blue Mountains to Lithgow. All these works were to the technical standards of Bradfield's 1915 report.

Thus, in Sydney, railway electrification was more than the technical issue of railway traction. It was part of a great social and political movement to improve the city's

Australia's first urban freeway, the Cahill Expressway, being built above the tracks of the new Circular Quay station. The train, typical of Sydney's suburban trains in the 1926–90 period, is on a trial run on 16 January 1956. The railway's public opening is only months away, but the days are numbered for the trams in the streets below. (SRNSW H 560016)

amenity. Railway electrification came as part of a package for remaking Sydney as a modern city. That package has been a brilliant success, even if not fully implemented quite as Bradfield envisaged. Sydney's status as a world city was secured by the infrastructure accompanying railway electrification in the 1920s, even if the costs brought down the second Lang government. Thus, Sydney was behind Melbourne in welcoming electric trains, but it was in Sydney that those trains had the greatest impact.

In both cities the increases in rail patronage following electrification were modest rather than spectacular (although greater in Sydney than Melbourne, reflecting the much greater investment in Sydney). There were two reasons for this. The Great Depression began in 1929, just as the railway electrification projects were completed. At the same time, growth in car ownership meant that those who were more prosperous increasingly took to the roads. The Depression did lead to a pause in the growth of car ownership, but only a pause. For instance, the number of cars in New South Wales rose from 28 665 in 1921 to 170 039 in 1929, then fell to 144 749 in 1931, but had recovered to 216 443 in 1939. Or, in other terms, there were 2.1 vehicles per 100 persons in 1921, but 11.9 in 1939, a relative increase of 567 percent.[27] This was precisely the period when the railways were electrified. Even the massive investment in the Sydney Harbour Bridge benefited motor as much as rail traffic, since the bridge included a roadway.

Nevertheless, in Sydney, with two new suburban lines opened during the 1930s as well as the Harbour Bridge and city underground to stimulate business, growth was steady, despite the Depression. Electrification provided a boost in passenger numbers, even if not quite to the extent Bradfield had envisaged; from 117.6 million in 1925, they rose to 137.5 million in 1930, a gain almost entirely lost in the first year of the Depression that followed.[28] It is significant, though, that the annual rate of increase

Newcastle and Brisbane were the last Australian cities where steam remained in charge of suburban trains. In 1967 a late afternoon commuter train headed out of Newcastle behind a 50 year old 30 class locomotive bound for Toronto while another 30 class tank locomotive waited to take out the next load of passengers. (Tony McIlwain)

was higher between 1920 and 1925 (that is, before electrification) than in the following five years.[29] Patronage grew rapidly during the war from a Depression low-point of 119 million in 1931, and, while not exactly buoyant throughout the post-war period, has been healthy since. It peaked at about 260 million in 1955, fell gradually to 205 million by 1980, but recovered to 240 million in 1996–97 and reached 296 million in 2007–08.[30]

In Melbourne, it was a different story. Suburban passenger patronage was relatively stable after the initial boost provided by electrification. Patronage declined during the Depression and rose during World War II, with the result that in 1955–56 journeys numbered 161 million, virtually the same as the 160 million of 1926–27. From that point, though patronage fell, reaching a low point of 93 million in 1977–78. In 1981 Melbourne at last acquired a new piece of city railway infrastructure – the underground city loop – but it was 50 years too late. Patronage recovered slightly, and by 1995–96 had reached 111 million. In general, though, suburban train usage per capita was only half in Melbourne what it was in Sydney in the 1990s, a result in part of the differing philosophies of electrification.[31] This was bad news for Melbourne's suburban railways, for so long the best in the country – their length and operating costs were similar to Sydney's, but their usage less than half. The solution would be dramatic reform and privatisation in the 1990s, after which patronage rose at an extraordinary pace, reaching 200 million for the first time in 2007–08.

The electrification of Melbourne and Sydney's suburban railways, and the associated work such as the Sydney Harbour Bridge and city railway in Sydney, have been among Australia's greatest ever infrastructure projects. More than anything else, these have contributed to urban amenity and the modern shape of these cities. Electric railways have also had much to do with driving the real estate market, which are the motors of so much economic activity in both cities.

Australia's other cities did not electrify their railways in the 1920s. The result was prolonged stagnation of their suburban railways and a flight into car transport on their peripheries. With very limited resources, the railway commissioners in other states did what they could to improve suburban services and maintain market share in the face of competition from trams, buses and private cars. In all states, the 1920s and 1930s saw the introduction of petrol, and later diesel railcars. At first these were intended for rural services, but railway administrations soon discovered their advantages on lightly trafficked suburban services as well. Although their capital cost was high, operating costs were low, they were relatively fast, cleaner than steam trains, and unquestionably modern. They were used on off-peak and some peak services in Adelaide, Perth and South Brisbane by

Brisbane's Central station, with its cramped location between two tunnels, was a grimy place when steam was still king in 1965. (James McCarthy)

the late 1930s. Brisbane and Newcastle, though, remained the domain of the steam locomotive for much longer, and many of their passengers commuted to the city in the late 1960s in the same carriages, often hauled by the same locomotives, as their great grandparents back in the first decade of the century.

By the 1950s, when Sydney had begun electrifying its outer suburban railways, the first closures began around Adelaide and Brisbane. Most of the lines closed in Adelaide were light railways partly on streets, but in Brisbane the system was radically pruned. The nadir was reached when the Beenleigh to Tweed Heads and Southport lines were closed in 1961 and 1963. This part of Queensland was developing rapidly and had become known as the Gold Coast. For the shysters who had taken over the local Country Party branches and council, this convenient railway had no use: it was closed and its real estate sold to benefit a handful of influential speculators. As with the closure of the Brisbane's trams a few years later (where the Queensland ALP was the guilty party), the corrupt Queensland political environment of the 1960s destroyed what was poised to become valuable infrastructure. The egregious folly of this vandalism took only a few decades to realise, and the line was rebuilt at vast expense in the 1990s.

Brisbane, the third largest capital, was where the pressure for suburban electrification was greatest. Like Melbourne and Sydney, it had a number of city stations, one of which (Central) was wedged between two tunnels. Traffic was busy, even intense for the infrastructure available, and until the mid-1950s it was all worked by steam locomotives burning none-too-clean Ipswich coal. Report after report, beginning in the late 1940s, recommended the electrification of Brisbane's suburban railways, but the money could never be found, as both major political parties, Labor and Country, relied heavily on the bush for support.

At that stage there was no broad consensus between the Queensland Labor and Liberal parties on the need for urban improvements to Brisbane, as there had been in Melbourne and Sydney. This was partly because of the far stronger role of Brisbane City Council compared to its counterparts in Sydney and Melbourne (and consequent lesser involvement of state government in urban issues); and partly because the Country Party dominated conservative politics and country Labor members dominated the ALP. During the 1950s, new carriages were delivered in anticipation of the imminent electrification of Brisbane's railways. Based on Sydney's suburban cars but with a modern stainless steel finish, they were designed to be converted to electric traction, but never were, spending their entire careers hauled by steam, later diesel, locomotives. In the 1950s, the contrast between the cities that had electrified their suburban railways and those that had not was stark. With their electrified railways, Sydney and Melbourne experienced growth and high property prices. Without such railways, Brisbane, Adelaide and Perth were stagnating. Lang had been right.

An FJ Holden leads a parade of cars and trucks across Brisbane's Victoria Bridge into the city in 1952. The era of mass motorisation of Australian society had just arrived. Petrol rationing had ended and roads were becoming congested. A decade later American traffic consultants Wilbur Smith and Associates would recommend the abandonment of Brisbane's tramways in an attempt to resolve the congestion, yet the trams in this photograph have about five times the seating capacity of all the cars and buses visible, while taking up less than half the road space. (John Oxley Library 62835)

Chapter 7

THE MOTOR CHALLENGE

ROAD AND RAIL IN CONFLICT IN THE MID 20TH CENTURY

THE SELECTORS WERE desperate: two players were sick and the first post-war test against the visiting Englishmen was to be played in Brisbane in two days' time, on Saturday, 26 June 1920. The best substitute players were in Sydney. New South Wales Rugby League officials received the telegram from Brisbane and scoured the city for players, eventually finding 'Junker' Robinson and 'Smacker' Blair. They rushed to the station, but missed the lunch-time departure of the Brisbane Express. The next day's train would arrive too late for the players to make the test because it was a 29-hour trip. The officials conceived a radical idea: they would lend 'Junker' and 'Smacker' a car so they could drive to Tweed Heads, whence they could take the Saturday morning train to South Brisbane, arriving at 10am. It was a long shot though. No-one in a hurry drove from Sydney to Brisbane in those days because the coast road was just a series of dirt tracks linking the ferry crossings of the New South Wales northern rivers.

To speed the players on their way, the car was loaded on the SS *Hunter* for the overnight trip to Newcastle, clearing Sydney Heads at 11pm Thursday. By dawn on Friday they were on the road out of Newcastle, with 24 hours to drive almost 800 kilometres and cross more than a dozen ferries to reach Tweed Heads. Resting only for the vehicular ferry crossings, 'Junker' and 'Smacker' did their best, pushing the car over the rough and sinuous dirt roads as fast as they dared. But they missed the Saturday morning train. Driving through to Brisbane was impossible because the Nerang and Coomera Rivers were in flood. The selectors hurriedly drafted two Brisbane players and, even without 'Junker' and 'Smacker', Australia won the test eight–four.[1]

In 1920 driving long distances was for the adventurous or, in this case, the desperate. Cars were much better than they had been a decade earlier, but the roads were not. Within a decade, though, all that would change, and a new era of mobility would begin. For Australians on the move, the constraints of train timetables and the shipping news would be absolute no longer.

BUYING CARS AND BUILDING ROADS

DURING THE EARLY 20th century, a new cult of mobility developed based on the motor car supplanting the horse culture of the previous century. Car ownership, though, remained very much an elite affair until the 1950s; and poor rural roads and the total absence of interstate highways meant that the railway remained the major focus of personal mobility. This began to change in the 1920s, though, as 'Junker' and 'Smacker's' epic drive showed.

Most of Australia's rural roads were in poor shape in the early 20th century. The best were in New South Wales, but even there earthworks were limited and surfaces rough. The bridges and vehicular ferries of New South Wales, though, were undoubtedly very numerous and of high quality, as they needed to be in view of the relatively sparse rail network and the quantity of large rivers and creeks, many of which were navigable. In much of Queensland and Western Australia, many roads were still 'natural roads', meaning that there were no earthworks or drainage at all, and the only improvements were the odd culvert or (more rarely) bridge. South Australia and Tasmania had some adequate rural roads, and their situation approached that of New South Wales but on a smaller scale. Finally, Victoria, the richest state with the best railways, had the worst roads relative to its density of population and wealth, because so much had been invested in its railways. Rural roads' main transport functions were confined to local needs, taking produce to the nearest railway station or port. The beginnings of the motor age changed all that dramatically.

The motor age was anticipated by a decade by a new form of transport which in many ways had similar (if more modest) requirements. This was the bicycle, which came to Australia in the 1870s and was extremely popular in the 1890s and thereafter. Early bicycles were not cheap, although prices fell rapidly, but they were almost free to run and sufficiently simple for their owners to maintain them. These were big advantages compared to the saddle horse. Moreover, in cities, a bicycle could be put in a shed between usage, requiring none of the space, feed and attention required by a saddle horse. For these reasons, bicycles have always been more popular in cities than in the countryside. Indeed, to this day, and for precisely the same reasons as in the 1890s, the bicycle

Vehicular ferries were particularly common on coastal roads in New South Wales, and they had their hazards, as seen in this 1920s view. Already the New England Motor Omnibus Company was competing with trains in this part of Australia. (Author collection)

This advertisement in the Sydney *Daily Telegraph* of 21 May 1927 astutely spruiks the advantages of personal motor transport over taking the train or bus. (Ian Dunn collection)

remains the favoured means of personal transport for many urban teenagers, just as the saddle horse is for their country cousins.

Bicycles, though, had two disadvantages compared to the saddle horse – they demanded human effort, and they needed smooth streets. The human effort factor was a matter of choice, and, in sport-crazy *fin-de-siècle* Australia, was in many ways a positive advantage. The popularity of cycling, though, increased the pressure on municipal authorities in particular to improve the quality of streets, especially in suburban areas where cycling was most popular. At that time, most suburban roads were every bit as bad as rural roads, and in many respects worse because they were used more intensively. Most were dusty in dry weather and muddy in wet, many degenerating into quagmires in prolonged wet periods. Equestrians could be a touch disdainful of these conditions or at least could affect to be; cyclists could not. Often the best-paved streets were those with tramlines, since the tramway authority was responsible for paving the roadway between the tramlines. Cyclists naturally enough tended to use these parts of the streets, which made for smooth if not particularly safe cycling.

Cyclists were numerous enough to have some political clout, and made vociferous demands for improved street paving. Melbourne's first cycling club even included a clarion call for better streets in its name. This was the Melbourne Boneshakers Club, which held its first race meeting in 1878.[2] Early bicycles were the cumbersome penny-farthings, which were harder to mount and every bit as nasty as a horse from which to fall. The development of the safety cycle, essentially the modern design with equal-sized wheels and a chain drive, made cycling safer than riding a saddle horse and far more accessible to women. The rigour of Victorian dress codes has been exaggerated, but riding a penny-farthing violated some notions of female decency. While there were always women willing to commit such violations, provoking no genuine outrage in the community as a consequence, the safety cycle posed no such sartorial dilemma. It also could be scaled down for children to use.

The motor age began in Australia, as elsewhere in the world, at the very beginning of the 20th century. The first Australian experiments in car construction were in the late 1890s. These involved both steam and internal combustion experiments, both of which were successful, although it soon became clear that internal combustion had considerable advantages over steam. Steam remained favoured, though, for early buses and trucks (called steam wagons) and for mobile machinery such as traction engines and steamrollers (as we still call them). Australia's first petrol car was made in Melbourne by Colonel Harry Tarrant in 1897. Although experimental, Tarrant learnt enough to begin manufacture on a commercial basis in 1901. In a technology transfer pattern typical of the times, he was joined in the enterprise by a Melbourne bicycle maker, Howard Lewis. By 1909 Tarrant was a manufacturer, importer and distributor, building his own cars as well as acquiring the Ford franchise. This was the year that Henry Ford began production of his T Model, the world's first mass-produced car, so it was an astute move on Tarrant's part. Tarrant also had the Melbourne dealership for more exotic marques such as Rover, Sunbeam and Mercedes.[3]

Initial public reaction to the motor car was far from universally favourable. Conservatives and socialists for once agreed in loathing it. Young men with money naturally enough loved the speed and freedom it gave, and of course were resented by many others for their pleasures. One early Queensland motorist believed his fellow citizens considered the car 'just another rich man's toy ... an emblem of class distinction and bloated capitalism owned by the snob who flashingly flaunted evidence of ill-gotten gains'.[4] However, doctors soon found cars to be superior to horses, and their early use of cars to make house calls did much to make them respectable. Doctors on duty, after all, could hardly be considered irresponsible speed-maniacs selfishly out on a spree frightening horses and old ladies. Speed always enables people, including doctors, to lead more productive lives. The railway and the tram already had proved that, but they were for public use so seemed less self-indulgent than the car, which was very much the preserve of the rich in its early years. Nonetheless, all but the very poor could enjoy a short car ride from 1904 when three licensed motor cabs began to ply Sydney's streets, and when meter taxis were introduced in 1909.[5]

Even though car numbers were very low in the first decade of the 20th century, their

Even as early as 1908 the erotic possibilities of motoring were already a cliché. The postcard is English but was popular in Australia. (Author postcard collection)

impact was considerable. No observer could doubt that their numbers were likely to increase.

The Australian Constitution, framed just before the motor age, was silent on the topic so regulatory responsibility lay with the states. Not surprisingly, it was the state with the most emphasis on moral improvement, South Australia, which led the way. In 1904 the South Australian parliament legislated for the registration of cars, and speed limits in towns and cities varying between 4 and 12 miles per hour (6 and 19 km/h).[6] The requirement of a man with a red flag to precede the vehicle (which did apply to trains in some situations) was never applied to motor cars in Australia – not even in Adelaide, not even during church hours.

In other states, initial regulation was by local councils, which imposed a wide range of speed limits. For instance, in Sydney the limit was 8 mph, in Parramatta 6 mph and in Hunter's Hill 10 mph. Very early in motoring history, Australian police regularly fined motorists for excessive speed. Often, though, the police tended to ignore the local limits and instead rely on the common-law charge of furious driving. This annoyed motorists, since it was so arbitrary. It was easy to see from its condition if a horse had been driven furiously, but very much more difficult to make such a judgment about a motor car. In New South Wales, the *Motor Traffic Act* of 1909 removed these anomalies and laid the foundation for statewide regulation, licensing of drivers, registration of cars and motor bikes (for a fee), and standardised speed limits, notably 15 mph (a sensible compromise) within 5 miles (8 km) of Sydney GPO. Trams were not covered by the Act and, as their trajectories was fixed, the NSWGR as owner, operator and regulator allowed them higher speeds, typically 20 mph in city streets and 40 mph

(32 and 64 km/h) in the suburbs. The Act wisely prohibited vexatious litigation against motorists for things such as soiling curtains or turning milk cows dry.[7] The Act has been much modified since, but the principles it enshrined remain the basis of traffic regulation in all Australian states.

Regulation was a response to the real dangers of motoring. No form of transport is more dangerous than road motor transport and the annual 'road toll' has been a miserable feature of Australian life since the first New South Wales motor fatality in 1905. Since then motor vehicles have killed close to twice the number of Australians as all wars.[8] In the transitional period from 1901 to 1930, motor vehicles were roughly three times as likely to cause a fatality as a horse in New South Wales, assuming only one in three horses was used for transport purposes on public streets and roads. In 1929, motor vehicles killed 415 people in the state while horse-drawn vehicles and bicycles killed 81 people. Despite their size, speed, accessibility and presence on public streets, trams (easily the biggest passenger movers) only killed two dozen and trains killed no members of the public who were legally on NSWGR property.[9]

Francis Birtles' camp beside his car on his pioneering transcontinental trip in 1912. Freedom, adventure and bushcraft are the themes of the image, which links new technology with traditional Australian outback values. (Francis Birtles collection, NLA vn3303272)

Seeing their pleasures threatened by moral improvers and legislation, motorists began to organise. Led by Sydney theatrical entrepreneur Harry Skinner, they established the Australian Motoring Association in 1903, later the Automobile Club of Australia and from 1920 the Royal Automobile Club of Australia. This was a national body from the beginning, with New South Wales, Victorian and South Australian branches. The flashy Skinner was all too typical of early motorists, and was just the kind of person moral improvers wanted kept in his place. Motoring organisations in all states vigorously opposed attempts to license cars and drivers or impose speed limits. Car travel soon became quite fast, even if at first there were few roads where their speed could be exploited. Attempting to beat the train's 16-hour journey between Sydney and Melbourne became a motoring obsession. The first attempt in 1908 took 25 hours and 40 minutes, but at that stage the road was still a 'bush track', although even then some 30 kilometres shorter than the rail route. In November 1921 HR Hodgson, something of dare-devil and a former member of the Royal Flying Corps, rode a motorcycle with sidecar from Melbourne to Sydney in a record 18 hours. Following the rapid improvement of cars and roads in the 1920s, Don Robertson drove between the two cities in 10 hours and 5 minutes, at which point the police prudently put a stop to such reckless fun. Robertson's time was faster than it is legally possible to drive the trip in 2010 and about 40 minutes faster than the train in 2010.[10]

So motoring, like horse riding, was a recreation as much as a transport mode and soon became a sport of remarkable diversity. Exploring the outback was a staple of Australian life and imagination in the 19th century, but in the 20th century became a motoring challenge. In 1912 the former outback cyclist Francis Birtles became the first man to drive a car across Australia and in 1915 he made his first drive through the trackless wilds of the Northern Territory, his Oldsmobile painted in traditional designs by Arnhem Land Aborigines. A popular event in the 1920s was the hill-climb. In October 1924, for instance, 121 motorists entered such a contest organised by the Royal Automobile Club of Victoria up Mt Ridley, 27 kilometres from Melbourne. The aim was to stay in top gear up the hill after a running start on the flat, although few achieved it. The fastest stop-to-pass run on the day, in a Minerva, averaged 65 mph (105 km/h), which would be illegally fast today, and the times of every entrant were reported in *The Argus*. However, most people wanting a day in the country still took the train, and on the same day ten special trains took over 10 000 passengers from Melbourne to a picnic in Bendigo.[11]

The car and the first wave of feminism swept the country simultaneously in the 1920s, and women took to motoring in a big way. Possibly cars had a bigger impact on women's lives than men's. Women who saw

he Reverend John Flynn photographed this outback tterbox in about 1930 to illustrate the advantages f motor cars in the outback. He used the image in is slide shows to raise funds for the Australian Inland lission. (John Flynn, NLA an24230064) their roles in traditional terms found cars made shopping, socialising and adultery easier, while more independent women were active in motor sports and in the burgeoning motor trade, owning or managing garages. Cars broke down the often fearful isolation of farmer's wives, who were able to participate in social and economic life as never before. The positive social and psychological impact of the car in the bush was not lost on John Flynn, head of the Australian Inland Mission and an enthusiastic motorist who quickly recognised cars' social utility for bush families. He was keen on trains and aeroplanes too, but saw that the car, relatively cheap and easy to handle and maintain, could provide reliable everyday transport for widely dispersed outback families in a way trains and planes never could. In 1931 the Dunlop Tyre Company estimated people on the land owned fully a half of Australia's 567 000 cars and trucks.[12] Then as now, for city people the car was merely a convenience and an at times selfish luxury; whereas for country people it so improved living standards that it was a necessity.

The Commonwealth parliament soon became aware of the importance of the new technology, and in 1902 imposed customs duties on imported motor bodies to encourage local manufacture. At this time, all cars were handmade, and most motor bodies were built by firms that also built horse-drawn vehicles. Just as there were varying qualities of horse vehicles, from the simple two-wheel buggy through the austere four-wheel surrey to broughams, victorias and such splendid vehicles, so motor bodies were available with many different levels of finish and appointments. This meant that carriage builders could easily adapt to the new technology which, so far as they were concerned, was not new at all. Only the means of traction and the details of design had changed. Most chassis continued to be imported.

This prompted a short-lived revival of the carriage-making trade, which had gone into decline in the 1890s with the popularity of the sulky (which needed no body). In 1917 the government banned motor-body imports, but a year later eased this law to a restriction of one import allowed per two local bodies built. The following decade was the heyday of the medium-sized motor-body builder, mostly former horse-carriage builders, or firms like Smith and Waddington of Sydney who also built timber trams and railway carriages.[13] Motor-body production reached about 90 000 by 1926. Of these, some 36 171 were produced by Holden Motor Body Builders, which had been founded in 1920 by the Adelaide carriage builders, Holden and Frost. They had produced their first motor body in 1917 and by the mid-1920s dominated the Australian motor-body industry.[14]

Car numbers, though, remained small. There were, for instance, only 3978 motor vehicles in New South Wales in 1911, just as the flood of Model Ts began to surge. They quickly replaced the horse-drawn carriage as the preferred means of city transport of the urban elite, as illustrated in photographs of Australian cities during the first decade of the 20th century. The saddle horse, always an affectation of the wealthy urban male, quickly disappeared from city streets because a motor car was an excellent social and psychological substitute. Horse power remained preferred, though, for deliveries and short-distance cabs. Hansom cabs remained part of the scene in Australian cities right up till the 1930s. In 1911 there were just three motor vans in Sydney, compared with 1303 horse vans. A decade later horses still predominated, with 1603 horse vans and just 376 motor vans. By 1927, though, these proportions were just about reversed, with 2016 motor vans but only 379 horse vans. A survey of Sydney traffic in July 1923 revealed that 39.2 percent of vehicle movements were by horse-drawn vehicles, 33.8 percent by car and 27 percent by motor van or lorry.[15] Of course, most people out and about in Sydney on that day were travelling on trams.

The introduction of the Model T Ford and the rapid improvement of motor technology during World War I led to an explosion in motor car use. In the five years from 1911 to 1916 motor vehicle numbers in New South Wales almost quadrupled from 3978 to 14 973. They then more than doubled in the next five years (when markets were interrupted by the war) to 33 214 in 1921; and quadrupled again to 127 160 in 1926.[16] American imports dominated the market. For example, in 1917, the worst year of the war, there were 15 000 cars brought into the country, of which 10 000 were Model T Fords, 2300 Dodges, 1500 Buicks and 1200 were

The increasing motorisation of society during the interwar period had a big impact on the typical New South Wales coastal resort town of Yamba. Until the 1920s most visitors came by river boat, but by 1940 its beachside park had become a car park (a fairly steep walking track leads to the beach below) and most of those camping or visiting for the day came by car. (Author collection)

other makes. The Model T had been designed with US conditions in mind. These were not so different from those in Australia, with its muddy or dusty roads and long distances. The Model T had simple, robust components, an austere but sturdy body, and high clearances, and so was ideal for rural conditions in both countries.

With the growth of the Australian car market, and given the high duties on imports, big manufacturers decided to establish plants in Australia during the mid-1920s. Ford set up a factory near Geelong in 1925. The next year, the other American giant, General Motors, also established itself in Victoria, at Fishermens Bend near Port Melbourne. General Motors made this a joint venture with Holden's of Adelaide, thus establishing the distinctively Australian and long-lived marque of General Motors Holden (GMH). Both Ford and GMH assembled imported chassis at the works and built local bodies to fit on them. Almost immediately, the old timber carriage-building tradition began to die out because these factories had metal presses. Body designs changed rapidly as metal bodies requiring steel pressings became the norm. Timber was still used for some features, but in 1937 the first all-steel car was produced, anticipating the shape of the post-war industry.

During the 1920s, the motor car became a feature of everyday life for a large proportion of the population for the first time. In 1920 there was one car for every 55 people in Australia; by 1929 this had increased to one for every 11 people, compared with one car for about every four people in the 1970s and one for every two in the first decade of the 21st century. What these figures indicate is that in 1920 a car was a rare luxury, but that a decade later it had penetrated most middle class and more than a few working class households as well. By 1970, most people in Australia who wanted a car enough could afford one, although a quarter of all households continued to choose not to have a car. Paradoxically, proportions of car ownership per head rose more strongly in poorer outer suburbs after 1950 compared with where initially they had been higher, in the richer inner suburbs. This reflected the greater need for private mobility in outer compared to inner suburbs, with their dense networks of tram and/or bus routes and railways.

During the crucial decade of the 1920s, car prices fell sharply while wages were rising. A new Chevrolet, for instance, cost £545 in 1920 but only £210 in 1926. This was less than a year's income on the minimum adult male wage, so was not particularly expensive. Cars were constantly improving too, becoming more comfortable and safer with pneumatic tyres, all-wheel brakes and enclosed bodies making them far more convenient than early models, which were only marginally more comfortable than a buggy.[17] The twenties also saw the growth of motor sport, with speedways mushrooming all over the country and motorists' organisations running all sorts of bizarre races and trials. With these activities, e advent of the motor vehicle brought people to many cations considered inaccessible during the railway age. artley, on the western slopes of the Blue Mountains in New outh Wales, had been an important little town complete with ourthouse before the railway was built. The railway passed rough Lithgow rather than Hartley, which fell into decline. s it was on the road to the Jenolan Caves, the coming the car enabled a modest revival, seen in this 920s family group posing in front of the already d courthouse. (Ian Dunn collection)

the motor car was starting to replace the horse, not just for transport but in the human imagination and psyche as well. As with a horse, car ownership was an opportunity to demonstrate taste (or, regrettably, sometimes its absence), affluence and masculinity (or sometimes feminine independence), while having the practical advantage of affording personal mobility.

This increased use of cars required improved roads. Early motorists were rich and influential and, moreover, it soon became clear that motor transport was more than a hobby but an effective means of transport. The problem was that places where cars were really needed – country areas – had a relatively small population to pay for the roadworks, whereas the cities, where cars were more a nuisance than a benefit, had the population and hence the tax base. The 1909 New South Wales Act provided the precedent for raising money for road improvements through vehicle registration,

Motoring and individual tourism went together from the beginning. About 1930 a woman tourist photographed her husband and dog (who rejoiced in the name of Caesar) on a motoring trip from Sydney to the new national capital in Canberra. Significantly, her motorist husband was none other than Harold Young, Chief Mechanical Engineer of the New South Wales Railways. (Eliza Young, author collection)

although this was not the Act's primary purpose. In 1920 the National Roads Association was established in Sydney to agitate for the formation of a well-funded board of roads for the state. Municipally maintained roads were often in a poor condition, especially if there were no tramlines in them. Two main Sydney roads were rebuilt in 1921 and 1922 through special arrangements. A 13-kilometre length of Parramatta Road west from Ashfield was funded by the state government, while an intercouncil trust was set up to rebuild Botany Road. Both these projects laid concrete road, and so set the standard for future new road building. These were ad hoc measures, but showed what could be done, so in 1924 the government established the Main Roads Board to build and maintain the state's main roads.

All New South Wales roads and bridges previously the responsibility of the Public Works Department (PWD) came under the new board. Metropolitan roads were classified as either local council or Main Roads Board responsibility by the government. Soon after it was established, it was given a huge and unexpected responsibility: the Sydney Harbour Bridge. This was being built by contractors, and the local engineers working on it were either from the PWD or the Railways. It was expected that it would be a NSWGR responsibility after completion, with the Railways maintaining the roadway with revenue raised from tolls. However, in 1928 the decision was taken to transfer the bridge from the Railways to the Main Roads Board, in order to improve railway finances by transferring bridge construction expenses elsewhere. Thus, after acceptance, the Sydney Harbour Bridge became (and has remained) the jewel in the crown not of the NSWGR, which initiated its construction, but the Main Roads Board or the Department of Main Roads as it became in 1932.[18] The new arrangements proved to be such a success that in 1937 the *Sydney Mail* actually asserted that 'with very few exceptions all our main roads are now wonderfully good'.[19] This was in a city where 'the execrable state of the roads' had been (and remains) a staple of public and press complaint since 1788.

There was a similar, although not as systematic, program in Victoria. As early as

1913 the Victorian government set up the Country Roads Board. Its aim, though, was very different from the later New South Wales Main Roads Board. It had no responsibilities at all in Melbourne, where roads and bridges would remain municipal concerns (except those parts of streets between tramlines, which were the responsibility of the tram operator). Its main aim was to build rural roads to ensure that farmers could have ready access to the state's railway stations. For its first decade, it only built local roads in areas where shire councils were unable to do so. Then, in 1925, it became responsible for Victoria's first state highway. Bizarrely enough, this ran from the East Gippsland town of Bairnsdale to the small town of Omeo. The reason was that there had been agitation for a railway on this route, which clearly could never pay. Turning the road into a state highway and upgrading it was the way the government placated the advocates of the Omeo railway. Thereafter, more roads in Victoria quickly became state highways, funded directly from Melbourne, but the government was reluctant to allow too much investment to roads. The investment in the state's railway infrastructure was just too great to allow that to happen. Victoria's wonderfully benign topography though meant that its roads soon became as speedy as its railways. Strangely enough, the Railways Minister who so ardently and successfully defended the railways from road competition through the 1930s (and was reviled as a communist by some Victorians for doing so) was the same Robert Gordon Menzies who as prime minister would abolish petrol rationing in 1950 and so begin the mass motor age in Australia.[20]

Victoria's great contribution to road building at this time was the Great Ocean Road from Torquay to Warrnambool. There were no railways in this part of Victoria and shipping was so dangerous that it was known as the 'shipwreck coast'. Although the transport need was real, the road was built to promote leisure travel. Its funding, conception and construction were unique because it was a 243-kilometre-long memorial to Australians who had died during World War I and was built largely by hand by more than 3000 former servicemen between 1920 and 1932. Until 1936 it was a toll road charging two shillings per motor car.[21] As with so many examples of transport infrastructure, the Great Ocean Road soon created its own traffic, becoming probably Australia's greatest motoring tourism icon and making possible the development of Victoria's premier beach resort of Lorne.

Thus, the 1920s saw the beginnings of state government funding of roads in a modern and systematic way – the New South Wales and Victorian precedents were followed elsewhere in the country. In addition, the Commonwealth began to fund road projects as well, even though it was not obliged to do so under the Constitution. The Commonwealth passed a *Main Roads Development Act* in 1923, under which it could offer funding to states

Victoria's Great Ocean Road has been Australia's premier tourist road since it was built. By the late 1950s airlines and hire car companies were using its delights to attract business from interstate visitors. (BR Linklater, NLA an7649535)

to assist with road building; and in 1926 the Commonwealth and states signed the Federal Aid Roads Agreement, which regularised the process. Thus by 1930 Commonwealth revenue, which included the excise on imported petrol, was being used to build and rebuild roads. By this period too the technology of road building had much improved, and the reinforced concrete highway, often with an asphalt layer on top, had become the norm, replacing earlier and more expensive Telford and macadamised roads.

While buying a car was no more expensive as a proportion of income in the 1920s than it would be in the 1980s, running a car was a different story. Taxation was high and needed to be, since roads had to be improved and there were relatively few cars to pay for it. New South Wales car owners paid an annual registration fee of £1 plus a weight tax of generally 2s 9d per half hundredweight (56 pounds or 25 kilograms). This amounted to £6 10s on a typical car, or well over $1000 in 2010 values. Insurance cost close to twice as much again and in 1925 petrol was 3s a gallon, or about $6.50 a litre in 2010 values, roughly five times its 2010 price.[22] This was partly because of the high Commonwealth excise (needed to fund roads) and partly because oil production, refining and distribution were still immature and inefficient. During the 1920s a network of bulk petrol terminals was established throughout the country, supplied either by rail or sea. Oil companies owned ships and rail tankers, which they brightly painted in their distinctive liveries as mobile billboards. Local distribution to service stations was by road. Sea and rail distribution survive in some places, although road distribution direct from refineries has become more common since the 1980s. This entire infrastructure was paid for by the first mass motorists of the 1920s.

The Great Depression and World War II affected motoring more than most of the economy, since all oil and most cars were imported. Car registrations in New South Wales fell from a pre-Depression 1929 peak of 170 039 to 144 749 in 1931. Thereafter they recovered, passing the 1929 level in 1935 and peaking again at 207 446 in 1940. Registrations fell again to 172 028 in 1942, and were still at only 188 412 in 1945. Petrol rationing through the 1940s kept car demand low, and as late as 1950 there were still only 269 250 cars on New South Wales roads, less than 100 000 more than the 1929 figure.[23] So, for the 20 years after 1929, the additional impact of the motor car was actually quite limited and this was the period when tram traffic in Sydney and Brisbane reached such phenomenally high levels.

THE MID-20TH CENTURY AUSTRALIAN RAILWAY

DURING THE 1920s railways began to respond to the growth in mobility afforded by growing car ownership. They no longer held a monopoly on medium- and long-distance land travel, and had to fight to maintain their share of traffic, especially lucrative first class traffic. Responses were of two kinds. Negatively, state governments regulated competitors to preserve as much of their railways' traffic as possible. More positively, all railway administrations sought to offer their passengers ever-greater speed and comfort. Victoria was particularly concerned about the situation, because its railways were the most highly capitalised in the country, and also uniquely claimed to serve virtually the entire population of the state.

Victorian Railways Chief Commissioner Harold Clapp sponsored the publication of this cartoon in the *Victorian Railways Magazine* of June 1928. It depicted the rivalry of road and rail as a game of chess to be played out until one or the other was defeated. (Author collection)

Victorian Railways had in Harold Clapp an aggressive Chairman of Railway Commissioners who was determined to keep VR's finances buoyant. Although Melbourne-born, he was American-educated and had a clear grasp of what competition could mean. He took road transport on its own terms, and began operating VR's own coach services from 1925, some running directly parallel with mainline railways, for instance from Melbourne to Geelong. However, he could see that VR could not maintain profitability if private road services were permitted to proliferate and run in competition, each undercutting the other and going progressively bankrupt. Thus, in December 1927 the Victorian parliament passed the *Motor Omnibus (Urban and Country) Act*, which provided for the licensing of all bus routes worked by vehicles carrying more than six passengers. Essentially, no licence would be issued for a route competing directly with a railway.[24] The most aggressive Victorian bus proprietor, though, Reginald Ansett, kept working at every loophole in the law to try to maintain a bus service from his hometown of Hamilton to Melbourne, a route over which the railway was less direct than the road.

The situation in New South Wales was more complex. Much of the state had sparse railways. Distances were longer and the roads out of Sydney had to cross the

In 1983 both the branch line railway (a century old) and the New South Wales 42-foot railmotor (60 years old) were nearing the end of their long lives. Back in the 1920s, the railmotor had been the epitome of progress in the bush, but by the 1980s was an anachronism. Here we see it crossing the Murrumbidgee at Gundagai on one of Australia's many inventive timber truss bridges, in this case the work of the imposing and influential civil engineer John Whitton. (Ian Dunn)

same mountainous terrain as the railways but around even sharper curves, so bus competition was not a serious issue on the main lines. Indeed, as late as 1940 the main competition on the NSWGR's northern lines was from ships. However, there was enormous bus competition with Sydney's trams and some suburban trains as well. There were also concerns about truck transport eating into rail freight revenue, although the NSWGR and the shipping companies seemed to be able to live comfortably enough with each other's competition in the north. New South Wales politics were more volatile than Victoria's in the late 1920s and 1930s, with changes of government at every election for much of the period. The first of many Transport Acts was passed by a conservative government in 1930, but there was a whole series over the next few years, as power and policies fluctuated. Their overall effect, though, was to limit competition and establish a licensing arrangement similar to Victoria's. Much the same kind of regulation occurred in the other states, for instance with South Australia's *Road and Railways Transport Act* of 1930.

To meet the growing demands for increased mobility, rail services improved

South Australian Railways' locomotive 509 was brand new when it lifted the overnight express to Melbourne up through the Adelaide Hills in 1926. Although built by Armstrong Whitworth in Newcastle-upon-Tyne, its massive design was largely the work of the American Locomotive Company of Schenectady, New York. The fourth and fifth cars behind the tender are heavy steel imports from the Pullman Car Company of Chicago. This American-style equipment differed dramatically from the British-style equipment used on this train until 1926, as illustrated on p 151. (Ian Dunn collection)

dramatically during the first half of the 20th century. They also became much more efficient and, relative to incomes, much cheaper. Train travel went from being a slow and inconvenient luxury to an experience almost everyone could afford. Moreover, even though few could afford a car, the relative speed of car travel raised the entire community's expectations, and railways responded by increasing their speeds as well. The same technology which made possible the motor car, the internal combustion engine, began to have an impact on rail operations remarkably early. The first application of the new technology on rails came in Victoria, which in 1911 ordered two railcars from the McKeen Motor Car Company of Omaha, Nebraska. These were astoundingly modern in appearance, streamlined with porthole windows, but they were no great success in service and lasted only three years. A year later, Queensland ordered five with only marginally better results.[25] Their technology was premature.

The McKeen cars may have been failures in operation, but the theory behind them was not. The idea was that an internal-combustion powered railcar could operate with small loads at relatively high speeds. In this way, trains could be operated at a fraction of the cost of larger steam trains and at much higher speeds. Railcars often replaced mixed trains, which conveyed freight as well as a single passenger car, and were a fabulously slow means of transport. Railcars were all about bringing modern mobility to the bush. As such they heralded the future.

The NSWGR and VR both built experimental railcars based on petrol truck chassis in 1919 and 1922 respectively. The Victorian cars were the first of a series of 19, while in New South Wales there was further design development culminating in the introduction of the celebrated 42-foot railmotors in 1923, with which the age of experimentation came to an end. This design, classified as CPH in 1937, was so successful that a total of 37 were built over the next seven years. Most had a working life of over 60 years. Four similar cars were built in Victoria, while South Australia imported steel railcars (known as Barwell Bulls after the state premier who ordered them) from the United States, and VR built ten similar steel petrol-electric cars between 1928 and 1931. Meanwhile, Queensland too developed a series of flimsy but effective and very cheap homegrown designs in the late 1920s, all based on truck technology. By 1930, then, the pattern of rural rail services in most of Australia was changing, as slow mixed trains averaging perhaps 15 km/h were replaced by moderately speedy railmotors, which could average 50 km/h or so even over light rural tracks.

While rail motors were adequate for light traffic, they could not provide a solution to competitive demand for higher speeds and greater comfort at lower costs on mainline services. South Australia, where rail finances were more parlous than elsewhere, took the most drastic action and in 1922 appointed an American, William Alfred Webb, as its railways commissioner. Within a few years Webb had transformed the system, turning it from an antiquated British-style railway into a modern if compact US-style railroad. Webb believed that only using larger locomotives to operate larger trains of high-capacity wagons could improve South Australian Railways' productivity. He bought new equipment, including some truly massive locomotives the likes of which had never been seen in Australia before, and tried to minimise the number of break-of-gauge stations. The new locomotives, of the 500, 600 and 700 classes, built in England but thoroughly North American in conception, began to arrive from 1926. They revolutionised train working and introduced real economies as well as providing faster services. Webb started using road delivery vehicles to provide a door-to-door service more competitive with road transport, and also built Adelaide's fine new terminal station. No other Australian railway went through such a revolutionary transformation in its operations or culture as South Australia's during the 1920s. None needed it more.

In New South Wales, which had kept more up-to-date than South Australia, there was also a big leap forward in freight haulage capacity. Once again the principles were North American, and it was an important step in the gradual shift from British to North American standards on Australian railways which occurred throughout the 20th century. In 1929 Clyde Engineering delivered the first of 25 massive 57 class freight locomotives to the NSWGR. Generally based on a Union Pacific Railroad type, these were the largest and most powerful locomotives yet on any Australian railway and sported such advanced technical features as three cylinders and a one-piece steel bed cast in Granite City, Illinois. Rather than heavy freight locomotives, Victorian Railway's prime power of the 1920s was four heavy pacifics of the S class built for working the Sydney Express between Albury and Melbourne. This was Australia's fastest train, a well as one of its heaviest. The Victorian S class were also three-cylinder locomotives, although their overall design was far more English than the US- style machines built for South Australia and New South Wales.

While new and more powerful locomotives could reduce transit times for passengers and freight and made for more efficient operations, they had little direct appeal to passengers. They looked for comfort, and railway administrations knew that they had to provide it if they were to retain the business, since by the 1930s the best motor cars were quite comfortable and roads were always improving. Trains, though, could offer their passengers space and luxurious touches no other form of land transport could ever match. Dining cars made their debut in Victoria, on the Sydney and Adelaide expresses leaving Melbourne in the evenings. They were soon followed by others on Commonwealth Railways. Victoria was the first state to offer its passengers the comforts of air-conditioning in 1935. By 1939 much of Commonwealth Railway's first class fleet used on transcontinental trains had been air-conditioned. Meanwhile, in New South Wales the emphasis was on accelerating journey times and improving the presentation of existing trains with refurbished

Australia's and the British Empire's first air-conditioned diesel train was the *Silver City Comet* of 1937, designed in Sydney with locally built cars and locomotive bodies but using diesel engines from Belfast and German hydraulic transmissions. The *Comet* was already 16 years old when photographed at a typical small outback station between Parkes and Broken Hill in 1953. (SRNSW H 530992)

and brightly painted rolling stock with refreshment services, hauled by some of the most colourfully painted locomotives the country had ever seen. It was not all just bright paint, though, as speed records were constantly being broken, and by the late 1930s trains between Sydney and Newcastle were faster than they have ever been since. These innovations were all consciously proclaiming the fact that the Depression was finally over, and style was back in vogue.

Late 1937 brought a bumper crop of rail innovation, beginning in September when New South Wales introduced a new fully air-conditioned diesel-powered lightweight aluminium train between Parkes and Broken Hill. Called the *Silver City Comet*, it was based on German and US high speed trains of the mid-1930s, and was wildly new technology for Australia, and indeed for the British Empire as a whole. The strange, wonderful and compelling thing about the *Comet* was its use in the outback. Then in November an even more impressive (if less technically innovative) train went into service between Albury and Melbourne, replacing the old Sydney Express. This was all-steel, all air-conditioned, and regally painted in the royal blue and gold which thereafter would become the proud livery of the Victorian Railways. Its precedent was the American streamlined flyers of the same period, and, like many of them, it used new and luxurious carriages hauled by decade-old steam locomotives freshly shrouded in extravagantly art deco streamlining. The train's name said it all: the *Spirit of Progress*.

War conditions delayed any further improvements, and meant that none was really needed. Petrol was so severely rationed that the main problem was keeping too many passengers off trains rather than trying to lure people onto them. However, railway planners knew well that such conditions would not last long after the war, and so planned for massive post-war improvements. Nowhere was this planning more aggressive than in New South Wales, which even during the war introduced a new series of express passenger steam locomotives, the 38 class. New South Wales planning involved the creation of a network of fast air-conditioned steel trains that would serve almost all the state, using the new faster and more powerful 38 class locomotives to bring most of the state within a day trip from Sydney. At that time, most long-distance journeys were still overnight.

So, with victory in sight, New South Wales began building not one *Spirit of Progress*, but a fleet of a dozen or so of them. By 1953 the plan had been realised, and the NSWGR boasted that it had the largest network of all air-conditioned trains in the world. As well as air-conditioning, these daylight express trains featured flushing toilets, reclining seats, wall-to-wall carpets, buffet cars, and finely detailed timber interiors. So, for the price of a second class ticket, passengers could enjoy such luxuries on a train at a time when very few Australian homes (especially in rural areas) or motor cars had anything like these amenities. To step into the cool calm ambiance of a daylight express on a hot day in Wagga Wagga or Dubbo or Tamworth or Grafton in the 1950s was like stepping into a vision of a barely imaginable luxurious future. They made their passengers feel as though they were on the set of a Hollywood movie. These trains, all leaving Sydney in a stately procession around eight every morning (Sundays excepted), made the state smaller and more accessible. With each train headed by a green 38 class locomotive, this early 1950s procession was the finest sight Australian railroading has ever offered, bringing enormous pride and sense of mission to every railway worker from commissioner to cleaner. But these trains were also rail's last hurrah as the prime transport mode in the state, not that anyone was aware of it at the time.

While nowhere else in Australia, and very few places anywhere in the world, could quite match the brilliant New South Wales daylight express trains, all Australian railways

American buffet-style counter dining was a feature of the new post-war fleet of New South Wales air-conditioned express trains. (SRNSW PR 1257)

introduced new high-quality passenger equipment in the 1950s. Victoria and South Australia built individual air-conditioned carriages, which they added to existing trains. This meant that, except in the busiest periods, most passengers could enjoy this comfort, although there was nothing like the same psychological and marketing impact of the New South Wales trains. Queensland and Commonwealth Railways matched the New South Wales precedent in their different ways. Queensland built a series of technically innovative long-distance air-conditioned trains to take over major through services on the coastal route from Brisbane to Cairns, and on the inland routes into the interior from Brisbane, Rockhampton and Townsville. The coastal train was called the *Sunlander*, a name which has stuck, and soon the other trains had similar names. Daringly, Queensland Railways painted these trains ivory, which was effective against the tropical heat but meant there could

Apart from heritage operations, 22 September 1987 was the last day of regular steam haulage on Australian railways. The South Maitland Railway Pty Ltd was the classic industrial railway built to serve mines, one of many around Newcastle, New South Wales. Its final operation between Stockrington colliery and Hexham, previously part of the Richmond Vale Railway, was a recent addition to the SMR's empire. The last locomotive prepared to drop its fire while workers at Hexham depot posed for a bitter-sweet celebration. (Author)

no longer be much tolerance for dirty carriages. Commonwealth Railways also acquired air-conditioned steel trains for its transcontinental services, although these came from a most unusual source. The New South Wales and Queensland trains were locally built, but the Commonwealth turned to Germany for its new transcontinental streamliners, their interiors incongruously decorated with marquetry pictures of German castles. All these trains were in service by 1951, which meant that post-war rail travel was far more comfortable and stylish than it had been before the war, let alone during it.

Innovation at this time was not confined to passenger cars; it was in the early 1950s that Australia's railways first starting using diesel traction on a large scale. Commonwealth Railways, with its long hauls through arid country, found that the new traction offered enormous benefits, and dieselised its main services with its first order in 1951. For other operators, the financial and operational benefits were less clear-cut, since the new technology was more expensive than the old, and the infrastructure and resources existed for a steam railway. Queensland Railways built the last Australian steam locomotive in 1958. Nonetheless, by the mid-1950s all Australia's railways were committed to phasing out steam power, which was achieved by 1973 on government railways and a decade later on coal railways near Newcastle.

New South Wales, Queensland and Western Australia, which had the finest steam fleets and the best coal, were the last states to use steam locomotives on regular traffic. Steam locomotives have remained prominent in heritage and tourist operations in all states since, but no longer play a crucial transport role. During the 1950s there was also some mainline electrification in both New South Wales and Victoria, beginning with Victoria's Gippsland line, electrified through to Traralgon in stages between 1954 and 1956. Then in 1957 the pioneering transmontane railway from Sydney to Lithgow (also Australia's steepest main line) was electrified followed in 1960 by the difficult main northern line out of Sydney as far as Gosford. There electrification stalled, and no further progress was made until the 1980s.

The NSWGR's air-conditioned daylight express trains introduced around 1950 were still in their prime in the winter of 1970, although mostly by then diesel hauled. A locally built diesel electric with largely American components was in charge of the *Central West Express* to Orange as it headed out of Lithgow. (Author)

The final important post-war development in Australian railway history was that at last the problems caused by break of gauge were addressed. The breaks in gauge had been disastrous during the war and made handling the heavy military traffic from the factories and bases of Victoria and New South Wales to northern Australia a logistical nightmare. In early 1942 Australia could not defend both Western Australia and north Queensland from invasion because the enemy controlled the seas, air transport was inadequate, and there was not enough rolling stock to move troops across the Trans-Australia railway and breaks of gauge prevented bringing more from New South Wales. Only the fact that the Japanese had even more serious transport problems had prevented a disaster.

In March 1945 Sir Harold Clapp, who had been Chairman of Commissioners of the Victorian Railways for most of the interwar period, presented a report to the Commonwealth proposing the conversion to standard gauge of the entire Victorian and most of the South Australian Railways. In 1946 the three governments plus the New South Wales government signed an agreement providing funding for this work, estimated to cost no less than £73 434 000. New South Wales, however, refused to ratify the agreement, since none of the money would be spent in that state, and the proposal lapsed. In 1956 a more modest Commonwealth proposal for mainline

In 1962 the NSWGR could claim with some justification that the *Southern Aurora* expresses between Sydney and Melbourne were 'the finest trains in the world'. It was a claim that excited public pride, not derision as such a claim certainly would provoke 50 years later. Such has been the decline of Australia's passenger trains relative to those elsewhere in the world. (Tony McIlwain collection)

standardisation from Albury to Melbourne, from Broken Hill to Port Pirie, and from Kalgoorlie to Perth and Fremantle met with a warmer response from the states, especially since the Commonwealth would foot 70 percent of the costs. The latter two sections would enable through running on one gauge from Sydney to Fremantle. WC Wentworth was the federal politician whose perseverance ensured the adoption of the plan, and Prime Minister Menzies, as a former Railways Minister, was always receptive to ideas of rail transport improvement, as long as they were affordable.

The Victorian section, easily the most urgent, was the first implemented, opening in early 1962. It was not so much a case of gauge standardisation as duplication, since a new standard gauge line was laid beside the broad-gauge tracks from the Murray to Melbourne. The main benefits were of course for goods traffic between Australia's two largest cities, or at least what was left of it following the deregulation of road hauliers in 1954. No longer did freight need to be transferred between wagons of different gauges at Albury, as had been the case since 1883.

However, the innovations were not confined to that. The NSWGR and Victorian Railways had built a new all-sleeping car stainless steel streamlined train to run every night between the two cities in just 13 hours. Christened the *Southern Aurora*, this began operation in April 1962 to great acclaim. NSWGR publicity asserted simply that it was 'the finest train in the world', and certainly its appointments were stunning. Modelled on the North American long-distance streamliners built between the late 1930s and the 1950s, by the time it was introduced its progenitors were running into real difficulties because of air competition. Travel in a train like that, more a hotel on wheels, could never be cheap, and to launch such a service at the dawn of the jet age was courageous indeed. The *Southern Aurora* really had been needed back in the 1930s, so it was a case of better late than never. Air travel in Australia was still expensive, and there were no long-distance freeways until the 1970s, so the 1960s were the last decade of rail's dominance of the interstate market. The *Southern Aurora* symbolised that dominance, but was an unsustainable symbol which would last just 21 years.

Meanwhile, the 1960s also saw work completed on the other two standardisation projects the Commonwealth had offered to fund back in 1956; and in 1969 freight traffic began to flow across the continent from Fremantle to Sydney on one gauge. Such hauls were where rail was really competitive, especially since the transcontinental road was still unsealed through the Nullarbor. As a result, the investment in standardisation was well rewarded with increased freight traffic. Finally, and years after it would have made a real impact on mobility, a passenger train began crossing the continent from Sydney to Perth twice a week from February 1970. It was a slightly updated version of the earlier *Southern Aurora*, and was very much a dinosaur when introduced. It has always been more of a tourist affair than real transport, but its introduction was an important symbol of the partial resolution of the gauge problem bedevilling Australian rail transport for over a century.

THE CAR TRIUMPHANT IN POST-WAR AUSTRALIA

EVEN BEFORE WORLD War II, there was ample evidence that the car would play an ever-increasing role in Australia's transport tasks. Railway administrations were well aware of it, which is why they performed so well in making their services more attractive during the late 1930s, and planned for such thorough improvements throughout the war years. For the railways, of course, the growth of the motor industry was a threat, but for many others it was a great opportunity. This was at all sorts of levels in the economy, from the local motor mechanic to service station proprietor to the multinational corporation. These were themselves a phenomenon largely spawned by the oil and motor industries, which seemed to be ever more concentrated in a handful of companies in a few of the world's richest countries.

For the wartime and post-war Commonwealth Labor governments, the motor industry seemed to provide solutions to two great problems. The first was the need to create employment in the post-war economy. Labor politicians of the era had been scarified by their experiences of the Great Depression, and full employment was their top priority. The second was their desire to offer workers improved living standards, including better housing and mobility. They believed that new suburbs on the fringes of cities could solve the social problems of the slums, as what 50 years later is the most expensive real estate in the country was then considered. Such suburbs could only be pleasant places to live if householders had a car, or at least the prospect of owning one, for their low densities meant they spread for considerable distances around the outer suburban railway stations. Locally made cars for a mass market could raise living standards and create employment, not just in their manufacture but also in the servicing and distribution they required, and so contribute to Labor's social as well as economic aims.

The government therefore invited motor manufacturers to submit plans for manufacture in Australia in return for tariff and quota protection. Motor and steel industry figures such as John Storey of Repco and Essington Lewis of BHP had been important figures in organising wartime production for Labor governments, so there was a level of co-operation and mutual regard between these very different sorts of individuals born of the common wartime struggle which made the enterprise possible. They also had worked beside railway administrators such as Harold Clapp and Harold Young, the NSWGR's Chief Mechanical Engineer, in wartime positions, so there was a flow of expertise from railway workshops into the new industries.

General Motors Holden, which was already a sizeable motor manufacturing business near Melbourne, took up the offer and the first 'Australian' Holden (as opposed to the GM cars built by Holden's to US designs with largely US components) was manufactured in 1948. GMH's General Manager, Lawrence Hartnett, was British born but an Australian patriot, as well as a skilled engineer and astute businessman. He strongly believed local design would lead to a better product and resisted Detroit's preference for building cars in Melbourne to an American design. Holden's plant included the first use of mass production techniques in Australia, featuring dedicated continuous production lines. There was a delicate balance struck between mechanisation and the employment aims of the plant. The Holden car was an immediate success and a powerful symbol of the growing maturity of Australian manufacturing. Its price was reasonable, and throughout the 1950s and 1960s fell in real terms. It was robust, parts and service were available everywhere, and it even enjoyed export success. Model revamps every year or two kept it looking up-to-date. It was generally smaller than comparable US cars, but larger,

The first 1948 FJ Holden in northwestern Victoria, as depicted in a Holden publicity postcard. (Author postcard collection)

Petrol was expensive until the 1950s and 2s 11d was a lot to pay for a gallon (about 4.5 litres) when many workers earned little more than £5 per week. During World War II motorists were rationed to 4 gallons a month. The proprietor of this service station in Drouin, Victoria, was astute enough to appeal to American servicemen, of whom there were plenty about in 1944. (NLA an24207635)

& SON
GOODYEAR
TYRES
BUICK
POWER CHIEF
POWER CHIEF
WHITE CHIEF
GALLONS
PLUME
POOL
PETROL
2/11 PER GALLON
AMERICANS!
GAS 47 CENTS

more robust and more reliable in hot weather than British cars of the same price. Not surprisingly, it became popular in British colonies in Africa and southeast Asia.

The success of the Holden spawned imitators and competitors. Ford, Chrysler, Volkswagen and the British Motor Corporation decided to produce cars in Australia. The market was growing rapidly: new registrations of passenger vehicles averaged 74 000 in the three years from 1948 to 1950; increasing to 160 000 between 1955 and 1957; and to 302 000 over the period from 1962 to 1964. Between 1954–55 and 1964–65 employment in the industry grew from 48 000 to 81 000, an increase of 68 percent, compared with 23 percent for manufacturing as a whole.[26] From 1950 on, car numbers increased dramatically. In New South Wales, for example, motor car registrations increased from 170 039 to 269 250 over the more than 20 years from 1929 to 1950, or by just 58.3 percent. Over the following ten years, though, to 1960, they increased to 623 467, or by 131.6 percent. Then over the next ten years to 1970, registrations increased again to 1 110 652 or by a further 78 percent.[27] In other words, car numbers were increasing at a rate where they doubled every decade in the post-war period. The increase was fastest during the 1950s, off a low base, but was sustained thereafter. During and after the war petrol had been rationed by coupon, and rationing was a central issue in the 1949 federal election. Robert Menzies, leader of the new Liberal Party, promised to end rationing, won the election, and did as he'd promised. Thus he heralded the beginning of the motor age as assuredly as his predecessor Ben Chifley had in presiding over the completion of the first Holden at Fishermens Bend.

As an economic and social policy, the succouring of the motor industry was a great success, but it had unintended and undesirable side effects. A lot more cars meant a lot more congestion and a lot more deaths on the roads, and it soon became clear that, in cities at least, the spread of the car had its limits. The installation of the country's first traffic lights on the corner of Market and Kent Streets in Sydney in October 1933 was a harbinger of things to come. Indeed, as early as 1914 congestion had led to the introduction of one-way streets in inner Sydney. This was because Australia's busiest city also had its narrowest streets, and the one-way system (on Pitt and Castlereagh Streets) was based on existing one-way single-track tramlines. In more spacious Melbourne and Adelaide, one-way streets are virtually unknown nearly a century later.

The motor age was to have an enormous impact on the shape and structure of Australia's cities. This was most evident in the planning for Australia's first motor-age city, Canberra. Its American designer, Walter Burleigh Griffin (1876–1937), was influenced by the ideas of the Chicago architect Frank Lloyd Wright (1867–1959). Wright envisaged new cities, where the population lived in bungalows and could use the freedom afforded by the car to have far more space and light around them than had been the case in cities hitherto. Griffin designed local railways and tramways for Canberra but none was ever built, although the tramway reservations remain in the centre of the city's streets. In practice, Canberra became a city dependent on the car, and so was a model for new suburbs built on the outskirts of older Australian cities.

'garden suburbs' by various state governments. Daceyville in southern Sydney was built adjacent to an under-utilised tramline; however, such transport planning was absent when the idea was generalised after 1945. At this time urban construction resumed after a long hiatus during the Depression and World War II. The post-war suburbs, both private developments and public housing alike, tended to have far

A Mobil publicity card for its service stations issued in the early 1950s. (Author postcard collection)

Griffin also designed two new suburbs in the 1920s at Mount Eliza outside Melbourne and Castlecrag in Sydney. Both incorporated Wright's urban planning principles.

Griffin's were expensive suburbs, but there was experimentation with the concept for working class housing in the second decade of the 20th century with the construction of

larger blocks than had been the case previously. Although urbanisation continued to follow railway lines, their inhabitants needed cars for many purposes. These suburbs encouraged the proliferation of trips for which public transport was ill-suited in areas of low population density.

The relationship between urban planning and the motor car was symbiotic. Suburbs were built which would have been inconceivable without the car, and life in these suburbs required a car (or two or more) in each household. An unintended consequence was the crowding of the streets of inner suburbs with cars from beyond, leading to congestion and delays to tram traffic. This became acute in the 1950s, especially in Sydney. The motor age also led to a proliferation of new sorts of structures, such as service stations and, especially in the 1950s, drive-in theatres. Most service stations were owned by or associated with one of the big American, British or Dutch international oil companies, but there were some Australian brands such as Golden Fleece and Ampol. By the 1970s there were drive-in bottle shops and food outlets in most Australian suburbs.

Car parks had been built in city centres as early as the 1930s, but they proliferated after 1950. The motor age also made possible the development of the suburban shopping mall, surrounded by vast quantities of free parking. The first were developed in the early 1960s at Chadstone near Oakleigh in Melbourne and Roselands, in Sydney's southwestern suburbs. Neither was near a railway station or tramline, unlike most previous shopping centres.[28] Similar developments followed throughout the country. The most disastrous impact was in Newcastle, where the formerly large and busy city centre, well served by trams and trains, went into decline, while most of the city's shoppers drove to large shopping malls on its fringes. Sensible urban planning never would have allowed Newcastle's malls to be built in outer locations ensuring the traditional city's drift into desuetude. Newcastle has suffered from the worst post-war planning of any city in Australia, and it continues with ridiculous council plans to close its city railway.

In the bush the motor car was almost entirely beneficial and without the destructive consequences it had for cities. More cars and increased mobility increased pressures for improved roads in the countryside. Happily, in post-war Australia the economy was buoyant most of the time and revenues existed for this purpose. Even during World War II, inadequate roads as much as inadequate railways had been recognised as a serious problem. While there was no attempt to use roads for heavy wartime haulage where a parallel railway existed, there was always the concern that this might be necessary if enemy bombing destroyed rail links. This never did happen, but the consequences would have been dire, especially if the Japanese had managed to bomb something as critical as the Hawkesbury River railway bridge just north of Sydney. During the war years, a road bridge was built at Peat's Ferry, just upstream from the railway bridge, which was itself being replaced. The new road bridge replacing the ferry opened in 1945 and the new railway bridge in 1946. The efforts of both the NSWGR and the New South Wales Department of Main Roads in building these two bridges, which rested on some of the deepest caissons in the world, were extraordinary, especially considering that both departments' resources were severely stressed by other demands of war.[29]

However, the main wartime road-building effort was far from the coast and the centres of population. This was the construction of the Stuart Highway from the railhead at Alice Springs to Darwin, completed after a year's work in 1943. Prior to this there was only a sandy track between the two places because most traffic to Darwin went by sea. For more than a year enemy action interrupted sea traffic, making this strip of bitumen through the inland an absolute necessity. During the war other missing link roads were built to connect railheads in western Queensland with the Northern Territory, and an inland sealed road was built parallel to the Queensland coast from Ipswich to Charters Towers, in case the Japanese were able to disrupt traffic on the coastal railway from Brisbane to Cairns.

After the war, there was a rapid process of sealing the surfaces of main roads in at least the more densely populated southeast of Australia. Indeed rural areas were the main focus of the various state main road authorities. In Victoria it was even called the Country Roads Board, while in New South Wales the Department of Main Roads over the 30 years from 1926 to 1955 spent £91 372 997 outside Sydney and only £23 911 473 in the greater Sydney area, even though this was where half the population lived and more than half the cars were registered.[30] In rural areas, road improvements often involved merely the resurfacing and improved drainage of existing roads, but in cities something more radical was required. Melbourne and Adelaide, with their wide streets and spacious air, did not need to invest early in urban freeways, but for cramped Sydney, with its extremely difficult topography, increased car use required new urban roads quickly. Brisbane had much the same problem as Sydney, although on a much smaller scale.

Not surprisingly under these circumstances, Sydney was the first Australian city to prepare a plan for urban freeways on the model established in the 1930s in the United States and above all in Los Angeles. Planning Sydney's urban freeways began as early as 1943. This was about the same time as the NSWGR was planning its magnificent post-war express trains. The Department of Main Roads planners assumed that Sydney's population would reach about four million by the end of the century (they were absolutely right) and that car ownership would rise to about one car for every two adults (once again right). The plans envisaged construction of 145 kilometres of freeway in greater Sydney and 1400 kilometres of main roads. These freeway plans were the equivalent of Bradfield's plan for Sydney's public transport during World War I. At this stage no other Australian city thought in such planning terms, or indeed needed to.

The first freeway in Australia was short but crucial. It was built in the heart of Sydney, indeed at the very spot where European

WRECKING THE SYDNEY HARBOUR BRIDGE: A TRANSPORT PLANNING DISASTER

Australia has no more important (nor expensive) urban transport link than the Sydney Harbour Bridge. Its development both before and after its opening in 1932 tells the story of the decline of Sydney's transport planning from the brilliant and farsighted Bradfield plan to the craven and venal caricature of policy of the last six decades.

Built as part of the Bradfield plan for the electrification and extension of suburban railways, the bridge was designed for four railway tracks. The planned northern suburban railways to Epping and Manly had not yet been built when it was finished, so the eastern pair of railway tracks was used to bring north shore trams into an underground station at Wynyard in the city. Trams encountered no delays from motor traffic crossing the harbour or in the city, so this was an effective and efficient transport solution, as seen with two O class trams (above) in 1952. (W Bindle NAA Series A1200, Item L14643) But Sydney soon would lose this excellent arrangement.

In June 1958 the Cahill government closed the north shore tram system. It then compounded its folly by converting the tramlines for use by motor traffic and turning the underground tram station at Wynyard into a car park, an absurd waste of such valuable infrastructure. On 2 July 1959, two additional motor lanes opened where the tramlines had been. (right above) The vandals were so proud of their destruction they commissioned the Australian News and Information Bureau

to photograph 'traffic flowing freely' through the toll gates that evening. (NAA Series A1200, Item L49372)

However, a lane devoted to motor traffic has only a fraction of the capacity of a tramline and a tiny fraction of a railway's. The result, evident in this 1964 image (left), was that within a few years congestion was worse than ever. (J Fitzpatrick NAA Series A1200, Item L32700)

Amazingly, successive New South Wales governments have failed to take 'time to think' and learn from this planning disaster. They keep making the same stupid mistakes.

settlement of the continent began, across the head of Circular Quay. This Cahill Expressway, named after the quondam railways fitter, latterly premier Joe Cahill, opened in March 1962 and was associated with two other transport decisions. It was built across the top of the recently completed Circular Quay railway station of 1956, and its approaches were built on the formation of the Harbour Bridge tramlines abandoned in 1958.[31] The next important urban freeway was the Warringah Freeway leading to the Harbour Bridge from the north. This required the demolition of the tramway arch on the northern approaches to the bridge and opened in 1968. In an absolutely literal sense, Australia's first urban freeways were built on the ruins of its greatest tramway system.

Before 1970, no other Australian city invested in urban freeways as Sydney did, for the simple reason that none other was as congested. Surprisingly perhaps, Perth was the other city to build roads of this standard, but these were associated with the building of the Narrows Bridge across the Swan River. Brisbane too began planning freeways and, as in Sydney, these required the destruction of its trams to build the new Victoria Bridge and the Riverside Expressway beneath it. During the 1960s, then, the age of the urban freeway tentatively came to Australia. The technological achievements, even in the first decade, were impressive, especially those immediately around the Sydney Harbour Bridge, always the cynosure for Australia's finest transportation engineering. Whether they represented the best solution to the problems of increasingly crowded cities, and to those of one increasingly crowded city in particular, is another issue altogether.

DEREGULATION AND THE NEW TRANSPORT CULTURE

AS ROADS AND the vehicles using them improved after 1950, they began to become capable of taking loads and speeds previously only possible on rail. Road transport had some advantages over rail, both technical and cultural. Its main technical advantage was flexibility, as reflected in its abilities to achieve door-to-door delivery with the one vehicle, to take alternative routes during surface maintenance, and to stop more frequently with less loss of time. Culturally, post-war road transport was dominated by small entrepreneurs, just like the bullockies and teamsters before them. Such individuals had a sharp sense of customer focus, and were price and time competitive. The railways had developed a bureaucratic culture which, while very good on matters such as safety and reliability, was not so responsive to customers' needs. The railways in all states (and especially in Victoria) also laboured under a heavy capital debt burden which was never repaid, and working conditions where union rules meant that productivity was less than it could have been.

All states protected their railways from road competition by legislation, mostly introduced around 1930. The New South Wales legislation had been challenged unsuccessfully in the High Court as early as 1933, so this regime remained in force until the mid-1950s. Then, in 1954 another challenge was launched in the Hughes and Vale case. Once again, the High Court upheld the legislation, but Hughes and Vale took the case to the Privy Council in London, which declared it invalid. With that precedent, the High Court subsequently declared similar legislation in other states invalid. Suddenly the interstate road transport industry exploded.

The road hauliers' victory in the Hughes and Vale case only applied to interstate transport. Traffic within state borders remained subject to the anti-competitive restrictions of the 1930s legislation. However, political pressure for its removal became intense. Even groups which had benefited enormously from the construction of loss-making railways (especially farmers and Country Party voters) turned against these same railways they had wheedled out of the taxpayer, since there was now a potentially cheaper and more efficient service on offer. In addition, railway lines were not always built to take the shortest line between two points, whereas often there was a road which did. This meant that buses, and certainly cars, often could offer faster transit times than trains, so there was pressure for deregulation from passengers as well as shippers.

Thus there was a political push to remove restrictions on road transport operations within states. South Australia was the first to move, when in 1963 it repealed its 1930 *Road and Railways Transport Act*. Others soon followed. Most importantly, New South Wales removed its restrictions on road freight in 1973 and in 1972–73 the NSWGR (in the very last year of its corporate existence after a life of 118 years) was worked at a loss for the first time ever in its long history as Australia's most profitable railway.[32]

Thus, in the early 1970s, a new era of Australian transport history was beginning. The details of the shape it would take were not yet clear, although the broad outlines were. The huge state enterprises, above all the state railways, which had dominated Australia's land transport investment and functions for a century, would no longer enjoy the same commanding role. Changing technology, increased road investment, and a new regulatory environment would ensure that patterns in Australian transport in the last decades of the 20th century would be very different from what they had been up till about 1970. Indeed, it was in transport that the first salvos of the neo-liberal movement in Australian public life were being fired, and the state railways were its targets. Neo-liberalism would intensify in the 1980s and triumph in the 1990s, above all in transport policy. Problems of distances and the need to move people and goods across them remained at the heart of Australian social, economic and political discourse.

The first Qantas Empire Airways Short S-23C Empire Flying Boat *Carpentaria* (VH-ABA) entered service with the airline in June 1938. In terms of comfort and style, Sir Hudson Fysh always considered these the finest aeroplanes Qantas ever flew, and he headed the airline from its beginning until the era of the Boeing 747. *Carpentaria* is at anchor at Rose Bay in Sydney, probably in 1940 or 1941. The red, white and blue flashes on the tail and hull (flying boats have hulls, not fuselages) indicate wartime, and the London–Sydney flying boat service ended as the Japanese swept through Malaya in February 1942. (Qantas Heritage Collection)

Chapter 8

FREE SKIES TO CROWDED AIRPORTS

CIVIL AVIATION

IN MAY 1935 CIVIL aviation was already a quarter of a century old. Aeroplanes had crossed the Atlantic and Pacific Oceans, and proved themselves as weapons of war in France 20 years earlier. But flying was still dangerous, mishaps were often fatal; and they could happen to the most experienced aviators. George V had been on the throne for 25 years and to celebrate his jubilee there was a series of special airmail flights. One of these, from Sydney to New Zealand, struck trouble. On 15 May 1935 Sir Charles Kingsford Smith was flying his famous but by then rather elderly aeroplane *Southern Cross* loaded with commemorative jubilee airmail when the manifold fell off the port engine, causing loss of oil pressure. His navigator, PG Taylor, with great courage, walked along the wing and transferred oil in a thermos flask from the starboard to port engine no fewer than ten times, as Smith struggled to fly back to Sydney. All on board survived that flight, although the mail did not. Most of it was jettisoned, sack by sack, to keep the plane flying.

THE HEROIC AGE OF AUSTRALIAN AVIATION

VAST DISTANCES, LONG flights over water, courage, and risk were the hallmarks of early Australian aviation. By 1935 its commercial and mobility advantages were clear and progress had been enormous, but civil aviation was not yet secure or routine. Australia had been significant in the origins of aviation because of the work of the wealthy Sydney gentleman-inventor, Lawrence Hargrave (1850–1915), who devoted much of his life to the development of flight. He had engineering experience in the Pyrmont workshops of the Australasian Steam Navigation Company, as well as artistic talent, and had undertaken serious anthropological research in New Guinea. As an inventor, he was responsible for two important steps towards aviation. His rotary compressed air engine of 1889, while never sufficiently developed to propel an aircraft, anticipated much future engine development. He was also the inventor of the aerodynamic box kite and in November 1894 lifted himself into the air with an arrangement of box kites at his Stanwell Park property, inherited with the nearby coal mines which made his career as an independent inventor possible.

The box kite was the basis of most early German and French aeroplanes. Hargrave refused to patent the concept, believing in the free exchange of ideas, and was honoured for his work with a medal from the Bavarian government. He had rather less success with his many designs for a steam engine to power an aeroplane. After the first flight of the Wright brothers in North Carolina in December 1903, Hargrave realised that his role as an inventor was over, largely because he was so far from the centres of aircraft development in the United States and Europe.[1]

It was some time before aeroplane manufacture became a commercial reality. The significance of the Wrights' invention was not really appreciated until their visit to France in 1908, and the first man to demonstrate its commercial and military potential was the Frenchman Louis Blériot, who flew across the English Channel from Calais to Dover in 37 minutes on 25 July 1909. The American aviator, Calbraith Rogers, flew across the Union from New York to Los Angeles in 1911, but the journey took him seven weeks and he had 80 stops and five major crashes on the way, for a trip that could be done in safety and comfort by train in five days. Rogers died when his biplane crashed a year later, bringing the death toll of aviators to 127 in just eight years. More encouragingly, French aviator Roland Garros crossed the Mediterranean flying 824 kilometres non-stop in 1913.[2]

Meanwhile, in Australia, the Commonwealth government was so impressed by Blériot's feat that in 1909 it offered a prize of £5000 to the Australian inventor of an aeroplane suitable for military purposes. The conditions were onerous: it had to carry two persons and be capable of 'poising' in the air. Twenty-one aviators entered but none ever claimed the prize. The first Australian to design a working aeroplane, the young Victorian electrical engineer John Duigan (1882–1951), did not enter due to his accurate perception that the conditions were impossible. At any rate, he made his first successful flight in an aeroplane of his own design and construction, with a Melbourne-built engine, on his family grazing property near Mia Mia on 16 July 1910. Duigan later became a brave aviator, wounded over France in World War I.[3]

The first two controlled flights in the country had been made in March 1910 using imported machines, one by the famous American daredevil Harry Houdini. In 1911 the Aerial League of Australia was set up to regulate what was starting to be an industry. It issued the first pilot licence to William Ewart Hart on 16 November 1911. Six weeks later Hart established a flying school at Penrith, but within days his biplane had crash-landed on the railway at Mt Druitt, unable to cope with an overweight pupil. Happily trains were infrequent, so aviator, biplane and burdensome pupil all survived, two of the three to fly another day. Hart and American 'Wizard' Stone staged Australia's first air race from Botany to Parramatta Park on 29 June 1912. The stake was £250, which Hart sorely needed to pay damages owing a farmer who had sued him for disturbing cattle. With local knowledge Hart won in 24 minutes while 'Wizard' landed lost in Lakemba.[4]

This was great fun, but visiting French aviator Maurice Guilleaux showed that aeroplanes were not just toys when he carried Australia's first airmail from Melbourne to Sydney in July 1914. The outbreak of World War I the same month would prove aviation's utility. In Britain the industry went from employing a couple of hundred to 350 000 persons between 1914 and 1918, and built over 50 000 aircraft.[5] In Australia, the Commonwealth established the Australian Flying Corps, as part of its contribution to the war effort, and the Central Flying School at Point Cook in Victoria to train airmen. These men, or at least those who survived, acquired the skills needed to fly aeroplanes in the harsh conditions of combat, becoming the pilots who established civil aviation in Australia.

They returned with aeroplanes as well as skills, and many offered joy flights to the public, enjoying reckless freedom in a new industry, regulated only by their own Aerial League. This situation could not last long and an international convention in Paris in October 1919 established civil aviation regulations. Australia was a signatory to the International Convention for the Regulation of Aerial Navigation which determined the principle of the sovereignty of airspace over a country's territory, the principle of freedom of safe passage of aircraft, and licensing of aeroplanes and pilots. Australia's response was the *Air Navigation Act* of 1920, establishing a Civil Aviation Branch, overseen by the Controller of Civil Aviation and administered by the Department of Defence. Colonel Horace Brinsmead, based at Victoria Barracks in Melbourne, became Controller of Aviation and his Branch was divided into three sections: Superintendent of Aerodromes; Superintendent of Flying; and Superintendent of Aircraft and Engineering.

The Act meant the Commonwealth acquired sites for airports and facilities, requiring staff to establish and maintain aerodromes

and to clear land for emergency landing sites. The Act required pilots, engineers and aircraft to be licensed, and proper skills standards set for the industry. The first Commonwealth licences were awarded in 1921 when there were just 56 aircraft, 104 ground engineers and 49 pilots licensed. Meanwhile, the Commonwealth was well aware that civil aviation had much to recommend itself to a country with large distances where population was so sparse that railways would never be viable and roads would remain primitive. Prime minister Billy Hughes had a technically progressive streak, so offered a sensational prize of £10 000 for the first flight completed from England to Australia in less than 30 days. This was roughly the time the journey took by steamer.

The winners were the South Australian brothers Keith (1890–1955) and Ross Smith (1892–1922). Both had flown in World War I, Ross extensively in the Middle East campaign. Indeed, just as the war ended in November 1918, he was co-pilot on the pioneering British flight of a Handley-Page 0/400 bomber from Cairo to Calcutta, which he then prolonged to Timor in an unsuccessful attempt to be the first to fly through to Australia. A year later, with the incentive of Hughes' prize before them, they flew much the same route in a similar aircraft, a Vickers Vimy, from Hounslow near London to Darwin in 28 days. Both were immediately knighted, although Ross did not live long enough to enjoy either wealth or status, dying in a plane crash in England in April 1922. Keith went on to be Vickers' Australian representative for the rest of his life.[6]

The Smiths' England–Australia flight and Ross Smith's subsequent death established the pattern for the heroic age of Australian aviation, stretching through the 1920s and into the early 1930s. Australian aviators' feats at this time had three outstanding characteristics. First, extremely long flights were an Australian speciality, since Australia's international and domestic geography demanded them. Second, it was extremely hazardous. Many of Australia's pioneer aviators died in their machines, pushing

In December 1911 Australia's first licensed aviator WE Hart established a flying school at Penrith, New South Wales, easily accessible by train from Sydney. Jack Turner captured this sensational image of dominant and emerging transport modes as Hart's biplane flew over the station, where I and J class locomotives were ready to take the tonnage on to Sydney. (Jack Turner from the Hudson Fysh collection, NLA vn3722803)

them to (and beyond) the limits of mechanical and human endurance. Third, there was a strong element of entrepreneurship, and many pioneering flights won prizes, often used to fund airlines or further flights. Distance was the key to the relentless pressure on these fliers, and the war experience in the Royal Flying Corps – where death was always an immediate possibility and where so many of their friends had been lost – gave them the psychological qualities to embark on such dangerous even foolhardy ventures.

The most famous of the aviators of the 1920s was Charles Kingsford Smith (1897–1935), son of a former clerk on the Canadian Pacific Railway. In his teens he trained as an engineer with the Colonial Sugar Refining Company. It was a typical aviator's background, with family interests in technology and transport. Returning from war service, 'Smithy' had a varied and not especially successful career as pilot and businessman. Disappointments were more frequent than successes, including being barred from the 1919 England–Australia race and failing to secure any of the airmail contracts tendered in the 1920s. His response was to form a partnership with the 'reckless and restless' Charles Ulm (1898–1934) to fly demonstration flights. These made their reputations.

Their inspiration was Charles Lindbergh's pioneering solo flight across the Atlantic from New York to Paris in May 1927. This made Lindbergh one of the most famous men in the world. Smith and Ulm's first demonstration was less adventurous, a round-Australia circuit in 10 days 5 hours in June 1927, but helped them secure backing for the first trans-Pacific flight. In June 1928 they flew from Oakland in California to Brisbane in ten days or just 83 hours 38 minutes flying time. This flight in a three-engine Fokker named *Southern Cross* was monumental in its impact much as Lindbergh's had been, although it was made by a larger plane with a crew of four, not a lone wolf. They flew three non-stop legs, from Oakland to Hawaii, then on to Suva, and finally from Suva to Brisbane (where the *Southern Cross*, following its withdrawal after nearly a decade in Smith's ownership, is now exhibited). The Honolulu to Suva flight of 2740 miles (4410 km) took 33 hours – slightly longer in time but rather slower than Lindbergh's flight – and was full of unknown tropical meteorological hazards. At its end fuel was critically low. Then in August 1928 Kingsford Smith flew non-stop from Point Cook near Melbourne to Perth and in September with Ulm non-stop from Sydney to Christchurch in New Zealand.[7]

1928 was something of an *annus mirabilis* for Australian aviation. For, as well as Kingsford Smith's flights in *Southern Cross*, the Bundaberg-born aviator Bert Hinkler (1892–1933) made the first-ever solo flight from England to Australia in an Avro Avian over just 15 days in February. Hinkler had worked in the Sopwith aircraft factory in England in 1913 and 1914, before war service. After the war he made his career in aviation in England. Barred from the 1919 race to Australia, he established

Refuelling Charles Kingsford Smith's Fokker tri-motor *Southern Cross* at Sydney's Mascot airport on 11 June 1928, just after the plane's monumental trans-Pacific flight. Kingsford Smith and Charles Ulm signed the photograph. (Ian Dunn collection)

a number of early European records, flying from London to destinations such as Turin in Italy and even to Riga in Latvia. He also was chief test pilot for Avro for a number of years. His career peaked with his solo flight to Australia, which was followed by some successful and one failed solo trans-Atlantic flights. It was on this last that he died when his plane crashed in the Italian Apennines in April 1933.[8] Even more improbable than Hinkler's career was that of Sir George Wilkins (1888–1958), a South Australian who became one of the world's last great explorers, mostly of the Arctic, and in April 1928 became famous for his pioneering flight over the Arctic from Alaska to Spitsbergen off Norway. It was an unusual place for an Australian aviator to make a name for himself.[9] More practically, 1928 was also the year when the world's first flying doctor service was established in Queensland.

Patrick (always known as PG) Taylor's (1896–1966) reputation was made in more familiar circumstances. War service in the Royal Flying Corps was followed by work as a commercial pilot and a number of marriages. Unsurprisingly, as they were brave handsome men whose war service had combined a life of comfort, even indulgence, on the ground with the immediate possibility of death in the air, many early Australian aviators led complicated emotional lives. He met Charles Kingsford Smith when Smith was running Australian National Airways Ltd and, after the airline's collapse, joined 'Smithy' and Ulm in some adventurous flying. It was on one of these ventures in May 1935 that Taylor so distinguished himself by walking along the wings of the *Southern Cross* with thermos loads of oil. Taylor went on to make pioneering flying boat flights from Port Hedland, Western Australia, to Mombasa in Kenya in June 1939 and from Sydney to Chile via Tahiti and Easter Island in 1951. These were the first flights between these continents. The Catalina flying boat he used for the latter, *Frigate Bird II*, is exhibited at Sydney's Powerhouse Museum.[10]

Kingsford Smith and Ulm were not as lucky as the future Sir Patrick Taylor, who survived to enjoy his old age sailing around Pittwater near Sydney. Both were close to ruined by the collapse of their airline, and in 1932, the year he was knighted, 'Smithy' was even reduced to giving joy flights and running (at a loss) a flying school at Mascot. They managed to scrape together sufficient resources for their last ventures – some together, some separately – between 1933 and 1935. The hazards were still enormous on the long flights over water. We know of Taylor's courage because he and Smith survived their brush with death above the Tasman in May 1935. However, we know nothing of how Ulm died, somewhere in the Pacific between California and Hawaii, on 3 December 1934; or how Smith died, somewhere in the Gulf of Bengal between Allahabad in India and Singapore, on 7 November 1935.

The deaths of Hinkler, Ulm and Kingsford Smith in consecutive years marked a sad coda to the heroic age of Australian aviation. It had been characterised by the extremely long flights over water which claimed the lives of all three. The last great pioneering air race was in October 1934 from London to Melbourne via compulsory stops in Baghdad, Allahabad, Singapore and Darwin, and any other stops the pilots cared to or had to make. It was organised to celebrate the centenary of the city of Melbourne and called the MacRobertson Air Race after the Melbourne confectioner who sponsored it. The winners, in a British DH88 Comet built especially for racing, completed the journey in just less than three days. More significantly, though, the second aircraft to arrive was a new Douglas DC2 commercial airliner flown by a regular KLM Royal Dutch Airlines crew. This all-metal aircraft was very much a harbinger of the future.

Flying, though, was still an adventurous business. Two of the 20 entrants crashed, one with the loss of all crew, and even the KLM DC2 was forced down by storms onto Albury racetrack, just 300 kilometres from its destination. Taking off from the sodden field was so difficult that most of the plane's passengers and mail had to make the last leg by train. Nonetheless, the Dutch (and the Americans who had made the plane) made a crucial point: a modern commercial airliner with a significant load of passengers and mail was almost as fast as and far more comfortable than a racing machine, and its flights could be profitable too. Thus, by 1935, although aviation was not yet quite routine, commercial flying was certainly an increasingly important part of the Australian transport scene, especially where roads and railways were poor.

PIONEERING CIVIL AVIATION, 1921-45

AS SOON AS the legislative framework for civil aviation was established by the *Air Navigation Act* of 1920, the Commonwealth moved to begin airmail services, calling for tenders for four routes, two over busy intercapital routes, two in remote districts beyond railheads. The latter two were from Geraldton to Derby in Western Australia and from Charleville to Cloncurry in Queensland while the intercapital routes were from Sydney to Adelaide and Brisbane.

These tenders were not fiercely contested, as financing airlines was anything but easy. The Geraldton to Derby route was won by Western Australian Airways Ltd (WAA), established in 1921 by Major (later Sir) Norman Brearley. He had had a distinguished career in the Royal Flying Corps and had been severely wounded and forced down in no man's land. It had been a lucky escape but the experience would stand him in good stead for flying in the wilds of the outback. The route involved flying 2028 kilometres along the west coast of Australia via Carnarvon, Onslow, Roebourne, Port Hedland and Broome weekly as a return trip for passenger, mail and parcels service. Initially he had used two Avros he had brought to Perth for barnstorming – flying around giving exhibition flights – but on winning the contract Brearley ordered six Bristol aircraft from England. However, he was unable to pay for them until financial support came from HV McKay, proprietor of the famous Harvester Works in Melbourne. With McKay's assistance, WAA became the first regular airmail service to operate in Australia when it took off in December 1921. Although the first flight ended in tragedy, with a pilot and a passenger killed, WAA persevered and in 1924 extended the route to Perth. Within ten years the airline was flying the British Empire's longest air route – from Wyndham to Perth and on to Adelaide – in a DH66 aircraft. The airline was subsidised for its airmail services, but was unable to withstand the financial pressures of the Depression and its fleet of 21 aircraft was acquired by Adelaide Airways Ltd in 1936.

The winners of the Sydney–Brisbane and Sydney–Adelaide tenders took far longer to get into the air. The Sydney to Adelaide tender for a weekly return air service via

Hudson Fysh, in flying kit with cigarette, signs receipt of airmail bags from a post office official at Charleville in 1922, with one of Qantas' first aeroplanes, a de Havilland DH4c behind him. Arthur Baird, the airline's long-term maintenance manager, looks on. The photo was probably taken on the day of QANTAS' first regular airmail service, 2 November 1922. (NLA vn3723003-v)

Cootamundra, Narrandera, Hay and Mildura had been won by the Larkin Aircraft Supply Co (Lasco), but the contract was not finalised until October 1923. However, because of lingering Commonwealth doubts as to the airworthiness of Larkin's machines, the company's founder, Herbert Joseph Larkin (1894–1972) formed Australian Aerial Services Ltd in 1924 as a partnership with Major Frank Roberts who had won the Sydney to Brisbane tender. Services on the Adelaide to Sydney route commenced at last on 2 June 1924, but it was a disaster due to continual poor and dangerous weather at notoriously foggy Cootamundra and the whole route was dropped the following year. The Brisbane service never began. Undaunted, Larkin went on to establish Murray Valley Aerial Services Ltd in 1930, servicing Melbourne, Adelaide and some points between them, but it too did not prosper. 'Tactless and impatient' and twice married, Larkin constantly argued with Commonwealth authorities and was no stranger to litigation. He sold his insolvent airline assets to New England Airways in 1934 then moved to Europe forever in 1937.[11]

By far the most successful tenderer in 1921 was for the least promising route, from Charleville to Cloncurry in outback Queensland. However, the small population it served was more than compensated for by the fact that flying conditions were very safe and there were no roads, railways or ships offering competition as on the other routes. The successful tenderer was a small company founded in November 1920, the Queensland and Northern Territory Aerial Services Ltd, usually known by its improbable acronym QANTAS. Given the very high mortality rate of early Australian airlines (and indeed of their passengers and crews), the survival of QANTAS (later spelt Qantas) to be the world's second oldest airline (after KLM Royal Dutch Airlines, whose operations had begun a year earlier with a summer only service between Amsterdam and London) appears miraculous. But it was no miracle: it was due to good planning; initially modest and achievable aims; sound business practice; and continuity of management more reminiscent of the government railways than of the transient airlines of the interwar period. Hudson Fysh, the pilot of its first flight in 1922, retired as Chairman in 1966, his last decisions concerning the ordering of Boeing 747 'jumbo jet' aircraft.

The airline's founders were Fysh (1895–1974), Paul McGinness (1896–1952) and Fergus McMaster (1879–1950). Fysh and McGinness had both been military aviators in the Middle East and had hoped to enter the 1919 England–Australia air race. They lacked the resources for this, so instead contracted to survey the route from Katherine in the Northern Territory to Longreach in Queensland. This took them 51 days in a

In 1928 the fully enclosed de Havilland DH61 Giant Moth class biplane *Apollo* was the latest thing in speed and comfort in Australian skies. It had just arrived in Brisbane with the first airmail Qantas carried to the city on 23 April 1928. (NLA vn3722860-v)

Model T Ford, and convinced them that air services could be viable in this part of the country, where there were neither railways nor trafficable roads but where there was a sparse population making good money in a widely dispersed pastoral industry. McMaster was one of these men, a wealthy grazier near Cloncurry. McGinness literally stumbled across McMaster whose car had broken an axle in the Cloncurry River, and promptly persuaded the grazier to support the venture. It would prove to be an investment McMaster never had any cause to regret. Arthur Baird, McGinness' and Fysh's former flight sergeant, was the company's first employee as engineer, a position he retained until retirement in 1949. Baird proved to be an inspired choice, for he was brilliant at his job, both in the early improvising days and later as manager of a large maintenance and engineering team. His engineering leadership, together with its good fortune of flying in the clear inland skies during the hazardous and experimental early years of civil aviation, gave Qantas an excellent safety record, although it is a myth that it has never lost a passenger's life. This record and its consistent profitability enabled this local enterprise to become one of the world's leading airlines.

The company was based at Longreach, until it moved to Brisbane in 1929. Taking delivery of its first aircraft, an Avro 504K in January 1921, QANTAS relied on charter work until the scheduled airmail service began between Charleville and Cloncurry on 2 November 1922. Expansion through the 1920s was rapid because the airline provided services that were a genuine necessity and could cut days or even weeks from travel time, rather than a decidedly uncomfortable and dangerous luxury only cutting hours, as was the case with operations between Sydney, Melbourne and Adelaide. When services began to Brisbane in 1929, the airline had outgrown its outback origins, although these remained at the core of its business. It was an unromantic and mundane way to start an airline compared to Kingsford Smith's heroics, but it was safe, profitable and useful.

Kingsford Smith, meanwhile, had established his own airline, Australian National Airways (ANA), in January 1930. Things had gone wrong from the beginning, with Smith and Ulm being stranded on a remote Western Australian dry river bed for more than a fortnight in April 1929 while flying the *Southern Cross* to England to buy aeroplanes for the venture. Two men died while trying to rescue them. Smithy was always more interested in adventures than running an airline, so while ANA was settling down in 1930, he was breaking solo records with flights from Ireland to Newfoundland and from London to Darwin in less than ten days. ANA quickly developed a network linking Brisbane, Sydney, Melbourne, Adelaide, Launceston and Hobart, but it did not endure long. On 31 March 1931 ANA's almost new Avro 10 aeroplane *Southern Cloud* crashed in the Snowy Mountains on a Sydney–Melbourne flight with the loss of all passengers and crew. It was Australia's first major aviation disaster. The wreck was not found until 1958. Kingsford Smith, instead of staying around to try to recover ANA's position, preferred flying experimental airmail routes between Australia and southeast Asia. ANA's collapse was the inevitable result.

There was a perception of unfairness of the Commonwealth's treatment of ANA, for it received no contracts or subsidies whereas the more successful WAA and QANTAS did. Kingsford Smith's mercurial personality and political naivety in flirting with the quasi-fascist New Guard did not help the airline either. ANA flew more miles and carried more passengers, but it did these over routes parallelling good rail services (or steamer services in the case of Tasmania) which could carry far greater quantities of mail more cheaply, more reliably and quickly enough for next day delivery. Even on ANA's busiest route between Sydney and Melbourne, most passengers – even the richest – continued to prefer the relative comfort and complete security of a sleeping berth, despite the change of train at dawn in Albury, to the risk of a sudden death in the skies. In contrast, WAA and QANTAS flew where there were mostly clear skies; exceptionally poor roads; and either no trains or very slow and infrequent ones: Brisbane to Cloncurry, for instance, was a four-day train trip.[12]

During the 1920s and 1930s there was a rapid improvement in aeroplane design, and from 1924 enclosed cabins became the norm for passenger and mail aircraft. These meant that passengers were no longer true aviators, wearing goggles and helmets. Multiple engines, often three at this time, also improved aircraft reliability. The really big step, though, came with the new generation of all-metal planes. The US-designed and built Lockheed Electra and the Douglas DC2 were the first of these. Although a KLM DC2 had flown to Melbourne in the air race of 1934, it was not until the lifting of the ban on importing non-British aircraft in 1937 that they were used in Australia. The new generation of all-metal planes had climate control, retractable landing gear, good insulation and cruising speeds of around 170 miles per hour (275 km/h). They were an enormous advance on the largely timber and linen aircraft of the early 1930s.

The United States was manufacturing far more comfortable and advanced passenger aircraft suitable for Australian conditions than Britain, whose short distances and highly developed rail network meant that aviation had little in the way of a domestic transport role. They showed the ability to perform the long-distance tasks Australia needed with KLM's introduction of a DC2 service from Amsterdam to Batavia (modern Jakarta) in just five and a half days in May 1935. This service was comparable in importance and distance to the England–Australia route, and at this stage the Dutch, using American aircraft, were well in front of the British.

By 1931 aviation was sufficiently developed for the Commonwealth to consider an experimental airmail service between Australia

Elegantly dressed passengers pose beside Qantas Empire Airways' DH86 RMA *Brisbane* (VH-USD) at Archerfield aerodrome in Brisbane, probably in 1935. A fur coat might seem superfluous on a flight from Brisbane to Darwin, but the DH86 was unpressurised. Its design was also flawed and DH86 failures account for most of Qantas' losses of passenger and crew life not caused by wartime conditions. (NLA vn3722860-v)

and Britain. Flying was still a dangerous business, though, and the venture's first casualty was none other than HC Brinsmead, Controller of the Civil Aviation Branch. He was a strong advocate of the development of a passenger and mail air service from England to Australia, and was en route to England to negotiate the concept when his plane crashed just after take-off from Bangkok.[13] He survived but was so badly injured that he never worked again. The outward leg in April 1934 was less than a brilliant success, since the Imperial Airways DH66 taking the mail from Karachi to Darwin crashed at Kupang in Dutch Timor. However, the return leg went smoothly. QANTAS carried the mail from Brisbane to Darwin, from where Charles Kingsford Smith took it on to Akyab in Burma in his 'old bus', as he now referred to the *Southern Cross*. From Burma, the British company Imperial Airways took the mail on to London via India. The relative success of this trial prompted the Commonwealth to call tenders in 1933 for 'Aeroplane services for the conveyance of Mails, Passengers and Goods' between Britain and Australia on a regular basis. The Australian end of the service was to be divided into three parts: the overseas from Singapore to Darwin; the eastern from Darwin to Brisbane and on to Cootamundra; and the Western from Katherine to Perth.[14]

(Hudson Fysh collection, SLNSW a1538003).

The choice of Cootamundra as the terminus of the England–Australia air route was extremely curious. It was based on the principles that the town was midway between Sydney and Melbourne and not far from Canberra, and that passengers and mail could proceed from there to Sydney or Melbourne by rail. It was a less than ideal choice though because Cootamundra was plagued by the foggy weather which had been Larkin's nemesis back in 1924. Moreover, the express trains between Sydney and Melbourne passed through the town in each direction at the unwelcoming hours of 2 and 3am. The proposal was widely and rightly ridiculed, but the Commonwealth persevered, and at first passengers and mail from London to Sydney and Melbourne indeed were deposited at Cootamundra. This unlikely terminus was reached by a Butler Air Transport DH84 Dragon connecting with the Darwin–Brisbane QANTAS flight at Charleville.[15]

QANTAS' successful tender for the northern section began its transformation from an outback carrier to an intercontinental airline. In January 1934 Imperial Airways and QANTAS set up a subsidiary owned half by each called Qantas Empire Airways (QEA or, more commonly known simply as Qantas) with Hudson Fysh as Managing Director. On 10 December 1934 the first regular service left Brisbane for Darwin and connection with Imperial Airways services on to Singapore, India and England. The Duke of Gloucester, then on a Royal Tour of Australia, presided over the inauguration of the service by DH50 and DH61 biplanes at Brisbane. These were by then decidedly old-fashioned aircraft, but Qantas was not given to extravagance. In any case, importation of more advanced American metal planes was still prohibited. From February 1935 until July 1938 larger four engine DH86 biplanes operated the service, and from April 1935 Qantas took over the Darwin to Singapore leg from Imperial Airways, thus becoming an international airline.[16]

Had it wished, Qantas could have imported Lockheed Electras or Douglas DC2s from the United States after 1937 but, as this was an imperial service, the airline had no choice other than to stick with British machines. Thus was ushered in the era of the Empire flying boats, built by Short Brothers of Rochester, England. These took off and landed on harbours, rivers or lakes, and the new termini were Sydney, where Qantas set up a base at Rose Bay, and Southampton. Cootamundra's improbable career as the terminus of the world's longest air service came to an end, and Qantas moved its headquarters from Brisbane to Sydney. A decade earlier they had been in Longreach.

Services began in July 1938 (with Lady

Imperial Airways operated Short Empire flying boats from England to Australia before Qantas took over the eastern leg in 1938. The first to arrive was *Centaurus*, seen here moored in the Brisbane River in December 1937. (Ian Dunn collection)

Mountbatten a passenger on the first flight out of Sydney) and ran three times a week. The decision to introduce flying boats was taken in London without any consultation of either the Australian government or Qantas, but the concept was sound enough. The same plane flew through, with Qantas and Imperial Airways changing crews at Singapore. Passengers and crews slept overnight in hotels en route. At the same time the KNILM (Royal Netherlands Indies Airways) began operating a DC2 service from Batavia to Sydney, connecting with KLM flights from Amsterdam. Compared with the Dutch services via Batavia, the Qantas and Imperial Airways flying boats were slow, but they were certainly comfortable. Indeed, Hudson Fysh considered them the most comfortable aircraft ever built, and argued they were more suitable than KNILM's DC2s for services over long stretches of water. In the single year of peace they operated they made a solid profit, maintained a perfect safety record, and were on time for 94 percent of their flights.[17]

Qantas' Empire flying boat services continued until 4 February 1942, when the last left a besieged Singapore just ten days before its fall to the Japanese. Over the next few months enemy action and accidents destroyed half the fleet of ten. Most Qantas services ceased during the war and its aircraft with their crews were either taken into military service or chartered for military use. Flying boat services were revived in July 1943, using American Catalina machines flying non-stop from the Swan River in Perth to Koggala Lake in southern Ceylon (Sri Lanka). From there, connecting services were provided on to England by the British Overseas Airways Corporation (BOAC, as Imperial Airways had been renamed following its nationalisation). This 5652-kilometre non-stop leg was the longest flown by a commercial airline to that time. At an average journey time of 28 hours, it remains the longest in time ever flown on a regular basis. Passengers, all of whom were on official business and sworn to secrecy, were presented with the 'Rare and Secret Order of the Double Sunrise' in recognition of their participation in these extraordinary flights. The main cargo was fuel; so only very urgent mail and three passengers could be carried. The operation ended just before the war did, on 18 July 1945 and, despite its hazards, lasted for two years without a single serious incident.

Meanwhile, so far as internal services were concerned, the 1930s saw a proliferation of airline companies. The most important was the reconstituted Australian National Airways Pty Ltd. This had its origins in Holyman's Airways, founded in 1932 by the Holyman family. After a number of mergers and takeovers, it grew on the (all too literal) wreckage of Kingsford Smith's company. The Holymans were wealthy Tasmanian shipowners with pastoral interests in the Bass Strait islands, so they were well aware of the advantages of civil aviation in serving isolated and island communities and also had far greater resources than Kingsford Smith had ever had.

Life could be very sweet indeed in the rear cabin of an Empire flying boat, as this Qantas publicity photograph from 1939 made abundantly clear. Their appointments were strongly influenced by art deco maritime and railway styles, as a distinctive school of aircraft interior design had yet to emerge. (Qantas Heritage Collection)

While the older Holymans had been ships' captains before becoming shipowners, the younger generation (led by the future Sir Ivan Holyman, 1896–1957) were pilots who made a successful transition to being airline owners and operators. This was a great contrast with 'Smithy' who, for all his great reputation, manifestly lacked business and political nous.

Holyman's Airways began with services between Launceston and Melbourne, using a DH84 Dragon, DH86s (one of which was lost in Bass Strait with all aboard), DH89 Rapides and later DC2s. However, their strong financial situation, based on shipping, meant they were able to buy many small airlines at cheap prices in the depressed market of the early 1930s. In 1936 Adelaide Airways had taken over Western Australian Airlines, and in 1937 this group merged with Holyman's to form the second ANA. Meanwhile, the New South Wales regional carrier, New England Airways, was absorbed in a new grouping called Airlines of Australia at the same time. Holyman in turn took over Airlines of Australia in 1942, giving ANA a clearly dominant position in Australian civil aviation. Thus, the Holymans' ANA was the airline with which most Australians flew on the main domestic routes linking Brisbane, Sydney,

Melbourne, Tasmania and Adelaide during the 1930s and into the war years.

Ivan Holyman's wife Hazel was also an unlikely aviation pioneer. She did not especially like flying, but in 1936 began training hostesses for ANA when Marguerite Grueber and Blanche Due became ANA's and Australia's first airhostesses. The provision of hostesses on aircraft was a significant step in the transition from the adventurous days of pioneering and decidedly uncomfortable flying to the safer, comfortable and even luxurious airliners of the late 1930s. This was just one year after the ever-progressive KLM had introduced the concept of the airhostess to the world. The aviation era coincided with the first wave of feminism, and women had been conspicuous among pioneer fliers. In an important Australian connection, the British pilot (or aviatrix in the twee language of the day) Amy Johnson made a solo flight from England to Australia in 1930. However, the introduction of airhostesses meant that for the first time women could have careers with airlines.

The other successful tender for a leg of the England–Australia service, Butler Air Transport, was very much a one-man operation, headed by Cecil Arthur Butler (1902–80). Butler had been a ground engineer with Larkin at Hay, before becoming a pilot and marrying into sufficient money to set up an airline. After the end of the airmail contract between Charleville and Cootamundra in 1938, he operated services around New South Wales and Queensland and during

Airlines of Australia was one of the transient enterprises of the 1930s and in 1938 was flying de Havilland DH89s, as seen here preparing for take-off in less than ideal weather conditions. The DH89 Rapide was a smaller and more reliable version of the DH86. (NLA vn3723313-v)

the war manufactured aircraft parts for the government.[18]

One of the most interesting pioneering airlines was Guinea Airways Ltd, which started in the mid-1920s as a one-plane operation called Guinea Gold, flying from Lae to Wau in the New Guinea goldfields. The airline bought heavy Junkers W31 and W34 aeroplanes from Germany to carry bulky freight to the extremely isolated area. It was even claimed that in the mid-1930s, Guinea Airways were carrying more freight than all other airlines in the world combined.[19] The reason was simple: there were no roads, no railways, no navigable rivers, and scarcely any bridle paths into the region. The New Guinea goldfields could never have been exploited without air transport, and this was a real first for the new technology. For the first time ever, large pieces of machinery like dredges were airlifted in sections to their worksites.

Under these circumstances, Guinea Airways were profitable and in 1936 bought two Lockheed Electra 10a all-metal aeroplanes to start more comfortable passenger services. These American aircraft were no great success in New Guinea, so the airline began operating an Adelaide–Darwin service. This was the start of its big move into South Australia and Northern Territory whose aviation market it soon dominated. The Territory services were especially popular because, although the population was not great, there was no railway to the rest of Australia and ships were infrequent and slow. By 1940 it had three Lockheed Electra 10a machines and three Super Electras (14h) in service and so was a serious air operation on the Australian mainland. This was just as well, since in 1942 Japanese fighters destroyed most of its New Guinea fleet and the area of its operation came under Japanese occupation. Under the post-World War II regulation of air services, in 1946 Guinea Airways was restricted to flying in South Australia and the Northern Territory, using DC3s, but retained its by then incongruous name until bought by Ansett in December 1959 and renamed Airlines of South Australia.

Ansett was the other big success story of the pre-World War II airlines. Founded by

British wooden and American all-metal aeroplanes alike were stranded by floodwaters at Port Hedland aerodrome in 1939. MacRobertson-Miller Airlines' Lockheed Electra 10a was identical to those operated by Ansett at the same time and could no more take off than the DH86 in the background. (State Library of Western Australia, the Battye Library 217213PD)

Reginald Miles Ansett (1909–81, known as Reg), the airline had its origins in his bus and trucking business and his consequent squabbles with Victoria's tough-minded Railways Minister, Robert Gordon Menzies. Ansett had acquired his flying licence in 1928, but began his transport enterprises with a car service between Ballarat and Maryborough. When Menzies legislated to prohibit road competition with Victorian Railways in 1935, Ansett bought a six-seat Fokker Universal aeroplane and began flights between Melbourne and Hamilton on 17 February 1936. His timing was fortuitous, since the Commonwealth began subsidising airlines at this time. Ansett Airways Ltd was listed on the Melbourne Stock Exchange the following year, and Ansett moved his operations from Hamilton to Melbourne's Essendon Airport, quickly extending services to Adelaide and Broken Hill.

Holyman, always looking for struggling airlines to absorb into his empire, moved in on Ansett and attempted to buy the airline. Independent in stance as ever, Ansett resisted and even managed to buy three Lockheed Electra 10a aircraft, despite the strain it put on his slender resources. Ansett's successful resistance to ANA was despite the desire of the company's chairman, Melbourne banker Ernest O'Sullivan, to sell the airline, which could not afford to pay the import duty on its Electras, then sitting on Melbourne's docks under customs bond. Reg Ansett could be charismatic, and persuaded a meeting of shareholders to trust him and not sell out. They were swayed by Ansett's rhetoric, O'Sullivan's proposal was defeated, and the chairman resigned. It was a narrow escape (and not the last) from extinction for Ansett. World War II was both kind and hard on Ansett. He was forced to abandon all his regular routes except Hamilton to Melbourne and see his rival ANA take over nearly all the remaining domestic traffic, but he secured a lot of charter work, especially for US forces, which meant that when the war ended his company was prosperous and ready for its great era of expansion.[20]

Not quite an airline but an important aviation service was the Australian Aerial Medical Service, which began operations out of the QANTAS base in Cloncurry in May 1928. It was yet another milestone in this great year for Australian aviation. This was the idea of prominent Presbyterian clergyman, the Reverend John Flynn (1880–1951), who had founded the Australian Inland Mission and devoted his life to improving the life of the peoples of the outback. Flynn was a convivial man and a great publicist, indefatigably touring the cities and the outback giving slide shows about the mission's work. He had many friends and supporters, ranging from the poorest and most marginalised to the wealthiest and most powerful in the country. Victorian industrialist HV McKay's will bequeathed funds to set up the service and, when McKay died in 1926, Flynn set about getting doctors into the air over outback Australia.

As an inveterate outback traveller, Flynn knew Hudson Fysh well, so QANTAS agreed to provide a DH50a four-seater and pilot at the very good rate of two shillings per mile. QANTAS operated the service until 1949, and in 1954 it became the Royal Flying Doctor Service with its own fleet of aircraft.[21] The service involved the meeting of two new technologies, aviation and the wireless, since the doctors were summoned to outback properties with small private radios, treadle powered when electricity was not available. Radio became an important part of aircraft control, and the relationship between the wireless and aviation in the 20th century was similar to that between the railway and the telegraph in the 19th. In both cases, new communications technology made new transport technology safer.

AIRCRAFT MANUFACTURE IN AUSTRALIA

DURING THE 1920s it was easier to establish a viable aeroplane manufacturing business than it would be later, because early aircraft were so simple. The materials needed – quality timber and linen – were relatively cheap, and Australia had an excellent skill base in carpentry. Much the same skills were needed to make an aeroplane as a Cobb and Co coach or a railway passenger carriage. Only the engines required skills of a different order: these were mostly imported and in any case were not much more complex than motor car engines.

For these reasons, the 1920s were the golden age of the small aeroplane manufacturer in Australia. Leading the field was the ever-tempestuous Herbert Joseph Larkin who, following a failed partnership with Sopwith, established the Larkin Aircraft Supply Co (Lasco) in 1920. Based on Coode Island at Fishermens Bend in Port Melbourne, Lasco had a flying school, manufactured aircraft and published *Wings*, an aviation magazine. As early as 1929 Lasco designed and built Australia's first all-metal aircraft, the Lascoter which operated his Cootamundra to Mildura route via Junee, Urana, Berrigan, Tocumwal and Echuca. The failure of Larkin's airlines, however, brought Lasco into liquidation in 1934.[22] Arthur Butler, who went on to found Butler Air Transport, also built a successful all-metal high-wing monoplane as early as 1930, although it had no subsequent commercial use.

QANTAS built seven of its own aeroplanes in its Longreach hangar between 1926 and 1928, neither so long after nor so far from where the last Cobb and Co coaches were built. All were DH50 biplanes built under licence from the English company de Havilland which then dominated aircraft sales throughout the British Empire. The completion of the first was a significant enough event for Lady Stonehaven, the wife of the Governor General, to make the long trip to Longreach to christen the plane on 26 August 1926. Six of the seven were given names ransacked from the classical dictionary, beginning with *Iris* and culminating in *Hippomenes*. Western Australian Airlines also built two DH50s in its own hangars in 1926. The career of QANTAS as an aircraft builder was brief for, as technology improved and aeroplanes became bigger, their construction in remote Longreach became impossible. When de Havilland introduced its next generation of passenger and mail aeroplanes, the DH61, QANTAS' talented engineer, Arthur Baird, who had overseen the DH50 project, decided that building DH61s was beyond the company's capabilities, and it reverted to importing them from England. Neither QANTAS nor its successor Qantas ever built another aeroplane, nor even used any Australian-built machines other than trainers.

De Havilland itself entered the Australian aircraft industry, initially in a sales and service role from 1927. However, in 1930 it began component manufacture at Mascot Airport in Sydney, moving into manufacture of its DH82 Tiger Moths in 1938 and from 1942 making DH84 Dragon communications aircraft. That year it opened a second production line at the new airport at Bankstown in Sydney where it built no fewer than 212 DH98 Mosquito fighter-bombers. After the war, it completed the first of 20 light civil aeroplanes called the DHA3 Drover in 1948. This was Australia's first all-metal civil aircraft and was used extensively by the Royal Flying Doctor Service. More significantly, in 1949 the first of 250 British-designed DH100 Vampire jet fighters emerged from the hangars at Bankstown.

World War II was the major stimulus to aeroplane manufacture in Australia. The vast majority of its output was for military use. Australia's civil aviation requirements could never support a manufacturing industry specialising in large passenger and mail aircraft (although it was a different story for smaller machines), but an industry could be developed to handle large military orders. Besides de Havilland, two other large aircraft manufacturing concerns were set up in the late 1930s, both on Commonwealth initiative, although one was private and the other government owned. These were the Commonwealth Aircraft Corporation (CAC) and the Beaufort Division, later known as the Government Aircraft Factories.

Essington Lewis, General Manager of BHP, was behind the creation of CAC in 1936 when informed that, in anticipation of the coming conflict, the Royal Australian Air Force (or RAAF as the Australian Flying Corps had become) would need large numbers of aircraft and a local production capacity. BHP and General Motors Holden were the main partners in the enterprise, although other concerns joined later as well. LJ Wackett was CAC's manager and he set up a factory at Fishermens Bend with amazing speed. He chose a US design for both the airframe and engine, and the resulting aircraft was known as the Wirraway. The first flew in March 1939

Beaufort fuselages under construction at Chullora Railway Workshops in Sydney in 1943. Women doing such work was a wartime innovation. (Author collection)

and over the war years CAC completed a total of 755 planes. While the Wirraway was no Spitfire or Zero – indeed by the mid-1940s it was a design ten years old and seriously obsolete – it did give the RAAF a basic fighter. CAC also built 200 Wackett trainers (named after the company's manager) in 1941 and 1942, and 250 Boomerang fighters (a faster and more powerful development of the Wirraway) from 1942. Driven by wartime imperatives, the Boomerang was in production just 14 weeks after Wackett approved the first rough drafts of its design. CAC also produced prototypes for the Woomera bomber and CA15 fighter, neither of which went into production.

The Beaufort Division initially was directly owned by the Commonwealth through its Department of Aircraft Production, with management drawn from both private industry and the state railways. Sir Harold Clapp, Chairman of the Victorian Railways Commissioners, headed the Aircraft Production Commission, which oversaw the project, while John Storey (1896–1955) – an immensely talented engineer and industrial manager and son of a former New South Wales Labor premier – directed the Beaufort Division. He came from GMH to the task in the unpromising month of September 1939, setting up another factory at Fishermens Bend next to CAC to manufacture the Bristol Aeroplane Company's Beaufort bombers under licence.

Although these were advanced aluminium aircraft requiring complex and hitherto untried assembly processes, the first flew as early as August 1941. During 1942 they were delivered at the rate of 16 per month and in 1943 at 29 per month. The last of 700 was delivered in August 1944, by which time production had shifted to Beaufighter fighter-bomber, of which 364 were completed by the end of the war. Finally, the Beaufort Division built an Australian version of the Lancaster bomber, the Lincoln, the first of which flew in March

1946. These were the largest aircraft ever built in Australia. The Beaufort project relied initially on parts imported from Britain. After June 1940 these were no longer available and the aircraft and all their components were made in Australia. As well as the Fishermens Bend factory, the Beaufort Division drew on the engineering resources of the government railways, especially in New South Wales, where the Chullora Railway Workshops built the Beaufort's aluminium wings and fuselages. These were taken by train to Fishermens Bend for fitting out and completion. This led to interesting technology transfer, whereby the NSWGR became an enthusiastic user of aluminium in railway vehicles just after the war.[23]

Many organisations contributed to the Beaufort project, notably motor car assemblers and railway workshops as well companies with an aviation background. Adastra was a Sydney-based aeroplane manufacturer which turned assemblies brought from the railway workshops into aeroplanes ready to take to the sky. In 1944 Adastra issued this card to celebrate the 700th Beaufort. (Author collection)

The Australian aircraft manufacturing industry, which had employed a handful of persons in 1937, grew to employ more than 44 000 at its peak in 1944, and delivered about 3500 aeroplanes, many of them – notably the Beaufighter and the Boomerang – highly advanced. After the war, the story of Australian aircraft manufacturing was one of steady decline. Demand for military aircraft dropped, and both civil and military aircraft were ever more complex and specialised. In these circumstances, the best the Australian industry could do was look for a niche for itself, unable to compete with the enormous American industry. Even the British and French industries found this competition daunting. The Government Aircraft Factories filled two niches at almost opposite ends of the aviation spectrum with its two main post-war projects, the Jindivik pilotless jet aircraft, of which over 500 were made over a period of nearly 40 years from 1952, and the Nomad utility aircraft, especially designed for short landing and take-off, of which about 170 were built in the 1970s and 1980s.[24] On the whole, though, machines imported from the United States, Britain and later France met the aircraft needs of both the RAAF and civil airlines from the mid-1940s.

AIRPORTS AND AVIATION REGULATION

IN THE EARLY DAYS of aviation there were no airports. Aeroplanes simply took off and landed wherever there was suitable relatively smooth and dry ground. Showgrounds, sporting fields, farms and even beaches all were used. Probably the last significant instance was during the 1934 London to Melbourne air race, when the Dutch entrant, a DC2, landed in terrible weather on Albury showground, after the town's power supply was used to spell out its name in Morse code and its motorists formed a row of lights on the sodden showground to make out a runway. By 1934, though, such measures were for emergency purposes only and regular airports had been built in all major cities and many towns as well. The earliest permanent aerodromes were built just before World War I for defence purposes, including the Commonwealth's flying school at Point Cook and the New South Wales government's school at Richmond near Sydney.

One of the first civil aerodromes in Australia was at Mascot in Sydney. This was developed on a marshy grazing paddock bordered by a sewage farm, the Cooks River, a golf course and a declining racetrack, leased from the Kensington Racing Club in 1919 by Nigel Love (1892–1979), a former pilot in the Australian Flying Corps in France. Mascot was and remains an ideal site, close enough to the city to be readily accessible, but separated from it by an industrial area with its fair share of noxious industries. Under the *Air Navigation Act* of 1920, the new Civil Aviation Branch was responsible for licensing aerodromes, and Love was soon licensed. He began joy flights at Mascot, as well as assembling Avro aeroplanes there (including QANTAS' first), and even carried the first paying passenger between Sydney and Melbourne. It was, paradoxically, far more difficult to make a living from aviation in Sydney than in Longreach, and Love's company went into voluntary liquidation in 1923. With the expiration of Love's lease, the Commonwealth resumed the land in the same year. Love went on to make his fortune in the more prosaic business of flour milling, although he returned to aviation as a Wing Commander training young pilots during World War II.[25]

Meanwhile, the Civil Aviation Branch believed that aerodromes were far too important to be left to private entrepreneurs, and had begun a process of rapid airport construction and development. The branch's Superintendent of Aerodromes, Captain Edgar Johnston, had recommended this in a 1921 report, and it took over Mascot and Albert Park (in Adelaide) and set up Essendon in Melbourne, Maylands in Perth and Eagle Farm in Brisbane. By 1927 there were 45 Commonwealth aerodromes, 12 private licensed aerodromes, two private fields and 91 emergency landing grounds in the country. In 1922 it had opened Essendon Airport in Melbourne, and by 1925 there were three hangars there, one owned by Lasco, another by the Civil Aviation Branch and the third by an aeronautical engineering company. The branch began levelling and preparing gravel runways at the major aerodromes so they could be used in poor weather. Prior to this grass runways prevented take-offs if too wet, since they became heavy much like a racetrack. Gravel runways were not built at Sydney until 1932, and it was not until 1935 and 1936 that AWA installed wireless facilities at Mascot and Essendon respectively. Mascot was named Kingsford Smith Airport in 1936. As early as 1930 there was some concern that Mascot might be too close to Sydney, but the branch decided to persevere with it as a site, ultimately developing another field further from the city at Bankstown.

The branch moved the locations of city airports extensively, abandoning Adelaide's Albert Park for Parafield, and then acquiring a new site closer to the city at West Beach during World War II. At the same time, it developed Perth's new airport at Guildford. In 1930 it moved Brisbane's main airport from Eagle Farm to Archerfield, although later commercial aviation returned to the original site. The branch did not open Tasmania's first aerodrome, at Western Junction near Launceston, until 1930. At Hobart an interim airfield had been developed at Brighton, which was first used as early as 1920 and hosted ANA's regular services from 1931. However, it was not until 1936 that the branch began work on Hobart's permanent airport at Cambridge.

Men from the Royal Flying Corps and the Australian Flying Corps dominated the branch, which was still within the Department of Defence. This meant it had a command culture coupled with a strong ethos of service. Thus, it encouraged aero clubs rather than private flying schools to provide pilot training. Aero clubs spread rapidly across the country during 1926 and 1927. During the 1930s the branch expanded rapidly and underwent two major restructures, first becoming the Civil Aviation Board and then in November 1938 the Department of Civil Aviation. This at last separated civil aviation from defence, and meant that it now had its own Commonwealth minister in the government as well as a fully-fledged director general. During World War II these were AB Corbett and Sir Daniel McVey, both men of energy and authority. McVey became the architect of Australia's post-war civil aviation regime and was subsequently a Qantas director.

Between 1938 and 1940, the Department of Civil Aviation built control towers and new terminals at Parafield, Mascot and Archerfield based on standard British designs built everywhere from Baghdad to Rangoon. Technology improved rapidly during the war with the creation of a network of meteorological stations, increasing use of radio, and the introduction of radar. After the

One of the least changed standard pre-war British civil aerodrome terminals remains to the present at Archerfield in Brisbane, surviving intact because commercial aviation was moved to Eagle Farm aerodrome. This DC3 had just arrived on what was thought at the time to be Qantas' last domestic flight from Mt Isa on 1 April 1949. Qantas, though, would return to carry domestic traffic once again more than four war, the Department had the challenge of taking over the multitude of former RAAF wartime fields and adapting most of them to civil requirements. It developed controlled air space, whereby major airports had air traffic control services and were surrounded by large areas of controlled space, managed from the ground by radio and radar. By 1959, 24 aerodromes had air traffic control and facilities were poised for the beginning of the jet age.

Jets vastly increased traffic, and both Sydney and Melbourne airports were soon showing the strain. The Department adopted different strategies for each. Melbourne's Essendon airport was surrounded by housing and industry and had little prospect of expansion, so an entirely new site was developed on land bought at Tullamarine in 1961. The runway was completed in 1968, but the imminent introduction of 747 jumbo jets delayed its opening, and the runway was extended from 8500 feet (2591 m) to 12 000 feet (3658 m) before the new airport was opened on 1 July 1970. Finding a new site for an airport at Sydney was not so easy, for precisely the same geographical reasons that a century earlier New South Wales' railways had been extended with so much more difficulty than Victoria's. Therefore, during the 1960s Mascot's main north–south runway was extended twice into Botany Bay, reaching a length of 13 000 feet (3962 m) in 1972. The new international terminal opened at Mascot in 1970 proved to be inadequate almost as soon as it was completed after 747s started operating, demonstrating that the Department, for all its emphasis on planning, could barely cope with the growth in traffic brought by the jet age.

THE TWO-AIRLINE POLICY, 1945-90

WORLD WAR II left the Australian civil aviation industry in a parlous state, yet poised for rapid expansion. While many aircraft had been destroyed or chartered by the military, and most services were suspended, a whole new generation of pilots had been trained in the forces, and there were large numbers of military aircraft, many of which were suitable for conversion for civil purposes. The Douglas C47, a development of the DC2, which could be converted readily to the DC3, was the most famous example and others included Catalina flying boats and Lancastrian and Liberator bombers. Despite their high maintenance costs, flying boats, mostly American Catalinas and British Sunderlands and Sandringhams, served many domestic ports in the early post-war period. Their last service, operated by Ansett, was between Rose Bay and Lord Howe Island. This ended on 10 September 1974 when, following completion of an airstrip on the island, Ansett's Sandringham *Beachcomber* operated the last regular flying boat service in the world.

Around 1970 Sydney offered two of the world's greatest transport experiences of the time, both retro trips on exquisitely maintained equipment of great style but of a dying era. One was to board the air-conditioned Newcastle Express at Central station leaving at 9am or 4.55pm, which would cover the 51 miles (82 km) from Gosford to Broadmeadow in 59 minutes behind a 38 class steam locomotive. In the winter of 1970, a 38 class, no longer in green livery but austerely black, only had a few more months in charge of the expresses arriving in Newcastle from Sydney. (Below, Tony McIlwain)

The other was to catch Ansett's Short S-25V Sandringham 4 flying boat at Rose Bay for Lord Howe Island. The interiors of both the train and flying boat were stylish late art deco.

Both were uniquely perfect travel experiences no longer offered anywhere else in

THE LAST FLYING BOATS AND THE LAST STEAM EXPRESS

the world, and people travelled across the globe to experience them. (Right) Ansett's Sandringham *Beachcomber* (VH-BRC) was moored on the lagoon at Lord Howe Island in August 1973, a year before the world's last regular flying boat service came to an end. The boat is now displayed in her Ansett livery at the Southampton Museum in England. (Bob Smith 2545-115)

The wartime Labor government was keen on detailed post-war planning and often believed government enterprises could contribute to a national economy better than private ones. During the war years the government strictly controlled airlines but, despite its predisposition to nationalisation of private enterprises, it was astute enough to realise that the aviation industry had been driven by the energies and enthusiasm of the entrepreneurs who had created the private airlines. The Department of Civil Aviation released its *Post-war Reorganization: Proposal Outline of a Plan for Civil Aviation* in 1943. This document contained the first inklings of what would become the post-war two-airline policy, whereby the Australian domestic aviation industry would be dominated by one government and one private airline, with local routes remaining the preserve of independent entrepreneurs.

These ideas were incorporated in the *National Airlines Act* of 1945. This established a government-owned airline known as Trans-Australia Airlines (TAA) and regulated the services of private airlines, largely on the basis of the 1943 proposals. The Act survived a challenge to the High Court, since it did not actually nationalise an existing airline and was not seen to constitute a restraint on trade between states, so the two-airline policy became enshrined in Australian domestic aviation policy, lasting until 1990, and supported both by Labor and conservative coalition governments alike over that long period.

TAA began operations in September 1946 and soon demonstrated that it was every bit as enterprising an airline as its private counterparts. The government wisely remained at arm's length from its daily operations, which meant that its airline did not fall into the public service routine which in the post-war period came to debilitate so many aspects of the once-great state railway systems. While TAA's main task was operating the major interstate routes which had been dominated by ANA, it also took over Qantas' internal Queensland and Northern Territory flights from 1949. From 1960 it also took over Qantas' flights to and within Papua New Guinea. Qantas was influential in setting up TAA's operations, and in many ways the airline was a domestic clone of the international carrier. Its first General Manager, Captain Lester Brain, was a Qantas official, and TAA's adoption of Qantas standards and practices gave it an excellent reputation.

TAA was well capitalised, and as early as September 1948 introduced Australia's first pressurised aircraft, the Convair 200, and in 1953 the first propjets used on domestic service, the British-built Vickers Viscount 700. Despite a nasty accident in Hobart early in its history, TAA developed a good record of safety and punctuality, which meant it quickly became the preferred airline for domestic travel, leaving the older ANA in the doldrums.

In many respects the airline which did best out of the post-war period of flux was Ansett. This was despite early Commonwealth

The Qantas crew was smartly turned out and exuded confidence, ready to welcome passengers aboard a Douglas DC3 at Brisbane on the occasion of the airline's first flight to Papua New Guinea in 1946. (NLA vn3723412v)

hostility to Ansett's aspirations and its unpromising situation at the war's end. In 1940 Ansett had been very much a minor local airline, despite its ambitious but almost ruinously expensive purchase of Lockheed 10as back in 1937. It ceased flying regular routes altogether during the war, but, after the war, quickly re-entered the aviation market in rigorous, even desperate, competition with both ANA and the new TAA. In this three-cornered contest for supremacy of Australia's domestic air routes, Ansett was very much the puniest contender.

Ansett bought three C47s and converted them to DC3s and re-established routes linking Melbourne with Canberra and Adelaide, with stops at Mt Gambier and Wagga Wagga respectively. In the highly regulated atmosphere of the time, Ansett was not permitted to duplicate ANA's non-stop services. Reg Ansett was a fierce critic of the emerging two-airline policy, which he rightly felt was squeezing him out. He espoused strong neo-liberal political convictions, although would later change his tune when it suited him. He felt that Commonwealth policy was shutting him out of expansion and preventing the transformation of Ansett into a powerful airline. He was congenitally hostile to Labor's post-war regulatory approach, but things did not get much better for him when a Liberal-Country Party coalition came to power in 1949, because the new prime minister was the same Robert Gordon Menzies who had done so much to frustrate his business ambitions when Victoria's Railways Minister back in the 1930s. However, although Ansett was not especially friendly with Menzies, he was very close to the long-term Victorian Liberal premier of the 1950s and 1960s, Henry Bolte. This support would be valuable for Ansett, especially in the 1970s when Ansett became the target for unfriendly takeovers, and secured in Melbourne the political and economic power base the airline needed to thrive. Ansett was very much the Victorian airline, while TAA and Qantas equally were seen as Sydney airlines, despite Qantas' Queensland origins.

Reg Ansett was a creative entrepreneur, though, and diversified, buying ex-military flying boats, and moving into hotels. In 1946 he renamed the company Ansett Transport Industries, to reflect its wider operations. Ansett at this stage tended to operate as a cut-price airline, and was the first Australian airline to move into the leisure market and package holiday concept. In 1947 he began operating direct flights to Barrier Reef island resorts using Catalina flying boats, then a highly novel concept. He also continued to operate road services, concentrating on interstate trucking and coach operations in competition with the government railways. By 1962 his Pioneer Coaches were operating a fleet of 245 vehicles carrying passengers all over the country. Ansett was the first airline in Australia to move aggressively into airfreight, and in 1956 imported its first Carvair nose-loading freight aeroplane. Ansett's big opportunity came when Sir Ivan Holyman died, leaving ANA in managerial difficulty, with an ageing fleet, but without a strong leader. In a daring and unexpected move, Ansett bought out ANA to create Ansett-ANA in October 1957. Thus, ANA, which had become great through the Holymans' shrewd acquisition of struggling airlines at good prices, became a victim of its own tactics. Ansett thus acquired ANA's fleet of DC6s, but his other main rival, TAA, had superior British-designed and built Vickers Viscounts, so Ansett aggressively bought six of them to counter the government airline. Within months of taking over ANA, Ansett moved in on Butler Air Transport, which had good political connections in New South Wales, great employee loyalty, and in

Arthur Butler a charismatic, respected and vastly experienced leader. The takeover was hostile, contentious and of dubious legality: Ansett played the business game very hard and by April 1959 Butler Air Transport had ceased to exist. Butler retired, honoured and admired, to write a history of Australian civil aviation.[26]

From being the two-airline policy's greatest critic, Reg Ansett became its firmest supporter. This Pauline conversion was a powerful demonstration of how self-interest could dampen the ardour of even the most enthusiastic advocate of laissez faire economics. His was an increasingly powerful voice in Australian business and politics after the takeover of ANA, and he was able to prevent TAA importing French Caravelle aircraft, which would have been the first jets to be used on Australian domestic routes. After Ansett's takeover of ANA and Butler Air Transport the two-airline policy hardened, and the *Airlines Equipment Act* of 1958 required each airline to buy the same aircraft types and to introduce them into service simultaneously, which was interpreted as meaning on exactly the same day. Moreover, thereafter TAA and Ansett-ANA operated over the same routes, at exactly the same fares, and even to the same timetables. TAA's and Ansett-ANA's infrequent flights to and from Perth, for instance, departed five minutes apart for decades, ensuring that passenger preference of travel time in no way would influence which airline they chose.

Ansett's expansion during the late 1950s and 1960s included takeovers of regional airlines like MacRobertson-Miller in Western Australia and Guinea Airways, which became Ansett Airlines of South Australia. MacRobertson-Miller had been established by the same Melbourne confectioner who had sponsored the London–Melbourne race back in 1934. It served Western Australia effectively receiving government subsidies on the condition that profits did not exceed 7.5 percent. This inhibited investment in new aircraft, a situation that changed with the Ansett takeover. Meanwhile Butler Air Transport's internal New South Wales network became Ansett Airlines of New South Wales. Ownership of these regional airlines enabled Ansett to become the world's largest operator of Fokker Friendship aircraft, which were ideally suited for the light loads of such operations.

In October 1964 both Ansett and TAA began flying domestic services with jet aircraft, using the first of many Boeing 727s imported into Australia through the 1960s and 1970s, following the toss of a coin between Reg Ansett and the General Manager of TAA for the honour. The jet age was one of rapid traffic growth and unprecedented safety. The last serious crash of a large Australian domestic airliner involved an Ansett-ANA Viscount at Winton in Queensland in 1966. Jets were not just safe: they were fast, economical and highly productive. A progressive fleet acquisition policy (in which

The changes in regional services to country airports between July 1972 and December 2009 illustrate the volatility of airlines operating these routes. In 1972 East-West Airlines operated a fleet of Dutch-built Fokker Friendships, as seen at its home port of Tamworth (above). In the first decade of the 21st century a new airline, Regional Express (or REX), became the dominant force, operating Swedish-built Saab 340 aircraft, seen (left) at the very small port of Grafton. (Tony McIlwain, Author)

TAA's first Boeing 727 jet VH-TJA arrived at Melbourne's Essendon airport simultaneously with Ansett-ANA's first 727 on 16 October 1964. In April 1967 passengers were disembarking from the pioneering aeroplane at Sydney's Kingsford Smith airport. The silver tail was a short-lived experimental livery. (Bob Smith 4610-274)

Ansett and TAA were by law equals) and ownership of provincial airlines saw Ansett become the country's leading domestic airline by 1969, thus breaking TAA's 20-year hold on that status. This was very much due to Sir Reginald Ansett's decisive, personal, ruthless but often inspiring leadership, which lasted from the company's foundation almost until his death in 1981.[27]

Ansett dropped ANA from its name in 1968 and thereafter had a tumultuous history as various holding companies jostled for control. By 1979 Reg Ansett had lost control and TNT, News Limited and Air New Zealand all at times held controlling interests. Its impressive fleet was diverse, too diverse in fact for economic operations and the two-airline policy was being challenged. TAA and Ansett had never enjoyed a total duopoly, and the strongest surviving regional airline, Tamworth-based operator East-West Airlines, was repeating Butler's quest for national presence under the strong management of Brian Grey. The times suited East-West, as the two-airline policy with its highly regulated fares, aircraft types and schedules was clearly contrary to the neo-liberal spirit of the age. East-West was expanding and began flying interstate, but fell trying to raise additional capital in 1987. Ansett's parent company, then TNT-News Limited, bought the stock and East-West became part of Ansett.

That was not however the end of the story; in October 1987 the Commonwealth government announced that Australian domestic aviation would be deregulated from 1 November 1990. Before deregulation the industry was rocked by its greatest ever industrial dispute as the Australian Federation of Air Pilots attempted to secure improved salaries and conditions before the deregulation would start putting pressure on airlines to cut costs. Lasting from August until the end of 1989, the great pilot's dispute was a watershed in many ways. In the short term it was a disaster both for the airlines and the striking pilots. Ansett's traffic, for instance, fell by 30.5 percent in the year affected by the strike. The strike ultimately was smashed; some pilots never returned to the industry, and those who did had poorer conditions than when the strike began. Longer term, though, it proved two things. First that a Labor government would put the health of the civil aviation industry above loyalty to its union origins, for the Commonwealth condemned the strikers and actively assisted in strike breaking by providing air force planes and crews to carry the traffic. Second it showed that the railways had lost the heart for a battle to win interstate passengers. A decade before they would have run as many extra interstate trains as possible to handle the traffic. In 1989 they did nothing, just wishing it would go away, having reached the dismal conclusion that the more interstate passengers they carried, the more money they would lose.

So, in the medium term, the pilots' dispute was a big win for the two big airlines and left them well positioned to cope with deregulation. Brian Grey returned to the fray immediately after deregulation to launch Compass, a third domestic airline which he hoped would break the duopoly. Compass began flying in December 1990, provoking Australia's first airline ticket price war. However, Grey's pockets were not deep enough to sustain the battle and Compass collapsed within a year. A second airline with the same name failed within seven months in 1992. For the rest of the 1990s, two airlines would be all Australia would have, but they were very different from what had preceded them.

Ansett appeared superficially robust, growing in regional markets by acquiring or developing partnerships with Kendell and Hazelton, two significant New South Wales operators. However, tempestuous battles over its shares, including a disastrous period of Air New Zealand domination, seriously weakened the airline. Employees were becoming nervous and its operations unprofitable, its fleet was incoherent in its diversity, and its market share sustained only by aggressive advertising and sponsorships, combined with a customer reward program so generous it was unsustainable. Meanwhile, the government renamed TAA Australian Airlines in August 1986 in anticipation of deregulation and sale. The buyer, as it turned out, was Qantas. When it bought Australian Airlines in September 1992, Qantas returned to domestic traffic for the first time in over 40 years. Its enhanced fleet enabled effective marketing and vast economies through the use of aircraft on both domestic and international services. As Ansett lurched from crisis to crisis, the merged and privatised Qantas grew ever stronger.[28]

A third serious entrant began flying in August 2000, Brisbane-based Virgin Blue Airlines. With backing from Richard Branson's enormous UK-based Virgin group and a clear vision of itself as a discount operator (and so different and distinct in operations and marketing from Qantas and Ansett), it was able to thrive and grow. A little over a year after Virgin commenced operations Ansett collapsed so totally that there could be no lasting revival (although there was a very brief partial revival) and its assets were sold. It was a happy coincidence for Virgin and also enabled Qantas to boost market share with help in the form of leased aircraft from its **one**world

Discount carriers are increasingly important in the Australian aviation market. Easily the most important is Virgin Blue, while Tiger Airways is a well capitalised recent arrival. Its name proudly flaunts its southeast Asian origins, echoing the logo of its linear ancestor, colonial era Malayan Airways. Both fly Boeing 737s as seen at Sydney's Kingsford Smith Airport's Terminal 2 in December 2009. (Author)

partners. Virgin has expanded rapidly and profitably, with a new standardised fleet of Boeing 737s and a clear philosophy of being different from Qantas, rather than a pale imitator, which is what Ansett had become in its last years. In fact, Virgin was so successful that in 2004 Qantas set up its own subsidiary on the Virgin model, Melbourne-based Jetstar Airways. If imitation is flattery, Virgin should be flattered.

As a result, Australian domestic aviation in 2010 is dominated by three airlines, each with a distinctive profile and range of service offerings, all operating profitably and competitively with new equipment, and offering fares cheaper than ever. There has even been sufficient growth for a fourth entrant to the market, Singapore-based Tiger Airways, a consortium dominated by Singapore Airlines and Ireland's RyanAir. So the traumas of deregulation and the Ansett collapse have left Australian civil aviation in remarkably good shape.

Regional airlines were also restructured and stabilised in the wake of the Ansett collapse. Impulse Airlines had begun flying newspapers north from Sydney and had a brief career in the 1990s as a regional operator. Bought by Qantas in 2001, it was incorporated into a consortium flying regional routes around the country and trading as QantasLink. It operates Canadian-built Bombardier Dash 8 turboprop and Boeing 717 jet aircraft exclusively, in the Qantas tradition of minimising aircraft types. Regional operators Kendell and Hazelton were cast adrift when Ansett collapsed, but a Singapore-Australian consortium bought and reorganised them as Regional Express (or REX). REX has standardised its passenger fleet with Swedish Saab 340 aeroplanes and operated profitably in regional areas along the eastern seaboard and in South Australia since 2002. Between them, QantasLink and REX have brought unprecedented stability and efficiency to regional aviation, an unexpected and perhaps even surprising outcome of deregulation.

POST-WAR INTERNATIONAL AVIATION

UNTIL THE 1980s there was only one Australian international airline, Qantas Empire Airways, later simply Qantas Airways. In 1947 the Chifley Labor government nationalised Qantas Empire Airways, buying out the shares held both by BOAC and Qantas at market prices. Hudson Fysh recognised that nationally owned airlines were becoming the norm everywhere except in the United Sates; so, far from resisting nationalisation, he worked closely with the government to make it a success. Chifley personally approved making a special payment to retiring chairman Fergus McMaster in recognition of his services. Fysh became chairman of the nationalised Qantas, while the directors of the original QANTAS voted to wind up the company and sell its assets, since TAA was taking over its routes in Queensland. Fysh would remain chairman of Qantas until he retired in 1966, 45 years after he had been one of its founders.[29] Fysh and Chifley agreed to retain the name Qantas rather than adopt something like the anodyne Australian Overseas Airways Corporation, which was favoured in some quarters. In this the businessman and Labor prime minister were at one in understanding the potent qualities of nationalism and modesty in retaining the name Queensland and Northern Territory Aerial Services for the nation's international airline.

The transformation of QANTAS into the Qantas of the early 1950s was achieved through a partnership of government and private enterprise. The most amazing thing about the rise of Qantas was its bush origins. Yet the isolation and harshness of the bush had made QANTAS such a needed, respected and profitable airline in the first place. Its original base, astride the main air route from Darwin to Sydney and Melbourne (and hence from England to Australia), had given it the edge in tendering for the first England–Australia airmail services.

Thus, aviation technology had enabled QANTAS to turn into positive advantages the distances, harsh environment and sparse traffic of the outback – the very same factors which had so inhibited the development of transport and communication in Australia and made life so difficult for the builders of remote projects like the Overland Telegraph and transcontinental railways. Its outback location gave QANTAS opportunities to expand far beyond its origins. However, it was its extremely astute management, both when privately and government-owned, that enabled it to take advantage of these opportunities and transform itself into one of the world's largest and longest-lived international carriers.

A major theme in Qantas' post-war history is decolonisation, as it moved from being Qantas Empire Airways to Qantas the Australian Airline. This was a long and at times painful process. For much of the period, traffic on its busiest route, the Kangaroo route from Sydney to London, was operated in a British Commonwealth pool which brought together BOAC, Air India and QEA. In late 1947, just after nationalisation, Qantas began its first service outside British possessions. This was a weekly flight using a Lancastrian (a converted British bomber) from Sydney to Tokyo via Darwin and Manila. This was intended to serve the Australian troops occupying parts of Japan following its defeat, but was the beginnings of Qantas' entry into an important market – travel between a revived post-war Japan and Australia. The Lancastrians were soon replaced by DC4s and a service added to Hong Kong.

Post-war aircraft purchases were a contentious issue, and Fysh was determined to buy the most modern and efficient aircraft

The first Qantas Lockheed Constellation of 1947, in its original unpainted livery, as depicted on a promotional postcard. (Roy Judd collection)

possible. This meant American aircraft. The Lockheed Constellation, with its elegant shape and triple tail, was the aeroplane of choice for long routes from 1947. For shorter and less busy routes Qantas used the Douglas DC3 and DC4, developments of the wartime C47 (or Dakota, itself based on the DC2 of the type which KLM had flown to Melbourne so impressively as long before as 1934). By 1949 Qantas had four Constellations, fifteen DC3s and five DC4s, as well as its flying boats and a few older British machines.[30] Passenger capacity was still low and flying very much for the rich. The early Constellations only had 33 seats and took 60 hours to fly from Sydney to London.

During the early 1950s, the British were developing the world's first passenger jet aeroplane, the Comet, and put heavy pressure on Qantas and the Australian government to order them. However, Fysh was sceptical of the Comet's economics, and successfully resisted its purchase, ordering instead Lockheed's development of the Constellation, the larger and more powerful Super Constellation. This proved to be a wise decision, for the Comet was not only

Qantas Lockheed Super Constellation VH-EAB *Southern Horizon* ready for departure across the Pacific from Sydney's then very austere terminal on 26 March 1956. The engines have started and the ground crew stand at ease while everything is readied for take-off. (SRNSW H 580453)

uneconomic, it was also unsafe, and soon began crashing at alarming rates. Comet failures wrought havoc with BOAC's operations and reputation, and the British passenger aircraft industry never really recovered from the blow. It was a narrow escape for Qantas from what would have been a disastrous purchase.

Qantas moved into the trans-Pacific market at the end of 1953, when it acquired British Commonwealth Pacific Airlines, an imperial enterprise with considerable Australian management that had begun flying across the Pacific in competition with the US giants, Pan American and Trans World Airlines, just after the war. This was known as the Southern Cross route, and had been preceded a year earlier by the inauguration of Qantas' trans-Indian Ocean route to Johannesburg via Perth, Cocos Islands and Mauritius in September 1952. The fortnightly South African service was none too profitable, but the Pacific route quickly became one of Qantas' most important. In January 1958 these long trans-oceanic services were united with the establishment of round the world services by Qantas Super Constellations. Qantas was the first, and one of very few airlines ever, to operate commercial services around the globe. The trans-Atlantic services did not survive the deregulation and intense competition on that route after 1980 but, for more than 20 years, Qantas was a world pioneer in encircling the globe with its own aircraft.

The next year Qantas achieved another first when it became the first airline outside the United States to operate Boeing 707 jet aircraft. Boeing had learned from the mistakes of the Comet and drew on its own experience as builders of US high-altitude bomber aircraft to develop the 707, the world's most successful jet passenger aircraft to that time. Services using 707s began in July 1959 and, by the time Sir Hudson Fysh retired in June 1966, the airline was operating 19 of them. Propeller aircraft were phased out and the fleet standardised with 707s. Boeing's jet aircraft were expensive to buy but, with triple the capacity and double the speed of the Super Constellations, their productivity was amazing: fares began to fall and profits rose. They were also extremely reliable and safe. It was the roar of the 707 jet, not the Empire flying boat or the Constellation, which sounded the death knell of the ocean liner. The maiden voyage of P&O's *Oriana* and the first flight of a Qantas 707 occurred within a year of each other, each breaking Anglo-Australian speed records. One was the last fling of the past, the other heralded the future.

The contemporary age truly began for Qantas in 1967, when the airline changed its name from Qantas Empire Airways to simply Qantas Airways Limited. The Empire of its name no longer existed, and the old imperial traffic sharing arrangements on the Kangaroo route were fading, especially as on their long flights to London the 707s no longer needed to stop in India, once so important a part of the imperial aviation network. In the same year Qantas ordered from Boeing the first of its 747 jumbo jets (having decided not to buy the first series a year earlier), which was delivered in September 1971. The 747 is the most successful design in aviation history, dominating the world's skies for four decades. The economies of size it introduced enabled spectacular falls in the real price of flying, bringing international flights within the budgets of most Australians. By 1979 Qantas operated an all-747 fleet, making for highly efficient maintenance but inhibiting flexibility in developing routes which could not justify the jumbo's capacity. The response was to start acquiring smaller but similarly efficient Boeing 767s from 1986.

While the 747 has been improved considerably over its long service life, with a large number of variations, it was not until September 2008 that there was a dramatic step up in capacity with the introduction of the first of eight French-built Airbus Industrie A380s, with their full-length double-deck cabin. As with the 747, the A380 brings greater comfort and, crucially, economy of operation to Qantas' fleet, enabling the airline to maintain profits (and hence investment and safety) while keeping fares low in the difficult context of increasing fuel prices.

One of Qantas' first Boeing 707s at its Sydney maintenance base in 1962 with a group of maintenance personnel trainers. These were the men who assured the airline its unparalleled safety record in the jet age. (Roy Judd collection)

Qantas' competitors for international traffic changed greatly over this period. In the early post-war years BOAC and Pan American Airlines, with its Boeing Stratocruisers developed from the B29 bomber, were the most significant; but the 1970s saw the rise of Asian airlines, initially British colonial operations like Hong Kong-based Cathay Pacific, but later carriers from southeast Asian nations like

Malaysia, Singapore and Thailand. By the 1990s the economic centre of the world clearly was moving from the north Atlantic to the western Pacific and the dominant international airlines serving Australia reflected this. European airlines increasingly were unable to meet Asian competition, which became ever more varied and intense, with new entrants from Japan, Korea, China and the Gulf gradually moving into the Australian travel market. All these operate much the same aircraft, products either of Boeing of Seattle, USA, or Airbus Industrie of Toulouse, France.

Qantas changed greatly in the wake of internal civil aviation deregulation in 1992, when it absorbed Australian Airlines and thereby returned to domestic operations after a break of more than 40 years. Within months the privatisation of Qantas began with the sale of a 25 percent share to British Airways (although this proved to be transient), reviving a connection dating back to the 1930s. Full privatisation was completed by 1995, and Qantas became a publicly listed company on Australian stock markets. The new arrangement with British Airways was not an imperial revival but part of a new international aviation regime characterised by airline alliances. These enabled airlines to make operational economies on less busy routes while competing on busier ones, and to offer integrated ticketing and seamless connections and to share customer loyalty programs, an innovation which really took off in the 1990s. The era of frequent flyers' accounts in the new international currency of miles flown had arrived.

Two major airline alliances operated in Australia. In 1999 Ansett joined Star Alliance, established in 1997, bringing it into association with, among others, Lufthansa, Thai and United Airlines. Meanwhile, Qantas was a founder member of **one**world in 1999, together with British Airways, American Airlines, Canadian/Canadien and Cathy Pacific. Membership of these alliances grew rapidly and transformed how international airlines operated at the beginning of the 21st century, effecting operational economies and offering passengers global ticketing convenience and loyalty incentives. Such was their success that by 2010 all but two of the world's major airlines, accounting for about three-quarters of all air travel, were members of one of three major alliances.

Deregulation in 1992 allowed Ansett to begin international flights, partly with its domestic fleet, partly with 747s leased from Singapore Airlines. These served Asian and New Zealand destinations and increased the airline's profile, but were never profitable. They ended with Ansett's collapse in September 2001, but from 2004 the newcomer in domestic aviation, Virgin Blue, also moved into the international market, albeit modestly at first serving Pacific islands through its subsidiary Polynesian Blue. In 2009 another Virgin subsidiary, V Australia,

entered an altogether more serious and competitive market launching trans-Pacific flights to Los Angeles using Boeing 777 aircraft.

The strongest rival (but hardly a threat) to Qantas' dominance of international civil aviation from Australia is its own subsidiary discount airline Jetstar, which began operations to New Zealand in 2005 and soon after took over a number of Qantas routes to Asian destinations. These are mostly leisure routes, but do include business routes such as Sydney–Osaka. Jetstar also began its Singapore-based operation Jetstar Asia in 2004 showing a confident, gritty and perhaps surprising determination by an Australian company to take on Asian discount airlines on their own turf. Jetstar uses an all Airbus fleet.

Thus, the early 21st century has seen the development of a two-tier world aviation system, with 'full-service' airlines linked in alliances providing integrated worldwide transport services in all classes beside discount airlines offering cheaper point-to-point fares but little integration between flights. Qantas, through Jetstar, has a foot in both camps; and Virgin subsidiaries as well as Asian-based operators like Tiger Airways and Air Asia are emerging as serious international discount options.

The recent history of Australian civil aviation is primarily about entrepreneurship in an environment of increasing deregulation, sometimes extreme economic fluctuations, and competiveness in both fares and service. The development of the two-tier system reflects the reality that it is not possible for one airline to compete too rigorously on both. Certainly, even with an international aviation sector dominated by Qantas, Australian international travellers have an ever-increasing range of choices in price and service offered by profitable and stable airlines. That is a much better outcome than could have been expected in the dark days of September 2001, when Ansett collapsed and the whole future of civil aviation was assailed by its use for terrorist attacks in the United States.

In 2010 Qantas operates over 30 Boeing 747 aeroplanes on routes across the globe. The type has dominated the airline's international fleet since the early 1970s, an extraordinary record of longevity for any design of transport equipment. Sometimes the airline paints them in special liveries, but none has been more striking than the Aboriginal motifs carried by VH-OJB *Wunala Dreaming* between 1994 and 2003 and by the new aircraft VH-OEJ since 2003. The first jumbo to carry the name and livery is seen here in a magnificent Qantas promotional photograph dating from 1994. (Qantas Heritage Collection)

Transport planners' dilemmas near Maitland, New South Wales, in May 2007. Coal traffic to the port of Newcastle is handled efficiently and is massively profitable. The QR National coal train carries 5000 tonnes and represents world's best practice. By contrast, the CityRail local railcar operating between Maitland and Newcastle would have to be full of adult passengers to generate enough revenue to cover its direct costs of wages, fuel, maintenance and track access. It certainly could not generate the profits needed to pay for investment in the service, which requires every bit as much track and careful management as the coal train. Yet it is needed and is part of the solution to the problem of sustainable mobility for Australians. The question is how to pay for it. The traditional answer was for profitable parts of a railway's operations to subsidise the unprofitable parts but, as the former have spun out of public ownership, it is no longer an option. (John Lacey)

Chapter 9

CONGESTED CITIES, CONTESTED BUSH

CONTEMPORARY TRANSPORT DILEMMAS

GELIGNITE JACK MURRAY (1907–83) was a bit of a lad – a practical joker, exuberant, more than a touch reckless – and people loved him for it. Bondi garage proprietor by profession, he was the most famous motor sport competitor of his time. His unmistakeable signature was exploding a stick of gelignite in a dunny as he accelerated away to begin another stage of an outback rally. 'Gelignite wouldn't hurt a flea,' he famously observed. Whatever happened to the fleas is unrecorded, but apparently his pyrotechnic pranks never injured anyone. At any rate, incontinence was not prudent when Gelignite Jack was around. Murray was the most celebrated competitor in the Redex Round Australia reliability trials of the mid-1950s, driving a 1948 Ford V8 former taxi nicknamed the 'Grey Ghost' on account of its practical but unrefined grey primer paint job. The crowd of 20 000 attending the concluding ceremony of the 1954 Redex trial at Sydney Showground witnessed the victorious Murray emerge from the 'Grey Ghost' neither crowned with a laurel wreath, nor drenched in champagne, but irreverently wearing a gorilla mask.[1]

'Gelignite Jack' Murray's 1948 Ford V8 the 'Grey Ghost' featured on the cover of the 1954 Redex trial brochure. (Andrew Moore collection)

TRANSPORT CULTURES

AN EXTREME CASE Murray may have been, but his individualism and larrikinism were hallmarks of motoring in general and motor sport in particular. Motoring, after all, is about pleasure as much as transport and its defining characteristic is the freedom for people to go where they want when they want, constrained only by the depths of their pockets and their mechanical ability. Other transport modes bring pleasure to many, but most of these (the saddle horse and bicycle sometimes excepted) are necessarily communal. The car is above all individual.

In its heyday, roughly from the 1920s to the 1970s, Australian motor sport reflected this individualism and competitors were mostly enthusiasts who either used private wealth or had to work to afford the sport. Sponsorship existed but did not dominate. Cars which participated in events like the Redex reliability trials and the Hardie-Ferrodo 500 race at Bathurst were registered vehicles driven by their owners. The experience gleaned from these events, especially the reliability trials, went into design and product development. By the late 1970s they had become less accessible to enthusiasts and degenerated into little more than carefully choreographed advertisements, the cars specially prepared by manufacturers and driven by contractors. Jack Murray found the 1979 Repco Rally tedious because of its

REDeX
RELIABILITY TRIAL
Annual
1954
AUTOMOTIVE REPAIR SERVICE
COMPILED FROM OFFICIAL RECORDS AND

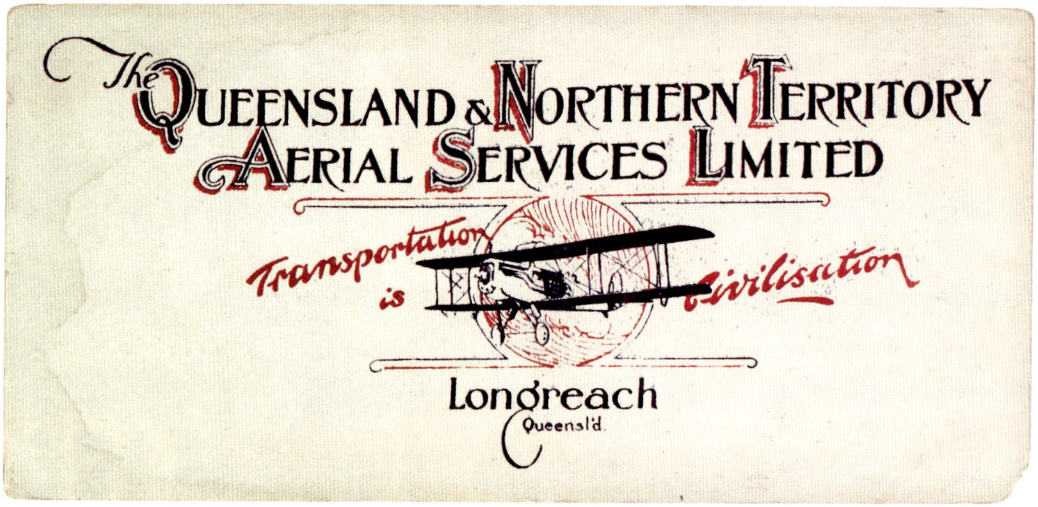

commercial pressures and lack of socialising: he never competed again.

The individualism and larrikinism of exemplary motorist Gelignite Jack contrast sharply with the values of heroes of other transport modes. No personalities could be more different from Murray's than those of the great commissioners of the state railways, who commanded their empires like generals, working through professional subordinates to command workforces of thousands, all trained to follow standardised operational and maintenance procedures aimed at ensuring maximum efficiency and consistently punctual service. Certainly they had courage and could be men of action and initiative when circumstances required. Victorian Railways Chief Commissioner Richard Speight once took charge of a fatal accident scene after the train on which he was going home from work crashed into another. As a young guard Queensland Railways Commissioner Charles

Evans led his passengers, including the judge Sir Redmond Barry, to safety after his train was blown off the line in a massive storm on the Darling Downs. However, it was not their heroism but their organisational skills and capacity for detailed hard work which took Speight and Evans to the top.

The aviation industry had its share of dynamic individualists and heroes, especially in its early decades, but the most charismatic, notably Charles Kingsford Smith, were failures when it actually came to running an airline. Reg Ansett's skills were those of an entrepreneur rather than a manager, and ultimately he fell by the sword he wielded. Hudson Fysh combined managerial, entrepreneurial and technical skills with personal conviction and in many ways was Australia's outstanding transport manager of the 20th century. He chose his subordinates wisely, notably Arthur Baird who was in charge of Qantas maintenance for 30 years, and ensured the airline was standardised and efficient in maintenance and operations. He believed in what he was doing too and chose the motto 'Transportation is Civilisation' for Qantas' letterhead. It is no accident that Qantas and Queensland Railways, whose letterhead of the 1930s was equally unequivocal about its role, are Australia's only big transport concerns which have survived from the 1920s. Both have had strong leaders with absolute conviction and faith in the value of their enterprises as businesses and as forces for good in the lives of the Australian people.

THE CAR MANUFACTURING INDUSTRY

ALTHOUGH MOTORISTS were an individualistic lot, making cars is every bit as regimented and disciplined a business as running a railway or an airline, with the advantage that consumers merely buy a new product every few years and are not actually on the property in large numbers every day. The success of General Motors Holden in designing and manufacturing cars in Australia from 1948 inspired imitation, encouraged by the protectionist economic policies of the 40 years after 1945. For at least three decades, Australian-built cars dominated the market and manufacturers invested in large manufacturing plants, concentrated in Victoria but also significant in South Australia and New South Wales. Some manufacturers developed a design capability, as Holden had back in the 1940s. In the 1950s Ford Australia built cars in its Victorian plants to the same designs as Ford produced in the United Kingdom, but it introduced a local design with the first six-cylinder Falcon of 1960. This was the first locally designed and manufactured rival to the Holden.

Chrysler soon followed Ford and Holden's lead. Back in the 1930s Chrysler had been an aggressive importer of its marques including De Soto, Dodge and Plymouth, and a local company had begun producing locally

Lowering an engine into a new Falcon in 1966 at Ford Australia's factory at Broadmeadows in Melbourne's northern suburbs. (Wolfgang Sievers, NLA vn3296975)

built bodies for imported Chrysler chassis. The local Chrysler distributors bought out an Adelaide body maker and so set the scene for increased levels of local production in the post-war period. Just as Ford had its British range to offer Australian motorists, Chrysler's American parent company acquired the French and British companies Simca and Rootes (makers of the Hillman and Humber marques), giving it a balanced range of both larger North American and smaller European style cars. Such a balance has been essential in the Australian market. In 1962 Chrysler became the third manufacturer to develop a design and manufacturing capability in Australia, opening its plant at Tonsley Park near Adelaide to produce a third Australian six-cylinder family-sized car, the Valiant.

The Holden, Falcon and Valiant were distinctively Australian and in the 1970s were known as the 'big three', such was their domination of domestic car sales. Their success owed more than a little to patriotism for, although the companies were wholly American owned, the cars were genuinely Australian from concept, through design and manufacture, to showroom. They were practical for transport purposes, simply if robustly engineered, and relatively cheap. They were good enough to be adapted for motor sport and, at their apogee in the 1970s, they morphed into distinctively Australian muscle cars at the high performance end of their range. These were both for competition and street use, for it was a time when petrol was cheap and nobody much cared about the environmental costs. Moreover, Australia had developed a thriving automotive components industry (including John Storey's Repco) which meant that most parts sourced from outside the big factories were also of domestic manufacture.

A little smaller than typical American family cars of the time, the 'big three' were designed to cope with Australia's rougher roads better than American products and had a touch of European sophistication to them as well. As in so many aspects of Australian culture and technology, they were a compromise between American and European practice infused with a uniquely Australian bush-bred toughness. Australian cars were tested in the outback, either around Alice Springs or between Bourke and Charleville, depending on where the manufacturer was located, to ensure their components could withstand the rigours of driving on unsealed, liberally potholed bush roads. Australian motorists expected their cars to be able to cope with such conditions, which American and European customers did not; and this characteristic helped Australian manufacturers develop export markets, especially in the Middle East and southern Africa, where conditions were not so very different.

There was a fourth big player for a while. In 1952 the British Motor Corporation began operations in a factory it built on the site of the former Victoria Park racetrack at West Kensington in Sydney. There it manufactured

English designs from the Austin and Morris stables, which had been imported for many years and had benefited from imperial tariff preferences. During the late 1960s, rebranded as Leyland Australia, the Victoria Park factory enjoyed enormous success with its smaller, technically advanced, front-wheel drive models, which were broadly similar to their English equivalents but benefited from outback testing and local development. Leyland then made a huge mistake and undertook design and manufacture of the greatest failure in Australian automotive history, the P76, so named because it was hoped to dominate the local market by 1976. Larger than the 'big three' family sedans, it was famed for having a boot designed to fit a 44 gallon drum. However, customer demand for such capacity was limited and the P76 was launched at the worst possible time, when fuel prices started to rise after a long period of relative decline, denting the popularity of the Australian family sedan forever. Unable to sustain losses on the P76, the Leyland factory closed in 1974. Almost no-one was aware of it at the time, but it was the beginning of a rapid decline in the Australian automotive manufacturing industry.

Ironically, Leyland's fine small and medium cars, whose production ceased with the P76 fiasco, were the prototype of what was to come, as the world centre of automotive excellence and innovation moved from the United States and Europe to Japan. The Japanese car industry developed impressively during the 1950s, at first replicating British models, then refining and improving them. Japanese industry had built to high standards during the war, as the Japanese military had demanded industrial excellence, and in the 20 years after defeat beat its swords into ploughshares, producing automobiles and high speed trains instead of fighter planes and tanks. By the 1980s the typical Japanese car sold in Australia was recognisably a descendent of the Leyland medium-sized front-wheel drive cars of the 1960s. In the last two decades of the 20th century Japanese makers developed the finest mass production motor cars of all time, characterised by refined and sophisticated design and 'total quality management' in manufacture. 'Friday cars', completed on a Friday when workers' thoughts were on the weekend, or 'lemons', cars riddled with manufacturing flaws, were almost unknown among the products of Japanese factories. The surviving big three manufacturers established links with Japanese carmakers to introduce both their excellent car designs and Japanese standards of total quality management.

Chrysler was the first to move when the American parent company bought into Mitsubishi and began assembling Mitsubishi models at Tonsley in 1971. The Mitsubishis were far superior products to the Simca and Hillman models they replaced and a great market success. So successful that when Chrysler went bankrupt in the United States, Mitsubishi took over the plant in

Motorisation in Russell Street, Toowoomba, in 1971. Leyland (in front of the bus and on extreme right) and Holden cars dominate road traffic, halted to allow steam, in the form of Queensland Railways' PB15 class No 448, to pass for one of the last times. The P plate on the Leyland was an early regulatory step to curb the exuberance of youthful motorists. (Eric Marggraf, QR Heritage)

The first Ford Falcon of 1960, designed and manufactured in Victoria, from a Ford promotional postcard emphasising the possibilities for family recreation made possible by a family-sized car. (Author postcard collection)

1980, promptly dropped the Valiant, and concentrated on developing Australian versions of Japanese designs, the Sigma and Magna. By the 1980s 'Japanese' was a byword for high quality and good value: Australian customers increasingly preferred a Japanese to an American or European marque. The Japanisation of the Australian motor industry was under way.

The stunning success of this story has been Toyota Australia. In 1963 Australian Motor Industries of Port Melbourne assembled the first ever Toyota car built outside Japan. It was not a particularly good car, thoroughly English in conception, rather fragile, and with a twee name to match, the alliterative Toyota Tiara. AMI had been operating in Melbourne since the 1920s under various names, assembling cars from parts imported from Britain and the United States, which it continued to do until 1978. Most of its marques were decidedly niche, although it had won a mass market for its Vanguard in the 1950s. Making Toyotas soon came to dominate AMI's activities, as new and far superior models (all beginning with the letter C) were introduced through the 1960s. Toyota struck a mighty blow with the introduction of the Camry in 1987, a little smaller than Holdens and Falcons, an excellent design developed locally and still in production, though much refined.

By 1991 Toyota was the Australian market leader, having taken over AMI in 1987, and then in 1994 moved its operations to a totally new plant at Altona on Melbourne's western fringe. The new factory was an automated modern operation with, for Australia, unprecedented quality control standards. It also began exporting on a scale never before seen for an Australian automotive manufacturer, including cars in kit form for assembly in Toyota's southeast Asian plants. For Toyota, the move into Australia has been exceptionally good business, marrying Australian product development and testing (which have been areas of Australian expertise since the first Holden was produced in 1948) with Japanese production methods and quality.

Other Japanese manufacturers have not succeeded as well in the country. Mitsubishi Australia ceased production at Tonsley Park in 2008 to become an importer. By then Tonsley Park was only producing one model and was clearly not viable. Nissan suffered a similar fate after a propitious beginning. The crucial figure in Nissan's early success was Sir Lawrence Hartnett, who had been responsible for developing the first Holden back in the 1940s. In 1960 he saw Nissan's Datsun Bluebird at the Melbourne Motor Show and thought it had potential as a small car in the Australian market. He was right: the Bluebird and its derivatives, notably the rally drivers' favourite, the Datsun 1600, were fine machines, certainly superior to the mostly British small cars like the Triumph Herald then being sold in Australia. Hartnett began assembly of kits imported from Japan at the Pressed Metal Corporation in Sydney and in 1972 opened a manufacturing plant at Clayton in Melbourne, taking over assets once used by Volkswagen. However, Nissan never really succeeded as a local designer and manufacturer, and in 1992 closed the plant and reverted to importing its products.

The transience of manufacturers in Australia is largely due to changing government policy. The 1945 to 1984 period was characterised by high tariffs and quotas, which restricted imports to 20 percent of all sales. Under these conditions local manufacturing made sense, even if unaccompanied by local design and development. However, prices were high and the Australian car fleet tended to be old, inefficient in fuel use and environmentally damaging as a result. The Hawke government was sensitive to affected manufacturers' and trade unions' concerns, but realised that increasingly free trade was the pattern of the future and that high levels of protection of the car industry were unsustainable in the long term. Consumers, far more numerous than car builders and keen to buy cheaper and better cars, totally concurred. Hawke's industry minister John Button began phasing out import quotas in 1984 and anticipated gradual tariff cuts to improve the industry's efficiency. Hawke and Button realised this would mean a reduction in the number of plants and manufacturers but believed the structural adjustment would be worth the cost. They were right.

Tariffs on imported cars fell from 57.5 percent in 1987 to the general tariff of 5 percent in 2010, at which level it is more a revenue raising than a protectionist tax. In 1990 there were eight plants operated by five makers in Australia: in 2010 three manufacturers produce cars in four plants. Two of the three, Holden and Toyota, use their Australian arms to design cars which are important to their range of international offerings and have large export programs. The third, Ford, with no large export program, is clearly the most vulnerable. Tariff reductions and the abolition of quotas have left Australia with a smaller but far more efficient car industry, making cars of real quality which are in demand in many parts of the world. For the consumer, Australian cars – and imported ones too – are cheaper and better than ever. This is a better result than many advocates of protection would have expected back in the 1980s. Australia is one of only 15 countries in the world with a capacity to take a car from concept through design, testing and manufacture to the showroom.[2]

Challenges will always remain as the requirement for energy efficiency means the development of whole new means of traction and new countries with low cost structures move into the industry. Korea, with no historical background in heavy industry at all, has shown what can be achieved in terms of creating a motor car manufacturing capability, and what Korea achieves today China almost certainly will tomorrow. The high levels of automation in modern car plants mean that differentials between workers' incomes are not as important as once they were in determining which nations' industries succeed and which do not. Countries with higher wage structures than Australia like Japan, France and Germany compete very effectively on world markets. Currency fluctuations now have a greater effect on car prices than tariffs and wages, and these are always volatile, in 2009 and 2010 working against the Australian industry but at other times very much in its favour.

Quality of design and build and the efficiency of factories are what really matters in the contemporary globalised motor market; by these yardsticks the Australian industry has performed very well since 1990. Government subsidies still do exist, including new ones introduced by the Rudd government for the development of alternative traction. This is increasingly the big issue for the motor industry, both because world oil supplies are limited, meaning that petrol prices undoubtedly will increase very considerably in the medium term, and because transport is a major generator of greenhouse gases and hence global warming. These subsidies have many critics but they are transparent, targeted and of defined duration. They also contribute to improved design and hence competitiveness rather than bolster inefficiency in the way tariffs did. Despite its rationalisation since John Button launched his car plan and the reality of increasingly free trade, in 2010 car making remains Australia's largest manufacturing industry and it does make some products at least which are globally competitive. In this, as in so many other things, it occupies the position held a century earlier by the railway rolling stock industry.

TRUCKS AND FREIGHT TRANSPORT DILEMMAS

TRUCKS CHANGED EVERY bit as much as cars between 1945 and 1990. In the immediate post-war period British manufacturers dominated sales and most were on rigid bodies. British army surplus 'blitz wagons' were a popular and economical choice for the trucking industry just after the war, but new imports increasingly were American. Mack and Kenworth replaced Thorneycroft and Albion as the truck manufacturers of preference. The articulated truck, popularly known as the semi-trailer in Australia, quickly came to dominate interstate road freight traffic and, after deregulation of intrastate freight, that too.

Power and speed of prime movers were always increasing, new technology such a turbo-charging and aerodynamic design improving efficiency. For most of the post-war period articulated trucks were limited to a gross weight of 38 tons, much the same as the horse drawn flat-top wagons of the

An ex-army 'blitz wagon' in civilian service for Booringa Shire in the early post-World War II period. Council employees pose on a primitive timber bridge near Mt Moffat, Queensland. (Frank Hurley, NLA an23148170)

late 19th century. After interstate and city fringe freeways were built the limit was raised to 50 tonnes and a new configuration permitted, the B-double, in which the prime mover tows two trailers. The maximum axle load for road trucks is now 9 tonnes, which is similar to the standard axle load on Queensland Railways in the steam era.[3] This means that trucks can now handle comparable tonnages to trains, albeit in many more units.

B-doubles are controversial and, although intended only for high-quality roads, all too often operate on roads and streets for which they are unsuitable causing delays and congestion. The B-double was an extension into densely populated areas of the concept of the road train, a prime mover towing (usually) three trailers which became popular in northern Australia in the 1950s. While the road train is useful and appropriate to the population levels and infrastructure where it is permitted, the B-double is widely disliked throughout southeastern Australia, considered little more than a shameless profit grab by an industry that shows little concern for the inconvenience and damage they cause. The trucking industry in Australia is relatively unregulated by international standards. There are no restrictions on operations at weekends or at night (as in many European countries), nor any requirement for speed and location recorders on trucks. The discrepancy between these requirements for road and rail operators is striking and often a matter for comment in enquiries into serious level crossing accidents, where there is always plenty of data on the train's performance but often no data at all on what the truck has been doing, other than drivers' all too often woeful records of traffic infringements and irresponsible driving.

Under these circumstances, popular hostility to the trucking industry is understandable. In 2008 in New South Wales, the most typical state in terms of the variety of its road conditions, articulated trucks were involved in 10.45 percent (54 out of 517) of all fatal accidents, but only 1.52 percent (1184 out of 77 671) of all accidents. Even more alarmingly, in 2009 there were only 81 217 articulated trucks in Australia compared to 12 023 098 cars, so 0.68 percent of the vehicles caused 10.45 percent of the fatalities. In other words, an articulated truck is 15 times more likely to cause a fatality than a car, although it must be said that these trucks spend more time on the roads than cars do.

In fact, apart from truck accidents, Australian roads are quite safe and New South Wales roads are the safest in the country, with just 5.4 fatalities per 100 000 of population and a national rate of 6.7 per 100 000 in 2008, both lower than most similar countries except parts of Scandinavia, Britain, the Netherlands and Japan. Canadian and US fatality rates are about double those in Australia. Deaths on New South Wales roads each year rose from 411 in 1945 to a peak of 1309 in 1970, remained at about that level for two decades then declined to a low point of 374 in 2008, since when the trend has been upwards again.[4] This was in the context of a growing vehicle fleet. In 2009 there were 12 023 098 cars in Australia, or about one for every two people, compared to roughly one car for every eight people in 1945. The annual growth rate in car registrations was 2.5 percent in the early 21st century, but the growth rate in articulated truck registrations was 4.1 percent.[5]

The reason for the high growth in articulated truck registrations is that they are relatively cheap to operate since they are

This section of the Pacific Highway near Byron Bay is considered dangerous and has a low speed limit, but its alignment is really quite good and infinitely superior to and much faster than the parallel railway between Bangalow and Byron Bay, which was closed in 2004. On New Year's Eve 2009, cars can readily overtake the B-double on the ascent, and the truck is permitted to run right through the night and into the next day, even though it will be a public holiday. (Author)

given unlimited road use for a very modest registration fee, while trains are required to generate profits on the infrastructure they use. A comparison of the costs of trucking companies and rail operators to use the infrastructure they need is instructive. The rail access charge for a typical express freight train weighing 2500 tonnes over the 810 kilometres from Newcastle to Brisbane is $8618, or 0.426 cents per gross tonne/kilometre. Trucks in Australia do not pay road access charges but a fixed annual registration fee. In New South Wales this fee is $14 340 for a 50 tonne B-double. Assuming 300 interstate trips of 1000 kilometres per annum, this is a charge of about 0.096 cents per tonne/kilometre, a little over a fifth of the sample rail access charge.[6] However, truck operators pay more excise tax on their diesel fuel than train operators, who benefit from an off-road rebate. This is less easy to quantify because fuel consumption varies and the excise is not specifically tied to road construction and maintenance (although it once was) but is part of general revenue.

The consequences of trains paying 0.426 cents and trucks 0.096 cents per gross tonne/kilometre to use infrastructure are obvious. Operationally, rail offers many economies of scale over trucks and, despite the higher access fees, is cheaper on a terminal to terminal basis, if slower. To some extent the discrepancy in the cost of access is justified as railways are more expensive to build, operate and maintain than roads, but not five times as expensive. Shippers, whose prime responsibility is to operate profitably, naturally prefer trucks to trains if they provide a service which better balances price and time. Moreover, trucks are faster as the alignments of all major highways have been improved dramatically at taxpayers' expense whereas the alignments of most railways remain much as they were when built. The worst interstate railway, between Sydney and Brisbane, makes a total of 177 circles in its 962 kilometres, which is a simply deplorable alignment.[7] Yet politicians cannot see the same electoral advantage in spending money on improving rail alignments as they do in spending it on the same thing for roads. Public pressure for improving the far worse railway is much less than for improving the parallel Pacific Highway, and politicians are always inclined to grease the squeaky wheel rather than make transport policy on the basis of need and efficiency. And no wheel in the country is squeakier than the road lobby.

A further factor is that road transport provides a more convenient service for shippers, because trucks deliver directly to the customer while trains deliver their freight to a terminal. This means that the inherent economies of rail are diluted on relatively short hauls, where terminal to destination costs are a larger proportion of the total, but become more apparent on long hauls. The result is that rail is the dominant mode in carrying transcontinental freight between the eastern states and Perth, but road dominates on shorter hauls. Rail moves about 57 percent of non-bulk freight between Perth and the eastern states, 37 percent between Melbourne and Brisbane (even though the rail route is longer and slower than the road route and goes through the bottleneck of Sydney), but less than 10 percent on the busiest routes between Sydney and Brisbane and between Sydney and Melbourne. Back in 1972 rail moved about 30 percent of freight between Sydney and Canberra but now moves precisely zero.

All this has occurred in a context of falling freight prices. Between 1970 and 2000 the average cost of interstate general freight fell from about 8 cents per tonne/kilometre by rail and 10 cents per tonne/kilometre by road to about 2.5 and 5.5 cents respectively in constant value terms.[8] This reflects a stunning improvement in the productivity of both modes, although in 1970 railways collected and delivered goods at hundreds of stations and sidings in each city rather than at one terminal. This was convenient for shippers, but operationally complex (because of the need for shunting and operating many small local freight trains) and unsustainably expensive for the railways. By abandoning this diversity of collection and delivery points, rail freight operations became profitable, which many certainly were not in the 1970s.

Clearly cheap freight rates bolster national economic competitiveness, but the questions can and should be asked whether the quest for cheap freight has gone too far and whether Australians in future should pay more to move goods and themselves around the country, whether by road or rail, in order to fund improved roads and railways. How to establish adequate and fair charges for rail and road operators' access to networks is one of the great challenges facing Australia as a nation. Certainly better infrastructure is badly needed and it is an absurd illusion, although a common one, that it can come without shippers, passengers and motorists paying for it.

ROAD AND FREEWAY CONSTRUCTION

MOVEMENT OF HEAVY goods over long distances by road in Australia dates from the Pacific War. The 1943-built bitumen strip of the Stuart Highway between Alice Springs and Darwin (where there was no through railway) was the road train's first haunt. The US army also built an inland road from Ipswich to Townsville in case enemy action disrupted the coastal railway, and these two roads were the precedent for post-war policy in northern Australia. During the 1950s Queensland, Western Australia and the Northern Territory built thousands of kilometres of 'developmental roads' through the outback. These were the solution to providing transport into remote areas which could be productive but only at very low densities of stock and people. Such districts could never justify a railway unless there was a mine (as at Mt Isa) or a large city (such as Darwin) at its end. Droving along stock routes had been the traditional solution, but the developmental road, at first gravel surfaced but increasingly sealed, and the road train were a far more effective combination. They brought fast and economical transport to much of the outback at a fraction of the cost of a railway. Moreover, the governments that built the roads were not confronted with the problem of trying to run the traffic at a profit, which was always the case when they built railways. They merely built and maintained the road, leaving the economics of operations to road hauliers, a far less complicated business than building and running a railway.

In more settled parts of the country, the growth in car numbers and deregulated interstate freight trucking created enormous demand and growing political pressure for improved highways. Until the late 1960s, this meant upgrading pre-war roads with wider sealed carriageways, improved signage and crash barriers, and overtaking lanes on hills. In New South Wales, steel truss bridges replaced vehicular ferries across rivers on the coastal highways north and south from Sydney. This was not enough, though, to meet demand. As with Victoria's pre-war Great Ocean Road, recreational motoring was the spur to investment in these coastal highways.

The sealing of Australia's major highways was a significant achievement of the 1950 to 1985 period. Many outback roads through mostly dry areas became quagmires after rain and often impassable for heavy vehicles. This was the scene on the Newell Highway at Bellata in northwestern New South Wales in 1963. (Tony McIlwain)

The terrain between Sydney, Newcastle and Wollongong is about as difficult as it gets for a civil engineer in heavily populated parts of Australia, yet weekend traffic was huge and delays frustrating. Around 18 000 vehicles crossed Peats Ferry bridge across the Hawkesbury most Sundays in 1960, while weekday usage was about 6000 vehicles.

New South Wales therefore led the way in building intercity motorways, partly funded by tolls, the first section through wild country north of the Hawkesbury River opening in December 1965. By December 1998 freeways connected the outskirts of Sydney with both Newcastle and Wollongong, including a new bridge across the Hawkesbury. The 128-kilometre freeway from Sydney to Newcastle had taken over three decades to build, which was hardly a stellar achievement.[9] Other states followed the precedent, all over much easier terrain, although South Australia's first long-distance freeway required construction through the Adelaide Hills to Murray Bridge. In Queensland the motorway from the Gold Coast to the Sunshine Coast involved a crossing of the Brisbane River downstream from the city on the spectacular toll-funded 64.5-metre-high Gateway Bridge, which opened in 1986. This was such a success that traffic grew from 17 000 to 100 000 vehicles a day in 20 years and it is now being duplicated as a result.[10] Whether this is an urban or intercity freeway is a moot point and an undesirable side effect of these freeways has been their growing use for long-distance commuting by car, ultimately a wasteful, environmentally damaging and unsustainable activity. This was not the intention in building them, but improved transport facilities always create new demand.

The Commonwealth began directly funding intercity freeways and highways under the Whitlam government's *National Roads Act* of 1974, appropriately enough first between the outskirts of Sydney and Canberra. It also funded upgrades of the Hume Highway between Goulburn and Melbourne and completion of the Sydney–Newcastle freeway without tolls. The 1974 Act designated Commonwealth funded National Highway links which brought together the hitherto separate state highways into a national network. Most car journeys on these roads are anything but national although many truck trips are, but it did enable motorists in ordinary cars to contemplate a trip across or around the continent with confidence. While the busy highways between Rockhampton and Adelaide were part of the network, these had been sealed roads since World War II. However, from 1974 work began on sealing the surfaces of highways across the Nullarbor, between Port Augusta and Alice Springs, and around the western and northern coasts linking Darwin with Perth and Brisbane. This work was completed at Commonwealth expense in 1986.[11]

Victoria's and most of South Australia's benign landscapes meant that upgrading and duplicating existing roads could achieve much the same results in terms of capacity, speed and safety which only freeways could offer New South Wales, where the challenges facing civil engineers were huge, and to a lesser extent Queensland where rapid population growth rather than topography was the big challenge. The greatest need for interstate highway improvement was Australia's busiest long-distance road for leisure traffic, the Pacific Highway between Newcastle and the Gold Coast. This road crosses many rivers and a deeply fractured landscape, features which also have made the parallel railway the slowest and poorest interstate rail link in the country. Just how dangerous this highway could be was proved in late 1989 when two crashes, involving three buses and a truck, at Cowper near Grafton on 20 October and Clybucca near Kempsey on 22 December, killed a total of 57 people. In both cases, as with almost every road accident, driver error and negligence were the true causes, but many people found it more comforting to blame the road. Opposition politicians habitually, disgracefully and irresponsibly delight in blaming allegedly inadequate government road funding rather than negligent motorists (who are really to blame but are also voters) for almost every serious road accident. Such cruel dishonesty has become a staple of what passes for political discourse on Australian transport policy.

Investment in rebuilding the Pacific Highway was already under way by 1989 and has been accelerated since. The road has benefited from numerous expensive deviations and many more are planned: by October 2009, 354 of its 677 kilometres between Newcastle and Tweed Heads had been or were being rebuilt as a dual carriageway.[12] Road safety enhancements have not been confined to rebuilding roads. In addition the regulatory framework of motoring was transformed in the last decades of the 20th century. The main features of this transformation were compulsory wearing of seat belts for motorists and helmets for motorcyclists, restrictions on the amount of alcohol motorists could imbibe, and discriminatory regulations against younger and older drivers who are overrepresented in accident statistics. Regulation also prescribed increasing safety features in new cars. The effects of these regulatory changes have been positive. While the number of accidents has increased with the growing number of vehicles since the 1970s, the number of fatalities and serious injuries has fallen, which was precisely the aim of increased regulation.

'CAR WARS', SUBURBAN RAILWAYS AND URBAN TRANSPORT PLANNING

WHILE INVESTMENT in highways and freeways linking cities has been relatively uncontroversial, urban freeway projects since the 1970s have provoked such bitter debate that the most exhaustive case study (of Melbourne) characterises them as the 'car wars'. At issue was the 1969 Melbourne Transportation Plan, 'often … characterised as one of Australia's great planning disasters'.[13] Even its name indicated it was American, as indeed it was, foreshadowing a city dissected by and ringed with freeways. Opposition to the plan divided the city for decades and made a big impact in Victorian and national politics. Activism against the plan made the career of clergyman politician Brian Howe, Labor deputy prime minister from 1991 to 1995, one of whose major achievements in that role was the Better Cities program, designed to bolster sustainable non-freeway based urban development. He was extremely bitter that the New South Wales government used funding from the program to build the Anzac Bridge, a freeway in effect, rather than invest it in light rail, for Howe's commitment was born of his struggle against urban freeways.

Wilbur Smith and Associates, the American consultants who produced the 1969 Melbourne study, had already done the same thing for Brisbane in 1965, leading to the abandonment of its trams, construction of the Riverside Freeway, and reductions in train services. The Whitlam government (1972–75) did not include any minister with quite the same commitment to urban planning as Howe would be under Hawke and Keating, but it did believe in an enhanced Commonwealth role in urban infrastructure. Whitlam often joked that his greatest achievements were in sewerage, which is both plausible and admirable if uninspiring. Certainly on transport policy his government attempted to strike a mean in the 'car wars', funding highways as no Commonwealth government ever had before but also funding design of an Australian Urban Passenger Train (AUPT) and promising Commonwealth assistance for the electrification of Brisbane's suburban railways. Despite their often tempestuous relationship and very different social visions, this was a project on which Whitlam and Queensland premier Joh Bjelke-Petersen could agree.

The first stage of Brisbane's technically advanced electrification project opened in 1979. For the first time in Australia the voltage was 25kV AC rather than 1500V DC, leading to economies of construction and operation. The new trains, the first air-conditioned suburban trains in the country, were stainless steel and based on the work done for the AUPT. The project was accompanied by resignalling, improved track and, for the first time in Brisbane, regular interval timetabling. When Victoria bought new air-conditioned suburban trains equipment in the early 1980s, they too incorporated many features from the AUPT design. Thus, Brisbane, with Australia's first new railway electrification project for 50 years, led the way in the late 20th century.

Meanwhile, in 1978 South Australian Railways were split between the Commonwealth and the state, the latter merging the suburban railways it retained with its bus and tram operations, beginning a trend towards increasing integration of transport modes in Australian cities, except Sydney. There the Granville disaster of 18 January 1977 had the opposite effect, leading to the breakdown of the unity of rail, bus and ferry operations established in 1973, which has contributed since to the state's subsequent inertia on intermodal ticketing. At Granville a derailment caused by 'the very unsatisfactory condition of the permanent way' killed 83 passengers on an early morning commuter train from the

The first series of Brisbane electric trains introduced in 1979 were the first air-conditioned suburban trains in the country. All are still in service and in January 2010 this one was serving Ascot, one of Brisbane's most attractive but underutilised stations beside Eagle Farm Racecourse. This quiet branch is one of only two suburban railways in Australia still controlled by semaphore signals, along with Melbourne's Hurstbridge line. (Author)

Blue Mountains to Sydney. The fragility of the timber carriages, all over 50 years old, contributed to the death toll. The real guilty parties were of course the politicians who had starved the state's railways of investment and given poor leadership for decades, but neither of those is a criminal offence.

The results of Granville were mostly positive. Most states were sufficiently alarmed to invest heavily in improved track and new steel rolling stock to replace surviving timber trains. Sydney replaced its entire fleet with double-deck suburban and interurban cars based on a French design introduced back in 1964. Sydney and Melbourne both extended their electric networks in stages, in Melbourne to service outer suburbs but around Sydney more substantially. Electric trains had reached Lithgow in 1957 and Gosford in 1960, and were extended to Newcastle in 1984 and Wollongong and Port Kembla in 1986. Subsequent extensions have taken southern electrification to Kiama.

These extensions benefited freight as well as passenger operations and appeared to anticipate a transfer of most coal haulage in the state to electric traction. However, it was not to be: electric operation of freight services was wound back in the late 1990s and did not outlast their privatisation in 2004. Electrification has seen an enormous increase in passenger capacity on these railways up to about a distance of 160 kilometres from Sydney, but there were no improvements to the railways' mostly very poor alignments; the new trains were often not as comfortable as the old, being designed for high capacity rather than for a clientele paying high fares; and they are slower than the best trains of steam days, which were very fine indeed. At least they are a lot cheaper. In 1956 it cost 25s 2d one way to ride the magnificent Newcastle Express in first class, at a time when many people earned under £10 a week, so something like $60 in 2010 values. In 2010 just $57 will buy a weekly ticket allowing unlimited travel, but the quality of service and journey times have declined to match the fares. The service has gone desperately down market.

While Sydney, Melbourne and most impressively Brisbane modernised their train fleets and extended electric services after 1980, the situation was on a knife edge in Adelaide and Perth while Hobart had abandoned its suburban passenger trains completely in 1975. In Adelaide the state authority which took over the suburban part of the old South Australian Railways acquired new diesel railcars that could be converted to electric traction and from 1990 all new sleepers it installed were gauge convertible. Apart from that, little happened there for three decades. Perth almost lost its suburban trains entirely. The original suburban spine had opened from Fremantle through Perth to Guildford in 1881 and services were later extended along the Bunbury line to Armadale. After little modernisation other than replacement of steam traction by a mixture of diesel railcars

Perth City station was a quiet place at night in 1970. One or two diesel mechanical railcars (imported from Cravens Railway Carriage and Wagon Company of Sheffield in 1954) sufficed for traffic on evening trains. Twenty years later the system would be electrified, patronage massively higher, and Perth City station rebuilt as the most stylish in the country. (Tony McIlwain)

and diesel hauled trains by 1970, the Perth to Fremantle section closed in 1979 and was replaced by buses.

Perth's suburban trains faced the possibility of total closure as the then Liberal state government was unremittingly hostile to passenger train operations. It got what it deserved at the next election and community pressure saw a revival of trains between Perth and Fremantle in 1983 with a promise of electrification. Technical standards were similar to Brisbane's and the rolling stock came from the same maker, ASEA Walker in Maryborough, Queensland. The impact was immediate and brilliant, so much so that an entirely new railway was built to the northern suburbs, the first section to Joondalup opening in December 2002 with subsequent extensions to Clarkson. Even more stunning though was the construction of the 82-kilometre Perth to Mandurah line, which included an underground section and station beneath the city, a new crossing of the Swan River and 11 stations. Built in four years by contractors Leighton Holdings for the extremely reasonable price of about $1.6 billion, it opened in December 2007. Within three months patronage had reached 80 percent of targets with about 40 000 passengers a day, up from the 16 000 a day who had used buses operating on the route previously. The overall patronage impact of the electrification, rebuilding and extension of Perth's suburban railways was a striking example of what could be achieved. In 1991 Perth's and Adelaide's railways both carried about seven million passengers. By

1997 Adelaide's patronage was unchanged but Perth's had reached nearly 30 million.[14]

The revival in Perth was imitated in Adelaide at last in 2008, when the state government announced its intention to electrify the city's suburban railways, extend them and convert them to standard gauge. In addition it was working on expansion of its one tramline into a light rail system physically integrated with the railways, which would include the running of trams on railways for part of their journeys and on streets in other parts. This will be a first for Australia although very much in the South Australian tradition of operating trains on suburban streets going back to the 19th century. The program will see restoration of rail services to Semaphore and a new line to West Lakes. While transport policy in Adelaide had not been especially dynamic for the 30 years before this announcement, it had been prudent and much of the preparatory work and equipment were in place.

While Adelaide will witness the largest tramway revival, it has happened elsewhere. Commonwealth funding provided under Howe's Better Cities program was the spur in Sydney. Trams returned to the city's streets in August 1997, when a light rail line was opened from Central station to Pyrmont after a construction period of just 16 months. It was extended to Lilyfield in 2000, but progress then stalled for a decade in the face of inexplicable and unexplained hostility from state governments, which appeared to prefer to spend more on studies for projects they clearly had no intention of building than on cheap extensions to light rail. Recognition of the wasteful folly of such an approach led to a revival of work on extensions in 2010. Construction of a similar light rail line on the Gold Coast began in 2010 for opening in 2014, once again with Commonwealth funding as the key to getting the project under way. The Gold Coast will become the first Australian city in over a century to have a new tram system commissioned where there was never one before.

Light rail trams are not the only option where passenger traffic is serious and expected to grow but may not justify heavy rail. Busways have become something of an Australian speciality. They are cheaper and more flexible than light rail, although their capacity is less and they are never likely to attract additional patronage to the same extent as light or heavy rail. Perth's Mandurah line has proved that beyond reasonable doubt. However, busways do enable buses to have some of the advantages of rail such as a separate right of way avoiding congestion, and higher speed limits than other road traffic (except in Sydney, where for some curious reason busways have lower speed limits than parallel roads). Australia's first were on the formations of abandoned tramlines in Moore Park in southeastern Sydney and date from the 1960s, but the first serious investment was in Adelaide, where the first stage of what became the world's longest and fastest

Nothing more than a painted yellow line separated motorists from the platform at Adelaide's Semaphore station in 1963. It was terminus of a branch which ran down the street from Glanville on the Outer Harbour railway. The line was closed in 1978 but is being rebuilt as a tramline. (James McCarthy)

No Australian city has embraced busways with more enthusiasm than Brisbane. The Inner Northern Busway dives from beside Roma Street railway station into tunnels leading to underground bus stations at King George Square and Queen Street. It opened in May 2008 and the photograph dates from December 2009. (Author)

guided busway was opened in 1986. It was built into the northeastern suburbs instead of an earlier plan for light rail along the route. It was new technology based on a system patented by Daimler-Benz called the O-Bahn. It requires small horizontal as well as normal wheels on each bus since it involves tracks on sleepers rather than a conventional road. In this respect it resembles early English coal tramroads of the 18th century with flanged rails rather than wheels, except that the flanged rails are reinforced concrete rather than iron.

Adelaide's O-Bahn was and is successful but has not been replicated elsewhere. Busways in Sydney and Brisbane are merely roads reserved for the exclusive use of buses, although with stations similar to those on a light rail line. In Sydney they are in the outer suburbs, where two radiating southwest and northwest from Parramatta opened in 2003 and 2006 respectively. The southwestern route's annual patronage is now above two million, which is a satisfactory result but a fraction of Perth's Mandurah railway. Brisbane got into busways earlier with the opening of the first section of the southeastern busway from the city to Woolloongabba in 2000, since extended beside the Southeastern Freeway as far as Eight Mile Plains with future extensions planned. Brisbane had already started putting its buses underground in the Queen Street bus station, which is unique in Australia. With sections of the Eastern, Northern and Inner Northern busways opened since 2008, Brisbane has acquired the outline of a busway network more resembling suburban railways than traditional bus operations, with complex underground and elevated stations. The investment is already over a billion dollars. Whether busways are a better option than rail for such traffic, though, remains a moot point. They certainly will not attract the same usage.

The software side of transport, notably ticketing, is as important to users as the hardware side of tracks and rolling stock. Ease of ticketing is an important factor in a traveller's choice of transport mode and most Australian cities have seen vast improvements since the 1970s. Adelaide, the first city to bring buses, trams and trains under common ownership in 1978, was the first to move to intermodal ticketing and easy transfers without fare penalty. Melbourne did the same in the early 1980s, but the process was more fraught because it was accompanied by the removal of conductors from trams. After some dismal experiments, of which the scratch ticket was the most notorious, Melbourne ended up with a zone-based system of admirable simplicity. This divided the city into three concentric zones (since reduced to two) with flat intermodal fares within or between them. It matters not at all to a Melbourne passenger what company operates the bus, tram or train, nor how many times he or she changes vehicles: ticketing is based simply on time and place.

Moreover, Melbourne's system requires low levels of technology, despite which it is moving towards electronic stored value cards that will further improve its efficiency. Fares under such a system are typically more expensive than traditional fare systems for a simple journey on one mode, but are much cheaper for journeys involving multiple modes and operators, which is as it should be and encourages wider use. Melbourne privatised its suburban train, tram and bus operations in the 1990s, as part of the Kennett government's largely successful attempt to bring costs under control and increase patronage. The fare system has worked well under this regime, because Victoria has worked out how to distribute revenue across multiple operators, a simple concept which Sydney apparently finds too hard to consider. Melbourne's extraordinary growth in patronage (four times the rate of Sydney's) in the first decade of the 21st century is at least partly due to its superior ticketing.[15] Brisbane and Ipswich, where the state owns the trains but Brisbane City Council and private companies own the buses, took longer to achieve integration, but now have the country's most technically advanced system with electronically read stored value *go* cards. Once again, it costs the passenger the same whatever mode is used. Weekly tickets have been replaced by a declining price for travel the more frequently a *go* card is used.

By contrast, Sydney has one of the worst and most primitive ticketing systems in the developed world and the least fair fares in Australia. Tickets are expensive for most users, but absurdly generous discounts are offered to sectional interests as electoral bribes. This encourages unviable and wasteful use, notably for very long-distance commuting, while discouraging motorists in crowded areas of the city to shift to public transport. There is no integration except in a limited way (depending on operator) and that only for season tickets, and the system discriminates massively against passengers who change vehicles. Different operators have different fare systems. There was an attempt in the early 2000s to introduce electronic ticketing, but it foundered after vast investment in the face of the government's inability to decide on, or apparently even to consider, a more rational fare structure.

Sydney's ticketing has changed scarcely at all in 120 years. In some instances integration has become less, notably when the Greiner government abolished through ticketing between trains and buses in the eastern suburbs and between ferries and buses. A much trumpeted minor modification in 2010 only entrenched the system's vices. It introduced no intermodal ticketing for casual users while reducing the price of season tickets for long distances to absurdly cheap levels. Fares that cheap can only discourage further investment, since the more traffic grows so do operational losses. As a result it costs a season ticket holder less to travel from Newcastle to Wollongong (240 kilometres) than for a casual user to go from Rozelle to Kings Cross (5 kilometres on a bus and train). As transport planning it's a dysfunctional system; as an election bribe it's brilliant. In short, it's a disgrace. It is hard to believe that Sydney's ticketing debacle could occur in a developed country: it is an abysmal reflection on the total lack of intelligent thought and commitment of state governments, both Labor and coalition, to the issue over many decades. It is the record of politicians who deeply and profoundly do not care, who could not be bothered educating themselves, and who feel they can get away with never facing the issue. The city deserves better.

Such a record, although very poor, is not surprising and conforms to the state's general record on urban public transport, even though its suburban railways are easily the country's busiest with close to 300 million passengers a year and ever increasing unmet demand for train travel. In 1998 its government announced an ambitious urban freeway plan involving five new roads. These were the Eastern Distributor under Darlinghurst; the M5 East from Beverley Hills to the Airport; the Cross City Tunnel from Rushcutters Bay to Darling Harbour (all three of these substantially underground); the Western Sydney Orbital from Casula to North Rocks; and the M2 from Naremburn to Gore Hill. All these were built in less than a decade, and were followed by the Lane Cove Tunnel whose completion meant that Sydney was ringed by the most impressive freeway system in the country, even if one in which three of the biggest investors (in the three tunnels) went broke. However, all this investment in urban freeways came at a cost: a lack of investment in urban railways. When announcing the road plan in 1998, Transport Minister Carl Scully released his Action for Transport 2010 plan, of which he claimed, 'This fully funded rail blueprint will deliver eight new rail lines by 2010, providing links will [*sic*] areas of Sydney where the population has expanded rapidly and where future urban growth is forecast to boom.'[16] Every announcement of a rail project for Sydney since has included the words 'fully funded'. Every time it has been a lie.

A series of announcements over the following few years raised similar hopes. Whereas the 1998 freeway plans have all been implemented (and others besides), the only rail achievements were the airport railway, already committed by the previous government, and the Chatswood–Epping railway. In 2000 the government commissioned Ron Christie, its Coordinator General of Rail, to report on long-term rail planning.[17] This was intended to refine the 1998 proposals, which had not been subject to serious research, and was the most thorough investigation of the city's transport requirements since the Bradfield Report of 1915. The government suppressed it for a

The old and new on Sydney's southern fringe. The coastal strip south from Sydney through Wollongong to Kiama has presented great challenges to generations of road and railway builders. Population has boomed while parts of the coastline are protected in national parks. The railway to Kiama, one of the most beautiful (if slow) train trips in the country, was electrified in stages from 1987. In November 1987 diesel railcars still handled people's mobility needs as seen at a busy seaside Kiama station (below). In February 2009 one of CityRail's latest medium-distance double-deck electric trains, a Kiama-bound OSCAR, paused at Otford just outside the Royal National Park (above). (Tony McIlwain, John Lacey)

year until it was leaked in February 2002. It then derided Christie's work, embarrassed by the extent of the needs he outlined.

New South Wales rail projects announced since 1998 and then abandoned have included high speed lines to Wollongong and Newcastle (complete with an image of a French TGV train in the publicity brochure); an underground line to Bondi Beach; and a Hurstville to Strathfield railway. For a brief period from 2005 the government claimed that a 'fully funded' project would see construction of new railways into the southwestern suburbs from Glenfield and into the northwestern suburbs from Epping, together with a new underground crossing of the city and harbour from Central to St Leonards to link them. This was then abandoned in favour of a metro from the city to the northwest, later truncated to the section northwest from Epping. It then abandoned this in favour of a metro from Central to Rozelle with possible future extension from Central to Parramatta along the route of Parramatta Road, apparently for no other reason than it would serve a large number of marginal government-held electorates. After spending close to $500 million on the metro, in 2010 the government once again abandoned a metro project, announcing an immediate start on light rail extensions, which could have been completed for the money it wasted on the metro. It also promised to revive the southwestern and northwestern railways, which already had been twice announced as 'fully funded' projects. However, construction of the northwestern line was not to begin for another seven years, which in the language of the New South Wales Treasury is never.

Planning in New South Wales appears to be stymied by a government culture of hostility, even hatred, towards rail projects and a desire to discourage people from using trains. Certainly the system is easily Australia's busiest and this has bred complacency: there is no need to attract people to the system as they come in droves whenever a service is offered. So its trains are the slowest in the country and costs of extensions are ludicrously exaggerated as an excuse for not building them. For instance, the government claims that the 11-kilometre southwestern line from Glenfield, with just two stations across extremely benign terrain with no engineering challenges whatever, would cost $1.36 billion, compared with $1.6 billion for the 82-kilometre technically complex Mandurah line in Perth. The cost estimate was clearly absurdly exaggerated: possibly the government was proposing to have some latterday Rum Corps build it.[18]

So deplorable a record raises the question whether the government ever seriously intending building any of the rail projects it announced and a further fundamental question of honesty in government. Australian governments generally attempt to fulfil their promises and implement their policies, yet New South Wales governments at this time felt no obligation even to appear to try, at least so far as transport planning was concerned. Repeated vacillation on such a stupendous scale and such a lack of achievement can hardly be accidental or the result of mere incompetence. It is difficult to avoid the harsh judgment that from 1996 to 2010 New South Wales governments, egged on by an insouciant, even positively hostile and destructive Treasury, perpetrated the worst example of deliberate and sustained political dishonesty, deception and negligence in the history of Australian transport planning.

Their irresponsibility was exacerbated by the policies of the Howard Commonwealth government, which funded numerous road projects but not one urban rail project in its entire life. For instance, Commonwealth funding for road projects in 2004–05 was $1 337 million whereas for rail it was zero, although in fairness it had funded the ARTC and Alice Springs to Darwin railway.[19] However, in 2009 the Rudd government was willing to invest in urban transport but the New South Wales government was unable to produce a viable plan. The blame for Sydney's transport mess lies unequivocally with the New South Wales government and Treasury.

RAIL FREIGHT RATIONALISATION AND PRIVATISATION

THE COMMONWEALTH investment in national highway links from 1974 was not accompanied by a comparable investment in interstate railways, which, except in Queensland, state governments allowed to fall into desuetude despite their rejection of the 1975 Commonwealth takeover offer. Australian National was the only profitable interstate railway at this time and used its operating profits to upgrade most of its transcontinental link from Port Augusta to Kalgoorlie through the late 1970s and 1980s. In New South Wales, and even more so in Victoria where there was no significant mineral traffic, the situation was increasingly dire.

From the 1960s the state railways had made serious efforts to improve the economics of their freight operations. The change in traction from steam to diesel was the most obvious but not the most profound change. When the transition was complete, train operations remained much the same as in the steam era. Indeed in the 1960s Victoria invested heavily in a new yard in Melbourne, shunted by gravity, which improved the marshalling of trains for despatch of individual wagons to dozens of stations in Melbourne and hundreds through the state. That, however, was the way of the past and within a decade the new yard was closed. It was clear that the forwarding of small consignments to hundreds of locations by rail, mostly in low-capacity four-wheel wagons, was no longer viable: the job could be done better, faster and cheaper by truck.

Both New South Wales and Victoria attempted to rationalise rail freight handling in the 1980s by setting up regional freight centres which would remain as the only stations served by rail. From these trucks would deliver goods either directly to customers or to smaller stations. The idea was good but proved as unviable as the multitude of small freight trains it replaced. It was not possible to carry freight profitably in this way and the freight centres also closed within a decade, marking withdrawal of the railways from the retail freight business in the two largest states.

This left railways with bulk traffic and as wholesalers of container services to transport companies. These were profitable, although the overall context was declining freight rates, road upgrades and reductions in truck travel times, which meant that a good performance in 1980 was a poor one by 1990 and hopeless by 2000. In Victoria bulk traffic was in decline as rail-delivered briquettes, made in the Latrobe Valley and once the main source of energy for many Victorian enterprises and domestic heating, were replaced by natural gas delivered by pipeline. Declining briquette traffic, among other operational factors, led to

Fortescue Metals' 3270-kilowatt General Electric locomotives were made in Erie, Pennsylvania, in 2007 for the Pilbara's newest heavy haul railway. A pair of them brings 200 or so ore cars grossing close to 30 000 tonnes down from Cloudbreak mine, past the 48-kilometre peg, and on to the loaders at Port Hedland. From there the ore will be shipped to contribute to the Asian economic miracle. (Toad Montgomery)

the de-electrification of the railway between Warragul and Traralgon in 1987.

Grain remained Victoria's main bulk commodity moved by rail, but it is never as lucrative as coal and other minerals. This meant that New South Wales and Queensland were better placed to maintain and improve rail freight profitability than Victoria. Queensland was particularly favoured as its big coal mines developed from the 1960s are in central Queensland, requiring new railways and ports in areas of low population. These high capacity, highly productive railways have generated the revenue which has kept Queensland Railways financially buoyant ever since. Between 1986 and 1989 most of these coal railways and the north coast railway between Rockhampton and Brisbane were electrified, an investment accompanied by track and signalling improvements. From the time of this achievement, Queensland can be said to have displaced New South Wales as Australia's most modern, impressive and certainly most profitable railway system.

New South Wales coal operations were and are more difficult, since they require trains to run through its three biggest cities. While in Newcastle, which handles the biggest tonnages, coal trains use separate tracks from other trains in the busiest sections, in Sydney and Wollongong the situation is deplorable, with coal trains sharing tracks with frequent electric suburban trains and enduring peak-hour curfews. It is so bad that, uniquely in Australia, some coal is delivered to the Port Kembla loader by road, dangerously and occasionally fatally. In the mid-1980s work began on an electrified railway, including the country's longest tunnel, which largely would eliminate these problems by taking coal trains west and south of both cities directly to Port Kembla. A change of government in 1988 saw the project abandoned – another example of the highly politicised shambles into which rail infrastructure planning in that state has degenerated.

Meanwhile, Western Australia saw a growth in mineral traffic even exceeding Queensland's, both between Kalgoorlie and Fremantle on the western leg of the transcontinental route and linking Pilbara iron ore mines with the ports of Dampier and Port Hedland. The first Pilbara railway opened from Mount Tom Price to Dampier in June 1966 and the second from Newman to Port Hedland in January 1969. There are now five, the most recent being Fortescue Metals' from Cloudbreak mine to Port Hedland, which opened in May 2008 and within six months had shipped its ten millionth tonne of ore. The other four, although trading under different names, are owned either by Rio Tinto Australia or BHP Billiton. These railways convey the highest tonnages in the world and have taken railway technology close to its limits, with axle loads up to 40 tonnes and trains with a gross weight of almost 33 000 tonnes. Except for Fortescue's line, they remain private railways in both senses of the word, serving only mines worked by their owners. Indeed Fortescue only had to build most of its railway because Rio Tinto refused to allow access, arguing that its tracks were not a public railway but an adjunct to its mines. Fortescue has had an open access policy from the beginning and is willing to host any operator's train for a fee, meaning it conforms to modern railway commercial practice elsewhere in the country.

While iron ore and coal traffic is the outstanding commercial success of the Australian railway industry and its greatest contribution to national income (its suburban passenger operations being its greatest contribution to national amenity), intermodal containerised freight traffic also became sufficiently profitable to be privatised. During the 1980s the state railways began operating what they called 'superfreighters' running between state capitals (where gauge differences allowed) at passenger train speeds, neither shunting at wayside stations nor changing locomotives at state borders. Customers, though, continued to receive invoices from all railways involved in a single shipment, and technical standards still varied from state to state.

In 1992 the Keating government established a company owned by the Commonwealth, Victoria and New South Wales to operate interstate intermodal trains with its own locomotives, the National Rail Corporation. At the same time it converted the Melbourne to Adelaide railway from broad to standard gauge. Accompanying this was the standardisation of some regional railways in western Victoria, anticipating conversion of all railways north and west of Melbourne. This however was stillborn because when the Victorian government upgraded its railways to Ballarat, Geelong and Bendigo for faster passenger traffic it baulked at the additional expense of $21 million to install gauge-convertible concrete sleepers. The Howard Commonwealth government could and should have contributed the difference, which was not a lot of money, but with sublime and insouciant irresponsibility ignored the whole issue.

It was a great opportunity lost and an episode that reflected poorly on both governments and indeed on Australian federalism. Sydney is well ahead of Melbourne in replacing timber sleepers with concrete and in renewing the 1920s vintage overhead on its suburban railways. This is why Sydney's suburban trains are more reliable in extreme heat than Melbourne's. When Victoria comes to make these replacements, as it must, the Commonwealth should insist that every single concrete sleeper is gauge convertible, so that Victoria can achieve what South Australia is doing: elimination of the broad gauge on all but heritage railways.

The Howard government was more proactive and effective on privatisation and unifying track management, if parsimonious in funding it. Keating's National Rail had gutted Australian National of its profitable transcontinental intermodal traffic, turning Australia's second most profitable railway (after Queensland) into a financial basket case. It therefore sold AN's passenger business and incorporated its track management into a new Australian Rail Track Corporation in 1998. Through leases negotiated with the states, by 2004 the ARTC came to control most freight trackage on the mainland outside Queensland. National Rail was sold in 2002 together with New South Wales' FreightCorp, the freight remnant of the old NSWGR. It later acquired Victoria's privatised freight operator. The new owners called the company Pacific National. Since 1995 other operators had begun running interstate intermodal trains, sometimes with their own locomotives and crews, sometimes with leased ones. A whole new system of freight train operations was created in the 1990s, whereby railways were no longer integrated technical and business enterprises, but separate track, freight train, passenger train and rolling stock providing concerns. This was the most profound change in the concept of what a railway was since they had been invented. Indeed until the 1990s the Liverpool and Manchester Railway of 1829 was generally defined as the world's first railway as much because of its integrated business model (it was the first to own the track and run all the trains) as for its technology.

The other great achievement of the Howard years was the completion of the Alice Springs to Darwin railway as foreshadowed in the 1911 agreement for the transfer of the Northern Territory from South Australia to the Commonwealth. This had a long and fraught history. In the immediate post-war period, when gauge standardisation and national planning were on the national agenda, Harold Clapp, who then had charge of planning, preferred to link the Northern Territory with the southern states through western Queensland and New South Wales, by a railway from Bourke to Darwin via Mt Isa. Clapp's reasoning was sound: why go to Adelaide if you could go as easily to Brisbane, Sydney and Melbourne? But, understandably enough, South Australia was ropeable and Clapp's scheme came to nothing.

Howard was congenitally disinclined to invest large sums of Commonwealth money in nation-building projects, which had always been a Labor speciality, but he made an exception in this case. A private company, AustralAsia Rail Corporation, built the line, with fairly modest investment (between $150 and $165 million each) from the Commonwealth, Territory and South Australian governments. The Tarcoola–Alice Springs railway was transferred to the company as a sweetener. The railway presented no great technical challenges, although at 1470 kilometres it was certainly long and something of a commercial risk. Built in less than three years, the prime minister opened it with much celebration in January 2004. Getting the railway built at last, 93 years after it was promised, was one of

Howard's finest achievements, certainly the one for which he will be remembered most fondly.

In the privatised environment the Howard government created, freight train operators and rolling stock leasing companies come and go. Producers and state government enterprises of varying degrees of commercial focus also sometimes run trains. The dominant intermodal rail company remains Pacific National, but it has had a tempestuous corporate history. Its main rival is now QR National, state government owned but stable, very good on technology, and efficient. The Queensland government has not invested in running freight trains throughout Australia as a service, but because it is profitable, so profitable that it may soon sell it, at least in part. Thus, rail freight business of the early 21st century has come to resemble the airline business of the 1950s, with frequent takeovers and issues like debt-equity levels affecting investment. It was an outcome no-one could have predicted even as recently as 1990.[20]

RAIL PASSENGER DECLINE

BY THE 1970s the post-war air-conditioned trains on Australia's railways were in need of replacement and the viability of local provincial train services was marginal. Branch line and some major services were abandoned throughout the country in the mid and late 1970s in the wake of deregulation. In South Australia, Australian National Railways briefly maintained services linking Adelaide with Mount Gambier, Whyalla and Broken Hill, but these soon expired and there are now no country train services in the state apart from transcontinental trains. In Western Australia only services to Kalgoorlie and Bunbury survived a savage pruning. Tasmania, already having no suburban trains in Hobart, abandoned passenger trains altogether in 1978. In New South Wales and Victoria country services remained on main lines and networks of connecting road coaches replaced branch line train services. In Queensland it was a similar story: mainline trains remained while local provincial services were left to private bus operators, although a few survived in far north Queensland (between Cairns, Kuranda and Forsayth and between Normanton and Croydon) on the strength of their tourist traffic.

Surviving passenger trains were modernised and accelerated. Overnight mail trains, carrying parcels and mail as well as passengers, lasted longer in New South Wales than elsewhere,

The twilight of the country passenger train in Tasmania (above) and South Australia (left). The Sunday evening Hobart to Launceston mail train leaving Ross in the Tasmanian Midlands in January 1973. (Author) In 1980, suburban (red) and country (blue) passenger trains both still operated out of Adelaide, although the latter would not last much longer. Given the dismal passenger loadings implied by the size of these trains, that can hardly be considered a surprise. (Tony McIlwain)

Loading parcels at Sydney station in 1940. This scene remained unchanged until 1987 when movement of parcels and mail by rail in New South Wales ceased. The vans were shunted onto overnight mail trains serving all parts of the state. (Ian Dunn collection)

but ceased running in 1987. No longer were evenings and early mornings at city terminals characterised by shunting of vans and handling of parcels and mailbags on their platforms.

New South Wales and Victoria led the way with new equipment in the early 1980s. The new trains had fixed formations that required no shunting, stopped less and were faster. New South Wales went for a then advanced British design, called locally the XPT, with a service speed of 160 km/h, while Victoria, where distances were shorter and alignments better, stuck with improved if conventional locomotives and cars whose service speed was 130 km/h. Prior to the 1980s Australian trains had not operated at speeds above 115 km/h (or 70 mph), which had been the speed limit in New South Wales and Victoria since the 1930s. The XPTs reduced travel times significantly, although there was no accompanying and much needed improvement in track alignment to enable them to reach their potential. Highways were being realigned and improved when the

XPTs entered service, meaning that travel times by rival modes were decreasing too. They were less effective when in 1990 they replaced overnight trains from Sydney to Brisbane and Murwillumbah, and in 1993 between Sydney and Melbourne (on runs where speed is not such a big issue), bringing to an end the era of comfortable travel by sleeping car, with the option of relaxation in dining and lounge cars.

Two decades later Victoria introduced a new generation of 160 km/h railcars as part of its regional high speed rail upgrade from 2004, with brilliant results. This was largely because their introduction coincided with a track upgrade program and completion of Melbourne's sumptuous new Southern Cross station on the site of what had been the slightly embarrassing city terminal in Spencer Street. Queensland introduced new rolling stock later than the southern states. Most of its long-distance trains with sleeping cars continue to use upgraded rolling stock dating from the 1950s and some generally similar later cars, but in 1997 Queensland began operating tilt trains, at first electric between Brisbane and Rockhampton and then diesel between Brisbane and Cairns. New South Wales briefly and successfully experimented with a Swedish tilt train offering a premium service between Sydney and Canberra in 1995, but a change of government saw the program abandoned and the subsequent decline of its

While the *Indian Pacific* and *The Ghan* are Australia's best known and longest distance traditional trains with sleeping, dining and lounge cars, Queensland Railways also offers its passengers such luxuries between Brisbane and Cairns and Brisbane and Longreach. Here QR's *Sunlander* rolls along among the cane fields to cross the Johnstone River near Innisfail. (QR)

regional services into depressing mediocrity.

The Howard government privatised Australian National's transcontinental services, *The Ghan* and the *Indian Pacific*, as the Great Southern Railway in 1997. The new operator extended the route of its north–south train *The Ghan* from Alice Springs to Darwin in 2004 and its trains now run profitably but expensively, primarily for the benefit of tourists, many international. While Great Southern's trains may be decidedly old fashioned as a means of transport, they certainly offer comfort and style unmatched on any other Australian trains, or indeed by any other land transport mode, although Queensland's sleeping car services come close.

Passenger train speeds where services have survived have generally improved. Queensland and Victoria have made very impressive improvements, although New South Wales, with the densest medium and long-distance traffic, has seen only regression since the 1980s, largely because other railways have improved the alignments of their tracks whereas New South Wales has not. The XPT schedules of the 1980s have been slowed for no apparent reason, although risible excuses that would disgrace a schoolboy who forgot his homework (such as it takes longer to close the doors) are occasionally proffered. Australia's busiest long-distance passenger rail route is between Sydney and the New South Wales north coast, yet there is little attempt to develop the traffic that would require, above all, greater speed and reduced journey times. On the contrary, government policy on concessions, maintenance and marketing seems aimed at deterring all but the poorest from using its trains, turning them into refuges for the elderly and the indigent, even in first class. Moreover, in 2004 the transport minister closed the north coast branch from Casino to Murwillumbah, even though it is in one of the most rapidly developing parts of the state, forcing passengers onto bus connections.

A comparison between 1948 and 2010 travel times on three major routes in the eastern states reveals much about the relative performance of the state railways. In 1948 the fastest train between Brisbane and Rockhampton took exactly 15 hours for the trip: in 2010 it is 7 hours 25 minutes. Between Melbourne and Bendigo the times were 2 hours 30 minutes in 1956 and 84 minutes in 2010. Between Sydney and Newcastle, much the same distance as from Melbourne to Bendigo and easily the busiest of the three routes, and hence the one which could generate the most revenue, the fastest train took 2 hours 18 minutes in 1948 and 2 hours 38 minutes in 2010. So, over six decades, the Queensland journey was accelerated by 50.6 percent and the Victorian journey by 40 percent while the New South Wales journey became 13.5 percent slower, a truly pathetic performance. Astonishingly, its governments appear to feel no shame about their underwhelming mediocrity, nor do oppositions have the nous to challenge it.

AIRPORTS AND HIGH SPEED RAIL

AUSTRALIAN AIRPORTS have had to cope with huge increases in passenger numbers since the 1970s as air travel has become accessible to a much larger proportion of the population. The process has been difficult at times, notably when a new international terminal opened in Sydney in 1970 but promptly proved to be inadequate because of the larger passenger numbers travelling on Boeing 747s, introduced at the same time. The terminal was quickly modified and since has been further extended. New international and domestic terminals were opened in Perth and Brisbane in different locations, although at the same airports, in 1986 and 1988 respectively. Melbourne had acquired a new airport at Tullamarine in 1970, so was ready for the new age of mass air transport.

Runway capacity was a serious issue at Sydney, the nation's busiest airport and one of its most convenient. Its very convenience though, was a problem, since it was so near a very large population. Airport noise became a serious political issue and in the 1990s a No Aircraft Noise Party even ran candidates in adjoining electorates. A solution of sorts was the construction of a third runway on land reclaimed from Botany Bay, which opened in 1992 after a breathtakingly short construction time. The new runway effectively doubled capacity since it was parallel to the existing main runway, and also enabled more flights to take off over the bay, improving the noise situation in many surrounding suburbs. Nonetheless, Kingsford Smith is one of the few major airports in the world that closes at night because of an 11pm to 6am curfew on jet operations.

A new airport for Sydney often has been seen as a longer term solution and many proposals have surfaced. The Whitlam government proposed a site at Galston, northwest of the city, attracting a massive community backlash; while the Hawke government chose a site at Badgerys Creek west of the city and actually began acquiring land for it, although the New South Wales government obviously was sceptical since it never created a rail reservation to enable passengers to reach it. Possibly, though, that failure may have been because it preferred not to have to think about its infrastructure responsibilities. In 2009 the Rudd government decided to abandon Badgerys Creek, meaning that the possibility of building a second airport in the Sydney basin has been lost. The air force base at Richmond is not a particularly good option, both because of expanding population and the prevalence of fogs. The issue remains problematic and will require vast sums of public money to resolve, even though the Howard government privatised capital city airports in 2002.

There is another and far better alternative to a new Sydney airport: high speed passenger trains. These would bring to an end air services between Sydney and Canberra, Newcastle and a host of regional ports and reduce demand for flights to Melbourne and Brisbane, thereby freeing up the airport's capacity for expansion of other routes. High speed rail projects began with the opening of the Tokkaido shinkansen (new main line) between Tokyo and Osaka in 1964. Since then the shinkansen network has expanded greatly and its trains have carried over eight billion passengers with an average delay per train of one minute (meaning the vast majority is on time) and not a single fatality due to accident or failure. The first shinkansen was built very consciously as 'a symbol of Japan', its immaculate operations reflecting Japanese quality and determination to be a leading industrial nation with socially and environmentally progressive policies. For the Japanese, the shinkansen was a peaceful way of asserting world leadership after the disastrous defeat of 1945, demonstrating the nation's brilliant capacity for technical innovation and social organisation.

High speed railways, like all transport systems, are every bit as dependent on social factors, notably quality management and an efficient, well-trained and enthusiastic staff, as they are on technology; and no people on earth do that better than the Japanese. The Japanese lead has since been followed by France, Germany, Spain, Korea, Taiwan and, most spectacularly of all, China. Most modern countries are happy to be judged by the speed and quality of their new passenger

Australia's first venture into increasing speeds since the 1930s was the then State Rail Authority of New South Wales' Express Passenger Train (XPT) introduced in 1982. Their first operation was on the *Central West Express* between Sydney and Dubbo, which it accelerated by two hours. In November 1986 an XPT in original livery worked the train through Locksley near Bathurst. At that time the steam era infrastructure and signals at Locksley were still intact. (Tony McIlwain)

railways: by that criterion Australia, where trains on the busiest intercity route (Sydney–Newcastle) are slower than they were in 1938, is a perversely and resolutely third rate nation.

Australia's lack of profile in high speed rail projects is mystifying. It is not as though there is insufficient traffic to justify them, for in 2002 two of the world's 11 busiest air routes were in Australia and both are less than 1000 kilometres, meaning that a four-hour high speed train trip is readily achievable. In general a rail journey time of four hours is the point at which rail becomes preferable to air for business travellers, provided the train is good. The busiest routes in 2002 were:[21]

Rank	Route	Region	Across	Journeys
1	Tokyo–Sapporo	Japan domestic	sea	9 510 000
2	Tokyo–Fukuoka	Japan domestic	sea	8 280 000
3	Tokyo–Osaka	Japan domestic	land	7 320 000
4	Hong Kong–Taipei	East Asia international	sea	5 460 000
5	Seoul–Busan	Korea domestic	land	5 390 000
6	Sydney–Melbourne	Australia domestic	land	5 350 000
7	Seoul–Jeju Island	Korea domestic	sea	4 910 000
8	Tokyo–Okinawa	Japan domestic	sea	4 330 000
9	London–New York	Atlantic international	sea	3 900 000
10	Sydney–Brisbane	Australia domestic	land	3 500 000
11	Taipei–Kaohsiung	Taiwan domestic	land	3 460 000

Other more recent sources use different criteria, notably flights per week rather than passenger numbers, which produce different results, notably pushing Madrid–Barcelona, São Paulo–Rio de Janeiro and Jakarta–Surabaya into high places, but all such studies put Sydney–Melbourne in the top six (sometimes as high as third) and Sydney–Brisbane in the top 12, whatever criteria are used. Madrid–Barcelona has dropped down the list with the introduction of high speed trains between the two cities in 2008. Similarly, the busiest air route in the European Union out of London was once to Paris but, following the introduction of a high speed rail service, London–Dublin has become the busiest. Seoul–Busan and Taipei–Kaohsiung also have dropped much lower following the opening of high speed rail links. In fact, the busiest air routes in the world over land are now in Australia, Brazil and the United States, three countries notorious for their short-sighted lack of investment in high speed passenger railways.

A Very Fast Train between Sydney and Melbourne via Canberra was first mooted by CSIRO Chairman Paul Wild in 1984. The Hawke and Keating governments were uninspired by the proposal, but the Howard government was more receptive, provided a private company invested most of the capital. It successfully called tenders for such a railway between Sydney and Canberra, with the possibility of future extension to Melbourne. However, the four prospective groups tendering were unable to secure from the Commonwealth Treasury the conditions they required to make the investment, even though the issue got as far as being discussed in the Howard cabinet in 1998.[22] New South Wales governments have behaved disgracefully on the topic and have been outright hostile throughout, only ever playing the role of spoiler, even though it is the state with most to gain. Notably it has rebuilt and amplified its suburban railway to Revesby without any resumptions to improve its alignment to allow very high speeds, even though this has been identified as the preferred route out of Sydney towards Canberra and Melbourne. The consequence is that, if the ECVHST project (explained in the following paragraph) is implemented, it will need to be rebuilt again. Such short-sighted folly is unbelievable but typical.

The Commonwealth released its *East Coast Very High Speed Train Scoping Study* in 2001. It examined a new passenger railway linking Brisbane with Sydney, Canberra and Melbourne called the East Coast Very High Speed Train or ECVHST, suggesting that the most urgent and viable section was between Newcastle and Canberra via Sydney. It also considered that the northern and southern extremities connecting Brisbane with Ballina

Melbourne's new Southern Cross station in December 2006, with a train of the new railcars ordered for the high speed regional rail project picked out by the sun. A rake of 1980s equipment (the N cars) waits for its departure on the other side of the platform. (Author)

and Melbourne with Albury also had merit and could be built simultaneously. Its author, Robert Thornton, argued that travel times from Sydney to Melbourne and Brisbane of four hours were possible, attracting the high volume, high value patronage necessary for the project's viability. However, he did not consider that the ECVHST could be built unless 'a significant degree of intergovernmental goodwill, agreement, and commitment to the concept were achieved across the five jurisdictions affected'.[23] The study's pessimism about the prospects of attracting sufficient private investment to the ECVHST without government 'goodwill, agreement, and commitment' meant that the Howard government had little further interest in it. Because most of the capital would need to come from public funds, federal transport minister John Anderson rejected further action, describing it as 'an exercise in false hopes'.[24]

The Rudd government is interested in the project

QR's tilt train to Rockhampton crossing the Mary River in December 2002. The problems of operating a high speed train on a railway built over the course of a century to widely varying construction standards are all too evident, with three types of span and considerable vertical curvature on the bridge. (QR)

and is considering its inclusion in its Nation Building Program. Its need may not be urgent while air traffic can cope with demand at a reasonable cost, but that cannot last forever. There is no alternative to high octane aviation fuel to maintain air traffic, and such fuel inevitably will become more expensive as world oil supplies decline. So route identification and acquisition of a suitable reservation for the entire ECVHST route at the very least is prudent, although that would require the co-operation of the New South Wales state government, whose record so far hardly has been characterised by 'goodwill, agreement, and commitment'. Construction can wait till the need is greater, although the time appears ripe for the Newcastle to Canberra section, especially since the Sydney–Newcastle railway is already close to saturation and provision of additional tracks is becoming necessary to cope with existing traffic. Naturally fares on the ECVHST will not be cheap, although comparable with air fares for longer journeys, with a wide range of prices depending on time of travel and ticket conditions. Fares for shorter journeys will need to be comparable with prices in real terms of rail tickets for such trips back in the 1930s, when trains were the fastest and best way to travel and express passenger trains were profitable.

CONCLUSION: 'THE INIQUITY OF THE FATHERS'

WITH A SMALL but concentrated population and a large landmass, Australia always has been a challenging land for those who seek to reach it or cross it. Many have died attempting one or the other and some still do. For the most part, though, contemporary challenges are posed neither by the elements nor the terrain, but by lack of political will and capital. Australia is a nation with a rapidly growing transport task and often pitifully inadequate infrastructure. Because transport of minerals is immediately and immensely profitable, this is where the nation excels. Infrastructure for such purposes is generally excellent, and in many cases among the finest in the world, except around Sydney. Inadequacies are soon remedied as tonnages and profits grow inexorably.

Performance in the cities and in moving people and goods between cities has been far patchier and sometimes woeful. The deplorable condition of east coast interstate railways and the disaster of creating suburbs, indeed whole regions, without transport speak for themselves. Many Australian attempts at planning urban transport have been ill-conceived.

Most states are improving their planning performance but the largest has been paralysed by indecision and the politics of spite, its ministers often incapable of discerning good advice from bad and its Treasury apparently determined to blight proper transport planning. Except in aviation, where their performance mostly has been very good, Commonwealth governments can choose or not choose a deep involvement in transport policy at will. The Howard government was activist in some respects, yet strangely quiescent in others, policy development and action stymied by its residual neo-liberalism and instinctive distrust of government investment. It is unfair to say that the exceptions were all based on perceived electoral advantage, but too many were.

There is a game of catch-up to be played and so far the Rudd government has run hard. Whether it can sustain its momentum and turn good intentions and admirable rhetoric into material achievement is another matter. In addressing their transport needs since human beings first came to this continent, Australians can find much of which to be proud as well as much at which to wince. Fortunately improved technology enables past neglect to be rectified and projects to be achieved quickly, provided the political will, social organisation and money are there. The overall context though, as oil runs out, energy becomes more expensive and the environment needs more protection, is difficult for transport development.

Past neglect means the cost of improving transport infrastructure is far higher than it would have been if investment had been timelier. John Whitton constantly made this point back in the 1860s but it is still often ignored. In transport infrastructure policy, the harsh words of the Old Testament are literally true, with poor decisions and inadequate planning indeed 'visiting the iniquity of the fathers upon the children unto the third and fourth generation'[25]. That is much longer than the electoral cycle, although too few Australian politicians seem to realise that cruel intergenerational injustice is the consequence of their negligence. In contrast, great transport planners such as Thomas Higinbotham, John Whitton, JJC Bradfield and Harold Clapp knew it instinctively. Present and future generations will continue to pay dearly for the parsimonious neglect of their forefathers, but there is little choice if Australians wish to move themselves and the goods they need within and between their cities.

NOTES

INTRODUCTION

1 In every other Australian capital city (and in most comparable cities around the world) it is possible to use the same ticket on different transport modes regardless of operator, but not in Sydney. Sydney's notoriously nasty ticketing attracts constant and richly deserved negative comment. See, for example, *Sydney Morning Herald*, 24 and 28 August 2009.
2 Queensland Department of Infrastructure and Planning Regional Overview. Available online at <www.dip.qld.gov.au/resources/plan/wide-bay/3-regional-overview.pdf>.
3 Unpublished manuscript. Edward Octavius Cotton, *Notes on the Tasmanian Aborigine,* 1887. University of Tasmania Library Special and Rare Materials Collection. Available online at <eprints.utas.edu.au/1887/1/W9-C4-1(11).pdf>.
4 Rebe Taylor, *Unearthed: The Aboriginal Tasmanians of Kangaroo Island,* Kent Town SA, Wakefield Press, 2002.
5 This account generally follows Regina Ganter, 'The View from the North' in Martyn Lyons & Penny Russell (eds), *Australia's History: Themes and Debates*, Sydney, UNSW Press, 2005, pp. 41–62.

CHAPTER 1

1 John Bach, *A Maritime History of Australia*, Melbourne, Pan Books, 1982, p. 70.
2 *Australian Dictionary of Biography (ADB)*, vol 2, pp. 546–7.
3 Malcolm J Kennedy, *Hauling the Loads: A History of Australia's Working Horses and Bullocks*, Melbourne, Melbourne University Press, 1992, pp. 49–50.
4 Bach, *A Maritime History of Australia*, p. 72.
5 Geoffrey Blainey, *The Tyranny of Distance*, Melbourne, Sun Books, 1983, p. 114.
6 Bach, *A Maritime History of Australia*, pp. 79–80.
7 On the clipper ships, see Basil Lubbock, *The Colonial Clipper*, Glasgow, Brown, Son & Ferguson, 1968.
8 Graeme Davison, *The Rise and Fall of Marvellous Melbourne*, Melbourne, Melbourne University Press, 1978, p. 21.
9 William F Stark, *The Last Time around Cape Horn: The Historic 1949 Voyage of the Windjammer* Pamir, New York, Carroll & Graf, 2003 describes this last voyage.
10 On the history of P&O and its mail operations, see Malcolm R Gordon, *From* Chusan *to* Sea Princess*: The Australian Services of the P&O and Orient Lines*, Sydney, Allen & Unwin, 1985.
11 On the voyages of the *Royal Charter*, see Blainey, *The Tyranny of Distance*, p. 210. On the *Chusan*, see Gordon, *From* Chusan *to* Sea Princess, p. 22.
12 On the services to Panama see Will Lawson, *Pacific Steamers*, Glasgow, Brown, Son & Ferguson, 1927.
13 For the operation of these mail trains in Adelaide, see Malcolm Thompson, *Rails through Swamp and Sand: A History of the Port Adelaide Railway*, Adelaide, Port Dock Railway Museum, 1988.
14 The evidence for the operation in New South Wales of these special English mail trains, presumably consisting of nothing more than a mail van or two, comes from a reference in Alex Grunbach, *A Compendium of New South Wales Steam Locomotives*, Sydney, Australian Railway Historical Society, 1981, to Locomotive No 16 of the NSWGR (a light, not very powerful but very speedy machine) being fitted with Westinghouse brakes in order to work the 'English Mail Specials', between Albury and Junee (p. 30).
15 *Argus*, 4 November 1921.
16 Lawson, *Pacific Steamers*, pp. 32–34.
17 For a general history of shipping companies on the England–Australia run, see Thomas King Fitchett, *The Long Haul: Ships on the England–Australia Run*, Adelaide, Rigby, 1980.
18 Philippe Ramona, *Paquebots vers l'Orient*, Saint-Cyr-sur-Loire, Editions Alan Sutton, 2001.
19 On the services of P&O and the Orient SN Company, see Gordon, *From* Chusan *to* Sea Princess.

CHAPTER 2

1 *ADB*, vol 3, pp. 344–5.
2 *Daily Examiner*, 10 March 1954, quoted in Stuart Lee, *Riverboats of the Clarence*, Yamba NSW, Port of Yamba Historical Society, 2003, p. 53.
3 Lee, *Riverboats of the Clarence*, p. 258.
4 *ADB*, vol 1, pp. 140–2. See also Tom Mead, *Empire of Straw: The Dynamic Rise and Disastrous Fall of Dashing Colonial Tycoon Benjamin Boyd*, Sydney, Dolphin Books, c. 2000.
5 Thomas King Fitchett, *The Vanished Fleet: Australia's Coastal Passenger Ships 1910–1960*, Adelaide, Rigby, 1976, pp. 19–21.
6 See Lee, *Riverboats of the Clarence* for a history of the remarkably dense services on the Clarence River.
7 Fitchett, *The Vanished Fleet*, pp. 7–9.
8 Mike Richards, *Workhorses in Australian Waters: A History of Marine Engineering in Australia*, Sydney, Turton & Armstrong, 1987, p. 37.
9 Richards, *Workhorses in Australian Waters*, pp. 133–7.
10 Fitchett, *The Vanished Fleet*, pp. 16–17, 23.
11 Fitchett, *The Vanished Fleet*, pp. 72–73.
12 Fitchett, *The Vanished Fleet*, pp. 103–7.
13 Bach, *A Maritime History of Australia*, p. 18.
14 Mary Shelley Clark, *Ships and Shores and Trading Ports: The Social and Working Life of Coastal Harbour and River Towns in New South Wales*, Sydney, Waterways Authority of New South Wales, 2001, p. 93.
15 See Mike Richards, *North Coast Run: Men and Ships of the NSW North Coast*, Sydney, Turton & Armstrong, 1977 for the history of the lines serving these difficult ports.
16 On Granite Island, see EE Morris (ed.), *Cassell's Picturesque Australasia*, London, Cassell, 1889, p. 382. On the Clarence, see Clark, *Ships and Shores and Trading Ports*, pp. 33–34.
17 Richards, *North Coast Run*, p. 98.
18 Morris, *Cassell's Picturesque Australasia*, p. 861.
19 The dates are those of the opening of railways to the ports, which are well documented in Howard Quinlan & John R Newland, *Australian Railway Routes 1854–2000*, Sydney, Australian Railway Historical Society (New South Wales Division), 2000.
20 Vaughan Evans, 'Ship Building and Repair' in Don Fraser (ed.), *Sydney from Settlement to City, an Engineering History of Sydney*, Sydney, Institution of Engineers Australia, 1989, pp. 126–7.
21 Richards, *Workhorses in Australian Waters*, pp. 107–10.
22 Richards, *Workhorses in Australian Waters*, pp. 128–31.
23 Evans, 'Ship Building and Repair', pp. 130–45.
24 Richards, *Workhorses in Australian Waters*, pp. 129–30.
25 Richards, *Workhorses in Australian Waters*, p. 128.
26 Morris, *Cassell's Picturesque Australasia*, p. 377.
27 David Wardle, *Murray River Paddle Steamers*, Canberra, Traction Publications, 1970, p. 6.
28 Lyn Griffiths & Bill Jeffrey, *River Boat Trail South Australia*, Adelaide, South Australian Department of Environment and Natural Resources, nd [c. 2000], pp. 20, 25, 30.
29 On the river trade, see Gwenda Painter, *A Different River: River Trade and Development along the Murray Valley*

Network, South Melbourne, Hyland House, 1983; Peter Christopher, *Paddlesteamers and River Boats of the Murray*, Stepney SA, Axiom, 2000; and Morris, *Cassell's Picturesque Australasia*, pp. 364–84.

CHAPTER 3

1 On James Rutherford's life see Sam Everingham, *Wild Ride: The Rise and Fall of Cobb & Co*, Melbourne, Penguin, 2007.
2 Morris (ed.), *Cassell's Picturesque Australasia*, pp. 792–5.
3 Kennedy, *Hauling the Loads*, p. 7.
4 Kennedy, *Hauling the Loads*, p. 30.
5 Kennedy, *Hauling the Loads*, pp. 25–6.
6 Max Colwell, *Australian Transport: An Illustrated History*, Sydney, Paul Hamlyn, 1972, pp. 29–34.
7 Patsy Adam Smith, *Romance of Victorian Railways*, Adelaide, Rigby, 1980, p. 156.
8 This account is based on TL McKnight, *The Camel in Australia*, Melbourne, Melbourne University Press, 1969.
9 Kennedy, *Hauling the Loads*, pp. 78, 81, 93, 96, 106.
10 Kennedy, *Hauling the Loads*, pp. 51–5.
11 Fraser (ed.), *Sydney from Settlement to City*, p. 12.
12 On this road, see George Hawley Stancombe, *Highway in Van Diemen's Land*, Western Junction TAS, the author, 1969.
13 Morris (ed.), *Cassell's Picturesque Australasia*, p. 641.
14 Morris (ed.), *Cassell's Picturesque Australasia*, pp. 862–3.
15 Richard Raxworthy, *The Unreasonable Man, the Life and Works of J.J.C. Bradfield*, Sydney, Hale and Iremonger, 1989, p. 23.
16 Robert Lee, *The Greatest Public Work, the New South Wales Railways, 1848–1889*, Sydney, Hale & Iremonger, 1988, p. 40.
17 Don Fraser, *Bridges Down Under: The History of Railway Underbridges in New South Wales, Sydney*, Australian Railway Historical Society, 1995, pp. 42–43.
18 National Trust of Victoria, *Timber Bridges Study*, Melbourne, The National Trust, 1997, p. 42.
19 Roads and Traffic Authority of NSW, *Timber Bridge Management*, Sydney, Roads and Traffic Authority, 2002, pp. 4–6.
20 Fraser (ed.), *Sydney from Settlement to City*, pp. 289–92.
21 Fraser (ed.), *Sydney from Settlement to City*, p. 106.
22 This description of freight vehicles is based on Kennedy, *Hauling the Loads*, pp. 31–9 and H McGregor, *The Horse and Buggy Days*, Canberra, Roebuck Books, 1981.
23 On early coaching, see Colwell, *Australian Transport*, pp. 50–61, and Kennedy, *Hauling the Loads*, pp. 43–46.
24 *The Australian Encyclopaedia*, Sydney, The Grolier Society, 1963, vol 2, p. 220.
25 RJ Unstead & WF Henderson, *Transport in Australia*, London, A & C Black, 1970, p. 33.
26 Green's complaint is included in Marcella Hunter, *Australia Post, Delivering More than Ever*, Sydney, Focus Books, 2000, p. 37.
27 Kenneth Austin, *A Pictorial History of Cobb & Co: The Coaching Age in Australia 1854–1924*, Adelaide, Rigby, 1977, p. 89.
28 Kennedy, *Hauling the Loads*, pp. 65–7.
29 Kennedy, *Hauling the Loads*, p. 130.
30 Leith Yelland, *Pads, Tracks and Waters, South Australia's Pastoral Stock Routes*, Adelaide, South Australian Department of Primary Industry and Resources, 2002, p. 53.
31 Raxworthy, *The Unreasonable Man*, p. 23. See also TL McKnight, *The Long Paddock: Australia's Travelling Stock Routes*, Armidale NSA, University of New England, 1977.
32 Kennedy, *Hauling the Loads*, pp. 125–6.
33 Kennedy, *Hauling the Loads*, p. 130.
34 Keith Willey, *The Drovers*, South Melbourne, Macmillan, 1982.
35 In 'Clancy of the Overflow'.
36 Yelland, *Pads, Tracks and Water*, p. 90.

CHAPTER 4

1 *Argus*, 26 November 1861.
2 *Argus*, 22 October 1862.
3 Henry Lawson, 'The Roaring Days', first published in *The Bulletin*, 21 December 1889.
4 On early railway building in New South Wales, see John Gunn, *Along Parallel Lines, A History of the Railways of New South Wales, 1850–1986*, Melbourne, Melbourne University Press, 1989, pp. 1–78, and Lee, *The Greatest Public Work*, pp. 1–66.
5 Robert McKillop & David Sheedy, *Our Region, Our Railway: The Hunter and the Great Northern Railway 1857–2007*, Sydney, Australian Railway Historical Society (New South Wales Division), 2008, pp. 7–14.
6 On the South Australian horse tramways, see Ron Stewein, *A History of the South Australian Railways* Volume 1 *The Early Years*, Melbourne, Australian Railway Historical Society (Victorian Division), 2007, pp. 50–89.
7 On the gauge issue, see Lee, *The Greatest Public Work*, p. 18, and Robert Lee, *Colonial Engineer: John Whitton (1819–1898) and the Building of Australia's Railways*, Sydney, UNSW Press, 2000, pp. 24–7, 81–2, 117, 213–14.
8 Harrigan, Leo J, *Victorian Railways to '62*, Melbourne, Victorian Railways Public Relations and Betterment Board, 1962, pp. 79–86.
9 Lee, *Colonial Engineer*, pp. 123–82.
10 John Kerr, *Triumph of the Narrow Gauge: A history of Queensland Railways*, Brisbane, Booralong Press, 1998, pp. 2–22.

CHAPTER 5

1 Ron O'Connell, 'Where miles mean nothing', EE Christensen, *Official Rugby League Year Book*, Sydney, New South Wales Rugby League, 1951, pp. 67–8. O'Connell travelled more than most because he played in tests in Brisbane and Sydney. The author is grateful to Dr Karen Entwistle for this reference.
2 Statistics from NSWGR Annual Reports (various names) in Lee, *The Greatest Public Work*, p. 175.
3 Coghlan, *Labour and Industry in Australia*, vol 3, p. 1411.
4 Coghlan, *Labour and Industry in Australia*, vol 3, pp. 1408–13.
5 Joseph Jones, Commissioner of Railways, to Higinbotham, 12 January 1869, quoted in Harrigan, *Victorian Railways*, p. 87.
6 Harrigan, *Victorian Railways*, p. 92.
7 The Woy Woy tunnel on the Sydney–Newcastle line was the longest until the opening of Cox's Gap tunnel, also in New South Wales, in 1987. The Hawkesbury River Bridge, also between Sydney and Newcastle, is the second largest railway bridge in Australia, has the deepest foundations and the second longest span of any Australian railway bridge except the Sydney Harbour Bridge of 1932. This latter structure is a railway bridge with a roadway slung between the two double track railways, one of which since has been converted to road use.
8 On Whitton, see Lee, *Colonial Engineer*.
9 Lee, *The Greatest Public Work*, p. 175.
10 On the origins of the North Coast line, see Dunn, *'The Railway from Nowhere to Nowhere'*.
11 Burke, *Chasing the Sunshine*. The only comparable narrow-gauge trains were the Union Express, which operated weekly from Capetown to Johannesburg and Pretoria in South Africa; the weekly International Express from Bangkok in Siam to Prai

(later Butterworth) near Penang in British Malaya; and the twice weekly service from la Calera (connecting with Santiago) to Iquique in Chile.
12 Kerr, *Triumph of the Narrow Gauge*, pp. 37–8, 43–56.
13 Callaghan, 'Horse and Steam, Wheat and Copper', p. 48.
14 Cooley, *Railroading in Tasmania*, p. 81.
15 Higham, *One Hundred Years of Railways in Western Australia*, p. 9.
16 David J Gordon MHR, 'Through the Heart of a Continent: The Straight Route Transcontinental Railway South–North Links Adelaide to Darwin', *The Australasian Traveller*, 8, 1 November 1912, pp. 129–32.
17 For the history of this railway see Lee, *Fruits of Federation*.

CHAPTER 6

1 Figures from Garry Wotherspoon, 'The "Sydney Interest" and the Rail 1860–1900' in Max Kelly, *Nineteenth Century Sydney*, Sydney, Sydney University Press, 1978, p. 12. The census was taken after the separation of Victoria, so Melbourne was not a factor in the large population outside Sydney.
2 Statistics from Michael Cannon, *Life in the Cities: Australia in the Victorian Age: 3*, Melbourne, Thomas Nelson, 1975, pp. 14–16.
3 On the Port Phillip excursion steamers, see Thomas King Fitchett, *Down the Bay: The Story of the Excursion Steamers of Port Phillip*, Adelaide, Rigby, 1973.
4 Morris (ed.), *Cassell's Picturesque Australasia*, p. 104.
5 AM Prescott, '"A Thousand Miles from Care": The Manly Ferry' in Gary Wotherspoon (ed.), *Sydney's Transport: Studies in Urban History*, Sydney, Hale & Iremonger, 1983, pp. 63–80.
6 On Sydney ferries, see Graeme Andrews, *The Ferries of Sydney*, Sydney, Reed, 1975.
7 REN Twopeny, *Town Life in Australia*, London, Elliot Stock, 1883, p. 16.
8 Twopeny, *Town Life in Australia*, p. 21.
9 Cannon, *Life in the Cities*, p. 51.
10 *The Tramways of Adelaide, Past, Present and Future*, Adelaide, *The Critic*, 1909 [reprinted in facsimile by the Australian Electric Transport Museum, Adelaide, c. 2000], p. 29.
11 Don Fraser, 'Roads and Streets' in Fraser (ed.), *Sydney from Settlement to City*, pp. 48–51.
12 Twopeny, *Town Life in Australia*, p. 14.
13 Morris, *Cassell's Picturesque Australasia*, p. 66.
14 Twopeny, *Town Life in Australia*, p. 15.
15 On horse buses, see Dick Audley, 'Sydney's Horse Bus Industry in 1889' in Wotherspoon (ed.), *Sydney's Transport*, pp. 81–100.
16 Table compiled from police records in Lester Hovenden, 'The Impact of the Motor Vehicle, 1900–39', in Wotherspoon (ed.), *Sydney's Transport*, p. 142.
17 *The Tramways of Adelaide*, p. 9.
18 Michael Cannon, *The Land Boomers*, Melbourne, Thomas Nelson, 1976, pp. 75–8.
19 Cannon, *The Land Boomers*, pp. 75–8.
20 This account is based on that in Harrigan, *Victorian Railways*.
21 Twopeny, *Town Life in Australia*, pp. 16–17.
22 Twopeny, *Town Life in Australia*, p. 211.
23 Ian A Brady, 'Jubilee of Sydney's Electric Trains', *ARHS Bulletin* 37, 461 (March 1976), p. 49.
24 This account owes much to SE Dornan & RG Henderson, *The Electric Railways of Victoria*, Sydney, Australian Electric Traction Association, 1979, pp. 5–32.
25 Calculated from Prescott, '"A Thousand Miles from Care"' in Wotherspoon (ed.), *Sydney's Transport*, p. 62.
26 The words are those of Country Party leader Colonel Bruxner, quoted in Raxworthy, *The Unreasonable Man*, p. 70.
27 *Official Year Book of New South Wales*, 1938–1939, p. 413.
28 Figures from the *Annual Reports* of the NSW Railway Commissioners.
29 The annual rate of increase 1920–25 was 7.62% compared with 4.70% for 1925–30. See Robert Gibbons, 'The "Fall of the Giant": Trams versus Trains and Buses in Sydney, 1900–61' in Wotherspoon (ed.), *Sydney's Transport*, p. 160.
30 Calculated from figures in the relevant *Year Books of New South Wales* and RailCorp *Annual Reports*. The definition of a suburban journey varied over this period, so the figures are approximate.
31 Marc Fiddian, *Trains, Tracks, Travellers: A History of the Victorian Railways*, Pakenham VIC, South Eastern Independent Newspapers, 1997, pp. 134, 143–5.

CHAPTER 7

1 'Many Changes before Victory', EE Christensen, *Official Rugby League Yearbook*, Sydney, New South Wales Rugby League, 1958, pp. 68–9.
2 Colwell, *Australian Transport*, p. 123.
3 SA Cheney, *Horses to Horse Power*, Adelaide, Rigby, 1965, pp. 36–7.
4 JFF Reid 'Pioneer Touring in Queensland' quoted in John William Knott, 'Speed, Modernity and the Motor Car: The Making of the 1909 Motor Traffic Act in New South Wales', *Australian Historical Studies*, 26, 103, 1994, p. 229.
5 Hovenden, 'The Impact of the Motor Vehicle' in Wotherspoon (ed.), *Sydney's Transport*, p. 143.
6 Colwell, *Australian Transport*, p. 131.
7 Hovenden, 'The Impact of the Motor Vehicle' in Wotherspoon (ed.), *Sydney's Transport*, p. 146; Knott, 'Speed, Modernity and the Motor Car', pp. 240–1.
8 About 106 000 Australians have died in military service in war since 1901 and about 190 000 Australians on the roads. Updated statistics from John William Knott, 'Road Traffic Accidents in New South Wales, 1881–1991', *Australian Economic History Review*, 34, 2, September 1994, p. 80.
9 Knott, 'Speed, Modernity and the Motor Car', pp. 224–6.
10 *The Argus*, 4 November 1921, reported Hodgson's trip. Other journeys are detailed in John William Knott, 'The "Conquering Car": Technology, Symbolism and the Motorisation of Australia before World War II', *Australian Historical Studies*, 31, 114, April 2000, p. 24.
11 *The Argus*, 6 October 1924, reported the two Victorian events. Birtles, who in 1927 became the first man to drive a car from England to Australia, wrote a spirited account of his adventures: *Battle Fronts of the Outback*, Sydney, Angus & Robertson, 1935.
12 Knott, 'The "Conquering Car"', pp. 12–13, 24. Flynn's picture collection in the National Library of Australia speaks volumes about his transport obsessions.
13 Hovenden, 'The Impact of the Motor Vehicle' in Wotherspoon (ed.), *Sydney's Transport*, p. 144. Smith and Waddington later concentrated on buses, trains and trams and in 1943 was reconstituted as the New South Wales operation of Commonwealth Engineering, an unusual example of a company moving out of cars and into railway rolling stock as its staple product.
14 *The Australian Encyclopaedia*, vol. 7, 1963, p. 50.
15 Peter Spearritt, *Sydney since the Twenties*, Sydney, Hale & Iremonger, 1978, p. 159.
16 Spearritt, *Sydney since the Twenties*, p. 159.
17 Hovenden, 'The Impact of the Motor Vehicle' in Wotherspoon (ed.), *Sydney's Transport*, p. 140.
18 Raxworthy, *The Unreasonable Man*,

pp. 92–4.
19 Quoted in Fraser (ed.), *Sydney from Settlement to City*, p. 61.
20 National Trust of Victoria, *Timber Bridges Study*, pp. 18–19.
21 David Rood, 'Road's still great, 75 years on', *The Age*, 10 April 2007.
22 This analysis of motoring costs in the 1920s is based on Knott, 'The "Conquering Car"', pp. 5–7.
23 Spearritt, *Sydney since the Twenties*, p. 163. These car figures exclude motorbikes, vans, trucks and buses.
24 Harrigan, *Victorian Railways*, pp. 257–8.
25 John Knowles, 'The McKeen Cars of Queensland', *ARHS Bulletin*, 53, 780, October 2002, pp. 363–71.
26 *The Australian Encyclopaedia*, vol. 7, 1963, p. 50.
27 Calculated from figures in Spearritt, *Sydney since the Twenties*, p. 163.
28 See Graeme Davison with Sheryl Yelland, *Car Wars: How the Car Won our Hearts and Conquered our Cities*, Sydney, Allen & Unwin, 2004, pp. 104–08.
29 Fraser (ed.), *Sydney from Settlement to City*, p. 119.
30 Spearritt, *Sydney since the Twenties*, p. 163.
31 Fraser (ed.), *Sydney from Settlement to City*, p. 61.
32 Gunn, *Along Parallel Lines*, pp. 477–9.

CHAPTER 8

1 *ADB*, vol 9, pp. 196–8.
2 *Daily Times*, Chattanooga, Tennessee, 4 April 1914, viewed 21 November 2009 <earlyaviators.com/erodgers.htm>; A Scott Berg, *Lindbergh*, London, Macmillan, 1998, pp. 61–2.
3 *ADB*, vol 8, p. 360.
4 Neville Parnell & Trevor Boughton, *Flypast: A Record of Aviation in Australia*, Canberra, Australian Government Publishing Service, 1988, p. 14.
5 CH Gibbs-Smith, *Aviation: An Historical Survey*, London, HM Stationery Office, 1970, pp. 1–35.
6 *ADB*, vol 11, pp. 654–6.
7 FitzSimons, Peter, *Charles Kingsford Smith and those Magnificent Men*, Sydney, HarperCollins, 2009; *ADB*, vol 9, pp. 599–601.
8 *ADB*, vol 9, pp. 305–07.
9 *ADB*, vol 12, pp. 488–90.
10 *ADB*, vol 12, pp. 183–5.
11 *ADB*, vol 9, p. 674.
12 ANA was flying 940 000 kilometres, WAA 480 000 kilometres and Qantas 160 000 kilometres in regular service at the time. See C Arthur Butler, *Flying Start: The History of the First Five Decades of Civil Aviation in Australia*, Sydney, Edwards and Shaw, 1971, pp. 20f.
13 *ADB*, vol 7, pp. 415–16.
14 *ADB*, vol 7, p. 30.
15 John Gunn, *The Defeat of Distance: Qantas 1919–1939*, Brisbane, University of Queensland Press, 1985, pp. 177–9.
16 Gunn, *The Defeat of Distance*, pp. 208–09.
17 Gunn, *The Defeat of Distance*, pp. 244, 281, 356.
18 *ADB*, vol 13, p. 319.
19 *Aviation Retrospect: From Civil Aviation Branch to Department of Aviation*, Canberra, Australian Government Publishing Service, 1985, p. 8.
20 Kenneth Bond OAM, 'The 2002 Sir Norman Brearley Oration', 22 August 2002, is a fine account of Ansett's history by a man who worked for the airline for 54 years, beginning as a 14 year old recruited by Ansett himself at Hamilton airport in 1940, viewed 15 November 2009, <www.spiritsofansett.com/history/Bond/Brearley.htm>.
21 *ADB*, vol 8, pp. 532–3.
22 *ADB*, vol 9, p. 674.
23 *ADB*, vol 16, p. 320–3.
24 SS Schaetzel, 'Post-War Aeronautical Design and Development in Australia', Sir Charles Kingsford Smith Memorial Lecture, Royal Aeronautical Society, Sydney, October 1986.
25 *ADB*, vol 10, p. 153. On Mascot see Jim Eames, *Sydney Airport: Eighty Years as the Gateway to Australia*, Sydney, Focus Books, 2000.
26 *ADB*, vol 13, p. 319. The book is Butler, *Flying Start*.
27 Bond, 'The 2002 Sir Norman Brearley Oration'.
28 On the convoluted business history of Ansett, see Stewart Wilson, *Ansett. The Story of the Rise and Fall of Ansett 1936–2002*, Canberra, Aerospace Publications, 2002.
29 John Gunn, *Challenging Horizons: Qantas 1939–1954*, Brisbane, University of Queensland Press, 1987, pp. 212–20.
30 Gunn, *Challenging Horizons*, p. 263.

CHAPTER 9

1 Andrew Moore, 'Murray, Eric John (1907–1983)', forthcoming *ADB* entry. The author is grateful to Professor Moore for this manuscript.
2 Malcolm Roberts, 'Once More around the Block', *Policy*, 24, 3, 2008, pp. 13–16, is a succinct analysis of protection of the Australian motor industry which takes a less sanguine view of current policy than the author.
3 *New South Wales, Road Transport (General) Act* 2005, General Class 3 Truck and Dog Trailer Combination Notice under Division 5 of Part 2 of the Road Transport (Mass, Loading and Access) Regulation 2005. Available online at <www.rta.nsw.gov.au/heavyvehicles/downloads/permitnotices/ttn2005.pdf>, viewed 3 January 2010.
4 NSW Centre for Road Safety, Road Traffic Crashes in New South Wales, Statistical Statement for the year ended 31 December 2008. Available online at <www.rta.nsw.gov.au/roadsafety/downloads/accidentstats2008.pdf>, viewed 3 January 2010. For truck accident statistics see Table 11, p. 30; for international comparisons of fatality rates see Table 2, p. 18; and for fatalities per year since 1945 see Table 4, p. 20.
5 Australian Bureau of Statistics, 9309.0 – Motor Vehicle Census, Australia, 31 March 2009. Available online at <www.abs.gov.au/AUSSTATS/abs@.nsf/mf/9309.0>, viewed 3 January 2010.
6 The rail access charge for a typical train is calculated from the published ARTC charges. These involve both a flat charge per 1000 tonnes over the route and a train/kilometre charge, each of which is variable according to the type of train depending on axle load and speed. See ARTC Pricing Schedule. Available online at <www.artc.com.au/library/Pricing%20Schedule%20Effective%2001072009%20%20Access%20Seeker%20updated%2018Jan10.pdf>, viewed 19 January 2010. B-double registration fees were increased to the level cited from 1 January 2010, a move which required legislation. See Parliament of New South Wales, Road Transport (Vehicle Registration) Amendment (Heavy Vehicle Registration Charges) Bill 2009, Legislative Council Debates, 28 October 2009. Available online at <www.parliament.nsw.gov.au/prod/parlment/hansart.nsf/V3Key/LC20091028043>, viewed 19 January 2010.
7 Philip Laird, 'The Sydney to Brisbane railway; yesterday, today and tomorrow', *Australian Journal of Multi-Disciplinary Engineering*, 7, 2, 2009, pp. 171–8.
8 These statistics are from Bureau of Infrastructure, Transport and Regional Economics, *Road and Rail Freight: Competitors or Complements?* Canberra, Department of Infrastructure, Transport, Regional Development and Local Government, 2009. Available online at <www.bitre.gov.au/publications/23/Files/IS34_RoadRailFreight.pdf>, viewed 23 January 2010. Bureau of Transport Economics, *Freight between Australian Cities*, Canberra, Department of Transport and Regional Services, 2003.

Available online at <www.bitre.gov.au/publications/87/Files/is22.pdf>, viewed 23 January 2010. Productivity Commission, *Road and Rail Freight Infrastructure Pricing*, Canberra, Australian Government, No 41, 22 December 2006, Figure 2.11. p. 32. Available online at <www.pc.gov.au/__data/assets/pdf_file/0003/47532/freight.pdf>, viewed 23 January 2010.

9 Sydney–Newcastle Fwy: construction information. Available online at <www.ozroads.com.au/NSW/Freeways/F3/ConstructionInfo.htm>, viewed 1 January 2010.

10 About the Gateway Bridge. Available online at <www.qldmotorways.com.au/aboutus/history/gatewaybridge.aspx>, viewed 1 January 2010.

11 See <www.ozroads.com.au/NationalSystem/nathwys.htm> , viewed 1 January 2010.

12 Upgrading the Pacific Highway. Masterplan for the highway upgrade, available online at <www.pacifichighwayupgrade.com.au/masterplan.htm> , viewed 1 January 2010.

13 Graeme Davison with Sheryl Yelland, *Car Wars*, p. 170.

14 Imran Muhammad, Nicholas Low & Leigh Glover, *Mega Projects in Transport and Development*. See also Peter WG Newman, *The Rebirth of the Perth Suburban Railways: A Personal and Policy Perspective*, Murdoch WA, ISPT Murdoch University, 1991.

15 From 1995–96 and 2006–07 suburban rail patronage increased by 81 percent in Melbourne (from 111 to 201 milllion) but by only 23 percent in Sydney (from 240 to 296 million). Given that road congestion is worse in Sydney than Melbourne, there can be only two reasons for the discrepancy: Sydney's unfriendly ticketing and inadequate capacity.

16 Hon Carl Scully, *Eight Major Rail Projects for Sydney*, media release, 23 November 1998. Available online at <www.rumble.net/transport_2010/eight-major-rail.html>, viewed 20 December 2009. The NSW government has suppressed this material and it is only available on a non-official website.

17 Ron Christie, 'Long-term Strategic Plan for Rail, Greater Sydney Metropolitan Region', Sydney, Office of the Coordinator General of Rail, June 2001. This plan has been suppressed on NSW government websites and is not in any public library in Australia, such is the repression of information about transport planning in New South Wales.

18 *SMH*, 17 November 2009.

19 Bureau of Transport Economics, *Australian Transport Statistics 2007*, Canberra, Department of Transport and Regional Services, 2007. Available online at <www.btre.gov.au/publications/46/Files/ATS2007.pdf >, viewed 23 January 2010.

20 The privatisation of rail freight traffic is discussed in Robert Lee, *The Railways of Victoria, 1854–2004*, Melbourne, Melbourne University Publishing, 2007, pp. 226–46 and *Fruits of Federation*, pp. 105–16.

21 Christopher Hood, *Shinkansen: From Bullet Train to Symbol of Modern Japan*, Abingdon and New York, Routledge, 2006, pp. 1, 37.

22 See Paula Williams, 'Australian Very Fast Trains – A Chronology', 6 April 1998, Australian Parliamentary Library Background Paper 16 1997–98. Available online at <www.aph.gov.au/library/pubs/bp/1997-98/98bp16.htm>, viewed 25 January 2010.

23 Peter B Thornton, *East Coast Very High Speed Train Scoping Study*, Sydney, ARUPTMG, 26 November 2001. Section 15, p 5. Available online at <www.infrastructure.gov.au/rail/trains/high_speed/pdf/ECVHST_Scoping_Study.pdf>, viewed 25 January 2010.

24 The government made the announcement on 24 March 2002. Hon. John Anderson (Minster for Transport and Regional Services), *Government Ends Scoping Study on East Coast Very High Speed Train Network*, media release, 26 March 2002. Available online at <parlinfo.aph.gov.au/parlInfo/search/display/display.w3p;query=Id%3A%22media%2Fpressrel%2FOH766%22>, viewed 25 January 2010.

25 Numbers 14:18 in the King James version.

BIBLIOGRAPHY

Andrews, Graeme, *Australia's Maritime Heritage*, Sydney, Cromarty Press, 1984.
——, *The Ferries of Sydney*, Sydney, Reed, 1975.
Austin, Kenneth Ashurst, *A Pictorial History of Cobb & Co: The Coaching Age in Australia 1854–1924*, Adelaide, Rigby, 1977.
Australian Dictionary of Biography (ADB) (16 vols), Melbourne, Melbourne University Press, 1966–2002.
The Australian Encyclopaedia (10 vols), Sydney, The Grolier Society, 1963.
Aviation Retrospect: From Civil Aviation Branch to Department of Aviation, Canberra, Australian Government Publishing Service, 1985.
Babbage, Jack & Barrington, Rodney, *The History of Pichi Richi Railway*, Quorn SA, Pichi Richi Railway Preservation Society, 1984.
Bach, John, *A Maritime History of Australia*, Melbourne, Pan Books, 1982.
Badger, Ian J, *Australian Horse Drawn Vehicles*, Adelaide, Rigby, 1977.
Baird, Kim, *South Coast Limited: A History of the Victor Harbor and Milang Railway Lines in South Australia*, Adelaide, Australian Railway Historical Society, 1972.
Bayley, William A, *The Great Zig Zag Railway at Lithgow*, Bulli NSW, Austrail Publications, 1977.
Beilby, Peter, *Australian TV: The First 25 Years*, Melbourne, Thomas Nelson, 1981.
Birtles, Francis, *Battle Fronts of the Outback*, Sydney, Angus & Robertson, 1935.
Blainey, Geoffrey, *The Tyranny of Distance*, Melbourne, Sun Books, 1983.
Blake, Leslie James, *Covered Wagons in Australia, 1913–1987*, Adelaide, Rigby, 1979.
Brady, Ian A, 'Jubilee of Sydney's Electric Trains', *ARHS Bulletin*, 37, 461 (March 1976).
Brand, M, *Transport in Australia* (Making Australian Society Series), Melbourne, Nelson, 1979.
Bureau of Infrastructure, Transport and Regional Economics, *Road and Rail Freight: Competitors or Complements?* Canberra, Department of Infrastructure, Transport, Regional Development and Local Government, 2009. Available online at <www.bitre.gov.au/publications/23/Files/IS34_RoadRailFreight.pdf>, viewed 23 January 2010.
Bureau of Transport Economics, *Australian Transport Statistics 2007*, Canberra, Department of Transport and Regional Services, 2007. Available online at <www.btre.gov.au/publications/46/Files/ATS2007.pdf >, viewed 23 January 2010.
——, *Freight between Australian Cities*, Canberra, Department of Transport and Regional Services, 2003. Available online at <www.bitre.gov.au/publications/87/Files/is22.pdf>, viewed 23 January 2010.
Burke, David, *Chasing the Sunshine: The Story of Queensland's* Sunshine Express, South Brisbane, Queensland Museum, 2009.
——, *Road through the Wilderness*, Sydney, UNSW Press, 1991.
Butler, C Arthur, *Flying Start: The History of the First Five Decades of Civil Aviation in Australia*, Sydney, Edwards and Shaw, 1971.
Callaghan, WH, 'Horse and Steam, Wheat and Copper: South Australia's Western System', *ARHS Bulletin* 53, 771–2, January and February 2002, 8–27, 46–63.
Campbell, Bob, *Getting There by Tram in Western Australia*, Perth, PETS, 1999.
Cannon, Michael, *The Land Boomers*, Melbourne, Thomas Nelson, 1976.
——, *Life in the Cities: Australia in the Victorian Age: 3*, Melbourne, Thomas Nelson, 1975.
Chamberlain, Brian, *Early Steam in Tasmania*, Launceston, the author, 1987.
Cheney, SA, *Horses to Horse Power*, Adelaide, Rigby, 1965.
Chinn, Norman & McCarthy, Ken, *New South Wales Tramcar Handbook, 1861–1961* (2 vols), Sydney, SPER, 1975–76.
Christopher, Peter, *Paddlesteamers and River Boats of the Murray*, Stepney SA, Axiom, 2000.
Clark, Mary Shelley, *Ships and Shores and Trading Ports: The Social and Working Life of Coastal Harbour and River Towns in New South Wales*, Sydney, Waterways Authority of New South Wales, 2001.
Clune, Frank, *The Overland Telegraph: An Epic Feat of Endurance and Courage*, Sydney, Angus & Robertson, 1955.
Coghlan, TA, *Labour and Industry in Australia from the First Settlement in 1788 to the Establishment of the Commonwealth in 1901* (4 vols), London, Oxford University Press, 1918.
Colwell, Max, *Australian Transport: An Illustrated History*, Sydney, Paul Hamlyn, 1972.
Cooke, David, Estell, Don, Seckold, Keith & Beckhaus, John, *Coaching Stock of the NSW Railways* (2 vols), Sydney, Eveleigh Press, 1999, 2003.
Cooley, Tomas CJ, *Railroading in Tasmania, 1868–1961*, Hobart, the author, c. 1961.
Dornan, SE & Henderson, RG, *The Electric Railways of Victoria*, Sydney, Australian Electric Traction Association, 1979.
Davis, Pedr, *Australians on the Road*, Adelaide, Rigby, 1979.
Davison, Graeme, *The Rise and Fall of Marvellous Melbourne*, Melbourne, Melbourne University Press, 1978.
Davison, Graeme with Yelland, Sheryl, *Car Wars: How the Car Won our Hearts and Conquered our Cities*, Sydney, Allen & Unwin, 2004.
Dunn, Ian A, *'The Railway from Nowhere to Nowhere': The Grafton to the Tweed Railway, 1894–1932*, Sydney, Eveleigh Press, 2002.
Eames, Jim, *Sydney Airport: Eighty Years as the Gateway to Australia*, Sydney, Focus Books, 2000.
Ellis, RF, *Rails to the Tableland*, Brisbane, Australian Railway Historical Society, 1976.
Everingham, Sam, *Wild Ride: The Rise and Fall of Cobb & Co*, Melbourne, Penguin, 2007.
Fiddian, Marc, *Trains, Tracks, Travellers: A History of the Victorian Railways*, Pakenham VIC, South Eastern Independent Newspapers, 1997.
Fitchett, Thomas King, *Down the Bay: The Story of the Excursion Steamers of Port Phillip*, Adelaide, Rigby, 1973.
——, *The Long Haul: Ships on the England–Australia Run*, Adelaide, Rigby, 1980.
——, *The Vanished Fleet: Australia's Coastal Passenger Ships 1910–1960*, Adelaide, Rigby, 1976.
FitzSimons, Peter, *Charles Kingsford Smith and those Magnificent Men*, Sydney, HarperCollins, 2009.
Fraser, Don, *Bridges Down Under: The History of Railway Underbridges in New South Wales*, Sydney, Australian Railway Historical Society, 1995.
——, *Sydney from Settlement to City, an Engineering History of Sydney*, Sydney, Institution of Engineers Australia, 1989.
Gibbs-Smith, CH, *Aviation: An Historical Survey*, London, HM Stationery Office, 1970.
Gordon, Malcolm R, *From* Chusan *to* Sea Princess*: The Australian Services of the P&O and Orient Lines*, Sydney, Allen & Unwin, 1985.
Griffiths, Lyn & Jeffrey, Bill, *River Boat Trail South Australia*, Adelaide, South Australian Department of Environment and Natural Resources, nd [c. 2000].
Grunbach, Alex, *A Compendium of New South Wales Steam Locomotives*, Sydney, Australian Railway Historical Society, 1981.
Gunn, John, *Along Parallel Lines, a History of the Railways of New South Wales, 1850–1986*, Melbourne, Melbourne University Press, 1989.
——, *Challenging Horizons: Qantas 1939–1954*, Brisbane, University of Queensland Press, 1987.
——, *The Defeat of Distance: Qantas 1919–1939*, Brisbane, University of Queensland Press, 1985.
——, *High Corridors: Qantas 1954–1970*, Brisbane, University of Queensland Press, 1988.
Gunzburg, Adrian, *A History of W.A.G.R. Locomotives*, Perth, Australian Railway

Historical Society, 1984.
Harrigan, Leo J, *Victorian Railways to '62*, Melbourne, Victorian Railways Public Relations and Betterment Board, 1962.
Higham, CJ, *One Hundred Years of Railways in Western Australia, 1871–1971*, Perth, Australian Railway Historical Society, 1971.
Hills, RL & Patrick, D, *Beyer Peacock, Locomotive Builders to the World*, Glossop, Transport Publishing, 1982.
Hood, Christopher, *Shinkansen: From Bullet Train to Symbol of Modern Japan*, Abingdon and New York, Routledge, 2006.
Hunter, Jean, *Up and Down the Mary, 1888*, Maryborough, Wide Bay Historical Society, 1992.
Hunter, Marcella, *Australia Post, Delivering More than Ever*, Sydney, Focus Books, 2000.
Institution of Engineers, Australia, *The Electrification of Sydney and Suburban Railways*, Sydney, Institution of Engineers, 1927 (reprinted by the Australian Railway Historical Society, 1987).
James, EBM, *The Overland Telegraph Line: From Katherine to Tennant Creek and Alice Springs*, Canberra, Australian Heritage Commission, 1984.
Keating, John D, *Mind the Curve! A History of the Cable Trams*, Melbourne, Melbourne University Press, 1970.
Keenan, David R, *Melbourne Tramways*, Sydney, Transit Press 1985.
——, *Tramways of Sydney*, Sydney, Transit Press, 1979.
Kelly, Max, *Nineteenth Century Sydney*, Sydney, Sydney University Press, 1978.
Kennedy, Malcolm J, *Hauling the Loads: A History of Australia's Working Horses and Bullocks*, Melbourne, Melbourne University Press, 1992.
Kerr, John, *Triumph of the Narrow Gauge: A History of Queensland Railways*, Brisbane, Booralong Press, 1998.
Knott, John William, 'The "Conquering Car": Technology, Symbolism and the Motorisation of Australia before World War II', *Australian Historical Studies*, 31, 114, April 2000, 1–36.
——, 'Road Traffic Accidents in the New South Wales, 1881–1991', *Australian Economic History Review*, 34, 2, September 1994, 80–116.
——, 'Speed, Modernity and the Motor Car: The Making of the 1909 Motor Traffic Act in New South Wales', *Australian Historical Studies*, 26, 103, 1994, 221–41.
Knowles, John, 'The McKeen Cars of Queensland', *ARHS Bulletin*, 53, 780, October 2002, 363–71.
Laird, Philip, 'The Sydney to Brisbane Railway: Yesterday, Today and Tomorrow', *Australian Journal of Multi-Disciplinary Engineering*, 7, 2, 2009, 171–8.
Lawson, Will, *Pacific Steamers*, Glasgow, Brown, Son & Ferguson, 1927.
Lay, Max G, *History of Australian Roads*, Special Report No. 29, Australian Road Research Council, 1984.
Lee, Robert, *Colonial Engineer: John Whitton (1819–1898) and the Building of Australia's Railways*, Sydney, UNSW Press, 2000.
——, *Fruits of Federation: The Grafton–Brisbane Uniform Gauge Railway and Clarence River Bridge*, Sydney, Loco Works Publications, 2009.
——, *The Greatest Public Work, the New South Wales Railways, 1848–1889*, Sydney, Hale & Iremonger, 1988.
——, *The Railways of Victoria, 1854–2004*, Melbourne, Melbourne University Publishing, 2007.
Lee, Stuart, *Riverboats of the Clarence*, Yamba NSW, Port of Yamba Historical Society, 2003.
Lubbock, Basil, *The Colonial Clipper*, Glasgow, Brown, Son & Ferguson, 1968.
Lyons, Martyn & Russell, Penny (eds), *Australia's History: Themes and Debates*, Sydney, UNSW Press, 2005.
McGregor, H, *The Horse and Buggy Days*, Canberra, Roebuck Books, 1981.
McKillop, Robert & Sheedy, David, *Our Region, Our Railway: The Hunter and the Great Northern Railway 1857–2007*, Sydney, Australian Railway Historical Society (New South Wales Division), 2008.
McKnight, Tom L, *The Camel in Australia*, Melbourne, Melbourne University Press, 1969.
——, *The Long Paddock: Australia's Travelling Stock Routes*, Armidale NSW, University of New England, 1977.
Maddock, John, *Mail for the Outback and Beyond*, Sydney, Kangaroo Press, 1986.
Mead, Tom, *Empire of Straw: The Dynamic Rise and Disastrous Fall of Dashing Colonial Tycoon Benjamin Boyd*, Sydney, Dolphin Books, c. 2000.
Morris, EE (ed.), *Cassell's Picturesque Australasia*, London, Cassell, 1889.
Muhammad, Imran, Low, Nicholas & Glover, Leigh, *Mega Projects in Transport and Development: Background in Australian Case Studies: Perth Urban Railway*, Melbourne, University of Melbourne Australasian Centre for the Governance and Management of Urban Transport. Available online at <www.abp.unimelb.edu.au/gamut/pdf/rail-background-report.pdf>, viewed 30 January 2010.
National Trust of Victoria, *Timber Bridges Study*, Melbourne, The National Trust, 1997.
Newman, Peter WG, *The Rebirth of the Perth Suburban Railways: A Personal and Policy Perspective*, Murdoch WA, ISPT Murdoch University, 1991.
Painter, Gwenda, *A Different River: River Trade and Development along the Murray Valley Network*, South Melbourne, Hyland House, 1983.
——, *The River Trade: Wool and Steamers*, Sydney, Turton & Armstrong, 1979.
Parnell, Neville & Boughton, Trevor, *Flypast: A Record of Aviation in Australia*, Canberra, Australian Government Publishing Service, 1988.
Parsons, Ronald, *Australian Coastal Passenger Ships: The Details and Brief Outline of the Career of every Steam and Motor Ship that Carried Passengers on the Australian Coast*, Magill SA, the author, 1981.
——, *Early Steam Ships in Australia: An Investigation into the Arrival and Development of Steam Ships in Australian Waters from 1830 till 1850*, Lobethal SA, the author, 2000.
——, *The Port of Maryborough*, Magill SA, the author, 1984.
——, *Ships of the Inland Rivers: An Outline History and Details of all Known Paddle Ships, Barges and other Vessels Trading on the Murray Darling*, Gumeracha SA, Gould Books, 1980.
——, *Southern Passages: A Maritime History of South Australia*, Netley SA, Wakefield Press, 1986.
——, *Steam Ships in Colonial Western Australia*, Magill SA, the author, 1980.
——, *Steamships to the Illawarra: The Development of the Steam Ship Service South of Sydney*, Lobethal SA, the author, 1991.
Pemberton, Barry, *Australian Coastal Shipping*, Melbourne, Melbourne University Press, 1979.
Pike, Glenville, *Conquest of the Ranges*, Mareeba QLD, Pinevale Publications, 1984.
Productivity Commission, *Road and Rail Freight Infrastructure Pricing*, Canberra, Australian Government, 41, 22 December 2006, Figure 2.11. p. 32. Available online at <www.pc.gov.au/__data/assets/pdf_file/0003/47532/freight.pdf>, viewed 23 January 2010.
Purtnell, Jean, *The Mosquito Fleet: Hawkesbury River Trade and Traders, 1794–1994*, Sydney, Daerubbin Press, 1995.
Quinlan, Howard & Newland, John R, *Australian Railway Routes 1854–2000*, Sydney, Australian Railway Historical Society (New South Wales Division), 2000.
Ramona, Philippe, *Paquebots vers l'Orient*, Saint-Cyr-sur-Loire, Editions Alan Sutton, 2001.
Raxworthy, Richard, *The Unreasonable Man, the Life and Works of J.J.C. Bradfield*, Sydney, Hale & Iremonger, 1989.
Richards, Mike, *North Coast Run: Men and Ships of the NSW North Coast*, Sydney, Turton & Armstrong, 1977.
——, *Workhorses in Australian Waters: A History of Marine Engineering in Australia*, Sydney, Turton & Armstrong, 1987.

Roads and Traffic Authority of NSW, *Timber Bridge Management*, Sydney, Roads and Traffic Authority, 2002.
Roberts, Malcolm, 'Once More around the Block', *Policy*, 24, 3, 2008, 13–16.
Schaetzel, SS, 'Post-War Aeronautical Design and Development in Australia', Sir Charles Kingsford Smith Memorial Lecture, Royal Aeronautical Society, Sydney, October 1986.
Stewein, Ron, *A History of the South Australian Railways* vol 1 *The Early Years*, Melbourne, Australian Railway Historical Society (Victorian Division), 2007.
Smith, Patsy Adam, *Romance of Victorian Railways*, Adelaide, Rigby, 1980.
Spearritt, Peter, *The Sydney Harbour Bridge*, Sydney, George Allen & Unwin, 1982.
——, *Sydney since the Twenties*, Sydney, Hale & Iremonger, 1978.
Stancombe, George Hawley, *Highway in Van Diemen's Land*, Western Junction TAS, the author, 1969.
Standage, Tom, *The Victorian Internet: The Remarkable Story of the Telegraph and the Nineteenth Century's Online Pioneers*, London, Weidenfeld & Nicolson, 1998.
Stark, William F, *The Last Time around Cape Horn: The Historic 1949 Voyage of the Windjammer* Pamir, New York, Carroll & Graf, 2003.
Taylor, Peter, *An End to Silence: The Building of the Overland Telegraph Line from Adelaide to Darwin*, Sydney, Methuen, Australia, 1980.
Thompson, Malcolm, *Rails through Swamp and Sand: A History of the Port Adelaide Railway*, Adelaide, Port Dock Railway Museum, 1988.
Thornton, Peter B, *East Coast Very High Speed Train Scoping Study*, Sydney, ARUPTMG, 26 November 2001. Available online at <www.infrastructure.gov.au/rail/trains/high_speed/pdf/ECVHST_Scoping_Study.pdf>, viewed 25 January 2010.
The Tramways of Adelaide, Past, Present and Future, Adelaide, *The Critic*, 1909 [reprinted in facsimile by the Australian Electric Transport Museum, Adelaide, c. 2000].
Twopeny, REN, *Town Life in Australia*, London, Elliot Stock, 1883.
Unstead, RJ & Henderson, WF, *Transport in Australia*, London, A & C Black, 1970.
Wardle, David, *Murray River Paddle Steamers*, Canberra, Traction Publications, 1970.
Watson, Stephen & Johnson, Ian, *The History of Melbourne's Tramways, 1885–1896* (map), Melbourne, the authors, 1996.
Willey, Keith, *The Drovers*, South Melbourne, Macmillan, 1982.
Wilson, Stewart, *Ansett: The Story of the Rise and Fall of Ansett 1936–2002*, Canberra, Aerospace Publications, 2002.
Wotherspoon, Garry (ed.), *Sydney's Transport: Studies in Urban History*, Sydney, Hale & Iremonger, 1983.
Yelland, Leith, *Pads, Tracks and Waters, South Australia's Pastoral Stock Routes*, Adelaide, South Australian Department of Primary Industry and Resources, 2002.

INDEX

Please note: Page numbers in *italics* refer to photographs.

DEPARTMENT OF RAILWAYS
NEW SOUTH WALES
TIMETABLE
COUNTRY
SERVICES
From 22nd JANUARY, 1956
Published by Authority of the Commissioner for Railways
(Crown Copyright Reserved)
Price: SIXPENCE
WICKHAM
TO
BURWOOD No. 3 PIT
SECOND CLASS
N 2
BURWOOD No. 3 PIT
CHILD'S TICKET
WYONG
TO
GOSFORD
SECOND CLASS
CHILD'S TICKET
CENTRAL
TO
NORTH SYDNEY
Via BRIDGE
BLACKHEATH
PLATFORM TICKET
ONLY
This Ticket is not transferable, and is available to attend one train only on date of issue, and must be handed to the Collector at Barrier. Holder of this ticket is prohibited from occupying a seat on train.
WICKHAM
TO
WHITEBRIDGE
SECOND CLASS
N 2
WHITEBRIDGE
SUNSHINE EXPRESS RAIL TOURS
WINELANDER
Roma St. to Stanthorpe
Stanthorpe to ROMA ST.
by special air-conditioned train
21st and 22nd February, 2009
634 km
TAA Ground Transportation Voucher
NOT TRANSFERABLE
PASSENGER'S RECEIPT
After touchdown...get straight to the point with Avis!
There's a friendly Avis team at every major airport in the country. You can book your Avis Rent a Car when you book your ticket. Or from your nearest Avis rental station.
Avis will have a car waiting for you no matter where you're going.
Avis have 160 rental locations around the country.
You're never far from a friendly Avis team.
we try harder AVIS
METROPOLITAN TRANSPORT TRUST
Ticket not transferable and must be shown on demand. Available for trip of issue only. Subject to Trust By-laws
№ 9955 Wi
17c.

N.S.W. GOVT. TRAMWAYS.
Available on trip of issue only and in section and direction punched. Void if punched more than once. Must be shown on demand or another fare paid.
OUT → Not Transferable. PLEASE DESTROY on ALIGHTING.
4d. A
20391
3d. B
WBD
70247
ST BE SHOWN ON DEMAND
10c-1/-
B C
03990
M. & M.T.B.
THIS TICKET MUST BE SHOWN ON DEMAND OR ANOTHER FARE PAID
NOT TRANSFERABLE
MULTIPLE ISSUE
CITY SECTION
10c
B Bb
IN OUT
276563
SCHOOL CHILD'S RAILWAY AND GOVERNMENT BUS
CONCESSION AUTHORITY
Available for travel at child's rate of fare by Government Train or Omnibus. This Authority is not available for travel on Special Train Services as advertised nor on Special Bus Services to Racecourse, Trotting or Coursing Grounds nor on other bus services as notified in the timetable or advertised otherwise.
FROM 1-4-68 TO 31-7-68
Issued to: LEE, Robert
Age: 16
Nº 81911
Pupil's Signature:
School: NORTH SYDNEY BOYS' HIGH SCHOOL
Teacher's Signature:
For Conditions—See Back
Form No. 202
THIS SIDE UP
YOUR RAIL TICKET FOR RELAXED TRA
10c
B Ax
282400
15c
A Ad
603306
FLIGHT TICKET
BOARDING CHECK: Please hand to your hostess on boarding the aircraft
CHECK-IN TIME:
Please observe important information inside front cover
FLIGHT No.
SEAT No.
IMPORTANT: SEATS NOT CLAIMED AT SEAT ALLOCATION COUNTER BY 20 MINUTES PRIOR TO DEPARTURE MAY BE RE-ALLOCATED.
16A
ANSETT AIRLINES OF AUSTRALIA
You'll enjoy the experience
GOVERNMENT TRAMWAYS.
1st SECTION.
PLEASE DESTROY ON ALIGHTING.
4d. A
77235
2nd Sections
5d. B
58395
1st SECTION.
5d. S
91157
1st SECTION
4d. S
79084
3218 253 840